Reshevsky at a San Francisco exhibition in 1921

Reshevsky's
Best Games of Chess

(Formerly Titled: Reshevsky on Chess)

By

SAMUEL RESHEVSKY

Dover Publications, Inc.
New York

Published in Canada by General Publishing Company, Ltd., 30 Lesmill Road, Don Mills, Toronto, Ontario.
Published in the United Kingdom by Constable and Company, Ltd., 10 Orange Street, London WC 2.

This Dover edition, first published in 1960, is an unabridged and unaltered republication of the work originally published in 1948 by Chess Review under the title *Reshevsky on Chess*. This work is reprinted by special arrangement with the Chess Review.

√ GV
1439
.R46
1960
PAP

International Standard Book Number: 0-486-20606-8

Manufactured in the United States of America
Dover Publications, Inc.
180 Varick Street
New York, N. Y. 10014

982213

CONTENTS

FOREWORD

WHEN I was a child touring Europe and the United States as a chess prodigy, my performances were the subject of much speculation. Everyone was curious to know "how an eight-year-old boy could beat gray beards at their own game." People continually pestered me for an explanation. I could not answer their questions then, nor can I do so now. Chess was, for me, a natural function, like breathing. It required no conscious effort. The correct moves in a game occurred to me as spontaneously as I drew breath. If you consider the difficulty you might have in accounting for that everyday motion, you will have some inkling of my dilemma in trying to explain my chess ability.

Today, spectators feel another kind of astonishment. It is my practice to spend the major part of my allotted time on the first fifteen or twenty moves of a tournament game. As a consequence, I am often forced to play at breakneck speed to avoid overstepping the time limit. After such a game, I am frequently asked why I took so long considering "obvious" moves. That's a question to which I am able to give a partial answer.

To a chess master, there is no such thing as an "obvious" move. Experience has shown repeatedly that wins or draws are thrown away by thoughtless play. Careful planning is the essence of chess strategy. Every move must be scrutinized with care. Each must be analyzed in the light of the plan under consideration. Nowhere is waste of time more severely punished than in chess. Let me hasten to explain, however, that I do not mean taking twenty minutes for one move but, rather, failing to make each move play its part in the scheme of things. By playing slowly during the early phases of a game, I am able to grasp the basic requirements of each position. Then, despite being in time pressure, I have little difficulty in finding the best continuation. Incidentally, it is an odd fact that more often than not it is my opponent who gets the jitters when I am compelled to make these hurried moves. So, you see, there are psychological considerations as well.

This collection of 110 of my best games is culled from the hundreds I have played. They range from my earliest efforts as a child prodigy to the present time. In them, the discerning reader will be able to trace my development from a "child wonder" to a contender for the world championship.

In my analyses, I have tried to anticipate the kind of question which the average player might ask. Wherever possible, I have pointed to the general principles which underly a given position. At the same time, I have attempted to satisfy the near-expert who wishes to explore the subtle mechanics of master chess.

If this book answers some of your questions, satisfies your curiosity or merely entertains you, it will have served its purpose.

SAMUEL RESHEVSKY

Roxbury, Massachusetts
February 16, 1948

Reshevsky's
Best Games of Chess

CHILD PRODIGY

T O ACHIEVE world-wide fame at the age of eight is a mixed blessing. Such was my lot in life. I was a "chess prodigy" and my childhood, from the time I left my native Poland in 1920, consisted of a series of public exhibitions throughout Europe and the United States. Wherever I went, great crowds turned out to see me play. For four years, I was on public view. People stared at me, poked at me, tried to hug me, asked me questions. Professors measured my cranium and psycho-analyzed me. Reporters interviewed me and wrote fanciful stories about my future. Photographers were forever aiming their cameras at me.

It was, of course, an unnatural life for a child, but it had its compensations and I cannot truthfully say that I did not enjoy it. There was the thrill of travelling from city to city with my family, the excitement of playing hundreds of games of chess and winning most of them, the knowledge that there was something "special" about the way I played chess, although I didn't know why.

I was constantly being asked how I was able to play such strong chess as a child, but of course I did not know the answer. I could sing and I could ride a bicycle and I could play chess, but I didn't know how or why I could do these things. I sang because I liked to sing—and I played chess because I liked to play chess. That was all I knew.

I had never studied the game. I was too young for that. I just picked it up from watching my father play at home. When I was four years old, I was able to play well enough to defeat most of the players in our village. By the time I was six, I had played with many Polish masters in Lodz and Warsaw, including Grandmaster Akiba Rubinstein, and had established a local reputation by giving simultaneous exhibitions in the leading cities of Poland.

In 1920, when I was eight years old, my career as a "chess prodigy" began in earnest. Accompanied by my parents, I toured the capitals of Europe, giving exhibitions at Berlin, Vienna, Paris, London and other cities.

On November 3rd, 1920, I arrived in New York with my parents and was immediately taken to the Marshall Chess Club, where I met Grandmaster Frank J. Marshall, then U. S. Champion, and A. B. Hodges, former U. S. Champion.

Several exhibitions were arranged in New York, including a clock game with Morris Schapiro, one of America's leading players at that time. The newspapers were particularly impressed by my showing at West Point Military Academy, where my score, in simultaneous play, was 19 wins and 1 draw.

Then began a tour of the United States which lasted for almost two years, until late in 1922. We travelled all the way to the West Coast and back, stopping at scores of cities and towns. I gave simultaneous exhibitions in chess clubs, public halls, theatres, department stores. At one store in Philadelphia, more than three thousand people turned out to see the exhibition.

When we returned to New York, I played in my first tournament with masters, at the Chess Club International.

The games in this section are from this exciting period of my life—from my first simultaneous exhibition after I left Poland, in 1920, to the thrilling moment when I defeated Janowski in my first tournament with masters.

EXHIBITIONS IN EUROPE

THE FIRST public appearance in Western Europe of young Samuel Rzeszewski, as my name was then spelled in English, was at the Kerkaupalast in Berlin. Playing 20 opponents, I scored 16 wins and drew 4 games. It was an auspicious beginning.

Game No. 1 is from this exhibition. As is generally the case in simultaneous displays, my opponent was a comparatively weak player. He conducted the opening timidly and I was able to build up a powerful position. However, I advanced too hurriedly and was lucky to be able to consolidate. Victory was finally achieved by means of a tactical finesse.

Game 2 is from another exhibition in Berlin, given a few days later. Here the player of the black pieces was demolished before he became aware of what was happening to him.

Game 3 is one of twenty games, played simultaneously, in an exhibition at Hannover. The opening is weird but the final winning combination is neat. Apparently I was able to see quite deeply into the position.

The fourth game is interesting and has considerable merit. The contest was staged in a special exhibition in London. My opponent was one of the compilers of the early editions of *Modern Chess Openings*. As I was completely ignorant of "book" openings, I suppose I should have been impressed by Griffith's knowledge of the subject—but I was too young to be troubled by such matters.

Another interesting aspect of the game is that it was played blindfold on both sides. This was considered a remarkable achievement for a child. So far as I was concerned, however, I found it somewhat easier to play a single game blindfold than twenty games in an ordinary simultaneous exhibition. I had a good memory and I was able to visualize the board without much trouble.

The important feature of Game 4 is that it was played well on both sides, with no real blunders to mar its artistic merit. I regard it as one of my best childhood efforts.

1.

RESHEVSKY–ZABLUDOVSKY
Simultaneous Exhibition
Berlin, 1920

RUY LOPEZ

Reshevsky	Zabludovsky
WHITE	BLACK
1 P–K4	P–K4
2 N–KB3	N–QB3
3 B–N5	P–Q3

The Steinitz Defense, which gives Black a cramped game. Modern theory favors 3 ... P–QR3; 4 B–R4, N–B3 etc.

4 P–Q4	PxP
5 NxP	B–Q2
6 N–QB3	NxN
7 QxN	N–B3
8 O–O	P–KR3?

A move which appears frequently in the games of weaker players. It loses time, creates a weakness and serves no useful purpose.

9 P–B4	BxB
10 NxB	P–R3
11 N–B3	B–K2
12 P–KR3	....

Partly to prepare for B–K3 without being molested by ... N–N5, and also as a preliminary to a later advance of the KNP. As is customary in this variation, White has decidedly the freer and more promising position.

12	O–O
13 Q–B2	....

B–K3 followed by QR–Q1 was a simpler and perhaps more effective course.

| 13 .... | N–K1 |

Too timorous. ... Q–Q2–B3 was indicated.

14 P–KN4	P–QB3
15 B–K3	P–QB4?

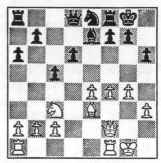

Creating a serious positional weakness in the form of a hole at his Q4.

16 QR–Q1	P–QN3
17 P–K5	....

It would doubtless have been more effective to postpone this advance by playing N–Q5 and doubling Rooks on the Q file.

17	Q–B2
18 N–Q5	Q–N2
19 Q–N2	R–R2

White threatened to win the Queen with N–B6ch.

| 20 KR–K1 | PxP |

Best; the threat was 21 NxBch, QxN; 22 PxP, NxP; 23 BxP and wins.

21 PxP	B–R5
22 B–B2	BxBch
23 QxB	K–R1?

Overlooking White's decisive reply. 23 ... Q–B3 followed by ... R–Q2 would have offered more resistance.

24 P–K6!	P–B3
25 N–B4!	K–R2
26 P–K7	....

There was an even quicker win with 26 N–N6!, R–N1 (if 26 ... KxN; 27 Q–B5 mate!); 27 Q–B5 and Black has no adequate defense to the threat of N–B8ch followed by Q–R7 mate.

| 26 . . . . | R–B2 |
| 27 R–Q8 | R–R1 |

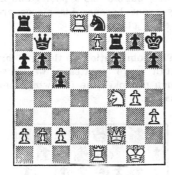

28 Q–N2! . . . .

This forces the issue.

28 . . . . QxQch

Now if 29 KxQ, RxP! and Black has extricated himself from his difficulties.

29 NxQ! **Resigns**

Black resigned, for if 29 . . . RxP; 30 RxQR, and White's Rook at K1 is protected!

2.

RESHEVSKY–DOERY
Simultaneous Exhibition
Berlin, 1920
KING'S GAMBIT

Reshevsky	L. Doery
WHITE	BLACK
1 P–K4	P–K4
2 P–KB4	PxP
3 B–B4	B–K2

This obsolete defense is not bad, but it gives White many attacking chances. Modern players prefer the more aggressive 3... P–Q4 or 3... N–KB3.

| 4 N–KB3 | B–R5ch |
| 5 P–KN3?! | . . . . |

More enterprising than 5 K–B1, which is, however, sounder.

5	PxP
6 O–O	PxPch
7 K–R1	N–KR3?

A slow continuation is fatal for Black in his undeveloped state. Correct is 7 ... P–Q4! 8 BxP, N–KB3; 9 BxPch, KxB; 10 NxB, R–K1 or 10 P–K5? B–R6 etc.

8 P–Q4	Q–K2
9 BxN	PxB
10 N–K5	B–B3

There is no satisfactory defense; Black's KBP is too vulnerable.

| 11 Q–R5 | R–B1 |

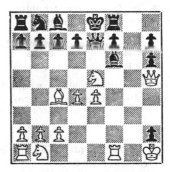

12 NxBP! **QxPch**

If 12 ... RxN; 13 BxRch, QxB; 14 QxQch, KxQ; 15 P–K5 winning easily.

13 KxP **QxPch**

Black has nothing better. If 13 ... Q–N3; 14 R–K1ch, B–K2; 15 RxBch, KxR; 16 Q–K5ch and wins the Queen. Or if 13 ... P–Q4; 14 N–Q6ch.

14 K–N3 **B–R5ch**

Desperation; if instead 14 ... R–N1ch; 15 N–N5ch, R–N3; 16 RxB wins (16 ... PxN; 17 B–B7ch. Or 16 ... QxB; 17 RxR).

| 15 QxB | QxB |
| 16 Q–Q8 mate | |

3.

RESHEVSKY–TRAUBE
Simultaneous Exhibition
Hannover, 1920

BIRD'S OPENING

Reshevsky	Dr. H. Traube
WHITE	BLACK
1 P–KB4	P–K3

1...P–Q4 gives Black more options.

| 2 N–KB3 | P–Q4 |
| 3 P–KN3 | .... |

Not a bad way of solving the problem of how to develop the KB, which is frequently troublesome for White in this opening.

3	N–KB3
4 B–N2	B–Q3
5 P–Q4	....

An alternative method would be to play P–Q3 intending a later P–K4.

| 5 .... | N–B3? |

This is out of place. 5...P–B4 or...QN–Q2 is in order.

| 6 N–K5 | N–K2 |
| 7 B–K3 | .... |

P–B4 is probably the move I would choose today. The text gives Black an opportunity to play 7... N–B4; 8 B–N1 (if 8 B–B2, N–K5 is annoying), BxN; 9 BPxB, N–Q2 followed by...P–KB3 with good counterplay in the center.

| 7 .... | P–B3 |
| 8 P–QR3 | .... |

Intending a general Queen-side advance.

8	P–KR3?
9 N–Q2	N–Q2
10 P–B4	P–QN3

This loosens up his position on the long diagonal to a dangerous extent, but he has a poor game in any event because his pieces are in each other's way.

| 11 P–QN4 | P–B3? |

The combination of this and his eighth move creates a weakness which provokes the following combination.

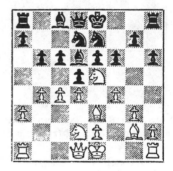

| 12 NxP! | NxN |
| 13 PxP | PxP |

Or 13...N–K2; 14 PxP regaining the piece with a winning position.

| 14 BxP | B–N2 |
| 15 Q–B2! | QR–B1? |

Even after the better move 15... Q–B2 White's last move would have been decisive: 16 QR–B1, QR–B1 (or 16...N–K2; 17 QxQ, BxQ 18 BxB, QR–N1; 19 RxB, K–Q1; 20 RxNch and wins); 17 Q–N6ch, K–Q1; 18 QxNP, R–K1; 19 B–B2 and White has more than enough compensation for the piece.

Or if 15...Q–K2?! 16 BxN, QR–B1; 17 Q–N6ch (not 17 BxNch?? KxB and Black wins), K–Q1; 18 BxB and wins.

| 16 Q–N6ch | K–B1 |
| 17 Q–B7 mate | |

4.

RESHEVSKY–R. C. GRIFFITH
Exhibition Game
London, 1920
Both players blindfolded
R U Y   L O P E Z

Reshevsky	R. C. Griffith
WHITE	BLACK
1 P–K4	P–K4
2 N–KB3	N–QB3
3 B–N5	N–B3
4 O–O	NxP

Even at the time this game was played, the Berlin Defense had virtually disappeared from serious chess. It frequently creates irremediable weaknesses, and the open positions which characterize the defense are often favorable for the development of a promising attack by White.

| 5 P–Q4 | B–K2 |
| 6 R–K1 | . . . . |

I did not know that the stronger alternative 6 Q–K2 is the book move. The point is that after 6 Q–K2, N–Q3; 7 BxN, QPxB? involves Black in serious difficulties: 8 PxP, N–B4; 9 R–Q1, B–Q2; 10 P–K6! PxP; 11 N–K5 etc.

| 6 . . . . | N–Q3 |
| 7 BxN | NPxB |

Black prepares for the time-consuming tour of the Knight which is a familiar element of this variation. Quite good here is the less well known 7 ... QPxB; 8 PxP, N–B4; 9 QxQch, BxQ giving Black excellent chances for the endgame.

8 PxP	N–N2
9 N–B3	O–O
10 N–Q4	. . . .

A good move which has several useful functions. It prevents the advance of Black's QP, it makes

P–B4 possible and in some cases White can play N–B5 with effect.

10	N–B4
11 P–B4	N–K3
12 B–K3	. . . .

Doubtless preferable to 12 NxN, BPxN which would leave Black with a poor Pawn position but give him more freedom than after the text.

12	NxN
13 BxN	P–Q4
14 Q–B3	. . . .

Today I would be strongly tempted to adopt the simple positional course of playing for control and occupation of the vital square QB5.

| 14 . . . . | B–KB4 |

Not 14 ... P–QB4; 15 NxP, PxB; 16 NxBch, QxN; 17 QxR and wins. The text seems necessary to stop the further advance of White's DP.

| 15 P–KN4! | . . . . |

The most enterprising continuation. The loss of a Pawn is only temporary.

| 15 . . . . | BxBP |
| 16 QR–B1 | P–QB4 |

16 ... B–K5; 17 NxB, PxN; 18 QxP followed by the loss of a Pawn is an equally unpromising course for Black.

17 RxB	PxB
18 NxP	P–QB4
19 P–B5	B–N4

White was threatening 20 P–B6, PxP; 21 PxP, B–Q3; 22 Q–B5, K–R1; 23 N–K7, R–K1; 24 Q–N5. If 19 ... P–B3; 20 PxP wins easily.

It is questionable whether 19 ... R–K1 would have been any better than the text, for example 20 P–B6, B–B1; 21 PxP, BxP (if 21 ... KxP; 22 R–B2 wins); 22 RxP and Black cannot safely capture the KP: 22 ... RxP? 23 RxR, BxR; 24 N–K7ch or 22 ... BxP? 23 RxB, RxR; 24 N–B6ch, K–N2; 25 RxR, QxN; 26 R–KB5 winning quickly.

        20 RxP   R–B1
        21 RxR   QxR

        22 P–B6!   R–K1

This loses the exchange. However, if 22 ... Q–Q2; 23 P–KR4!

and wins; for if 23 ... BxRP; 24 N–K7ch, K–R1; 25 PxPch, KxP; 26 N–B5ch or 23 ... B–Q7? 24 N–K7ch, K–R1; 25 PxPch, KxP; 26 Q–B6 mate! Or 23 ... B–K6ch? 24 RxB, PxR; 25 N–K7ch, K–R1; 26 PxPch, KxP; 27 Q–B6 mate.

Nor would 22 ... Q–Q1 be of much value, because White could simply win the QP if nothing better was available.

        23 N–K7ch   RxN
        24 PxR   BxP
        25 R–KB1   . . . .

Despite the previous exchanges, White still has a strong attack. If now 25 ... P–B3 he can win with 26 Q–Q5ch followed by 27 P–K6; or else 26 PxP, PxP (if 26 ... BxP? 27 P–N5 wins a piece); 27 P–N5!

        25 . . . .   Q–K1
        26 Q–Q5!   B–Q1

Allowing a decisive simplifying maneuver by White; on other moves, however, P–K6 would win very rapidly.

        27 RxP!   QxR
        28 QxBch   Q–B1
        29 QxQch   KxQ
        30 K–B2   Resigns

The Queen-side Pawns decide.

EXHIBITIONS IN THE UNITED STATES

UPON MY ARRIVAL in America in November, 1920, several exhibitions were arranged in New York. Two were held at the Lenox Theater and one at West Point. I also played exhibition games with individual players. Game 5 belongs to the latter category, but this contest should not be taken too seriously. My opponent, Charles Jaffe, was playing blindfold and was probably not doing his best. However, the manner in which his attack was refuted is entertaining.

Game 6, played against Morris Schapiro, is much more important since this was a serious contest with one of America's leading players at that time. The game, played at the rate of thirty moves an hour, took place in the home of Mischa Elman, the noted violinist, who must have been reminded of his own career as a *wunderkind*. On his 35th move, Schapiro went astray and gave me an opportunity to gain the victory in a rather curious manner.

Game 7 was played in one of the two simultaneous exhibitions at the Lenox Theater. The other games in this section, numbers 8 and 9, were likewise played in simultaneous exhibitions, during my tour of the United States. Game 8 is, perhaps, typical of simultaneous play; it is also a good example of how *not* to play chess. The final sacrifice was made possible by weak moves on the part of my opponent.

Some of my childhood games stand out in my memory because of unusual circumstances: for example, the game I played as a six-year-old against Grandmaster Akiba Rubinstein or the game against the German governor of Warsaw. If, however, I were asked to name the *best* chess game I played as a child, I would almost undoubtedly name Game 9; the only other serious candidate would be Game 4. Curiously enough, the opponents in both games were named Griffith. The contest with Dr. R. B. Griffith of Los Angeles was one of eight games played with clocks—a severe test for a child of nine. It was a long and difficult struggle, and I had to steer my way through a maze of complications to a drawn endgame.

5.

JAFFE–RESHEVSKY
Exhibition Game
New York, 1920
Jaffe played blindfold

KING'S GAMBIT DECLINED

C. Jaffe	Reshevsky
WHITE	BLACK
1 P–K4	P–K4
2 P–KB4	B–B4
3 N–KB3	P–Q3
4 P–QN4?	....

An attempt to combine the King's Gambit with the Evans Gambit. It is not a continuation which Black need fear.

4	BxP
5 P–B3	B–QB4
6 P–Q4	PxQP
7 PxP	B–N3

White's center looks powerful, but this impression is deceptive.

8 B–B4	N–KB3

9 Q–Q3	....

Black can answer 9 P–K5 with 9 ... P–Q4; 10 PxN, PxB; 11 PxP, R–N1 with a satisfactory game; whereas 9 P–K5, PxP; 10 BPxP, N–Q4; 11 B–KN5, Q–Q2; 12 Q–N3, P–QB3; 13 O–O would leave Black with a difficult game because of his undeveloped Queen-side and his opponent's attacking prospects on the other wing.

9	O–O

9 ... P–Q4 looks attractive, but it would be premature because of 10 PxP, NxP; 11 Q–K4ch, N–K2; 12 B–R3 etc.

10 O–O	R–K1
11 QN–Q2	....

On 11 P–K5, Black counters effectively with 11 ... P–Q4! 12 B–N5 (if 12 B–N3, N–K5), P–B3; 13 PxN, PxB; 14 PxP (or 14 N–N5, P–N3), Q–B3 with the better game.

11	P–N3!

In order to answer P–K5 with ... B–KB4. The move also has an additional purpose, which White fails to perceive.

12 P–B5	P–Q4!

Smashing White's center and ruining his attacking chances.

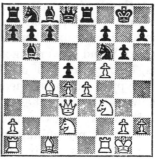

13 PxQP	BxP
14 Q–N3	N–N5!

The initiative has now passed to Black. White's feverish attempts to attack only hasten the end.

15 P–Q6	R–K6
16 BxPch	....

Loses at least the exchange; but after 16 Q–N2 or Q–Q1, QxP; White's game would also be untenable.

16	K–N2
17 Q–B4	....

17 Q–Q5? P–B3 or 17 PxP? QxBP
would lose a piece for White!

  17 . . . .   B–Q6
    Resigns

After 18 PxP, BxBP; 19 Q–Q5, Bx
R White would have no compensation for the loss of the exchange.

6.

SCHAPIRO–RESHEVSKY
Exhibition Game
New York, 1920

Time limit: 30 moves per hour

FRENCH DEFENSE

M. Schapiro	Reshevsky
WHITE	BLACK
1 P–K4	P–K3
2 P–Q4	P–Q4
3 N–QB3	N–KB3
4 B–N5	B–K2
5 P–K5	KN–Q2
6 BxB	QxB
7 Q–Q2	P–QR3

Not 7 . . . P–QB4 because of 8
N–N5. However, Black could play
7 . . . O–O; 8 P–B4, P–QB4 and if 9
N–N5, N–QB3 with a good game.

  8 N–Q1   . . . .

A rather old-fashioned continuation which indicates White's intention of building up a solid center.

8	P–QB4
9 P–QB3	N–QB3
10 P–KB4	N–N3
11 N–B3	B–Q2
12 B–K2	. . . .

12 B–Q3 looks more natural, but
Schapiro must have "feared" the
exchange of Queens which might
have resulted from 12 B–Q3, PxP;
13 PxP, Q–N5. After the text, if
12 . . . PxP; 13 PxP, Q–N5; 14 N–B3

and the exchange of Queens has
been avoided.

12	O–O
13 O–O	P–B4
14 PxP	. . . .

Going in for simplification after
all. The natural continuation is 14
N–K3, intending action on the
King-side with P–KN4 etc.

14	QxPch
15 Q–K3	QxQch
16 NxQ	N–R5

Black must seek compensation
for the theoretical inferiority of
his Bishop.

  17 P–B4!   . . . .

A very fine move. If now 17 . . .
PxP; 18 KR–Q1! with a powerful
game (18 . . . R–B2; 19 N–N5! R–
KB1, 20 BxP threatening RxB).

17	P–Q5!
18 N–B2	P–Q6!

Gaining a tempo which will be
useful.

19 BxP	NxNP
20 B–K2	N–R4
21 N–K3	P–QN4
22 PxP	PxP
23 QR–N1	N(4)–B5

Despite the ensuing simplification, Black will continue to hold
a slight initiative.

24 NxN	NxN
25 KR–Q1	B–B3
26 N–Q4	B–Q4

Black has managed to bring
about a considerable improvement
in the placement of this Bishop.

27 NxNP	N–K6
28 R–Q2	. . . .

R–Q3? would of course be a terrible blunder because of . . . B–K5.

28	BxRP
29 R–QB1	B–Q4
30 K–B2	N–N5ch
31 BxN	. . . .

K–N1 would have been simpler,

but the text is good enough for drawing purposes.

31	PxB
32 K–N3	R–R5
33 N–Q4	. . . .

N–B3 was also playable here.

33	P–R4
34 R–KB1	. . . .

White could have banished all danger with R–QB3 followed by P–R3.

34	K–R2

Threatening 35 . . . K–R3 with a view to 36 . . . R–R6ch; 37 K–R4, RxP!! 38 RxR, P–N4 mate!

35 P–B5?	. . . .

The losing move. Correct was 35 P–R4! R–R6ch; 36 K–R2 with a tenable position. The text leads to a curious finish.

35	R–R6ch
36 K–B4	

Amusing would be 36 K–R4, K–R3; 37 QR–KB2, BxP! 38 RxB, R–R6 mate!

36	K–R3!

With the astonishing threat of . . . P–N4 mate!

37 P–R4	PxP e.p.
38 N–B3	PxNP
39 RxP	RxPch
40 K–N3	QRxNch
Resigns	

The sudden collapse of White's game was remarkable.

7.

RESHEVSKY–CHERNEV
Simultaneous Exhibition
New York, 1921

GIUOCO PIANO

Reshevsky	I. Chernev
WHITE	BLACK
1 P–K4	P–K4
2 N–KB3	N–QB3
3 B–B4	B–B4
4 P–B3	P–Q3

Too slow, because it gives White a strong center. 4 . . . N–B3 is a more effective reply.

5 P–Q4	PxP
6 PxP	B–N3

On 6 . . . B–N5ch, White could reply K–B1 threatening to win a piece with 8 P–Q5 and 9 Q–R4ch.

7 P–KR3	. . . .

To prevent the pin by . . . B–N5, but this is too slow. More aggressive is 7 N–B3, N–B3; 8 B–N3, O–O (if 8 . . . B–N5; 9 B–K3, BxN; 10 PxB with a good game); 9 O–O etc.

7	N–B3
8 N–B3	O–O
9 O–O	P–KR3

He not only weakens his position with this move, but he overlooks the possibility of equalizing with 9 . . . NxKP! 10 NxN, P–Q4.

10	B–K3	R–K1

Again he misses an opportunity to play ... NxKP!

11	B–Q3	N–QN5

Loss of time. 11 ... B–Q2 would have been relatively better.

12	B–N1	B–Q2
13	P–R3	N–B3
14	Q–B2	N–R2

Another weak move; it makes possible White's reply, which opens up now lines and creates weaknesses in Black's game.

15	P–K5!	N–B1
16	PxP	PxP
17	N–K2	....

Missing the even stronger N–Q5.

17	....	R–B1
18	Q–Q3	Q–B6
19	N–B4	N–K2
20	Q–N3	N–B4?

It is true that 20 ... N–K3?? 21 N–R5 would lose the Queen for Black, but 20 ... N(1)–N3; 21 N–R5, Q–K3 would have left him with a relatively satisfactory position.

21	N–Q5	Q–Q1
22	NxB	QxN
23	QxQ	PxQ
24	B–B4	....

Black's chances of holding the position are slim indeed, for he has serious Pawn weaknesses and his

Knights are no match for White's far-ranging Bishops.

24.	....	P–Q4
25	B–Q3	N–N3
26	B–R2	N(4)–K2
27	QR–B1	RxR
28	RxR	B–B4

A trap: if now 29 BxB, NxB; 30 R–B7, NxP! In any event, White would renounce most of his advantage if he were to exchange one of his valuable Bishops.

29	B–N5!	R–QB1
30	B–B7!	B–K5
31	N–Q2	N–B1

Cherney points out that if 31 ... N–B5? 32 NxB wins a piece: likewise if 31 ... N–B4; 32 B–Q7 wins at least the exchange.

32	R–B3	N–K6
33	BxP	RxR
34	PxR	N–B5
35	B–B7!	N(2)–N3

The NP cannot be taken either way.

36	BxN	NxB
37	NxB	PxN
38	B–B4	K–B1
39	P–KR4	K–K2

This loses a second Pawn, but he has little choice: if 39 ... P–B4; 40 P–N3, N–N3; 41 P–R5, N–K2; 42 B–K6 and Black is helpless.

40	P–N3	N–K3
41	B–Q5	N–B2
42	BxNP	N–N4
43	BxP	NxBP
44	B–Q3	K–Q3
45	B–B4	P–B3
46	K–N2	N–Q4

Running into a lost K and Pawn ending; but his game was hopeless.

47	BxN	KxB
48	P–R5!	KxP
49	K–B3	K–Q4
50	K–B4	**Resigns**

8.

RESHEVSKY–BRUCKSTEIN
Simultaneous Exhibition
St. Louis, 1921

KING'S GAMBIT

Reshevsky	Bruckstein
WHITE	BLACK
1 P–K4	P–K4
2 P–KB4	PxP
3 N–KB3	P–Q3?

This has too cramping an effect on Black's position. Such natural moves as 3 ... P–Q4 and 3 ... N–KB3 give a much easier game.

4 P–Q4	B–N5

An aimless move. 4 ... P–KN4 would be better, transposing into the old classical lines of this gambit.

5 BxP	Q–B3?

This early development of the Queen can only result in loss of time later on.

6 B–N3	BxN?

Opening lines for White and strengthening his center.

7 PxB	P–QR3?

Waste of time.

| 8 N–B3 | N–B3 |
| 9 N–Q5 | Q–Q1 |

... QxQP? would lose at least the exchange. As a result of his previous inferior moves, Black's position is hopeless.

10 Q–Q2	KN–K2
11 B–QB4	P–QN4
12 B–N3	P–QR4?
13 P–QR4	P–N5
14 Q–Q3	Q–Q2
15 O–O–O	R–B1

Having weakened his position on both wings, Black is in a quandary about castling.

16 Q–B4	NxN

White threatened 17 N–B6ch!

17 QxN(5)	P–N3

Hoping to get out his Bishop. White decides to strike while the iron is hot.

18 P–K5!	N–Q1

The alternative 18 ... PxP; 19 KR–K1, QxQ; 20 BxQ, N–K2; 21 BxKP, KR–N1; 22 B–B6 is not inviting.

| 19 KR–K1 | N–K3 |
| 20 Q–K4 | N–N4? |

He should have tried ... B–R3ch followed by ... O–O. The text leads to a drastic finish.

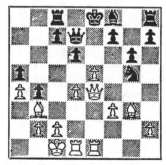

21 PxPch!	NxQ

If 21 ... K–Q1; 22 Q–K5 wins.

22 RxNch	Q–K3

He must return the Queen, for if 22 ... K–Q1; 23 B–R4ch etc.

23 RxQch!!	....

Much stronger than 23 BxQ. The point is that if 23 ... PxR; 24 BxP, R–R1; 25 PxP, B–R3ch; 26 K–N1, K–K2; 27 B–B3 followed by the advance of the QP and wins.

| 23 .... | K–Q2 |
| 24 R–B6 | Resigns |

9.

RESHEVSKY–R. B. GRIFFITH
Simultaneous Exhibition
Los Angeles, 1921
One of eight clock games

PHILIDOR'S DEFENSE
(in effect)

Reshevsky	Dr. R. B. Griffith
WHITE	BLACK
1 P–K4	P–K4
2 B–B4	N–KB3
3 N–KB3	N–B3
4 P–Q4	PxP
5 O–O	P–Q3

Prudently avoiding the complications of the Two Knights' Defense and the Max Lange Attack.

6 N–P	B–K2
7 N–QB3	B–Q2
8 P–KR3	O–O

Black's game is unpleasantly cramped as a result of his decision on move five to play safe.

9 P–B4	P–QN3

An unorthodox but trappy move. He threatens to win a piece with 10...NxN; 11 QxN, P–Q4 etc.

10 B–K3	R–K1
11 P–K5?!	....

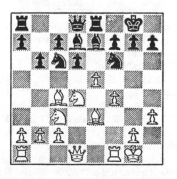

But this impetuous advance is rather weak and dissipates White's advantage by opening up the position for Black and allowing him to secure powerful counterplay. The simple 11 Q–B3 would have left White with an overwhelming game.

11	PxP
12 NxN	BxN
13 PxP	B–Q3!

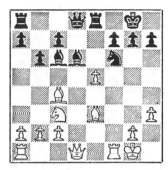

This excellent move, which stamps Black as a bold, imaginative player, seizes the initiative. It seems incredible to me that I was able to come through the following complications satisfactorily.

14 PxN	....

A promising alternative is 14 RxN, PxR; 15 Q–N4ch, K–R1 (if 15...K–B1; 16 B–R6ch); 16 BxBP, R–K2 (if 16...RxP; 17 B–R6); 17 P–K6 with Pawn and positional compensation for the exchange.

14	RxB
15 Q–N4	....

It would be pointless to rely on 15 PxP, Q–N4; 16 BxPch, KxP; 17 Q–N4, QxQ; 18 PxQ because of the powerful 18...R–N6!

15	P–N3!

Realizing that the apparently crushing 15...R–N6? is refuted by 16 BxPch! If 15...R–N6; 16 BxPch, KxB; 17 PxP dis ch, K–N1; 18 R–B8ch, BxR; 19 PxR(Q) dbl ch, KxQ; 20 QxR and should win.

16 Q–R4	....

But not 16 BxPch? KxB; 17 Q–

B4ch, R–K3 and Black's Bishop is immune from capture.

16	B–B4
17 K–R1	Q–Q2

Threatening mate in two moves.

18 K–R2	Q–Q3ch
19 K–R1	Q–Q2
20 K–R2	Q–Q3ch
21 K–R1	Q–Q2

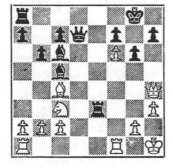

22 N–Q5?! . . . .

Avoiding the draw by repetition of moves, but inviting defeat.

22 . . . . QR–K1!

But not 22 . . . BxN; 23 BxB, Qx B; 24 Q–R6, B–B1 (forced); 25 QxR and White has won the exchange.

23 QR–Q1 . . . .

If 23 NxR? RxN; 24 K–R2, R–K5 winning the Bishop, for White dare not play 25 R–B4? because of . . . RxR; 26 QxR, B–Q3 etc.

23 . . . . R(1)–K5?

Apparently decisive, and yet it leaves White an ingenious resource. Borochow subsequently demonstrated that 23 . . . R(6)–K5!! would have won: 24 R–B4, RxB; 25 RxR, BxN; 26 RxKB, BxPch; 27 K–R2 (or 27 KxB, R–K7ch etc.), QxR with an easy win.

Another possibility is 24 R–B4, RxB; 25 N–K7ch, RxN; 26 RxQ (26 Q–R6, QxRch etc.), R(2)xR; 27 RxR, R–Q8ch; 28 K–R2, B–Q3ch; 29 R–B4, R–KB8 and wins.

24 Q–R6 . . . .

But not 24 R–B4? RxR; 25 QxR, RxPch; 26 PxR, QxPch; 27 Q–R2, Q–B6ch; 28 Q–N2, QxRch; 29 K–R2, B–Q3ch; 30 K–R3, Q–R4 mate (Borochow).

24 . . . . RxPch!

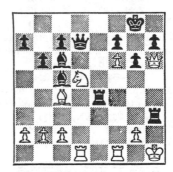

Best under the circumstances. If 24 . . . B–B1, Borochow gives the following interesting analysis: 25 N–K7ch, RxN (not 25 . . . QxN? 26 Px Q, BxQ; 27 R–Q8ch, K–N2; 28 RxP mate); 26 RxQ, BxQ; 27 RxR, RxP ch; 28 K–N1, B–K6ch; 29 R–B2, R–N6; 30 K–B1!! BxR; 31 RxKBP, P–KR4; 32 RxPch, K–R1; 33 KxB winning at least a piece.

In this variation, the reader must note the effect of 25 N–K7ch. Had the Black QR remained on K1, this move would have been unsatisfactory for White.

25	QxR	QxQch
26	PxQ	RxB

Black has simplified into an end-ing in which he has one Pawn for the exchange, and must soon gain a second Pawn. From now on, White has an uphill game all the way, and must play very carefully to hold the game.

27	P–B3	R–K5
28	R–Q2	R–K4
29	KR–Q1	R–B4
30	P–N4	B–Q3
31	K–N1	BxN
32	RxB	RxP

Black will eventually have two connected passed Pawns on the King-side. White's only counter-chance consists in playing for an exchange of Rooks and getting an open line for the remaining Rook.

33	P–R3	K–N2
34	P–B4	R–B6
35	R(1)–Q3	RxR
36	RxR	K–B3
37	K–B2	K–K3
38	R–K3ch	B–K4

If 38 ... K–Q2 the Black King is cut off from the King-side. If 38 ... K–B3; **39** R–K8 etc. If Black

wishes to make any headway, he must permit the entry of White's Rook.

39	P–QR4	P–KN4
40	R–Q3	K–K2
41	R–Q5!	P–KB3
42	K–B3	P–KR4
43	P–R5	B–B5
44	PxP	RPxP
45	P–N5	B–K4
46	K–K4	K–K3

As he cannot allow K–B5, he must permit White's next move.

47	R–Q8	P–B4ch
48	K–K3	P–N5
49	PxP	RPxP
50	R–K8ch	K–B3
51	R–KN8	B–Q3
52	R–KR8	B–B4ch
53	K–B4	B–Q3ch
54	K–K3	K–N4
55	R–R7	. . . .

White waits until his opponent commits himself with the further advance of the Pawns, which are less dangerous than they look. Sooner or later one of them will find itself on a black square and unable to advance.

55	. . . .	P–B5ch
56	K–K4	P–B6
57	R–R1	B–B4
58	R–R7	P–B7

See the previous note. Black's King can make no headway, and the game could be given up here as a draw.

59	R–R1	B–Q3
60	R–KB1	B–N6

If 60 ... P–N6; 61 K–B3 etc.

61	K–K3	K–B4
62	R–KR1	K–N4
63	R–KB1	K–B4

The game was abandoned as a draw nine moves later.

FIRST TOURNAMENT WITH MASTERS

IN OCTOBER, 1922, after the exhibition tour of the United States was completed, I was invited to play in a special tournament arranged by the Chess Club International of New York. It was my first tournament with players of master strength and my severest test up to that time.

There were six competitors: J. Bernstein, H. R. Bigelow, C. Jaffe, D. Janowski, E. Lasker and myself—a formidable line-up of opponents for a small boy!

In the early stages of the contest I was hopeful of winning second prize, but losses to Lasker and Bigelow put me out of the running. Against Jaffe I had a sure win, but I made a bad move and drew the game. I also drew with Bernstein.

The big moment of the tourney was when I won my game against Janowski, a famous master. I was so excited and happy that I rushed home in a taxi to tell my father and mother. I couldn't even sit down in the taxi. I jumped up and down all the way. When I got to the hotel, I ran up the stairs to our rooms, without waiting for the elevator, and broke the news to my parents: I had won from Janowski! And then I sang. I sang so loudly that nobody could talk. It was one of the happiest days of my life.

10.

JANOWSKI–RESHEVSKY
Club Tournament
New York, 1922

QUEEN'S GAMBIT DECLINED

D. Janowski	Reshevsky
WHITE	BLACK
1 P–Q4	N–KB3
2 N–KB3	P–Q4
3 P–B4	P–K3
4 N–B3	QN–Q2
5 B–N5	B–K2
6 P–K3	P–B3

It is more customary for Black to castle before committing himself to a definite line of defense.

7 B–Q3 . . . .

Here or on the next move, White has an attractive alternative in PxP, a move which is often seen in my later games.

7	P–QR3
8 O–O	PxP
9 BxBP	N–N3?

Naturally enough, there were many gaps in my knowledge of the openings in those days, which explains why I adopted such a clumsy maneuver instead of the natural ... P–QN4 followed by ... P–B4.

10	B–Q3	KN–Q4
11	BxB	QxB
12	Q–Q2	....

N–K4 or R–B1 would be even stronger.

12	....	NxN
13	PxN	P–QB4
14	QR–N1!	N–Q2
15	P–QR4	O–O
16	Q–B2	P–R3
17	KR–K1	P–QN3
18	R–N2	....

White has a fine, free game while Black's position is destined to be permanently cramped and under pressure.

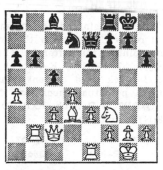

18	....	R–N1
19	KR–N1	Q–Q3
20	Q–K2	P–QR4
21	B–N5	R–Q1
22	P–R3	Q–B2
23	P–K4	....

Janowski is well satisfied with his strong position and is now ready to play for a K-side attack.

23	....	N–B1
24	Q–K3	B–Q2
25	N–K5	B–K1
26	BxB	RxB
27	P–KB4	P–B3

Creating a target for White's subsequent attack, but to leave White's Knight in its commanding position would have required a patience that was beyond me!

28	N–B3	N–Q2
29	P–K5	P–KB4

Hardly avoidable, but now Janowski has the target that he needs for opening up the King-side.

30	P–N4!	P–N3
31	NPxP	NPxP
32	P–Q5!	N–B1

32 ... PxP; 33 Q–Q3 is equally unpleasant for Black.

33	R–N2ch	K–R2
34	P–B4	Q–B2
35	K–R2	N–N3
36	QR–N1	R–N1
37	P–Q6	Q–QN2

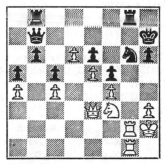

Janowski has strengthened his position from move to move in fine style, and he could now have forced the game as follows: 38 N–N5ch!! PxN; 39 RxP, R–N2 (or 39 ... Q–K5; 40 Q–KN3! and wins); 40 Q–KN3! Q–KB2; 41 R–R5ch, K–N1; 42 R–R6, NxKP (on other Knight moves, 43 Q–R4 wins); 43 PxN! Rx Q; 44 RxRch, Q–N2; 45 RxQch, Kx R; 46 RxP etc.

38	P–R4?	Q–B3
39	P–R5?	....

The Knight check should still win, whereas the apparently forceful text gives Black a way out.

39	. . . .	N–R1
40	N–N5ch	PxN
41	PxP	N–N3!!

An unexpected resource. From here on, the play is intricate and difficult all the way, and Black's escape verges on the miraculous.

| 42 | R–N3 | . . . . |

Against 42 Q–KR3 the best reply would have been 42 ... R–KR1! but not 42 ... N–B5?; 43 P–N6ch, K–R1; 44 Q–KN3, NxR; 45 Q–N5! R–KN2; 46 P–R6 and should win.

| 42 | . . . . | K–N2 |
| 43 | R–KR3 | R–KR1 |

Beginning a struggle for the KR file which is finally resolved in Black's favor.

| 44 | PxN | RxRch |
| 45 | KxR | . . . . |

A better alternative here is 45 QxR! R–KR1; 46 Q–R6ch! K–N1! 47 P–N7, R–R2; 48 K–N3, RxQ; 49 PxR, Q–K5; 50 P–Q7 forcing a draw.

45	. . . .	R–R1ch
46	K–N3	QxRP
47	Q–KB3	P–B5ch

Now it is Black who is calling the tune.

| 48 | K–N4 | Q–B7 |
| 49 | QxP | Q–K7ch |

Interposing the Queen here or on the next two moves would be fatal for White.

50	K–N3	Q–Q6ch
51	K–N2	Q–K7ch
52	K–N3	Q–R7ch
53	K–B3	R–KB1
54	Q–B6ch!	K–N1!

This preserves some winning chances, whereas after 54 ... RxQ

ch; 55 NPxRch, K–N1; 56 P–Q7, Q–Q7; 57 P–N7! Black cannot win because of the standing threat of P–B7ch etc.

| 55 | P–Q7 | RxQch |

| 56 | NPxR? | . . . . |

This surprising slip is the move that really throws away the draw. The point is that after 56 KPxR! Q–Q7; 57 P–B7ch, K–N2; 58 R–KR1! Black must content himself with a perpetual check, for if 58 ... QxQP? 59 R–R7ch, KxP; 60 P–B8(N)ch and wins!

| 56 | . . . . | Q–Q7 |
| 57 | R–KR1 | Q–Q6ch! |

But not 57 ... QxQP? 58 P–B7ch, K–N2; 59 R–R7ch and wins.

| 58 | K–N2 | QxPch |

This CHECK makes all the difference. Now the QP falls as well.

59	K–B2	Q–B4ch
60	K–N⌣	Q–N5ch
61	K–R2	Q–K7ch
62	K–R3	Q–Q6ch
63	K–R4	QxP
64	R–N1ch	K–B1
65	K–N5	Q–Q5
	Resigns	

A PRODIGY GROWS UP

M Y CAREER as a chess prodigy ended in 1924, when it was decided that a formal education was long overdue. I had been in America about four years and had learned to speak English—but little else. I had been too busy playing chess.

So, at the age of twelve, I went to school for the first time in my life! Six months with a private tutor equipped me to begin at the high-school level. After my graduation from high school, I studied accounting for two years at the University of Detroit, after which I transferred to the University of Chicago, where I obtained my degree in 1933.

While I was at school I played very little serious chess. In fact, I tried very hard to live down my reputation as a "boy wizard." Successfully, I might add. Before very long, the public had only dim recollections of the little boy in a sailor suit who used to give chess exhibitions.

Occasionally, someone would ask what had happened to the boy wonder with the tongue-twisting name—"the one who beat everybody at chess a few years ago"—but only a few intimate friends knew the answer. Young Sammy Rzeszewski was learning to read and write!

Most prodigies are popularly supposed to be failures in later life. I doubt that this belief is well founded. Among musicians, it is the rule, rather than the exception, that the child prodigy of one generation is the mature artist of the next.

There are fewer cases in chess. This much, however, is clear: if one decides to make chess a profession, a childhood devoted to the game cannot possibly be a handicap. In my own case, chess has always been the medium in which I feel most at home: at a chessboard I express myself in my mother tongue.

Hence the urge to play chess was still within me during my school years, even though I had dropped out of public sight as a chess player. I yielded to this urge in 1927, when the Western Championship Tournament was held in Kalamazoo, near my home in Detroit.

After four more years of concentration on normal studies, opportunity knocked again. Samuel Factor, one of Chicago's strongest players, was driving to Tulsa to take part in the Western Association Tournament. At his invitation, I accompanied him. School was out, and it was a chance for a pleasant vacation, if nothing else.

At Tulsa, I won the Western Association title without losing a game. It was my first tournament success. It was a minor event, but the taste of victory was sweet. Nevertheless, I had not yet consciously decided to make chess my profession. I still had two years of my university training to complete. I was only twenty years old and was still not quite certain of myself. Perhaps I had been lucky. (Other chess players often say that I'm very lucky!)

The next year, at Minneapolis, I failed in defense of my title. Immediately thereafter came the Pasadena Tournament, won by Dr. Alekhine, then world champion. The tournament was so hard fought that I managed to tie for third place even after losing four games!

But these tournaments taught me a lesson. Lack of knowledge of the openings had been unimportant in my barnstorming days as a child, but at this stage it was crippling! At best, I was running into time pressure and an abnormal number of adjourned games.

I simply had to learn openings. I went home to study chess for the first time in my life!

My studies bore fruit, for in 1934, after tying for first place in the Western Championship at Chicago, I took first prize without the loss of a game in the International Tournament at Syracuse, New York.

The following year I was invited to the famous Easter tournament at Margate, England. Here my most formidable rival was ex-world champion J. R. Capablanca. I won my encounter with this chess immortal and took first prize in this, my first foreign tournament. Later, I was equally successful against a somewhat weaker field at Yarmouth.

With these victories came recognition as one of the world's leading chess players. The prodigy had grown up.

WESTERN CHAMPIONSHIP TOURNAMENTS

THE GAMES which follow were played in four different Western Championship Tournaments. Since these tournaments are no longer being conducted, a few words about them might indicate their place in the American scene.

The Western Championships were first played in 1900 under the auspices of the Western Chess Association and were continued annually through 1933. At that time the Association expanded to become the American Chess Federation, and the tournament became known as the United States Open Chess Championship.

Meanwhile, other chess players in the United States had organized as the National Chess Federation, and in 1936 this group held a tournament which was called the United States Chess Championship. For a few years these two large bodies of chess players each claimed to represent the whole country, and each held separate "national" tournaments, but in 1939 they merged into the United States Chess Federation and have since conducted the tournaments of *both* earlier bodies on a combined and truly national basis.

The older of these, tracing its lineage back to 1900, is still called the United States Open Chess Championship and is open to any player. This has the excellent effect of encouraging large numbers of comparatively unknown players to compete and thus gain valuable tournament experience.

Incidentally, those who become interested in tournament play soon discover that love of the game will have to compensate them for the most part, since prize money seldom pays even for the food a contestant consumes during the course of a tournament—let alone his hotel bill and his fare to and from the event. In a few tournaments in the past, moreover, misunderstandings or poor organization have reduced the prize even farther. My prize "money" for winning the Tulsa Tournament in 1931 consisted of a few cordial words!

The other national tournament, the United States Chess Championship, is open partly to those who survive qualifying rounds and partly to those invited to play on the basis of past performance. Although this type of tournament does not tend to promote tournament play as widely as the older event, the caliber of play is consistently higher and it is therefore more highly regarded among top-flight players.

During the period 1927-1934, covered in the ten games which follow, most of this was history yet to be made. The Western Championships afforded me the most convenient opportunity to measure my strength against some of the strongest American players of the day.

11.

RESHEVSKY–PALMER
Western Championship
Kalamazoo, 1927

QUEEN'S GAMBIT DECLINED
Reshevsky   M. Palmer
WHITE   BLACK

1	P–Q4	P–K3
2	N–KB3	P–Q4
3	P–B4	P–QB3
4	P–K3	N–B3
5	N–B3	QN–Q2
6	Q–B2	....

The usual move (and best) is 6 B–Q3. After the somewhat passive text, Black should obtain a perfectly good game.

6	....	B–Q3
7	B–Q3	PxP
8	BxBP	P–QN4

Rather questionable, with White's Queen on the QB file. 8 ... P–K4 would have equalized without any difficulty. Whereas ... B–Q3 is a good move when Black strives for ... P–K4, it is a poor move in the text system of development.

9	B–Q3	P–QR3
10	B–Q2	....

The immediate N–K4 was also good.

10	....	P–B4

To delay this advance would invite a positional catastrophe. But

White's reply is embarrassing.

11	P–QR4!	BPxP?

This brings White's KN into play very strongly. His best chance was 11 ... P–N5; 12 N–K4, NxN; 13 Bx N, R–R2.

12	KNxP	P–N5
13	N–K4	N–K4?

He had nothing better than 13 ... B–K2, which, however, would lose at least a Pawn and leave him with a poor position. The text is much worse.

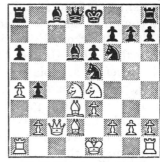

14	N–B6!	Q–B2

Black's predicament is hopeless. If 14 ... QxN; 15 QxNch wins a piece. If 14 ... NxBch; 15 QxN with the same result.

15	NxBch	QxN
16	NxN	B–N2

Or 16 ... QxN; 17 Q–B6ch etc.

17	N–B4	Q–Q4
18	P–K4	Q–Q5
19	B–K3	Resigns

12.

RESHEVSKY–BOROCHOW
Western Championship
Tulsa, 1931
Brilliancy Prize Game
INDIAN DEFENSE
(in effect)

Reshevsky	H. Borochow
WHITE	BLACK
1 N–KB3	N–KB3
2 P–B4	P–K3
3 P–KN3	P–Q3

Black is undecided about his choice of a defense. As the game goes, he loses a clear tempo by taking two moves to play ... P–K4.

4 B–N2	QN–Q2
5 O–O	P–K4
6 P–Q4	B–K2
7 P–N3	P–B3
8 N–B3	....

Not fearing 8 ... P–K5, which could be answered by 9 N–KN5, P–Q4; 10 PxP, PxP; 11 P–B3, opening up the game to White's advantage.

8	O–O
9 Q–B2	R–K1
10 R–Q1	Q–B2
11 P–QR4	N–B1
12 B–QR3	....

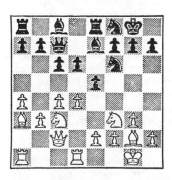

White intends to train his guns on the weak QP, a plan which will

be completed later on with the doubling of his Rooks on the Q file. Black's position is cramped and will remain so, with the result that he is condemned to passivity and more or less meaningless regrouping of his pieces. His line of defense must therefore be dismissed as inadequate.

| 12 .... | N–N3 |
| 13 P–R3! | .... |

The beginning of an action against Black's weakened center which is not completed until move 24.

13	B–B1
14 N–KR2	B–Q2
15 N–B1	....

The Knight is headed for KB5.

| 15 .... | QR–Q1 |
| 16 N–K3 | Q–B1 |

White is foiled for the time being, but he has another plan.

| 17 K–R2 | P–KR3 |

Black is frankly marking time. He might have tried 17 ... P–B4, but after 18 PxBP, PxP White's control of Q5 would have been strategically decisive.

| 18 R–Q2 | B–K2 |
| 19 QR–Q1 | N–B1 |

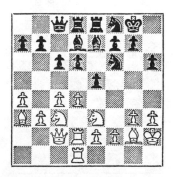

20 PxP! ....

Forcing the removal of Black's KB and gaining complete control of Black's weak Q3.

20	PxP
21 BxB	RxB
22 P–B5!	N(1)–R2
23 P–R4	QR–K1
24 N–B4	Q–B2
25 N–Q6	. . . .

A magnificent outpost for the Knight. As Black's situation is hopeless in the center and on the Queen-side, his only chance is to play for attack.

25	R–KB1
26 P–QN4	N–N5ch
27 K–N1	P–B4
28 P–K3	P–KN4
29 P–KR5	P–K5

Too slow. The only chance was ...P–B5, but Borochow was doubtless reluctant to play this move, because White would thereupon gain control of the square K4.

30 N–K2	. . . .

Now this Knight also takes up a powerful position.

30	N(2)–B3
31 N–Q4	NxRP
32 B–R3!	. . . .

Threatening to regain the Pawn advantageously by capturing the KBP.

32	P–B5

33 N(4)–B5!	. . . .

White cannot capture the KBP, but he can still capture KB5, which serves his purpose equally well!

33	BxN
34 NxB	PxKP

Or 34 ...RxN; 35 BxN and wins.

35 BxN	. . . .

And not 35 NxRch, QxN; 36 PxP, NxKP; 37 Q–N3ch, N–Q4 with a good game for Black.

35	N–B3
36 NxRch	QxN
37 Q–N3ch	K–R1
38 QxP	NxB
39 Q–Q4ch	. . . .

Had Black played 37...K–R2, White would win with 39 R–Q7 etc.

39	Q–K4

39...K–N1; 40 R–K1 is equally hopeless for Black.

40 QxQch	NxQ
41 R–Q8	Resigns

13.

RESHEVSKY–MICHELSEN
Western Championship
Detroit, 1933

KING'S INDIAN DEFENSE
(in effect)

Reshevsky	E. Michelsen
WHITE	BLACK
1 P–Q4	P–Q4
2 P–QB4	P–QB3
3 N–KB3	P–KN3
4 N–B3	B–N2
5 P–K3	N–B3
6 Q–N3	. . . .

This is a position which can arise from the Slav Defense or from the Gruenfeld Defense. White's last move is considered the strongest at this stage, as it exerts lasting pressure on Black's center.

6	O–O
7 B–Q3	. . . .

B–Q2 followed by R–B1 is more exact; if Black plays ...PxP, White saves a tempo in developing his KB.

7 . . . .   PxP

After this early capture, Black has little terrain and meager prospects. 7 ... P–N3 or ... P–K3, holding the center for some time to come, is a more promising course.

        8 BxBP   QN–Q2
        9 N–KN5   P–K3
        10 O–O   . . . .

Here I gave a great deal of thought to the possibility 10 BxP, PxB; 11 NxKP, Q–N3; 12 QxQ followed by NxR, with Rook and two Pawns for two minor pieces. This would have been unfavorable for White. The best course is to proceed with natural development.

        10 . . . .   N–N3
        11 B–K2   KN–Q2
        12 N–B3   P–K4

Black seems to have freed himself, but the position is less simple than it seems. What Black is really doing is opening up the position for White's pieces.

        13 R–Q1   Q–K2
        14 P–K4!   PxP
        15 NxP   N–B4
        16 Q–B2   N–K3
        17 N–B3!   . . . .

An important move, exemplifying the principle that when your opponent has a cramped game, it is wise to avoid exchanges. Black's KB is his only well placed piece.

while the other minor pieces are poorly posted. The result is that Black cannot get his Rooks properly developed, and his pieces are bunched together without any effective coordination.

        17 . . . .   B–Q2
        18 P–QR4!   QR–Q1
        19 B–K3   KR–K1
        20 P–R5   . . . .

Crowding back into a worse huddle than ever.

        20 . . . .   N–QB1
        21 P–K5!   . . . .

The strategically decisive move. ... N–Q3 is prevented, and N–K4 is threatened. Black's natural attempt to avoid strangulation leads to a quick catastrophe.

        21 . . . .   P–B3
        22 PxP   BxP
        23 N–K4   B–N2

After this Black must lose some material, but to part with the valuable KB would be just as serious.

        24 Q–N3!   P–N3

Losing the exchange; however, permitting the loss of the QNP would be just as bad.

        25 B–KN5   Q–B2
        26 BxR   RxB
        27 B–B4!   Resigns

He has no defense against the double threat of RxB or N–N5.

14.

FOX–RESHEVSKY
Western Championship
Detroit, 1933

QUEEN'S INDIAN DEFENSE

M. Fox	Reshevsky
WHITE	BLACK
1 N–KB3	N–KB3
2 P–B4	P–K3
3 P–Q4	P–QN3

My experience with this defense has taught me that it usually gives Black a cramped position, and that the best he can hope for is a draw. To my way of thinking, 3 . . . P–Q4 gives more scope for fighting play.

4 P–KN3	B–N2
5 B–N2	B–N5ch

5 . . . B–K2 is somewhat more promising, as it avoids undue simplification. The text is not obligatory, since Black's KB is at least as valuable as White's QB.

6 B–Q2	BxBch
7 QNxB	. . . .

As will be seen later on, the more customary 7 QxB is stronger. If then 7 . . . O–O; 8 N–B3, P–Q3; 9 Q–B2, Q–K2; 10 O–O with a much freer game for White. See Game 18 for an example of the recapture with the Queen.

7	O–O
8 Q–B2	P–Q3
9 O–O	Q–K2
10 P–K4	P–K4

We are now out of the opening stage. White has a good center formation, but he cannot be said to have any advantage because his QN is poorly posted. On QB3 this piece would threaten to occupy the important square Q5, whereas on its present post, the QN has little influence on the center. It is both curious and interesting that this difference in the position of the QN should have so much bearing on the evaluation of the position.

11 N–R4	. . . .

A better plan was P–Q5 followed by N–K1 and P–B4.

11	P–N3

11 . . . PxP would allow White to regain the Pawn advantageously with 12 N–B5, Q–K4; 13 P–B4 etc.

12 P–Q5	P–QR4

In order to prevent P–QN4; Black also has in mind the possibility of anchoring his QN at QB4 and wants to prevent its being dislodged by P–QN4.

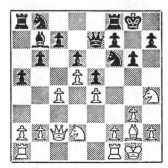

13 P–B4?	. . . .

A positional error which has serious consequences. The indicated continuation was 13 P–N3 (not 13 P–QR3, P–R5), followed by P–QR3 and P–QN4.

13	PxP
14 RxP	. . . .

The natural move is 14 PxP (retaining command of K5); but then Black wins a Pawn with 14 . . . N–R4! (but not 14 . . . NxKP or . . . NxQP because of 15 NxP! with a good game for White).

14	B–B1

The Bishop has no scope at N2 and is therefore returned to its original diagonal. From here it can be usefully developed to Q2 or N5 later on.

As a result of White's faulty thirteenth move, Black has the considerable positional advantage of being able to post a piece at K4 without having to fear that it will be driven off by Pawns. However, before Black can turn this advantage to account, he must first neutralize White's pressure on the KB file.

15 QR–KB1	N–R4

...N–N5 (intending ...N–K4) looks attractive, but it seemed more important to me to consolidate the King-side by posting the Knights at KR4 and KB3.

16 R(4)–B2	N–Q2
17 QN–B3	QN–B3

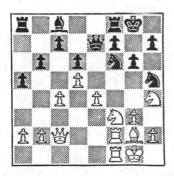

18 N–Q4	....

R–K2 (intending P–K5) would have been more to the point. Black would then continue with ...N–N5–K4.

18	B–Q2
19 R–K2	....

White has no plan, and just making moves always proves fatal.

19	N–N5
20 Q–Q2	QR–K1

Black is now ready to concentrate his forces on K4 and the KP.

21 P–N3	Q–K4
22 N(R4)–B3	Q–N2

23 R(1)–K1	R–K2
24 N–QN5	....

Vainly hoping to divert Black's forces.

24	N–K4!

For if 25 NxBP?; B–N5 wins at least the exchange.

25 NxN	QxN
26 N–Q4	....

26 NxBP? would be refuted by ...B–N5.

26 ...	KR–K1
27 B–B3	N–B3

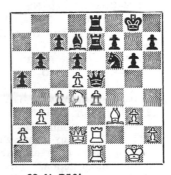

28 N–B5?!	....

A faulty plan but a good try: he overlooks Black's 33rd move. While it is true that the text hastens the end, White would have succumbed to the pressure sooner or later.

28	PxN
29 PxP	QxBP
30 RxR	RxR
31 RxR	QxB
32 Q–N5ch	K–B1!
33 RxB	Q–Q8ch!

This is the move that refutes White's combination. Since he cannot play 34 K–B2?? because of ...N–K5ch, he must allow Black's Queen to reach the K file.

34 K–N2	Q–K7ch
35 K–R3	NxR
Resigns	

White resigns, for 36 Q–Q8ch is met by 35 ...Q–K1.

15.

PALMER–RESHEVSKY
Western Championship
Detroit, 1933

KING'S INDIAN DEFENSE

M. Palmer	Reshevsky
WHITE	BLACK
1 P–Q4	N–KB3
2 P–QB4	P–KN3

A defense which I like because of its fighting qualities.

| 3 N–QB3 | B–N2 |

At present I prefer ... P–Q4 because it prevents White from obtaining a strong center.

4 P–K4	P–Q3
5 N–B3	O–O
6 P–KR3	KN–Q2

The usual continuation is ... QN–Q2 followed by ... P–K4, but I wanted to get my opponent out of the "books." In any event the text has the merit of freeing the KB for immediate action.

| 7 B–K3 | P–QB4 |

The alternative was 7 ... P–K4; 8 P–Q5, P–QR4; 9 B–Q3, N–R3; 10 O–O, QN–B4 etc.

| 8 Q–Q2 | N–QB3 |

Judging from the actual continuation, ... PxP followed by ... N–QB3 might have been better.

| 9 P–Q5 | QN–K4 |
| 10 NxN | NxN |

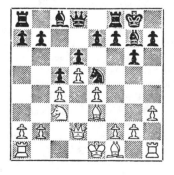

| 11 B–R6 | .... |

P–B4 would have been more energetic. Since Black's position is cramped, there is little point in White's offering to exchange.

| 11 .... | P–B3! |

To create a retreat for the Knight at B2 where it can be employed most advantageously for protective purposes in the event of a King-side attack.

| 12 B–K2 | B–Q2 |

Had this been played a move earlier, White would have been able to win a piece by BxB followed by P–B4.

| 13 P–KR4 | .... |

White is intent upon a King-side attack at all costs.

| 13 .... | Q–B1 |
| 14 P–B3 | .... |

Here again White misses the most energetic continuation: 14 Bx B, KxB; 15 P–B4, N–B2; 16 O–O–O followed by QR–KN1 and P–KN4.

| 14 .... | P–R3 |
| 15 P–KN4 | .... |

Still another inexact move. It was essential to play 15 BxB, KxB; 16 P–R4. If then 16 ... P–QN4? 17 BPxP!, PxP; 18 BxP, BxB; 19 Nx B, N–B5; 20 Q–B3 etc. and Black would not have enough play for the sacrificed Pawn.

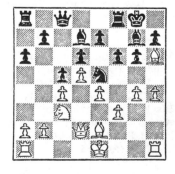

15 . . . .   P–QN4!

White's attack on the King-side
is inevitable; hence Black looks
for counter-chances on the other
wing.

16 K–B2?   . . . .

White has lost the thread of the
game. It is true that he could not
have won a Pawn with 16 PxP, Px
P; 17 NxP?, BxN; 18 BxB, NxPch
etc. The text, however, unnecessarily loses a Pawn. Correct was 16
P–N3 (not 16 PxP, PxP with a very
promising Queen-side game for
Black), PxP; 17 PxP, R–N1; 18
N–Q1 followed by N–K3 guarding
the QBP and making P–B4 possible.

16 . . . .   PxP

The win of this Pawn is not so
important as the fact that Black
acquires the QN file as a base of
operations.

17 BxB   KxB
18 QR–KN1   P–R3!

Very important. Without this
move White could have played P–
N5 and if ...P–B4; P–R5 opening
the KR file. As matters stand now,
19 P–N5 would be answered by 19
...BPxP; 20 PxP, P–KR4 and
White's attack is at a standstill.
Black's position is now fully secure
and he can safely afford to take
the initiative.

19 N–Q1   R–QN1!
20 N–K3   Q–N2!
21 P–B4   . . . .

Relatively better was 21 R–N1,
Q–N5; 22 Q–B1 (if 22 Q–B2, B–R5),
N–Q6ch; 23 BxN, PxB and Black
retains the initiative.

21 . . . .   QxNP!!

A painful surprise for White.
Practically all of White's remaining moves are more or less forced.

22 QxQ   RxQ
23 PxN   PxPch
24 K–K1   R–Q8!

The key-move of Black's combination. Once he captures the KP,
the combined action of his Rooks
is irresistible.

25 NxP   RxRP
26 N–K3   . . . .

White's position is most unpleas-
ant! If 26 N–Q2, R–R8ch; 27 B–Q1,
BxP; 28 RxB, RxR etc.
Or if 26 B–Q3, B–N4!; 27 K–Q1,
R–B6; 28 B–K2, R–B6! etc.

26 . . . .   RxKP
27 R–N3   R–R8ch
28 B–Q1   B–R5
29 K–K2   R–R7ch
30 K–K1   . . . .

If 30 K–Q3 (not 30 K–B3??, R–
B5 mate. If 30 K–B1, RxN etc.), R–
Q5ch; 31 K–B3, BxB; 32 RxB, Rx
R; 33 NxR, R–R6ch winning the
Rook.

30 . . . .   BxB
Resigns

16.

RESHEVSKY–WILLMAN
Western Championship
Detroit, 1933

QUEEN'S GAMBIT DECLINED

Reshevsky	R. Willman
WHITE	BLACK
1 P–Q4	N–KB3
2 P–QB4	P–B3
3 N–QB3	P–Q4
4 N–B3	P–K3
5 PxP	. . . .

By interpolating this exchange, White sidesteps the Cambridge Springs Defense in its usual and strongest form.

5	KPxP
6 Q–B2	QN–Q2
7 B–N5	Q–R4

. . . B–K2 would be more to the point. After the previous exchange of Pawns, this development of the Queen has little value.

| 8 N–Q2 | . . . . |

To take the sting out of . . . N–K5.

8 . . .	B–N5
9 P–K3	O–O
10 B–Q3	P–B4

Rather than retreat or exchange, Black prefers to play energetically in the hope of gaining the initiative.

| 11 BxN | . . . . |

The simpler course was 11 O–O and if . . . P–B5; 12 B–B5 with a strong bind on the position. Although I realized that it would expose me to a powerful attack, I determined to accept the challenge and play for the following win of a Pawn.

11	NxB
12 N–N3	Q–B2
13 PxP	P–QR4

13 . . . BxP is answered by 14 NxP!

14 P–QR3	P–R5
15 N–Q4	BxBP
16 NxRP	Q–R4ch

To retreat the Bishop would leave Black with an ending which would surely be lost in the long run. He therefore prefers to sacrifice a piece in the hope of profiting from the resulting complications.

17 P–N4	BxPch
18 PxB	QxPch
19 K–K2	B–N5ch
20 P–B3	B–Q2
21 N–N2	QR–K1

| 22 Q–Q2 | . . . . |

Although White has a piece for a Pawn, the position is not so simple as it might seem at first sight. White's King is in a precarious position, and Black has several dangerous attacking possibilities. In such positions, one must always be extremely careful because of the psychological tendency to relax after having obtained a distinct advantage in material.

Instead of playing his last move, White could also have parried the threat of ... QxKN with 22 K-B2, for if then 22 ... RxP; 23 KxR, R-K1ch; 24 K-B2 (not 24 B-K4, NxB; 25 PxN, RxPch; 26 K-B3, QxKN with a promising attack), QxNch; 25 K-B1 and White is out of danger.

22 . . . .   RxPch!?

It is a case of now or never, for if White is allowed time for K-B2, the attack will peter out completely.

23	KxR	R-K1ch
24	B-K4	Q-Q3
25	K-B2	PxB
26	QR-K1	. . . .

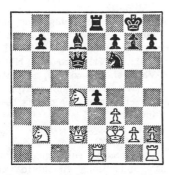

More precise would have been 26 N-B4, Q-B4; 27 N-K3 with nothing to worry about. After the text Black still manages to keep his opponent uncomfortable, despite the Rook down.

26	. . . .	B-N4
27	Q-B3	B-R3
28	N-B2	P-KR4
29	P-KN3	Q-K3
30	P-KR4	R-QB1

31 Q-Q2   . . . .

31 . . . .   N-N5ch

His best chance for putting up a long resistance was 31 ... Q-N3ch; 32 N-Q4 (not 32 N-K3, PxP; 33 KxP, Q-B3ch!), R-Q1; 33 R-Q1, B-Q6; 34 NxB, QxNch; 35 Q-K3. However, after the forced exchange of Queens, White would win the QP and eventually the QNP, after which victory would only be a matter of time.

32	PxN	Q-B3ch
33	K-N1	QxN
34	R-R2	B-Q6
35	N-K3	Q-K4
36	Q-KB2	P-QN4
37	R-N2	P-N5
38	Q-N2!	R-B6

This loses the important QNP, but if 38 ... Q-B4; 39 PxP followed by P-R6, with the attack beaten off and the initiative finally in White's hands.

39	QxP	PxP
40	NxP	Q-B2
41	N-K3	R-B4
42	Q-Q4	P-B4
43	K-R2	P-B5
44	PxP	R-R4
45	N-Q5	Resigns

Black deserves credit for his plucky fight against great odds.

17.

RESHEVSKY–OPSAHL
Western Championship
Detroit, 1933

COLLE SYSTEM

Reshevsky	E. Opsahl
WHITE	BLACK
1 P–Q4	N–KB3
2 N–KB3	P–K3
3 P–K3	. . . .

This opening is a favorite with many aggressive players, for if it is not handled carefully by Black, White quickly obtains a terrific bind.

3	P–QN3
4 B–Q3	B–N2
5 O–O	P–Q4

Since this shuts the diagonal of the QB, it is illogical in combination with Black's third and fourth moves.

6 N–K5	QN–Q2
7 P–KB4	. . . .

White's Knight is now very strongly entrenched at K5. If Black exchanges, White opens the KB file with BPxN, giving him formidable attacking possibilities.

| 7 . . . . | P–QR3 |

A superfluous precaution. He should have tried 7...B–K2 and if 8 B–N5, O–O; 9 N–B6, Q–K1; 10 N–Q2, P–QR3; 11 NxBch, QxN; 12 B–Q3, N–K5; 13 Q–B3, P–KB4 with better prospects than in the text continuation.

| 8 Q–B3 | P–N3 |

Black reasons that his KB will be more effective at N2 than at K2. At the same time he prevents any possibility of P–B5.

9 N–Q2	P–B4
10 P–B3	Q–B2
11 Q–R3!	. . . .

Preparing for a powerful assault in the event that Black castles King-side. At the same time KB3 is freed for the KN and certain sacrificial potentialities are introduced into the position.

11	B–N2
12 QN–B3	P–KR3?

Black wants to restrain his opponent from playing N–N5, but this move is too risky.

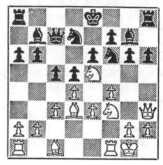

| 13 B–Q2 | . . . . |

Being intent on completing my development, I rejected 13 BxNP!, PxB; 14 QxKPch, K–Q1; 15 N–B7 ch, K–B1; 16 NxR, BxN; 17 N–K5 and White should win, as he picks up the KNP, while Black's King is still insecure and his pieces lack coordination.

13	N–K5
14 P–QR4	. . . .

I was not at all concerned about Black's opportunity to obtain two Bishops with ...NxB, because Black's Knight is well posted at K5, whereas White's QB has little scope for the present.

Here again a promising sacrificial line presented itself: 14 NxNP, PxN; 15 QxPch, K–Q1 (not 15... K–B1?; 16 N–K5 and wins); 17 QxKNP etc. But this line is by no means so promising as the variation given above.

14	QN–B3
15 B–K1	Q–K2
16 K–R1	P–KN4?

16 ... O–O–O should have been played. The text eases White's task by making the KB file available to him.

| 17 N–N1! | O–O–O |
| 18 Q–B3 | P–KR4 |

And here again Black had a better move in 18 ... N–Q2, intending ... NxN and ... P–B3. If (after 18 ... N–Q2) White tries 19 P–QN4, P–B5; 20 NxQBP? he loses a piece: 20 ... P–N5; 21 QxP, P–B4 etc.

| 19 PxNP | NxNP |
| 20 Q–B4 | N(3)–K5 |

Black's game has become very difficult. If 20 ... N(4)–K5; 21 B–R4, R–R3; 22 KBxN, PxB; 23 B–KN5 and wins.

| 21 BxN | BxN |

Leaving himself with a terrible weakness on the black squares, but other moves would lose at least a Pawn.

| 22 QxB | NxB |

If 22 ... PxB; 23 B–N3! with a winning position.

| 23 Q–B4 | P–B3 |
| 24 B–N3! | .... |

And now White's plan has become clear: he forces the exchange of the well placed Knight for the inactive Bishop, remaining with a mobile Knight against a hemmed in and useless Bishop. In addition, Black's Pawns are scattered and insecure.

24	NxBch
25 QxN	QR–N1
26 Q–R4	R–N3
27 R–B2	K–Q2
28 P–R5!	....

Played at just the right moment. This move initiates a maneuver which is extremely risky, as it in-volves the opening of the dormant Bishop's diagonal. However, careful play repulses the attack.

| 28 .... | P–N4 |
| 29 PxP | KR–KN1 |

Of course, if 29 ... QxP; 30 RxP and wins.

| 30 N–K2! | R–N5 |

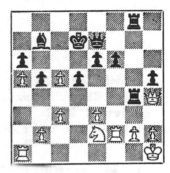

| 31 Q–R3! | .... |

Best. If 31 QxBP, QxQ; 32 RxQ, RxP with strong attacking chances. Or if 31 QxRP?, Q–N2! (threatening ... R–KR1 as well as ... RxP); 32 Q–R3, P–Q5! and White cannot meet the double threat of 33 ... R–KR1 and 33 ... RxP.

| 31 .... | P–Q5! |
| 32 N–B4! | .... |

The winning move. If 32 ... P–K4; 33 NxP wins easily, for if 33 ... BxPch; 34 RxB and Black's pinned Rook is helpless!

Or if 32 ... PxKP; 33 R–Q1ch, K–B1; 34 QxKP, P–K4; 35 N–Q5, Q–K3; 36 P–B6!, BxP (not 36 ... QxP??; 37 N–K7ch); 37 Q–B5 (another way is 37 RxP and if ... Qx R; 38 NxQ, RxP; 39 N–Q5 etc.), R–K1; 38 R(2)–Q2 and wins.

32	QxP
33 BPxP	Q–B3
34 R–Q1	....

Another way was 34 P–Q5, PxP; 35 NxRP etc.

| 34 .... | RxN |

Black is desperate because he has no worthwhile means of attack left.

35 PxR	Q–B5
36 P–B5!	Q–R5
37 PxPch	K–K2
38 QxP	R–N2
39 P–Q5	Resigns

A hard game!

18.

RESHEVSKY–FINE
Western Championship
Detroit, 1933

QUEEN'S INDIAN DEFENSE

Reshevsky	R. Fine
WHITE	BLACK
1 P–Q4	N–KB3
2 P–QB4	P–K3
3 N–KB3	B–N5ch
4 B–Q2	BxBch
5 QxB	....

The correct way to recapture (see Game 14).

5	P–QN3
6 P–KN3	B–N2
7 B–N2	O–O
8 N–B3	Q–K2
9 O–O	P–Q3

9...N–K5 also leaves Black somewhat short of equality; for example 10 Q–B2, NxN (if 10...P–KB4; 11 N–K5! with considerable positional advantage); 11 QxN, P–Q3; 12 KR–Q1, N–Q2; 13 N–K1, BxB; 14 NxB, P–KB4 (or 14... N–B3; 15 P–B3 followed by P–K4 and N–K3 leaving White with a freer game); 15 N–B4 and Black's weakness on the white squares gives White an edge.

10 Q–B2	P–B4
11 PxP	....

This gives Black a fairly easy game. Likewise if 11 P–K4, N–B3;

12 QR–Q1 (if 12 P–K5, QPxP; 13 PxKP, N–KN5; 14 KR–K1, P–B3; 15 PxP, QxP with a strong pressure on the KB file), P–K4! and White cannot prevent his opponent from occupying the important square Q5.

White's best line seems 11 QR–Q1, PxP; 12 NxP, BxB; 13 KxB, R–B1; 14 Q–Q3, as Euwe played against me at Nottingham.

11	NPxP!

More enterprising than the drawish ...QPxP, which would probably lead to an early slaughter on the Q file. Black is confident that he can defend the QP adequately, and he hopes to utilize the QN file later on.

12 QR–Q1	N–B3
13 P–K4	....

A difficult decision: this move is played to prevent a possible advance of the QP, but it opens up White's Q4 to invasion by the hostile QN.

13	KR–Q1
14 R–Q2	N–KN5!?

Black is not content with the simpler course ...P–K4 followed by ...N–Q5. Instead, he plans the removal of White's KN, in order to occupy White's Q4.

15 KR–Q1	KN–K4
16 NxN	N–Q5!

The safest course was 16...Px N, leading to further exchanges and very likely an early draw. The weakness of Black's Pawn position would be compensated for by Black's command of Q5.

16...NxN? would be quite wrong because of 17 N–N5 winning the QP.

17 N–N6!	....

More promising than 17 Q–N1, PxN etc.

Note that 17 RxN? would be a mistake because of 17...PxR leaving both Knights **en prise.**

17 . . . .   RPxN

Of course not 17 . . . NxQ?; 18
NxQch, K–B1; 19 RxN remaining a
piece ahead.

18 Q–Q3   P–K4!?

Black is still in an aggressive
mood. The text gives additional
support to the advanced Knight,
but creates strong counter-chances
for White (P–B4 etc.).

19 R–KB1   . . . .

Taking immediate advantage of
the opportunity offered by Black's
last move.

19 . . . .   B–B3

Fine is apparently ignoring the
gathering storm-clouds. Tarrasch
makes the interesting suggestion
here of 19 . . . P–KN4, which would
compel White to proceed with
great caution, since the results of
the immediate 20 P–B4, NPxP; 21
PxP, PxP; 22 RxP do not look too
inviting.

20 P–B4   QR–N1

The following advance could be
prevented by . . . P–B4, but after 21
KPxP and the resulting exchange
of Bishops, White would bring his
Knight to Q5 with devastating
effect.

21 P–B5!   Q–N4

Black is now ready to block the
KB file with . . . P–B3.

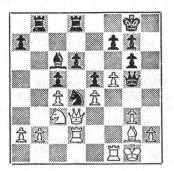

22 P–B6!   . . . .

This leads to exciting play.

22 . . . .   R–N2

If 22 . . . PxP; 23 R(2)–KB2 regains the Pawn advantageously.

23 R(2)–KB2   PxP
24 P–N3   P–B4?

Still playing to win, he mis-
judges the position. Fine's later recommendation of 24 . . . P–R4; 25
RxP, R(1)–Q2 is definitely better.

25 PxP   BxB
26 KxB   PxP

27 RxP!   . . . .

Fine later admitted frankly that
he had overlooked this move. It is
the natural consequence of White's
play up to this point, and it
achieves the following results: it
removes Black's Knight, his best
posted piece; it gives White's
Knight an unassailable post at Q5,
with devastating effect; all of
White's pieces cooperate beautifully against the exposed King,
while Black's pieces do not function harmoniously.

27 . . . .   NxR
28 RxN   Q–R3

The best chance was 28 . . . Q–
N2; 29 N–Q5, K–B1; 30 Q–K4, P–
B3! giving up a Pawn in order to
swing the QR from N2 to KB2.

28 . . . Q–N3 would have been refuted by the following interesting

line of play: 29 N–Q5, K–B1; 30
Q–K4, Q–R3; 31 Q–N4, Q–N2; 32
R–N5, Q–R2; 33 R–R5, Q–N1; 34
Q–R4 and wins.

| 29 Q–K4 | R–K2 |
| 30 Q–N4ch | K–B1 |

Any other move loses the Queen.

| 31 R–R5 | Q–N2 |

Or 31...Q–Q7ch; 32 K–R3, R–
K3; 33 Q–R4, R(1)–K1; 34 N–K4,
Q–K6; 35 R–R8ch, K–N2; 36 Q–R7
mate.

| 32 Q–R4 | K–K1 |

There was no defense. If 32...
P–B4; 33 R–R8ch, K–B2; 34 R–R7
etc.

| 33 N–Q5 | .... |

This wins at once.

| 33 .... | P–B4 |
| 34 NxR | Resigns |

For if 34...QxN; 35 R–R8ch, K–
Q2; 36 R–R7. A very tense struggle
throughout.

19.

RESHEVSKY–GRIGORIEFF
Western Championship
Chicago, 1934

QUEEN'S GAMBIT DECLINED

Reshevsky	V. Grigorieff
WHITE	BLACK
1 P–Q4	N–KB3
2 P–QB4	P–K3
3 N–KB3	P–Q4
4 N–B3	P–B3
5 P–K3	QN–Q2
6 B–Q3	B–K2

The Meran Variation, once so
highly thought of, has been discredited by the following line of play:
6...PxP; 7 BxBP, P–QN4; 8 B–
Q3, P–QR3; 9 P–K4, P–B4; 10 P–
K5, PxP; 11 NxNP, NxP; 12 NxN,
PxN; 13 Q–B3, B–N5ch; 14 K–K2,

QR–N1; 15 Q–N3! (an innovation
introduced by the author), Q–Q3 or
Q–Q4; 16 N–KB3! and White has
much the better game.

7 O–O	O–O
8 Q–K2	P–QN3
9 P–K4	....

A good alternative here is 9 P–
QN3 followed by B–N2.

| 9 .... | PxP |
| 10 NxP | B–N2 |

Naturally not 10...NxN? 11 Qx
N and White wins a Pawn.

| 11 N–B3 | .... |

Here again White could have
played P–QN3 followed by B–N2,
but it is generally a good idea to
avoid exchanges when your opponent has a cramped position.

| 11 .... | P–B4 |

A very natural move, but it
opens up the game prematurely.

12 PxP	NxP
13 B–B2	Q–B2
14 N–QN5!	Q–B3
15 B–B4	N–KR4

Black apparently relies on being
able to exchange this Knight for
the QB, or else on forcing...N–B5
eventually if the Bishop retreats
along its original diagonal. It was
not easy to foresee that this plausible speculation would turn out so
badly.

| 16 B–K5! | .... |

Provoking the following weakening move.

| 16 .... | P–B3 |

Black should have resisted temptation by playing...N–Q2.

| 17 B–KN3 | P–K4 |

White was threatening P–QN4
followed by QN–Q4. Black's last
two moves have created serious
weaknesses on the white squares.

| 18 N–B3! | .... |

Heading for the inviting square
Q5, in line with the previous note.

18 . . . .   **NxB**

There was no better disposition of the Knight, in view of its awkward and decentralized position.

19 BPxN!   **. . . .**

An exception to the usual principle that Pawn captures should be toward the center. In the present position, the opening of the KB file gives White an advantage that is far more important than strict adherence to the general principle.

19 . . . .   **N–K3**
20 N–Q5!   **Q–B4ch**

...B–B4ch would have the drawback of not providing for the elimination of the troublesome Knight.

21 K–R1   **BxN**

Black's game seems safe enough at a superficial glance, especially now that he has Bishops of opposite colors. But it is precisely this fact that gives him such a poor game: he lacks a Bishop now to guard the weak white squares.

22 PxB   **N–B2**

Amusing would be 22...QxP?; 23 B–N3, Q–B3; 24 Q–B4!, QxQ; 25 BxQ, K–B2; 26 N–N5ch winning a piece. Here we have an example of the value of opening the KB file.

If instead 22...N–Q5; 23 NxN, PxN; 24 QR–B1 with a position

much in White's favor.

23 QR–B1!   **Q–Q3**

23...QxP?? loses at once after 24 B–N3. Or if 23...Q–N4; 24 Q–K4, P–N3; 25 B–R4 winning a piece.

24 N–R4!   **. . . .**

The win of a Pawn with 24 BxP ch, KxB; 25 Q–B2ch, P–B4; 26 QxN is obvious, but White prefers a more forceful line. After 26...Qx Q; 27 RxQ, B–B3 Black could put up a lengthy resistance.

24 . . . .   **R–B2**

Allowing a neat finish, but the position was becoming untenable. Thus if 24...NxP; 25 B–N3 wins a piece; while if 24...P–N3 (to keep out the Knight); 25 Q–N4 is decisive. Against other moves, 26 N–B5 should win quickly.

25 BxPch!   **KxB**
26 Q–R5ch   **K–N1**
27 N–N6   **KR–B1**
28 R–B6!   **Resigns**

For if 28...Q–Q1 (if 28...Q–N5; 29 RxN wins easily. If 28...Q–Q2; 29 Q–R8ch, K–B2; 30 NxP ch, K–K1; 31 Q–R5ch winning the Queen); 29 Q–R8ch, K–B2; 30 Nx Pch, K–K1; 31 Q–R5ch and mate follows. Once more the opening of the KB file has been justified!

20.

RESHEVSKY–KASHDAN
Western Championship
Chicago, 1934

QUEEN'S GAMBIT DECLINED

Reshevsky   I. Kashdan
WHITE   BLACK

	WHITE	BLACK
1	P–Q4	N–KB3
2	P–QB4	P–B3
3	N–KB3	P–Q4
4	N–B3	P–K3
5	P–K3	QN–Q2
6	B–Q3	....

Regarding the opening, see the notes to Game 19.

6	....	PxP
7	BxBP	P–QN4
8	B–Q3	P–QR3
9	P–QR4	....

Not so good as 9 P–K4! etc. The text is less energetic and consequently gives B l a c k fighting chances.

9	....	P–N5
10	N–K4	P–B4
11	O–O	B–N2
12	QN–Q2	....

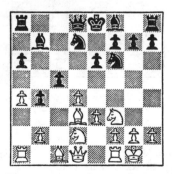

The position is approximately even. The fact that White has to make so many moves with the QN in order to find a good square (QB4) for this piece, indicates that White has gained nothing substan-tial from the opening.

12	....	B–K2
13	P–R5!	....

An important move which prevents the occupation of Black's QN3 by his pieces, and isolates his QNP artificially by preventing ... P–QR4; the move also has the virtue of fixing Black's QRP on a square where it will be subject to attack by White's pieces.

13	....	O–O
14	Q–K2	Q–B2
15	N–B4	KR–Q1

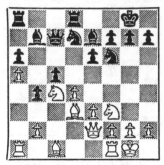

The alternative was 15 ... PxP; 16 PxP, N–Q4 (threatening ... N–B5); 17 QN–K5, NxN; 18 PxN, P–B4; 19 N–Q4, Q–Q2; 20 B–Q2. White can continue with KR–B1, intending N–N3–B5; it would be difficult for Black to cross this plan because of the need for keeping his QR at R1 to guard the QRP.

16	KN–K5	N–B1

Black can easily go wrong here, for example 16 ... N–K5?; 17 NxN winning the exchange. Or 16 ... Nx N; 17 PxN, N–Q2 (not 17 ... N–Q4??; 18 P–K4); 18 P–B4, P–B3; 19 PxP, BxBP; 20 P–K4, P–K4; 21 P–B5 with an overwhelming advantage.

17	R–Q1	N–N3

Now Black threatens to win a

Pawn (but not 17 ... PxP; 18 PxP, RxP?; 19 BxPch etc.).

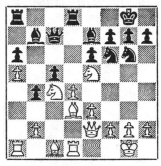

18 BxN!   . . . .

This move was played only after a very thorough study of the position. Needless to say, I was reluctant to give Kashdan his beloved Bishop-pair, but there seemed to be no satisfactory alternative. If, for example, 18 NxN, RPxN; 19 PxP, BxBP; 20 P-K4?, NxP! It seemed to me that the resulting effective position of my Knights would outweigh the strength of the two Bishops, and I believe that the further course of the game vindicated my judgment.

          18 . . . .   RPxB
          19 P-QN3   PxP
          20 PxP   N-Q4

Compelling White to renounce his intention of fianchettoing his Bishop, for if 21 B-N2?, N-B5 is disastrous for him. However, the Bishop renders valuable service at Q2 by attacking the QNP.

          21 B-Q2   B-KB3

The simplest continuation was 21 ... KR-B1; 22 QR-B1, Q-Q1 continuing to keep an eye on White's QRP.

          22 QR-B1   Q-K2
          23 N-N2!   . . . .

The removal of Black's attack on the QRP enables White to post this Knight on the powerful square QB5.

          23 . . . .   QR-B1
          24 N-R4   B-N4

A plausible notion which leads to trouble. Best was 24 ... BxN; 25 QxB, B-B3 followed by ... B-N4— or 25 ... RxR; 26 RxR, Q-Q2!; 27 N-B5, Q-N4. Or 24 ... BxN; 25 Px B, Q-K1; 26 N-B5, B-B3 and now 27 QxP?? would be refuted by 27 ... B-N4; 28 Q-R7, R-R1; 29 Q-N7, KR-N1.

          25 RxR   RxR
          26 N-B5   . . . .

The Knights are ideally posted.

          26 . . . .   BxB
          27 QxB   N-B6
          28 R-K1   R-Q1

Now we see what Kashdan had in mind when he played 24 ... B-N4. He has eliminated White's Bishop and has occupied the attractive post QB6. Furthermore, he has strong pressure against the QP and at the moment he threatens ... Qx N. And yet White's reply gives the game a decisive turn in his favor!

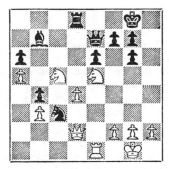

          29 Q-B4!   . . . .

This does not threaten 30 QxP ch, QxQ; 31 NxQ, KxN; 32 NxB because of 32 ... RxP. But White threatens ... to threaten.

          29 . . .   B-R1

Losing a Pawn, but a careful

study of the position shows that
he had no good move:

I. 29 ... N–Q4; 30 QxPch winning a Pawn.

II. 29 ... R–Q4; 30 N(K5)–Q3
with the two-fold menace of 31 Nx
NP and 31 Q–N8ch.

III. 29 ... R–KB1; 30 N(K5)–Q3,
N–Q4; 31 Q–Q2 wins a Pawn.

IV. 29 ... P–B3; 30 N(K5)–Q3
(not 30 NxP?, QxN; 31 PxQ, N–K7
ch; 32 K–B1, NxQ; 33 NxN, P–K4;
34 N–K6, R–Q6 with better chances
for Black), P–K4; 31 Q–K3 (if 31
PxP, N–K7ch; 32 RxN, QxN with
a highly complicated position), N–
Q4; 32 Q–N3 and Black is in difficulties.

V. 29 ... B–Q4; 30 NxRP, R–
R1; 31 NxQNP! and Black cannot
capture the QRP, nor can he play
31 ... QxN; 32 QxPch, K–R1; 33
R–K3 and wins; while if 31 ... Bx
QNP; 32 N(5)–B6 followed by Q–
K3 wins.

| 30 NxRP | P–N4 |

If 30 ... Q–N2; 31 Q–B3, QxN;
32 QxPch, K–R1; 33 R–K3 and
wins.

| 31 Q–N4 | Q–Q3 |
| 32 N–B5 | QxP |

Thus Black has regained the
Pawn, but the ending is lost for
him, as he cannot contend with the
formidable QRP.

33 QxQ	RxQ
34 N–B4	R–Q1
35 N–N6	N–Q4
36 R–R1	K–B1

If 36 ... R–N1 White has a strong
reply in 37 N–R6 etc.

37 P–B3	K–K2
38 K–B2	B–B3
39 N–R6!	....

The threat was 39 ... NxN; 40
PxN, R–QN1; 41 R–R7ch, K–Q3;
42 N–Q3, P–B3 with equality.

| 39 .... | K–Q3 |

The loss of a Pawn was unavoidable. If 39 ... NxN; 40 PxN, K–Q3;
41 R–Q1ch wins. If 39 ... B–N2; 40
NxNch, RxN (if 40 ... BxN; 41 Nx
P etc.); 41 NxP, R–N4; 42 R–R4
etc.

| 40 R–Q1 | B–N2 |
| 41 NxP | .... |

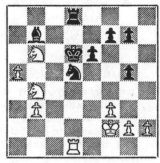

Thus the Pawn has fallen; the
two Knights aided by the QRP are
too much for the Bishop and
Knight. It is my belief that as a
rule, two Knights can accomplish
more than a Bishop and Knight.

| 41 .... | K–B4 |
| 42 N–B2 | .... |

More exact than 42 N(4)xN, Px
N; 43 R–B1ch, K–N4; 44 R–B7, B–
R3; 45 RxP, KxP and Black has
some drawing chances.

| 42 .... | R–KR1 |
| 43 P–N4ch! | K–N4 |

If 43 ... NxP; 44 N–Q7ch, K–B5
or ... K–N4; 45 NxN, KxN; 46 R–
N1ch.

| 44 NxN | BxN |
| 45 N–K3 | B–B3 |

If 45 ... KxP; 46 NxBch, PxN;
47 RxP and White wins easily.
Likewise if 45 ... RxP; 46 NxB,
PxN; 47 RxPch, KxP; 48 P–R6, R–
R1; 49 R–Q7 and Black has nothing
to play for.

| 46 R–QB1 | R–QB1 |

Black has little choice. If 46 ...
B–R1; 47 R–B7 wins. If 46 ... B–
K1; 47 R–B8 is decisive.

    47 N–B4   **KxP**

Or 47 ... R–Q1; 48 N–R3ch, Kx
P; 49 RxB, KxN; 50 R–B7 and
wins. After the text, White wins
a piece.

48	N–Q6	R–B2
49	P–R6	P–B4
50	P–R7	. . . .

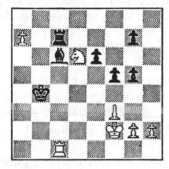

Another way was 50 N–N7, R–

B1; 51 P–R7, R–QR1; 52 RxB,
RxP; 53 N–Q8 etc.

50	. . . .	RxP
51	RxB	R–R7ch
52	K–N3	R–K7

Black might well have resigned
here. The rest requires no comment.

53	N–B7	P–B5ch
54	K–R3	P–N5ch
55	KxP	RxPch
56	KxP	RxP
57	RxP	K–B4
58	R–KN6	K–Q4
59	RxP	K–K3
60	N–K5	R–R7
61	R–N6ch	K–K2
62	K–B5	R–R4
63	P–B4	R–N4
64	R–K6ch	K–B1
65	K–B6	K–N1
66	K–N6	R–N1
67	P–B5	K–R1
68	P–B6	R–N1ch
69	K–R6	Resigns

INTERNATIONAL TOURNAMENT AT SYRACUSE, 1934

T HE INTERNATIONAL Tournament at Syracuse in 1934 was attended by many of the best players of the western hemisphere, besides masters from Germany and Italy. For me, the important point was that all of the newer crop of masters were entered: Dake, Denker, Fine Horowitz, Kashdan, Kupchik, Steiner, and others. Most of them were in their twenties at the time, and all of them could be expected to exercise a strong influence on master chess in the United States for a generation to come.

In a very real sense this tournament was a turning point in my chess career. The question was whether I could hold my own in competition with my contemporaries. If I could not, it would be quite clear that I could hardly expect to enter on chess as a life career.

When I won the tournament, and without losing a game, it served as encouragement to continue serious attention to chess. But for this encouragement, I would have renounced serious chess, although I would have continued to play the game occasionally with friends.

21.

RESHEVSKY–ARAIZA
Syracuse, 1934

QUEEN'S INDIAN DEFENSE

Reshevsky	J. J. Araiza
WHITE	BLACK
1 P–Q4	N–KB3
2 P–QB4	P–K3
3 N–KB3	P–QN3
4 P–KN3	B–N2
5 B–N2	B–N5ch
6 B–Q2	Q–K2
7 O–O	BxB
8 QxB	P–Q3
9 Q–B2	P–B4

Black can also fight for control of the center with 9 ... B–K5; but there would follow 10 Q–N3 and 11 N–B3 regaining the lost tempo.

10 N–B3   N–B3

After 10 ... O–O we would have the same position as in my Detroit game with Fine (see Game 18). The text is inferior.

11 QR–Q1   O–O

An attempt at simplification would not turn out well: 11 ... PxP; 12 NxP, NxN; 13 RxN, BxB; 14 KxB, O–O; 15 KR–Q1, KR–Q1; 16 P–K4 and White is in complete control.

12 P–Q5   PxP
13 PxP   N–QN5

As Black does not relish being slowly throttled after White's P–K4, he starts a counterattack which is not quite good enough. Nevertheless, the resulting intricate play must be handled with the greatest care.

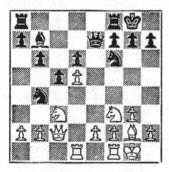

14 Q–N3   P–QR4

Threatening ... P–R5 as a means of exchanging the QRP for White's QP.

15 P–QR3!   ....

If instead 15 P–K4, B–R3; 16 KR–K1, P–B5; 17 Q–R4, N–Q2 with an excellent game for Black.

15 ....   P–R5

The natural follow-up to his previous move.

16 Q–B4   P–QN4!?

Black stands or falls by this move. ... N–R3? would lose a

Pawn without compensation.

17 NxNP   ....

Naturally not 17 QxP?? B–R3 and wins.

17 ....   BxP
18 Q–B4   ....

Leaving Black little choice, for if 18 ... N–B3; 19 QxQP, QxP?; 20 RxB or 20 N–B3 wins.

18 ....   QxP
19 N–B7   N–Q6!

The only move. Black hopes for the plausible reply 20 Q–K3, when there would follow 20 ... BxN! with the following possibilities:

I.   21 BxB, QxQ; 22 PxQ, QR–B1!

II. 21 QxN, QxQ; 22 RxQ, BxB etc.

III. 21 NxR, QxQ; 22 PxQ, BxR; 23 RxB, NxP.

In all cases Black would have at least equality.

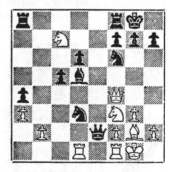

20 Q–Q2!   ....

After this fine move, Black must lose the exchange, as he has too much en prise.

20 ....   BxN
21 NxR!   P–B5

Relatively best was 21 ... QxQ; 22 RxQ, BxB; 23 KxB, RxN (better than 23 ... NxNP; 24 RxN, RxN; 25 KR–QN1 and White wins rather easily); 24 RxN, P–Q4 and White will have technical difficulties.

22	N–N6	P–Q4
23	BxB	QxB
24	Q–K3!	....

Much more effective than 24 Nx RP, P–Q5 (threatening ...N–K5 very strongly); 25 R–R1, Q–B3 and White still has many difficulties to contend with.

24 ....   Q–R4

The best chance was 24...QxQ; 25 PxQ, R–N1 (not 25...NxP; 26 R–N1, P–B6; 27 KR–B1 etc.). Black's stubborn retention of the Queen only hastens his downfall.

25 P–B3   R–K1

Black has nothing to gain from 25...NxP; 26 R–N1, N–Q6; 27 NxRP, R–R1; 28 N–B3 and the RP cannot be captured.

26	Q–Q2	Q–K4
27	NxRP	P–Q5

This results in the undermining of the advanced Knight's position; but there was no longer any good move.

28 P–N3!   N–Q4?

Loses a piece.

29	PxP	N(4)–B5
30	PxN	NxP
31	K–R1	Q–KN4
32	QR–K1	R–K6
33	R–KN1	Q–K4

Black resigned without awaiting his opponent's reply.

22.

RESHEVSKY–DENKER
Syracuse, 1934

B U D A P E S T   D E F E N S E

Reshevsky	A. S. Denker
WHITE	BLACK
1 P–Q4	N–KB3
2 P–QB4	P–K4
3 PxP	N–N5

This defense, after a brief flurry of popularity, has virtually disappeared from master play. The underlying conception is basically unsound, so that White can usually secure the better game by natural, sound development.

For example, the tricky 3...N–K5 can be answered in this way: 4 N–Q2, N–B4; 5 KN–B3, N–B3; 6 P–KN3, Q–K2; 7 B–N2, P–KN3; 8 N–QN1! White's QN travels to Q5, where it exerts effective pressure in the center.

4 P–K4   ....

The most aggressive continuation; the more conservative 4 B–B4 gives White a slight positional edge after 4...N–QB3; 5 N–KB3, B–N5ch; 6 QN–Q2, Q–K2; 7 P–QR3, KNxKP; 8 NxN (not 8 PxB??; N–Q6 mate!), NxN; 9 P–K3, BxNch; 10 QxB, O–O; 11 B–K2, P–Q3; 12 O–O, B–B4; 13 QR–B1 etc.

4 ....   P–Q3?

A faulty continuation; 4...KNx KP is in order.

5 B–K2   ....

White can accept the Pawn sacrifice with impunity by playing 5 PxP, BxP; 6 B–K2, P–KB4; 7 PxP, Q–K2; 8 N–KB3 (White can win a piece by 8 P–B5, but Black gets a strong attack after 8...BxBP; 9 Q–R4ch, N–B3; 10 QxN, N–Q5); BxBP; 9 B–N5, N–KB3; 10 N–B3 and it is difficult to see what Black has for the loss of the Pawn.

However, rather than run the risk of running into some prepared analysis, I relied on quick development.

    5 . . . .   NxKP
    6 P–B4   N–N5?

It is true that 7 BxN would not win a piece because of ... Q–R5ch in reply. But the text loses valuable time; Black should have played ... N–N3, or perhaps ... KN–B3 followed by ... QN–R3–B4.

    7 N–KB3   N–QB3
    8 O–O   B–Q2?

Rather frivolous in this critical situation. 8 ... B–K2 was necessary, in order to castle in good time and thus retreat the KN to K1 in the event that Black's KN is driven back as in the text continuation.

    9 N–B3   B–K2
   10 P–KR3   N–B3
   11 P–K5   PxP
   12 PxP   N–KN1

Home, Sweet Home! The Knight has made five moves in order to return to its original square!

   13 B–K3   P–B3?

This is suicidal. He should have tried 13 ... B–K3; 14 N–Q5, Q–Q2; 15 Q–N3! O–O–O; 16 QR–Q1, Q–K1 and although Black's position is seriously cramped, he can still put up some resistance.

   14 B–Q3!   PxP?

He might at least have played ... B–K3. The result could be no worse.

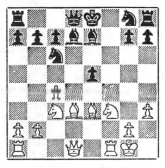

   15 N–KN5!   N–B3

Too late. However, if 15 ... BxN; 16 Q–R5ch (an amusing echo of Black's sixth move!), K–K2; 17 B–B5ch, K–K3; 18 Q–B7 mate.

   16 RxN!   . . . .

The decisive stroke.

   16 . . . .   BxR
   17 Q–R5ch   P–N3
   18 BxPch   PxB

Or if 18 ... K–B1; 19 Q–R6ch, B–N2; 20 B–B5ch, N–K2; 21 R–B1ch and mate follows.

   19 QxPch   K–K2
   20 B–B5 mate

23.

SEITZ–RESHEVSKY
Syracuse, 1934
QUEEN'S GAMBIT DECLINED

Dr. A. Seitz	Reshevsky
WHITE	BLACK
1 P–Q4	P–Q4
2 N–KB3	P–K3
3 P–K3	N–Q2

White wants to play the Colle System, as in Game 35. However, Black refuses to chime in with his opponent's intentions.

4 QN–Q2	....

Weak. White should have been warned by his opponent's omission of the customary ... N–KB3.

4 P–B4 followed by 5 N–B3 is natural and good, whereas after the cramping text, there is no objection to Black's building up a stonewall formation.

4	P–KB4
5 P–B4	P–B3
6 Q–N3?	....

And this is thoughtless, as his QB is completely ignored. Better was 6 B–Q3, N–R3; 7 P–QN3 followed by B–N2 and Q–B2, as in a famous game of Capablanca's.

6	B–Q3
7 B–Q3	N–R3!

This is one type of position in which the development of the Knight to the side of the board is quite satisfactory. The chief function of this move is to be able to answer a possible PxP with ... KPxP.

8 N–QN1	....

A belated admission that his fourth move was ineffectual.

8	O–O
9 B–Q2	Q–K2!

Preparing for aggressive action in the center and at the same time preventing B–N4.

10 N–B3	K–R1
11 QR–B1?	....

Another weak move. White is understandably reluctant to castle King-side, as Black has a good formation for a strong attack. Relatively best would have been O–O–O, although Black would have been left with an excellent game.

11	PxP
12 BxQBP	P–K4!

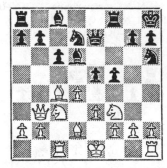

Black has freed himself. White has hardly anything better than exchanging; if for example 13 O–O?, P–K5; 14 N–K1, BxPch; 15 KxB, Q–R5ch; 16 K–N1, N–N5 and wins.

13 NxP	NxN
14 PxN	BxP
15 Q–B2	....

White continues to mark time. However, if 15 O–O, BxPch is decisive.

15	P–B5!
16 P–K4	P–B6!
17 P–KN3	....

17 PxP, RxP is equally devoid of attraction for White.

17	N–B4!
18 Q–Q3	....

18 PxN, BxNch would leave White in a hopeless state

18	N–Q3

Threatening to win the KP.

19	N–Q1	B–R6
20	B–N4	QR–Q1
21	Q–B2	KR–K1

Black's position steadily becomes more powerful.

22	B–Q3	. . . .

The KP needed more protection; but now Black wins a Pawn by force.

22	. . . .	Q–K3!

Menacing not only the QRP but also 23 ... B–N7; 24 KR–N1, Q–R6 etc. as well as 23 ... NxP; 24 BxN, B–B3 etc.

23	N–K3	QxP
24	P–N3	QxQ

Black has no objection to exchanging Queens, as his pressure on White's game still remains irresistible.

25	RxQ	B–B3
26	B–R5	R–Q2
27	P–KN4	. . . .

As good or bad as anything else. Black is now ready to wind up the game quickly, taking full advantage of White's exposed King and weakened Pawn structure.

27	. . . .	NxP
28	BxN	RxB
29	R–N1	B–KN7
30	B–Q2	B–K4!
31	K–Q1	RxN!
	Resigns	

24.

RESHEVSKY–MONTICELLI
Syracuse, 1934

QUEEN'S GAMBIT DECLINED

Reshevsky	M. Monticelli
WHITE	BLACK
1 P–Q4	N–KB3
2 P–QB4	P–K3
3 N–QB3	P–Q4
4 B–N5	QN–Q2
5 PxP	. . . .

Now that Black has declined my challenge to play the Nimzoindian variation, I steer the game into the channels of my favorite line of play in the Queen's Gambit Declined.

5	. . . .	PxP
6	N–B3	B–K2
7	P–K3	P–B3
8	Q–B2	O–O
9	B–Q3	R–K1
10	P–KR3	. . . .

Reserving the possibility of castling Queen-side. A promising alternative was 10 O–O and if 10 ... N–B1; 11 N–K5, N–N5; 12 BxB, QxB; 13 NxN, BxN; 14 N–K2! followed by N–N3. The Knight protects the King-side and leaves White free to prepare a general Pawn advance on the other wing which is exceedingly unpleasant for Black.

10	. . . .	N–B1
11	B–KB4	. . . .

To prevent ... N–K5, at least for the time being.

11	. . . .	N–N3

... B–Q3 at once would have been more exact, as the QN is poorly placed here.

12	B–R2	B–Q3
13	BxB	QxB
14	O–O–O!	. . . .

White plays for the attack, foreseeing that the later advance of his KRP will gain time.

    14 . . . .   B–Q2

The alternative was ... P–N4 followed by ... P–QR4. The success of such a thrust would have been problematical, since the advance of the Pawns could not be properly supported by Black's pieces, and serious weaknesses would be created for the endgame.

    15 P–KN4   KR–QB1

In order to make room for his KN at K1.

    16 K–N1   P–N3
    17 KR–N1   N–K1

If 17 ... P–B4; 18 PxP, RxP; 19 N–Q4 with marked advantage for White; or 18 ... PxP?; 19 P–N5 winning the QP.

    18 P–KR4   . . . .

The more prosaic Q–K2 would have been safer.

    18 . . . .   Q–B3!

    19 R–N3!?   . . . .

Sacrificing a Pawn for an interesting attack. The safer alternative was 19 Q–K2, NxP; 20 BxPch!, K–B1; 21 NxN, QxN; 22 B–B2 leaving White with a strong attack and even material.

    19 . . . .   BxP!
    20 RxB   QxN
    21 B–B5!   R–Q1
    22 P–R5!   N–Q3!

An interesting position. The text

is compulsory in view of White's threat of 23 QR–N1 (after 22 ... N–B1), P–N3; 24 R(4)–N3, QxRP; 25 R–R3 winning the Queen.

    23 PxN   QxB

And not 23 ... NxB? 24 R–B4 winning a piece.

    24 PxRPch   KxP?

Allowing White to freshen up the attack. ... K–R1 was preferable.

    25 R–R4ch   K–N1
    26 P–K4!   . . . .

Being a Pawn down, White avoids the exchange of Queens.

    26 . . . .   NxP
    27 NxN   PxN
    28 QR–R1   . . . .

As a result of Black's ill-judged twenty-fourth move, White has a strong attack on the KR file.

    28 . . . .   P–B3

But not 28 ... K–B1??; 29 RxP and Black cannot parry the double threat of R–R8 mate and R–K8ch winning the Queen. Or if 28 ... P–N3; 29 R–R8ch, K–N2; 30 R(1)–R7 ch, K–B3; 31 QxPch etc.

    29 RxP   Q–Q4?

After this second mistake, White's attack rages unabated. 29 ... R–Q4 was in order, after which White would have had a difficult fight on his hands.

    30 R(4)–R4!   . . . .

Black's position has become desperate. If now 30 ... K–B2 (White threatened 31 Q–N6, K–B1; 32 R–R8ch etc.); 31 R–N1, R–KN1; **32** Q–N6ch, K–B1; 33 R–K1 followed by R(4)–K4 and wins.

30	**P–KB4**
31 Q–K2!	**R–K1**

Else Q–K7 is crushing.

32 Q–R5	**. . . .**

Threatening Q–N6 with decisive effect.

32	**Q–K3**
33 R–B4	**Q–R3**

The only move. White was threatening 34 Q R7ch, K–B2; 35 RxPch, K–K2; 36 R–K5 etc. If 33 ... R–KB1; 34 Q–R7ch, K–B2; 35 RxPch, K–K1; 36 R–K5 etc. If 33 ... P–N3; 34 Q–R8ch, K–B2; 35 R–R7 mate.

34 QxQ	**PxQ**
35 RxRP	**R–K5!**

Black's best drawing chance. An attempt to protect his weak Pawns would only facilitate White's victory.

36 RxR	**PxR**
37 RxP	**R–Q1**
38 R–B4	**. . . .**

Here I could have saved myself some hard work by playing 38 R–B7!, RxP; 39 RxP, R–Q7; 40 R–K7, RxP; 41 RxP with an easy win.

38	**P–N4**
39 R–N4	**K–B2**

Black's only hope is to bring his King rapidly into the game. Thus if 39 ... R–KB1; 40 P–Q5, RxP; 41 RxKP winning easily. Or if 39 ... R–Q4; 40 P–R4, P–R3; 41 PxP, PxP; 42 K–B1, K–B2 (if 42 ... R–KB4; 43 K–Q2, RxPch; 44 K–K3 and wins); 43 K–Q2, K–K3; 44 K–K3, K–B4; 45 P–N3 and Black is in Zugzwang!

40 K–B2	**K–K3**
41 RxP	**RxP**
42 R–N7	**P–R4**

Strong, but the weakness of his KP will eventually prove fatal.

43 R–N6ch	**K–K2**
44 R–N5	**P–R5**
45 R–N6!	**K–Q2**

The play hereabouts is simple but subtle. If Black's King moves to the Queen-side, White wins with R–KB6 as in the text. If Black stays near his KB3, then White wins by means of P–R3 and R–N4.

46 P–R3	**K–B2**

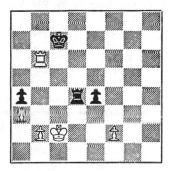

47 R–B6!	**. . . .**

Strangely enough, 47 R–N4? does not win! There follows 47 ... RxR! 48 PxR, K–B3; 49 K–B3 (if 49 P–N3, P–R6; 50 K–N1, K–N4; 51 K–R1, KxP; 52 K–R2, K–B6; 53 KxP, K–Q7; 54 P–N4, K–K7; 55 P–N5, KxP; 56 P–N6, P–K6; 57 P–N7, P–K7 drawing!), K–N4; 50 K–Q4, KxP; 51 KxP, K–N6; 52 P–B4, KxP; 53 P–B5, P–R6 and again the ending is a draw.

47	**K–Q2**
48 R–B4	**. . . .**

Decisive! Black has no resource against the coming P–B3

48	**R–B5ch**
49 K–Q2	**K–Q3**
50 P–B3	**R–Q5ch**
51 K–K3	**R–Q6ch**
52 KxP	**R–N6**
53 K–B5	**RxNP**
54 RxP	**Resigns**

25.

STEINER–RESHEVSKY
Syracuse, 1934
FRENCH DEFENSE

H. Steiner	Reshevsky
WHITE	BLACK
1 P–K4	P–K3

I rarely resort to this defense
because of my strong conviction
that either 1...P–K4 or 1...P–
QB4 is the best reply Black can
make to 1 P–K4.

2 P–Q4	P–Q4
3 N–QB3	N–KB3
4 B–N5	PxP
5 NxP	B–K2
6 BxN	PxB

...BxB equalizes, but I prefer
the more enterprising text because
it presents greater problems to
both players.

7 N–KB3	P–N3
8 P–KN3	....

Plausible but too slow, so that
Black has an opportunity to seize
the initiative. Correct was 8 B–
N5ch, P–B3; 9 B–B4, B–N2; 10 Q–
K2, N–Q2; 11 O–O–O, Q–B2; 12
KR–K1 and White has more free-
dom.

8	B–N2
9 Q–K2	Q–Q4!
10 QN–Q2	....

If instead 10 Q–N5ch, QxQ; 11
BxQch, N–Q2; 12 N(4)–Q2, O–O–O
and Black's Bishops give him
splendid prospects for the ending.

10	P–QB4!

An important move which gives
Black's pieces increased scope by
removing the QP.

11 PxP	....

P–B4 would not accomplish any-
thing, as it would only drive
Black's Queen to the powerful post
R4.

11	QxBP
12 O–O–O	N–Q2
13 B–N2	O–O–O
14 N–K4	....

Better 14 N–R4 so that if 14...
BxB; 15 NxB, Q–Q4; 16 Q–B4ch
with an even game.

14	Q–QR4
15 K–N1	N–K4

16 N–Q4	....

Black gets a distinct pull now;
but after 16 NxN, PxN Black's
Bishops would be very strong.

16	P–B4
17 P–KB4	....

Likewise after 17 N–N3, Q–R3;
18 QxQ, BxQ; 19 N–B3, N–N5; 20
RxRch, RxR; 21 P–KB4, B–B3
Black would have fine prospects
because of his powerful Bishops
and White's cramped position.

17	PxN
18 N–N3	....

Necessary, for if 18 PxN, QxKP
and Black has won a Pawn.

18	Q–R3!

Stronger than the plausible 18...
Q–R5, which would be answered by
19 PxN followed by QR–K1 winning the KP.

19 QxQ	BxQ
20 PxN	P–K6!

A passed Pawn on the sixth rank
which can be easily defended is
most powerful. All of White's en-

ergies must now be directed toward stopping this Pawn.

21 QR–K1   B–KN4
22 B–B3   KR–B1

Intending to open the KB file with ...P–B3. Black subsequently changes his mind about this.

23 N–B1   ....

From this point on, White is virtually in **Zugzwang**. Thus if 23 B–K2, BxB; 24 RxB, R–Q4 winning the important KP.

23 ....   R–Q7

The pressure increases steadily.

24 B–K4   P–R4
25 N–Q3   ....

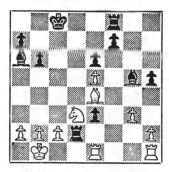

25 ....   R–Q1!

Deviating from my original intention of advancing the BP. 25 ... P–B3 would not have been advisable because of 26 N–B4!, BxN; 27 PxB, PxP; 28 PxP, P–K7; 29 K–B1, R–Q5; 30 B–Q3, BxB; 31 PxB, R–B7; 32 K–Q2 and White has drawing chances.

26 P–KR4   B–R3
27 KR–B1   ....

If instead 27 N–B4, B–QN2! 28 BxBch, KxB; 29 K–B1 (not 29 Rx P?, R–Q8ch; 30 RxR, RxR mate), P–K7 and White is in **Zugzwang**.

27 ....   P–K7
28 R–R1   R–Q5
29 B–B3   B–QN2!

It is this move that establishes

the soundness of the previous advance of the KP.

30 BxBch   KxB
31 P–N3   B–K6

Threatening 32 ... R(5)xN; 33 PxR, B–B7.

32 P–KN4   ....

A last try. However, there was no satisfactory continuation. If for example 32 R–R2, R(5)xN; 33 PxR, R–Q8ch etc.

32 ....   PxP
33 P–R5   P–N6
34 P–R6   P–N7
35 R–R3   R–Q8ch
36 K–N2   RxR
Resigns

26.

DAKE–RESHEVSKY
Syracuse, 1934

QUEEN'S GAMBIT ACCEPTED
(in effect)

A. W. Dake   Reshevsky
WHITE   BLACK

1 N–KB3   P–Q4
2 P–B4   PxP

More promising, and also more risky, is 2 ... P–Q5.

3 P–K3   ....

This transposes into the Queen's Gambit Accepted. The move which is calculated to give Black the most trouble is 3 N–R3.

3 ....   P–K3

An interesting alternative would be ...P–KN3, ...B–N2 and ...N–KB3, transposing into a form of the Gruenfeld Variation.

4 BxP   P–QR3
5 P–Q4   ....

White could interpolate P–QR4 here to prevent ...P–QN4, but this would create a permanent weakness at White's QN4.

5 ....   P–QN4

The more usual ...N–KB3 followed by ... P–B4 would have been simpler. After the text, it becomes White's ambition to stamp the advance of the QNP as premature.

    6 B–N3   B–N2
    7 O–O   N–KB3

7 ... P–QB4 and if 8 P–QR4, P–N5 would have given Black an easier game.

    8 P–QR4   P–N5

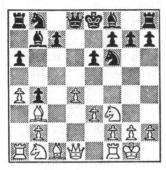

    9 P–R5!?   . . . .

After this move the game takes a highly critical turn. White is bent on artificially isolating Black's QNP by depriving it of its most natural support (... P–QR4). At the same time, the consequences of his intended B–R4ch have to be calculated with the utmost care.

    9 . . . .   B–K2

The natural move 9 ... P–B4 would not do because of 10 B–R4ch, QN–Q2; 11 N–K5 giving Black a difficult game.

    10 B–R4ch   . . . .

So that if 10 ... QN–Q2; 11 N–K5, O–O; 12 N–B6 with a strategically won game for White. However, the check ultimately turns out to be waste of time.

    10 . . . .   P–B3

This causes Black some temporary inconvenience, as the diagonal of his QB is blocked. However, the freeing move ... P–B4 cannot be prevented and White must lose time to guard his advanced QRP.

    11 QN–Q2   O–O
    12 N–N3   QN–Q2
    13 B–Q2   . . . .

Preventing ... P–B4 for some time to come.

    13 . . . .   B–Q3

This move prevents N–K5 and makes room for the Queen at K2.

    14 R–B1   R–B1
    15 Q–K2   N–K5

Black cannot permit White to gain additional space with P–K4.

    16 KR–Q1   . . . .

The position is very tricky. Thus if 16 Q–Q3, P–QB4!; 17 PxP (if 17 BxN, QxB; 18 PxP??, BxPch winning the Queen), QNxP; 18 NxN, RxN threatening to win the Queen with ... BxPch and thus gaining time to win the QRP.

    16 . . . .   Q–K2

Ordinarily it is good policy to exchange a Knight for a Bishop, but in this case White's QB has little scope while Black's KN is actively posted and is playing a vital role in preventing P–K4.

    17 B–K1   KR–Q1
    18 R–B4   P–QB4!

At last! The freeing move is made possible by a finesse which White has overlooked.

19 BxN ....

Optimistic. The simplest course was 19 PxP, QNxP; 20 NxN (but not 20 RxP, NxB; 21 RxQN, B-B3; 22 R moves, B-N4 and wins), BxN (if 20 ... NxN; 21 RxP); 21 RxR, RxR; 22 N-Q4 with an approximately even position.

19 .... **QxB!**

Dake has overlooked that if now 20 PxP, BxPch wins the exchange.

20 R(4)-B1 **PxP**

21 KNxP ....

This seems best, for if 21 QNxP (21 PxP gives White an isolated QP), RxR; 22 RxR, Q-R5 winning the QRP. Or 21 RxP, P-K4; 22 R (4)-B4, B-Q4; 23 RxR, RxR; 24 RxR, QxR and the ending is greatly in Black's favor because of his two Bishops and White's poor Pawn position.

21 .... **P-K4**

22 RxR ....

Better than 22 N-B3, Q-K3; 23 QN-Q2, NxN; 24 NxN, P-K5; 25 N-B4, B-B4 and Black has the better game.

22 .... **RxR**

23 N-B3 **Q-K2**

24 QN-Q2 **NxN**

But not 24 ... R-B7?; 25 Q-Q3 and White wins.

25 QxN **R-Q1**

26 Q-B2 **P-R3**

27 Q-N3? ....

A blunder which loses a Pawn. 27 P-K4 would probably hold the position, for example 27 ... B-B2; 28 RxRch, BxR; 29 Q-R4 etc.

27 .... **P-K5!**

28 N-Q4 **Q-K4**

29 P-N3 **QxP**

The rest is only a matter of time.

30 N-B2 **Q-N3**

Foiling White's plan, for capturing the QNP would now cost a piece (31 ... P-QR4).

31 N-R3 **P-QR4**

32 N-B4 **Q-B2**

33 Q-R2 ....

If 33 NxB, RxN; 34 RxR, QxR; 35 Q-B2, B-B3 and White's game is untenable, as he is helpless against an eventual invasion on the white squares.

33 .... **B-K2!**

34 R-B1 **R-QB1**

35 P-N3 **B-Q4**

36 B-Q2 **Q-R2**

Threatening ... P-R5.

37 Q-R4 **BxN**

38 RxB ....

38 PxB would have made the win slightly more difficult, although Black's connected passed Pawns are irresistible in any event.

38 .... **RxR**

39 PxR **Q-N3?**

40 Q-K8ch **B-B1**

41 P-B5 ....

A last desperate attempt.

41 .... **Q-Q4**

42 BxP **PxB**

43 P-B6 ....

The Pawn looks dangerous, but Black has the win well in hand.

43 .... **Q-B5**

44 Q-B8 **P-N6**

45 P-B7 **P-N7**

46 Q-N7 **QxP**

47 QxQ **P-N8(Q)ch**

48 K-N2 **Q-Q8**

The remaining play is easy but very instructive. After consolidating his position, Black begins the winning process, which consists in advancing the Pawns so as to force a break in the defenses of the White King, after which he will be helpless against Black's superior force.

49 Q-B8 **Q-Q3**

50 Q-R8 **Q-K2**

51 Q-B8 **K-R2**

52	Q–B5ch	P–N3	59	....	PxP
53	Q–Q5	Q–K3	60	P–R3	B–Q3
54	Q–R8	B–B4	61	Q–B6	B–K4
55	Q–R5	Q–B4	62	Q–K8	Q–N3ch
56	Q–B3	P–N4	63	K–B1	Q–K3

At last beginning the final phase.

57	K–N1	P–R4
58	Q–B4	P–R5
59	PxP	....

Else White will have to be perpetually on guard against the mating threat ... P–R6 in combination with ... Q–B6.

64	Q–Q8	....

The exchange of Queens would of course also be hopeless.

64	....	QxPch
65	K–K1	B–B6ch
66	K–K2	Q–B6ch
67	K–B1	Q–R8ch
	Resigns	

FIRST EUROPEAN VICTORIES

C HESS FANS probably wonder occasionally exactly how one goes about getting recognition as a grandmaster. There is no "ivory tower" method: one becomes a grandmaster in the heat of competition by defeating already established grandmasters. At the Syracuse tournament I had succeeded among my contemporaries: could I hold my own against recognized grandmasters?

It was with this challenge in mind, and the memory of the international careers of Morphy and Marshall, that I entered the tournaments at Yarmouth and Margate. Hence when the immortal Capablanca offered a draw at Move 35 of Game 28, I declined the offer. I thought I could win, and I could not hope to become a grandmaster by accepting draws in winning positions. As it turned out, I won both tournaments—and, with them, recognition as a grandmaster.

27.

SERGEANT–RESHEVSKY
Margate, 1935

R U Y   L O P E Z

E. G. Sergeant — Reshevsky
WHITE — BLACK

1 P–K4 — P–K4
2 N–KB3 — N–QB3
3 B–N5 — P–QR3
4 B–R4 — N–B3
5 O–O — B–K2
6 R–K1 — P–QN4
7 B–N3 — P–Q3
8 P–QR4 — . . . .

An interesting deviation from the routine 8 P–B3.

8 . . . . — B–N2

8 ... P–N5 would be inferior because of 9 P–R5!, O–O; 10 P–B3 and Black's position on the Queenside is unsatisfactory. 8 ... B–N5 seems best.

9 P–B3 — N–QR4
10 B–B2 — P–B4
11 P–Q4 — Q–N1

A surprising reply, but the more conventional 11 ... Q–B2 might easily involve Black in serious trouble, for example 12 RPxP, RPxP; 13 N–R3, B–R3; 14 P–QN4, PxNP; 15 PxNP, N–B3; 16 NxNP etc.

12 RPxP — RPxP
13 Q–K2 — . . . .

On 13 N–R3 Black would have a satisfactory reply in ... B–B3.

13 . . . . — P–B5
14 QN–Q2 — O–O
15 N–B1 — R–K1
16 PxP — . . . .

Not the best. The idea of occupying Q5 with the QN is plausible, but Black gains time and freedom while White carries out his plan. Two preferable courses were: (a) 16 B–N5 followed by N–K3; (b) 16 P–Q5 followed by P–KR3, P–KN4

and N–N3. A difficult maneuvering
game would result, with Black compelled to shift some of his forces
to the King-side.

16 . . . .   PxP
17 B–N5   Q–B2
18 KR–Q1   . . . .

Systematically playing for control of Q5.

18 . . . .   P–N3

With his QB at N2, Black must
think about preventing an eventual
N–B5 on White's part.

19 N–K3   KR–Q1

Here Black discards 19 . . . NxP
(if 19 . . . BxP?; 20 BxB, NxB; 21
BxB, QxB; 22 N–Q5 etc.) because
of the continuation 20 BxB, RxB
(or 20 . . . QxB? 21 N–Q5); 21 N–
Q5, BxN; 22 RxB winning back the
Pawn with a good position.

20 BxN   . . . .

This turns out poorly. Better was
20 RxRch, forcing the reply 20 . . .
BxR, for if 20 . . . RxR; 21 NxKP,
QxN; 22 BxN, BxB; 23 RxN, BxP;
24 BxB, QxB; 25 RxP and White
has the advantage.

20 . . . .   BxB
21 N–Q5   BxN
22 PxB   R–R3!

In order to blockade the passed
Pawn, with the hope of eventually
winning it.

23 Q–K3   . . . .

Here White might have played
23 P–QN4! forcing the reply . . .
PxP e.p. with resulting weaknesses
in both camps. This aggressive
course would have offered better
prospects than the text method.

23 . . . .   B–N2

In order to play 24 . . . QR–Q3,
whereupon 25 NxP? would not do
because of 25 . . . R–K1; 26 P–KB4,
P–B3 winning a piece.

24 N–N5   . . . .

After this Black is able to force
a decisive exchange. The position
was already ripe for some desperate move such as 24 P–KN4 in
order to restrain a later . . . P–B4.

24 . . . .   B–R3!

In order to exchange Bishop for
Knight, which will leave Black with
a strong Knight against a weak
Bishop. 24 . . . QR–Q3 would not do
because of 25 Q–B3, P–R3 (not 25
. . . P–B4? 26 N–K6 winning the exchange); 26 N–K4, RxP; 27 RxR,
RxR; 28 N–B6ch etc. 24 . . . P–R3;
25 N–K4, P–B4? would be hasty
because of 26 N–B5 followed by
N–K6.

25 Q–N3   . . . .

Black was threatening to win a
piece with . . . Q–K2 followed by
. . . P–B3.

25 . . . .   BxN
26 QxB   P–B3

27 Q–K3	QR–Q3
28 Q–K4	....

28 B–K4 is refuted by 28 ... P–B4; 29 B–B3, P–K5 winning the QP. Since the QP must fall in any event, White's relatively b e s t course was 28 P–B4, RxP; 29 RxR, RxR; 30 B–K4, R–Q1; 31 PxP, PxP; 32 R–KB1 with some counter-chances.

28	N–N2
29 R–Q2	N–B4
30 Q–B3	P–B4
31 QR–Q1	P–K5
32 Q–N3	N–Q6
33 BxN	BPxB
34 P–B3	Q–B4ch
35 K–R1	RxP

The beginning of the end.

36 PxP	PxP
37 R–K1	R–K1
38 R–K3	....

Q–K3 would have held o u t longer.

38	R–KB1

Immediately decisive; if now 39 R–K1, P–K6! or 39 R–Q1, P–Q7; 40 P–R3, Q–B5 and wins.

39 P–R3	R–B8ch
40 K–R2	R–N4
Resigns	

White resigns, as he must lose a Rook.

28.

RESHEVSKY–CAPABLANCA
Margate, 1935

QUEEN'S GAMBIT DECLINED

Reshevsky	J. R. Capablanca
WHITE	BLACK
1 P–Q4	N–KB3
2 P–QB4	P–K3
3 N–QB3	P–Q4
4 B–N5	QN–Q2
5 PxP	PxP
6 P–K3	B–K2
7 B–Q3	O–O
8 Q–B2	P–B4

I prefer ... P–B3 here, because the text, despite its apparently ag-gressive c h a r a c t e r, invariably leaves Pawn weaknesses in its train.

9 N–B3	P–B5

Since the QP will be weak in any event, Black tries to prevent a di-rect frontal attack on it. If instead 9 ... PxP; 10 PxP, R–K1; 11 O–O and White's coming occupation of K5 will definitely give him the bet-ter game.

10 B–B5	R–K1
11 O–O	P–KN3

But not 11 ... N–B1?; 12 BxB, RxB; 13 BxN, BxB; 14 Q–B5 win-ning the QP (a blunder committed once by Vera Menchik against Flohr, and by Dake against me in our game at Chicago, 1934).

12 B–R3	N–B1

Stronger is ... N–N3, permitting Black to utilize the Knight to greater advantage. Black's QP would have additional protection, and in the event of P–QN3 followed by PxP, Black could recapture with the QN. An attempt by White to shatter the QN's position with P–QR4 would be answered by ... P–QR4.

| 13 | BxB | RxB |
| 14 | BxN! | .... |

Highly important, because it prevents equalization by ...N–K5 and also removes a vital protection of the QP.

| 14 | .... | BxB |
| 15 | P–QN3! | Q–R4? |

Kashdan later recommended ... Q–Q2 followed by ... P–KR4, which surely gives better chances than the provocative text. 15 ... PxP? on the other hand, would not do because of 16 QxP winning a Pawn.

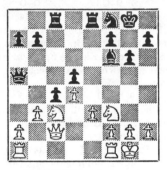

16 P–QN4!   ....

The key to White's plan. Since 16 ... QxNP; 17 QR–N1 would allow an uncomfortable penetration into his position, Black has no choice but to retreat with the Queen.

| 16 | .... | Q–Q1 |
| 17 | Q–R4! | .... |

The necessary sequel to his previous move. Black cannot avoid creating a target for attack on the Queen-side, for if 17 ... R–R1?; 18 Q–N5 winning a Pawn.

| 17 | .... | P–QR3 |
| 18 | P–N5 | R–K3 |

18 ... P–QR4 would not do because of 19 P–N6!, QxP; 20 NxP followed by NxBch and QxRP.

| 19 | QR–N1 | R–N1 |

Resigning himself to the defen-

sive. If 19 ... P–QR4; 20 P–N6!, RxNP; 21 RxR (not 21 QxRP??, RxR and wins), QxR; 22 NxP winning a Pawn.

| 20 | R–N2 | B–K2 |
| 21 | PxP | RxRP |

Forced; but now the weak QNP is exposed to attack.

| 22 | Q–B2 | N–K3 |
| 23 | KR–N1 | R–R2 |

Black's position assumes an ever more passive character.

| 24 | P–QR4! | N–B2 |
| 25 | N–K5 | Q–K1 |

N–B6 was threatened.

26 P–B4   ....

26 N–N5 would be premature: 26 ... NxN; 27 RxN, P–B3; 28 N–B3 (if 28 N–N4?, P–R4 wins the Knight), Q–Q2 and Black's chances have improved.

| 26 | .... | P–B3 |
| 27 | N–N4! | .... |

The Knight is headed for a useful career on the other wing.

27	....	Q–Q2
28	P–R3	K–N2
29	N–B2	B–R6
30	R–R2	B–Q3
31	N(2)–Q1!	....

White wants to exchange Knights, so as to remove a valuable support of the hostile QP. He therefore makes it possible for the KN to replace his colleague at QB3.

| 31 | .... | P–B4 |
| 32 | N–N5 | R–R4 |

Necessary, if the QP is to be defended adequately.

33	NxN	BxN
34	N–B3	Q–K3
35	Q–B2	P–N3

Here Capablanca offered a draw, but since I had a clear initiative and pressure on Black's weaknesses, I declined the offer.

| 36 | Q–B3 | R–Q1 |

The QP required additional protection, in view of White's contemplated 37 R–N5, RxR; 38 PxR, R–Q1; 39 R–R7—which would have left Black with a lost game.

37 R(2)–N2   Q–K2!

A clever move. The idea is that if 38 R–N5, Q–R6! 39 NxP, RxN; 40 QxR, QxPch; 41 K–B1 (if 41 K–R1, QxBP etc.), Q–Q6ch; 42 K–B2 (the King must not go to the first rank because of the reply ...QxR ch), BxP; 43 Q–B3, QxPch; Black would be left with an excellent game.

38 R–N4   R–Q2

Black has to sit tight and wait for decisive action by his opponent.

39 K–B1   . . . .

This and the next move are questionable. The straightforward course was to bring the King to QB2 followed by R–N5. The invasion of Black's Queen at QR6 would have been neutralized and the QP would have fallen in the long run.

39 . . . .   B–Q1
40 P–N4?   . . . .

There was still time to change my plan. My idea was to stabilize the King-side and then march the King over to the Queen-side to protect my Knight before proceeding with R–N5. However, this plan could have been demonstrated to be faulty if Capablanca had seized his opportunity on the 45th move.

40 . . . .   PxP
41 PxP   Q–Q3
42 K–N1   B–B2
43 K–B2   R–KB2

Threatening ...P–KN4, which White must prevent.

44 P–N5   B–Q1
45 K–K2   BxP?

Black is desperate in the face of the threatened R–N5, but he over-

looks the strength of 45...Q–K3! If then 46 R–N5, RxR; 47 RxR, Q–B4! with strong counterplay. In any event, it is difficult to see how White could have continued with his plans after 45...Q–K3! without the interpolation of a lengthy neutralizing maneuver against Black's intended ...Q–B4 followed by ...Q–Q6ch or ...Q–B7ch

46 RxNP   . . . .

Now Black has no recourse.

46 . . . .   Q–R6
47 K–Q2!   B–K2
48 R–N7   . . . .

Tying up Black's pieces.

48 . . . .   RxRP!?

An ingenious trap. He hopes for 49 NxR? Q–Q6ch; 50 K–B1 (if 50 K–K1, B–R5ch), B–R6ch; 51 R(7)–N2, P–B6 and Black wins.

49 QxP!   R–R4
50 QxP   R–R4
51 K–Q3   . . . .

White's King is a bit exposed, but not enough to matter.

51 . . . .   Q–R1
52 Q–K6   Q–R6
53 R–Q7!   . . . .

Winning a piece, for Black is helpless against the coming R–N3.

53 . . . .   R(4)–KB4
54 R–N3   Q–R8
55 RxB   Q–B8ch
56 K–Q2   Resigns

29.

MIESES–RESHEVSKY
Margate, 1935

CARO-KANN DEFENSE

J. Mieses	Reshevsky
WHITE	BLACK
1 P–K4	P–QB3
2 P–Q4	P–Q4
3 N–QB3	. . . .

If White adopts the Botvinnik-Panov line 3 PxP, PxP; 4 P–QB4, N–KB3; 5 N–B3, P–K3; 6 N–B3, Black's best course is 6...PxP; 7 BxP, B–K2; for after 6...B–K2; 7 P–B5 he would have great difficulty in freeing his position.

3	PxP
4 NxP	N–B3
5 N–N3	. . . .

5 NxNch is stronger, for White either obtains the Queen-side majority of Pawns, or else (after 5 ...NPxN; 6 P–KN3) Black remains with lasting Pawn weaknesses.

| 5 . . . . | P–K4 |

Playing to give his pieces more scope in the center by removing the important QP.

| 6 B–K3 | . . . . |

This move is not calculated to create any difficulties for Black, but if instead 6 PxP, QxQch; 7 Kx Q, N–N5 or 6 N–KB3, PxP; 7 QxP, QxQ; 8 NxQ, P–KN3 — in either event with an excellent game for Black.

| 6 . . . . | PxP |
| 7 QxP | Q–R4ch |

It would be disadvantageous for Black to exchange Queens at this point, for then White's QB would be well posted at Q4; in addition, Black would be facilitating the development of White's pieces!

| 8 Q–Q2 | . . . . |

Since, as the further course of the game indicates, White's chief interest is simplification, he should have played 8 B–Q2, Q–Q4; 9 QxQ, NxQ; 10 B–QB4.

| 8 . . . . | B–QN5! |

A finesse which forces P–QB3 and the resultant creation of a weakness at White's Q3.

9 P–QB3	B–K2
10 B–Q3	O–O
11 KN–K2	P–B4

In order to develop the QN to its strongest square.

| 12 N–B5 | . . . . |

White's eagerness to get a Bishop for a Knight misleads him in this instance. It would have been better to play 12 O–O, N–B3; 13 B–B5, P–B5; 14 Q–B2 etc.

12	BxN
13 BxB	N–B3
14 O–O	QR–Q1

White's faulty 12th move has enabled Black to develop his pieces very rapidly.

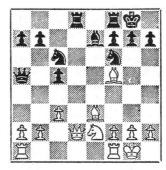

| 15 Q–B2 | P–KN3 |

Practically forcing White to relinquish the two Bishops, for at R3 the KB would be out of play, while 15 B–Q3, N–K4 would lead to much the same position as in the text continuation.

| 16 B–K4 | NxB |
| 17 QxN | KR–K1 |

Black continues to gain time effortlessly. The threat is ... B–N4 followed by ... BxB leaving White with a lost game.

18 Q–B2	P–B5
19 P–QN4?	....

A serious positional error which weakens his QBP and thus intensifies the strength of Black's contemplated occupation of Q6. N–Q4 seems best at this point.

19	Q–B2
20 KR–Q1	N–K4
21 B–B4	....

Naturally he does not want to permit ... N–Q6.

21	B–Q3

With the powerful positional threat of 22 ... N–B6ch; 23 PxN, BxB, when White's Pawn weaknesses must result in his downfall.

Nor would 22 B–N3, N–Q6; 23 BxB, RxB; 24 N–B1 be satisfactory because of 24 ... N–K8; 25 Q–R4, P–QN4!; 26 QxNP, RxR; 27 QxR ch, K–N2 and the discovered check will be fatal for White.

22 N–Q4	N–B6ch
23 NxN	BxB

White has avoided the danger of occupation of his Q3, but he is now faced with the ominous likelihood that the Bishop will be utilized against his QBP.

24 P–N3	....

A new weakness. Relatively best was RxR followed by R–Q1.

24	B–R3
25 P–QR4	B–N2
26 P–N5?	....

Still another weakness! Now Black can occupy his QB4 and prepare to seize undisputed control of the Q file.

26	Q–B4
27 QR–B1	R–Q4

Preparing to double Rooks o n the Q file and thus leaving White little choice.

28 RxR	QxR

29 N–Q4?	....

Overlooking Black's 30th move, which wins a Pawn by force. However, he had little choice:

I. 29 N–Q2?, R–K7; 30 R–Q1, N–B8 winning a piece, for if 31 P–B4?, Q–N7 mate, or 31 N–B1, Q–B8 and wins.

II 29 K–N2, R–Q1; 30 R–K1, Q–Q6 (30 ... P–B4; 31 R–K3, P–N4; 32 K–N1, P–B5; 33 PxP, PxP; 34 R–K4 gives White good drawing chances); 31 QxQ, PxQ; 32 P–B4, R–QB1; 33 R–Q1 (if 33 N–Q2, B–B6; 34 R–Q1, BxN; 35 RxB, RxP; 36 RxP, RxP; 37 R–Q7, P–N3 and Black should win), RxP; 34 RxP, RxP and Black's extra Pawn should be decisive.

The parenthetical line in Variation II (beginning with 33 N–Q2) was White's best chance.

29	BxN
30 PxB	R–K5!

White must have failed to realize the strength of this move, which enables Black to win a Pawn. The point is that if 31 QxP?, R–K8ch wins the Queen.

31 R–Q1	RxP
32 RxR	QxR
33 K–B1	K–B1

34 P–R5   . . . .

If 34 K–K2, K–K2 followed by the further advance of Black's King with an easy win.

34 . . . .   Q–Q6ch

The easiest way.

35 Q–K2   . . . .

Or 35 QxQ, PxQ; 36 K–K1, K–K2; 37 K–Q2, K–Q3; 38 KxP, K–B4 and wins.

35	QxQch
36 KxQ	K–K2
37 K–K3	K–Q3
38 K–Q4	P–B6
39 KxP	K–B4
40 P–N6	PxP
Resigns	

30.

FAIRHURST–RESHEVSKY
Margate, 1935

QUEEN'S GAMBIT DECLINED

W. A. Fairhurst	Reshevsky
WHITE	BLACK
1 P–Q4	N–KB3
2 P–QB4	P–K3
3 N–KB3	P–Q4
4 N–B3	P–B3
5 P–K3	QN–Q2
6 B–Q3	PxP
7 BxBP	P–QN4
8 B–N3	. . . .

This avoidance of the Meran Variation is unnecessary (on this point see the comments on the opening in Game 19).

8	B–K2
9 O–O	B–N2
10 P–K4	. . . .

Premature. The advance of the KP is attractive, for if it can be played successfully, Black's position will be badly cramped. However, if 10 Q–K2 (to prepare for P–K4), there follows 10 ... P–N5; 11 N–QR4, P–B4; 12 NxP, NxN; 13 Px

N, Q–R4! recovering the Pawn with a good game, while P–K4 is still impossible.

10 . . . .   P–N5

Forcing White's reply.

11 P–K5	PxN
12 PxN	NxP

But not 12 ... BPxP? 13 PxB, Px R(Q); 14 PxQ (Q)ch, RxQ; 15 Q–B2 followed by B–N2 winning.

13 PxP	O–O
14 R–N1	P–B4!

This natural and useful move parries White's transparent threat, for if now 15 BxP? BxN wins a piece.

15 B–N2?   . . . .

A clumsy move which is difficult to understand, since one readily sees that the QB cannot have much of a future on this square.

15	B–K5
16 R–B1	. . . .

The alternative B–B2 does not appear inviting, as the resulting exchange would leave White with his inferior QB. The text, on the other hand, has the drawback of placing the QR on a square where it is wholly ineffective.

16 . . . .   Q–N3

Black is steadily improving his position, and is now prepared to get his Rooks into action.

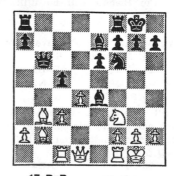

17 PxP   . . . .

Q–K2 was a better parry to the

threat of ... P–B5. The text brings Black's KB into effective play, and in addition it is quite likely that the Q file will fall into Black's hands because of his superior development.

17	BxP
18 Q–K2	QR–Q1
19 QR–Q1	. . . .

It took the Rook no less than three moves to reach this square!

19	B–N2

The retreat all the way to R1 would have been more exact. The basic idea behind the withdrawal of the Bishop is to create mating threats and also to make room for the Knight at K5, so that the resulting pressure on White's KB2 will force him completely on the auiuunlue

20 N–K5	B–R1
21 P–B4	. . . .

This opens the diagonal of his QB, but correspondingly limits the activities of the other Bishop.

21	Q–N2
22 N–B3	N–K5
23 B–R1	. . . .

White's position is very uncomfortable. If 23 B–Q4, BxB; 24 RxB, N–B6; 25 Q–Q3, RxR and wins.

23	RxR
24 BxR	. . . .

If 24 QxR, N–N4 wins a Pawn, for if 25 N–K1, N–R6ch wins the exchange.

24	R–Q1
25 B–B2	Q–B3

Provoking White's p l a u s i b l e reply.

26 N–K5?	. . . .

A decisive mistake, but if instead 26 BxN, QxB; 27 QxQ, BxQ and Black should win the ending without much difficulty. Or if 26 B–Q1, N–Q7; 27 R–K1, NxP etc.

26	N–N6!
27 NxQ	. . . .

Choosing to lose a piece. But likewise after 27 Q–B3, QxQ followed by ...NxR White's game would be hopeless.

27	NxQch
28 K–R1	BxN
Resigns	

31.

RESHEVSKY–REILLY
Margate, 1935

QUEEN'S GAMBIT DECLINED

Reshevsky	B. Reilly
WHITE	BLACK
1 P–Q4	P–Q4
2 P–QB4	P–K3
3 N–QB3	N–KB3
4 B–N5	B–K2
5 P–K3	QN–Q2
6 N–B3	O–O
7 R–B1	P–B3
8 Q–B2	P–QR3
9 P–QR3	. . . .

Both players are waging "the fight for the tempo"; Black does not want to play ...PxP until White's KB has moved to Q3.

9	R–K1
10 P–R3	P–R3
11 B–B4	. . . .

B–R4 is also quite playable; the text avoids exchanges.

11 . . . .   PxP

. . . P–QN4 is sometimes played in similar situations, but it would not be good here because of 12 P–B5, after which Black is unable to counter with . . . P–K4.

12 BxBP   P–QN4
13 B–QR2   P–B4

The natural freeing move for Black in all variations of this opening.

14 PxP   . . . .

An excellent alternative is 14 P–Q5, PxP; 15 NxQP, R–R2; 16 B–N1!, B–N2; 17 R–Q1! etc.

14 . . . .   NxP
15 B–N1   . . . .

If 15 O–O, Q–Q6! equalizes.

15 . . . .   B–N2
16 O–O   Q–N3
17 B–K5   QN–Q2

Better than 17 . . . QN–K5; 18 Nx N followed by Q–B7 with marked positional advantage.

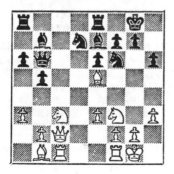

18 B–N3   . . . .

Best. After 18 B–Q4, Black can play 18 . . . B–B4; 19 NxP, QxN; 20 BxB, NxB; 21 QxN, QxP with even chances.

18 . . . .   QR–B1
19 Q–K2   P–N5
20 PxP   BxP
21 N–K5   BxN

The exchange leaves White with an unpromising position on the Queen-side, but his two Bishops offer some consolation.

22 NxN   NxN
23 PxB   N–B4
24 P–K4   . . . .

To play B–K5 in the hope of preventing . . . P–K4 would be pointless, for Black would reply 24 . . . P–B3; 25 B–N3, P–K4, when 26 Q–B2 or Q–R5 would be met convincingly by 26 . . . B–K5.

24 . . . .   P–K4
25 K–R1   Q–N3
26 KR–K1   QR–Q1
27 K–R2   Q–N4

Black is playing for attack on the King-side, oblivious of the fact that he is neglecting the other wing.

28 QR–Q1   . . . .

I wanted to dispute the open file, and at the same time I felt that simplification would favor me because of my Bishops.

28 . . . .   N–K3
29 Q–B4   . . . .

Beginning a quiet but highly effective maneuver with the Queen.

29 . . . .   N–B5
30 B–R2   N–K3

Serious waste of time. It would have been preferable to retreat the Queen to K2, leaving himself in a much better position to repulse White's contemplated pressure on the Queen-side.

31 Q–N4!   RxR

The surrender of the Queen-file is poor policy, but 31 . . . B–B1; 32 Q–R5! N–B5; 33 Q–B7 would also create a difficult situation for Black.

32 RxR   B–B1
33 Q–R4   R–B1

Black's position is steadily deteriorating. 33 . . . Q–K2 is bad because of 34 BxP, N–B4; 35 Q–Q4, QxBch; 36 QxQ, RxQ; 37 R–Q8ch, K–R2;

38 RxB, NxP; 39 BxP, NxP; 40 B–
N8ch, K–N3; 41 R–B6ch, K–N4; 42
RxP and White should win.

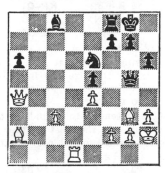

34 Q–R5!	N–B5
35 B–B4	P–R4
36 P–R4	....

White has the win well in hand
now, so that he must beware of
premature action on the Queen-
side; thus if 36 BxP? BxB; 37 QxB,
P–R5; 38 BxN, QxBch followed by
...QxP.

| 36 .... | Q–B3 |
| 37 Q–B7! | ... |

This completes the encirclement
of Black's game. In view of the
decisive threat of R–Q6, Black decides to stake everything on a desperate counterattack.

37	P–N4
38 PxP	QxP
39 BxPch!	....

Strange! After all of White's
maneuvering on the Queen-side,
the blow falls on the other wing.

| 39 .... | K–R1 |
| 40 K–R1! | .... |

Very important. If the KB retreats, then ...P–R5 regains the
Pawn.

| 40 .... | P–R5 |

40...Q–N2 looks strong, but
White has the winning reply 41 R–
Q8! Or if 40...B–N5; 41 R–Q5!,
NxR; 42 PxN threatening BxPch.

| 41 BxN | .... |

Now this capture is in order, as
Black cannot retake with a check.

| 41 .... | QxB |
| 42 B–N6! | .... |

The simplest.

42	Q–R3
43 QxPch	K–N1
44 B–B5	BxB
45 PxB	Resigns

32.

KLEIN–RESHEVSKY
Yarmouth, 1935

QUEEN'S PAWN OPENING

E. Klein	Reshevsky
WHITE	BLACK
1 P–Q4	P–Q4
2 N–KB3	P–QB3
3 B–B4	....

The customary P–B4 is stronger,
but apparently White does not care
to play against the Slav Defense.

| 3 .... | Q–N3! |

Playing for the initiative, and
confronting White with the choice
of sacrificing a Pawn for development (4 QN–Q2), or weakening his
Queen-side (4 P–QN3) or making a
defensive move (4 Q–B1).

| 4 Q–B1 | B–B4 |
| 5 P–K3 | P–KR3 |

Creating a retreat for the QB in
the event of N–R4.

| 6 P–B4! | PxP |

Although this gives White chances in the center, the capture
seemed necessary to me, as the further advance of the QBP might
have been unpleasant.

7 BxBP	P–K3
8 O–O	N–B3
9 N–B3	QN–Q2
10 R–K1	....

Beginning a struggle for the control of K4. If White can succeed in

playing P–K4, he will obtain a powerful position in the center, thus completely refuting Black's strategy.

10	B–QN5
11 P–QR3	BxN
12 PxB	. . . .

If White were drawishly inclined at this point, he could play 12 Qx B, N–Q4; 13 BxN etc. However, with two Bishops and some prospects of forcing P–K4, White hopes to secure the advantage.

| 12 . . . . | P–B4 |

Black must play aggressively to keep the powerful White Pawn center within bounds. Black holds in reserve a formidable weapon in the occupation of the QB file by his Rooks.

| 13 Q–Q1 | . . . . |

Rather slow. Two good ideas which suggest themselves here are: (1) 13 N–K5 intending P–B3 and P–K4; (2) 13 N–Q2 trying to force P–K4.

| 13 . . . . | O–O |
| 14 B–Q3 | BxB |

Simpler and safer than 14 . . . N–K5; 15 Q–B2, QN–B3; 16 N–K5, with the troublesome threat of P–B3.

| 15 QxB | N–R4 |

A certain amount of simplification will be useful, because Black's coming attack on his opponent's Pawn center can best be exploited in the endgame.

16 B–K5	KR–Q1
17 KR–N1	NxB
18 NxN	Q–B2
19 Q–N5	. . . .

Parrying the threat of . . . QxN and trying to seize the initiative.

| 19 . . . . | P–QN3 |
| 20 P–QR4! | . . . . |

This attempt to liquidate the Queen-side is the best counter to Black's contemplated play against the center Pawns.

| 20 . . . . | N–B3 |
| 21 Q–B6 | . . . . |

Loss of time. Best was 21 P–R5, BPxP; 22 BPxP (if 22 RPxP, RPxP; 23 BPxP, N–Q4 with a satisfactory game), PxP; 23 QxP, KR–QB1 and Black has a slight advantage.

21	QR–B1
22 QxQ	RxQ
23 P–R5	NPxP
24 RxP	N–K5!
25 KR–R1	PxP!

25 . . . NxQBP; 26 RxBP is quite playable for White.

| 26 BPxP | KR–QB1 |

Threatening mate.

| 27 P–N3 | . . . . |

Had White seen more clearly into the nature of the following endgame, he would have preferred 27 N–Q3, R–B6; 28 R(5)–R3, RxR; 29 RxR, R–B6; 30 RxR, NxR. Despite the reduced material, however, Black would still have had winning chances because of his outside passed Pawn.

27	R–B8ch
28 RxR	RxRch
29 K–N2	R–B7
30 RxP	. . . .

30 K–B3 is equally uninviting, for after . . . P–B4; 31 N–Q3, R–Q7; 32

R–R3, P–N4 White's pieces are badly tied up. The indicated winning plan for Black would be ... P–QR4–5 followed by the advance of his King to Q4.

30	RxPch
31 K–N1	P–R4
32 N–Q3	R–Q7
33 N–B4	P–N3

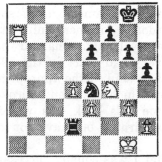

Black now enjoys three decisive advantages: (1) he has control of the "absolute" seventh, so that White's King is confined to the last rank; (2) White's KP lacks Pawn protection, and must therefore be guarded by a piece; (3) Black's King is headed, after due preparation, for the strongly centralized post K5.

The way in which these factors are combined to achieve victory make the following play exceedingly instructive.

34 R–R1	N–B6

Threatening either ... N–Q8 or ... N–K7ch in certain eventualities.

35 R–K1	. . . .

Note how concerned White has become over his KP! If instead 35 R–QB1, N–Q8; 36 N–N2, K–N2 and White will gradually be starved out of moves.

35	K–N2
36 N–R3	N–K5!

Maintaining the bind on White.

37 N–B4	K–R3

38 R–K2	. . . .

If 38 R–KB1, P–N4 is decisive:

I 39 N–N2, K–N3; 40 R–QB1, K–B4; 41 R–B1ch, K–N5; 42 RxP, K–R6; 43 N–K1, R–Q8; 44 R–D1, N–Q7 and wins.

II 39 N–R3, K–N3; 40 R–K1, K–B4; 41 R–B1ch, K–N5; 42 N–B2ch, NxN; 43 RxN, RxR; 44 KxR, K–B4!; 45 K–B3, P–N5ch; 46 K–B2, K–K5; 47 K–K2, P–B4 and wins.

38	R–Q8ch
39 K–N2	P–N4
40 N–R3	N–B6
41 R–QB2	R–Q6
42 K–B2	K–N3
43 N–N1	K–B4

The process of encirclement has been completed. If now 44 N–R3, P–B3 followed by ... K–K5 winning the KP. Or 44 N–K2, N–K5ch with the same result.

44 N–B3	N–Q8ch
45 K–K2	RxPch
46 KxN	RxN
47 K–K2	K–K5
48 R–B4	R–B4
49 P–R3	. . . .

White's position is hopeless. If 49 R–R4, P–B3; 50 R–N4, R–Q4; 51 R–N6, KxP; 52 RxP, R–K4ch; 53 RxR, PxR winning easily.

49	R–B6
Resigns	

CAREER OF A CHESS CHAMPION

THE sixty-nine games which make up this section were played during the years 1936 to 1942. In this time I won the chess championship of the United States and successfully defended my title three times in tournament play and twice in match play.

A remarkable feature of these tournaments is of such interest that I trust I will be pardoned for mentioning it—particularly since it is now more a psychological hazard than an asset. After getting off to a very bad start in the 1936 championship (of which more will be said in the appropriate place), I began a streak of victories which has been unbroken in tournament play up to the time this book was written (1947). I have been obliged to yield draws, but have not lost a game in seventy-six encounters.

It would be pleasant to say that I was equally successful in my tournaments abroad, but the record would not bear me out. In a half-dozen tournaments played in Europe, although I was beaten two or three times in each, I managed to place among the prize-winners so consistently as to be reckoned among the handful of players who could justly be considered world championship contenders.

To those who have never had occasion to do so, it must seem fascinating to wander about from one foreign country to another, observing many cities and men while practising one's chosen profession and enjoying one's favorite pastime. Reality is less romantic. Steamship lines, railway companies, and hotels are strangers to the ancient and royal game of chess, and either indifferent or hostile to its apostles. By the time one gets to a tournament, a hot bath and a comfortable bed are more desirable than even the most stimulating competition at chess. And sightseeing is even more out of the question. Such discomforts are transitory, however, but the product of the travels, the games of the chess masters, is a permanent contribution to chess literature.

FIRST U. S. CHAMPIONSHIP TOURNAMENT NEW YORK, 1936

To those who have not followed chess tournament and match play closely it may come as a surprise to learn that tournament play was not always the traditional way to win a championship. The would-be contender had to issue a challenge and put up a purse which would compensate the reigning champion for risking his title. Negotiations might drag on for years, and the titleholder might even, with little criticism, refuse to meet a challenger.

All of this was changed, so far as the United States championship was concerned, by the generosity of the late Frank J. Marshall, champion of the United States from 1909 to 1936. Realizing that the method used in golf and tennis to determine a championship offers more encouragement to rising players and stimulates interest in the game, the grand old man of American chess voluntarily retired and put his title at the disposal of the National Chess Federation with the understanding that it would be contended for biennially in tournament play.

For me, this tournament will long remain something of a nightmare. After winning my first round game, I had the misfortune to draw my second one and then lose the third and fourth! At this early stage it seemed as if the ultimate winner would be only three points down at the most and there were few people who would have taken seriously my chance to win the title. Somehow I managed to pull myself together and by winning round after round, I slowly gained on the leaders. At last in the twelfth round I achieved a tie for first place with Simonson. The pressure was intense as we fought it out on even terms up to the final round. Then, unexpectedly, he lost while I drew my game to finish first by a scant half a point. I had done the "miraculous" by winning nine and drawing two of my last eleven games. More important I had fulfilled my ambition of becoming chess champion of the country of my choice.

33.

RESHEVSKY–TREYSTMAN
U. S. Championship, 1936

QUEEN'S GAMBIT DECLINED

Reshevsky	G. Treystman
WHITE	BLACK
1 P–Q4	P–Q4
2 P–QB4	P–K3
3 N–QB3	N–KB3
4 PxP	. . . .

The "Exchange Variation," which
I have played with good results on
important occasions. The text is
usually adopted a few moves later,
but it can also be resorted to at
this early stage.

| 4 . . . . | PxP |
| 5 B–N5 | QN–Q2 |

Offering White an opportunity to
fall into the ancient trap 6 NxP??
NxN! 7 BxQ, B–N5ch and wins.

6 P–K3	B–K2
7 Q–B2	P–B3
8 B–Q3	O–O
9 N–B3	. . . .

KN–K2 followed by O–O–O leads
to sharper play, whereas the text
is more conservative and insures
White a solid position. Castling on
the Queen-side gives both sides
promising attacking possibilities,
but it has not yet been proven
conclusively in serious games that
either player has the better winning chances.

9	R–K1
10 P–KR3	N–B1
11 B–KB4	. . . .

The immediate O–O would give
Black an opportunity to simplify
with . . . N–K5.

11	B–Q3
12 BxB	QxB
13 O–O	B–K3

Black's difficulty is that he cannot hit on any promising plan; be-

fore he can undertake anything, he
must wait and see what White's
plans are.

| 14 KR–N1 | . . . . |

White reveals that he intends to
attack Black's Queen-side Pawns.
The threat is a difficult one to
parry, but QR–N1 would have
been more exact.

| 14 . . . . | R–K2 |

14 . . . P–QR4 (to prevent White's
next move) would have been met
effectively by N–QR4–B5 followed
in due course by P–QN4.

| 15 P–QN4 | R–B2 |

This only prevents P–N5 momentarily. However, an attempt to
blockade the Queen's wing by 15
. . . P–QR3; 16 P–QR4, P–QN4
would be answered by 17 P–K4!
with an overwhelming game.

| 16 Q–Q2 | Q–K2 |
| 17 Q–B2 | . . . . |

The Queen moves are explained
by my hesitancy to make a decisive
break before all preparations have
been completed. Black has nothing
better to do than mark time.

17	N–K1
18 P–QR4	N–Q3
19 R–QB1	QR–B1
20 Q–N2	. . . .

The best square for the Queen;
if now 20 . . . N–B5; 21 BxN, PxB;
22 P–K4 with an excellent game.

20	N–N3
21 P–N5	Q–B3?

21 ... P–QB4 was in order.

| 22 PxP! | .... |

Black is never given an opportunity to play the threatened BxP.

| 22 .... | PxP? |

After this he has a positionally lost game, as the backward QBP becomes a helpless target. 22 ... Rx P was relatively better.

| 23 B–R6! | R–Q1 |

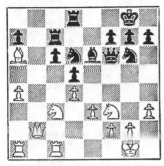

| 24 N–QN5! | .... |

Forcing a favorable exchange.

| 24 .... | NxN |
| 25 PxN | R–N1 |

If instead 25 ... BxP; 26 RxP, Rx R; 27 PxR, B–K3; 28 P–B7 with an easily won game.

| 26 Q–R3 | B–B4 |

Or 26 ... BxP; 27 RxP, RxR; 28 PxR and the passed QBP decides the issue.

| 27 R–B5 | .... |

White's well-posted pieces are now ready for the kill.

| 27 .... | Q–Q3 |
| 28 Q–R5 | B–K3 |

The QP required additional defense.

| 29 QR–QB1 | R–N3 |
| 30 PxP! | R(3)xP |

Black's position would also be untenable after 30 ... R(2)xP; 31 B–N7!, RxR; 32 PxR, Q–B2; 33 P–

B6, RxB (if 33 ... Q–N1; 34 R–R1, B–B1; 35 BxB, QxB; 36 N–Q4 and wins); 34 PxR, QxRch; 35 K–R2 and wins.

| 31 B–N7! | .... |

Forcing a powerful passed Pawn.

31	RxR
32 PxR	Q–K2
33 P–B6	B–B1

He has little choice.

34 BxB	RxB
35 QxQP	Q–K3
36 Q–QB5	....

This wins more rapidly than the exchange of Queens.

36	R–B2
37 N–Q4	Q–K2
00 N–N5	Resigns

For if 38 ... R–B1; 39 P–D7 followed by N–Q6, or NxP.

34.

ADAMS–RESHEVSKY
U. S. Championship, 1936

FRENCH DEFENSE

W. W. Adams	Reshevsky
WHITE	BLACK
1 P–K4	P–K3

One of the rare instances on which I have adopted this defense: I have a strong preference for 1 ... P–K4 or 1 ... P–QB4.

| 2 P–Q4 | P–Q4 |
| 3 N–QB3 | B–N5 |

I consider this more of a fighting defense than the line of play beginning with 3 ... N–KB3.

| 4 B–Q3 | .... |

Too tame. The most promising course is 4 P–K5 followed by P–QR3 with strong attacking possibilities for White.

4	PxP
5 BxP	N–KB3
6 B–N5	....

After this White is compelled to

part with one of his valuable Bishops. However, the alternative 6 B–Q3 also leaves Black with a good game: 6...P–B4; 7 P–QR3, BxN ch; 8 PxB, O–O; 9 N–B3, QN–Q2; 10 O–O, P–QN3; 11 Q–K2, B–N2; 12 N–K5, R–B1; 13 B–N5, NxN; 14 Px N, Q–Q4 etc. (Spielmann-Przepiorka, Meran, 1926).

6	....	P–KR3
7	BxN	QxB
8	N–B3	O–O
9	O–O	N–Q2
10	N–K2	B–Q3

Black's game is quite satisfactory. His position has considerable potential power, whereas White's pieces have little opportunity for harmonious cooperation.

11 P–B4 ....

This loosens up the position and is therefore bound to provide additional scope for the Bishops; hence the more conservative P–B3 was preferable.

11 .... P–B4

Eliminating White's control of K5 and therefore an important step in the freeing of Black's position.

12 R–B1 ....

A colorless move, but the apparently stronger 12 P–Q5 would be answered effectively by 12...P–K4 followed eventually by ...P–B4.

12	...	PxP
13	QNxP	P–R3

White has the Queen-side majority, but this is much less important than the fact that Black has the squares K4 and QB4 at his disposal.

14	P–QR3	N–B4
15	B–N1	B–B5!
16	R–B3	R–Q1
17	Q–B2	....

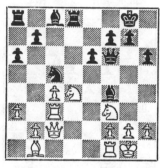

17 .... P–KN3!

Avoiding the trap 17...RxN?; 18 NxR, QxN; 19 R–Q1 and Black can resign: 19...Q–K5; 20 R–Q8 ch, K–R2; 21 Q–Q1 winning the Queen; or 19...Q–K4; 20 Q–R7ch, K–B1; 21 Q–R8ch, K–K2; 22 Q–Q8 mate.

18 P–QN4 ....

This turns out badly. He should have played N–K2.

18 .... P–K4!

After the anticipated 18...N–Q2 it would take Black considerable time to free himself.

19 PxN ....

He has little choice, for after 19 N–K2, B–B4; 20 Q–R2, N–R5; 21 R–N3, B–K3 the outlook for White's game would be very poor.

19 .... PxN

20 R–N3 ....

From a strategical point of view, White's Queen-side Pawns are disastrously weak. By attacking the QNP and therefore keeping Black's QB at home, he hopes to gain time to menace the QP.

| 20 . . . . | B–Q2! |

A little surprise, and **m u c h** stronger than 20 . . . B–B4; 21 Q–N2 with good prospects for White.

21 Q–N?   . . . .

The QNP is taboo after all. 21 RxP, B–B3; 22 R–N6 (if 22 R–N3, B–R5 wins. If 22 R–N4, BxN; 23 PxB, Q–N4ch; 24 K–R1, Q–R5 and mate follows. If 22 R–N2 Black can win in the same way or else he can play 22 . . . P–Q6; 23 Q–N3, either R–N1 and wins), B–B2 and White must lose at least the exchange.

| 21 . . . . | B–B3 |

Now the Bishops are functioning in ideal style.

| 22 R–Q1 | Q–K2! |

Now follows some interesting play which centers about the apparently weak QP.

At this point the QP is amply protected, for if 23 RxQP?, RxR; 24 QxR, R–Q1 and wins. After 23 NxP, B–K4 wins. Or even 23 NxP?, B–R5; 24 RxP, RxN!! and White is helpless!

| 23 R(3)–Q3 | QxP |
| 24 NxP? | . . . . |

This loses rapidly, although after 24 RxP, RxR; 25 QxR, QxQ; 26 Rx

Q or 26 NxQ, Black would have a vastly superior ending because of his powerful Bishops and because of the weakness of White's Queenside Pawns.

| 24 . . . . | B–K4 |
| 25 Q–Q2 | . . . . |

White's original intention may have been 25 N–K6, but then Black has the crushing reply 25 . . . RxR!

25	BxN
26 RxB	RxR
27 QxR	QxRP
28 Q–B6	Q–QN6!

Black has not only won a Pawn, but he has definite tactical threats as well.

| 29 R–K1 | . . . . |

If 29 R–QB1, R–K1; 30 BxP, QxP!; 31 R–N1, PxB winning easily.

| 29 . . . . | R–K1! |

With the delightful point that if 30 RxRch, BxR and Black wins a piece!

| 30 R–KB1 | QxP |
| 31 BxP | . . . . |

Overlooking Black's reply, **b u t** the position had already become quite hopeless.

| 31 . . . . | QxRch! |
| **Resigns** | |

Mate in three is forced.

35.

RESHEVSKY–KEVITZ
U. S. Championship, 1936

C O L L E   S Y S T E M

Reshevsky	A. Kevitz
WHITE	BLACK
1 P–Q4	N–KB3
2 N–KB3	P–K3
3 P–K3	P–B4
4 B–Q3	P–Q4

. . . P–QN3, reserving the option of advancing the QP one or two squares, is more promising.

| 5 P–B3 | QN–Q2 |
| 6 QN–Q2 | PxP? |

A serious mistake, for it opens up the K file for White and allows him to concentrate his forces on K5. Relatively better would have been 6 ... Q–B2; 7 O–O, B–K2; 8 Q–K2, O–O; 9 P–K4 with slightly better chances for White.

7 KPxP	B–Q3
8 O–O	O–O
9 R–K1	Q–B2
10 Q–K2	P–QN3

We see here another sad consequence of Black's faulty sixth move. The center lacks fluidity and therefore there is no good development available for the QB. A preferable course, however, would have been ... P–QR3 followed by ... P–QN4, with some later hopes of counterplay by ... P–N5.

| 11 N–K5 | .... |

This magnificently posted Knight can hardly be captured, because after the QP recaptures, White has excellent attacking chances.

| 11 .... | B–N2 |
| 12 P–KB4 | KR–K1 |

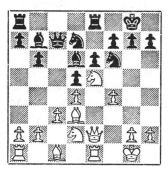

13 P–KN4!   ....

On with the attack! The formidable position of the advanced Knight justifies aggressive tactics.

| 13 .... | N–B1 |

Equally uninviting is the alterna-

tive 13 ... P–N3; 14 P–N5, N–R4; 15 N–B1 followed by N–N3 etc.

| 14 P–N5 | KN–Q2 |
| 15 N–B1 | R–K2 |

Black plans to drive away the unbearable Knight, but the result is a weak Pawn formation.

| 16 N–N3 | P–B3 |
| 17 PxP | PxP |

... NxP was safer, but Black is reluctant to give up his idea of dislodging the Knight. In any event, the KP would remain a serious weakness.

| 18 NxN | RxN |

If instead 18 ... QxN (not 18 ... NxN; 19 Q–N4ch winning a Pawn); 19 N–R5, R–B2; 20 Q–N4ch, K–R1; 21 P–B5, P–K4; 22 B–KR6 and Black is helpless against K–R1 followed by R–KN1.

| 19 N–R5 | R–B2 |
| 20 P–B5! | PxP |

After 20 ... P–K4 the game would proceed on pretty much the same lines as in the previous note.

21 BxP	K–R1
22 B–R6	B–B1
23 R–KB1	Q–K2

Losing a Pawn, which, however, had practically become inevitable.

24 QxQ!	BxQ
25 BxB	RxB
26 R–B5	R–Q1
27 N–B4	....

This explains White's readiness to exchange on move 24. White wins a Pawn, with more to come very shortly.

27	N–N3
28 NxP	N–R5
29 NxB!	RxN

| 30 R–B4! | . . . . |

More exact than 30 RxP, which would give Black counterplay by

30 . . . R–K7; 31 QR–KB1, R–N1ch; 32 K–R1, RxP etc.

| 30 . . . . | N–N3 |

30 . . . R–N1ch is worthless because of 31 K–B1 followed by RxP.

| 31 RxP | R–KN1 |

Black might well have resigned here instead of playing on for twelve additional moves.

32 K–B1	R–K5
33 R–B2	N–R5
34 B–B4	P–KR4
35 B–N3	R(5)–N5
36 R–K1	N–N3
37 R–B3	P–R5
38 B–B2	K–R2
39 P–KR3	R–B5
40 R–K7ch	K–R1
41 RxR	NxR(5)
42 R–K3	R–KB1
43 R–B3	K–N2
44 B–K3	Resigns

INTERNATIONAL TOURNAMENT
AT NOTTINGHAM, 1936

THE great chess tournaments have always come about as the result of a sponsor's generosity. As is well known to everyone who has done any globe trotting, international travel is an expensive affair. Moreover, chess masters are usually an impecunious lot. Unless the tournament committee is willing to advance them the money for traveling and living accommodations, most of them prefer to stay in their own back yards—much to the detriment of the game. And unless the tournament committee can find a patron or a group of patrons, it cannot furnish the advances or put up prizes calculated to tempt the best masters to participate.

The great Nottingham tournament of 1936 was made possible through the generosity of Alderman Derbyshire. He sponsored the event to commemorate his winning first place in the masters' tournament of 1886. The Alderman was one of the great patrons of chess. Many European tourneys owed their inception or their final success to his keen interest in and love for the game.

The list of contenders was impressive. In addition to the world champion Dr. Max Euwe, three ex-champions—Lasker, Capablanca and Alekhine — were competing. Rising young players like Flohr, Botvinnik, Fine and myself were balanced against stars of the older generation like Tartakover, Vidmar and Bogolyubov. To round out the group, several of the leading British masters were present.

With such a field it is understandable that the tournament was exceptionally hard fought. Only one and a half points separated first place from eighth! I finished in a triple tie for third, fourth and fifth, only half a point behind Capablanca and Botvinnik who shared first and second prizes. I was much encouraged by winning my games from Lasker and Alekhine. My defeat of the venerable Dr. Lasker was one of the quickest of his long and successful career.

36.

ALEXANDER–RESHEVSKY
Nottingham, 1936

ENGLISH OPENING

C. H. Alexander	Reshevsky
WHITE	BLACK
1 P–QB4	P–K4
2 N–QB3	N–QB3
3 P–KN3	P–KN3

Later I was to discard this defensive system for Black, as it gives White too strong an initiative.

4 B–N2	B–N2
5 P–K3	KN–K2
6 KN–K2	O–O
7 O–O	P–Q3
8 N–Q5	. . . .

An even more promising course is P–Q4, Black can hardly avoid the following exchange, as White's QN has too commanding a post at Q5. The result is, however, that White will be in a position to exert some pressure via the newly opened QB file.

8	NxN
9 PxN	N–K2
10 P–Q4	N–B4!

Virtually forcing the following exchange, which will leave the Knight a good square at Q3.

11 PxP	PxP
12 P–K4	N–Q3
13 B–K3	P–KB4

Since White has an easy initiative on the QB file already mapped out, Black must be prepared to create counterchances on the other wing.

| 14 PxP | BxP |

Although this gives White command of his K4, it is more promising than 14 ... PxP; 15 P–B4, P–K5 etc.

| 15 Q–N3! | P–N3 |

Rather bold because it intensi-

fies the backwardness of the QBP; but sooner or later Black would have to guard against the occupation of his QB4 by hostile pieces.

| 16 QR–B1 | Q–Q2 |
| 17 P–B3 | . . . . |

Here Alexander loses the thread of the game. He should have adopted the banal but strong plan of R–B6 followed by KR–B1, and the pressure on the BP would have effectively balanced Black's Kingside prospects.

The text threatens to win a piece with P–N4—a menace which is easily parried. Another point of the text is to make N–K4 possible; but, as will be soon later on, this only creates King-side chances for Black.

| 17 . . . . | P–KR4! |

Not only protecting the QB from harm, but holding the further advance of the KRP in reserve.

| 18 KR–Q1 | . . . . |

Pointless. There was still time to double the Rooks on the QB file.

18	R–B2
19 N–B3	QR–KB1
20 N–K4	. . . .

Offering the exchange of Queens with Q–R4 would have been a simpler course.

| 20 . . . . | NxN |
| 21 PxN | B–R6 |

22 R–B1? . . . .

A strangely tame move from
such an aggressive player as Alexander. The continuation 22 RxP!,
QxR; 23 BxB was much richer in
resources for White and would
have led to a game which it is difficult to appraise accurately.

22 . . . .   BxB
23 KxB   Q–N5

Thus White's opening of the KB
file has only turned against him.
If now 24 Q–B4, P–R5; 25 RxR (not
25 B–B2?, P–R6ch; 26 K–N1, Q–
B6), P–R6ch; 26 K–N1, RxR; 27
R–B1, RxRch; 28 KxR, Q–B6ch; 29
B–B2, Q–N7ch; 30 K–K2, K–R2!
and Black wins the KRP with a
quick victory in sight.

24 Q–Q3   RxR?

A fateful transposition! 24 . . . P–
R5! would have won much more
rapidly.

25 RxR   RxR
26 KxR   Q–B6ch
27 K–K1   B–R3?

Another inexactitude. This move
seems to win a piece, for if 28 K–
Q2?, Q–B7ch. As will be seen, however, the proper course was 27 . . .
Q–R8ch; 28 K–K2, QxPch; 29 B–
B2, B–B1 (threatening . . . B–B4);
30 K–B1, Q–R6ch etc. The win
would still present difficulties, but
it would be technically easier.

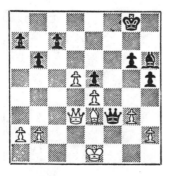

28 P–Q6! . . . .

This unexpected move is calculated to prolong White's resistance.

28 . . . .   PxP

Since the Pawn cannot be allowed to advance, White is able to ex-
tricate himself from the pin.

29 Q–Q5ch   K–R2
30 BxB   Q–R8ch
31 K–K2   QxPch
32 K–B3   Q–R8ch
33 K–K3   Q–B8ch
34 K–B3   QxB
35 QxQP . . . .

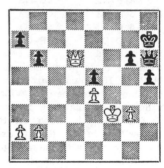

The ending which follows may
be logically divided into the following stages: (1) Black plays . . . P–
R5, creating a passed KNP; (2) he
guards his Queen-side Pawns from
attack; (3) he combines this defensive policy with continual menace of White's KP; (4) having thus
reduced White to passivity, he is
ready for combined action by his
King, Queen and KNP. All this is
easier said than done!

35 . . . .   Q–N4!
36 Q–K6 . . . .

If 36 Q–B7ch, K–R3; 37 QxRP,
Q–N5ch; 38 K–B2, P–R5! 39 PxP,
QxPch; 40 K–K3, Q–B5ch and
Black will win the KP with check.

36 . . . .   K–R3
37 Q–B8   Q–B3ch
38 K–N2   P–R5!

Thus the passed Pawn is created.

39	PxP	K–R4
40	Q–Q7	P–R4
41	Q–Q1ch	KxP
42	Q–K1ch	K–R4

These checks are only superficially irritating, since they are bound to come to an end soon without anything positive being achieved by White.

43	Q–Q1ch	K–R3
44	Q–R1ch	K–N4
45	Q–Q1	K–R3
46	Q–R1ch	K–N2
47	Q–QB1	Q–Q1
48	Q–B2	Q–N4ch

Now it is Black's turn! But there is this difference between the two series of Queen's checks: whereas White's checks accomplish nothing, Black materially improves his position by finally getting his Queen to KB7.

49	K–R3	Q–K6ch
50	K–N4	Q–B5ch
51	K–R3	Q–B6ch

52	K–R2	. . . .

If 52 K–R4, K–R3; 53 Q–Q2ch, Q–B5ch wins.

52	. . . .	K–R3
53	Q–B6	Q–B7ch
54	K–R3	K–R4!

54 . . . QxP would be inferior because of 55 Q–B6 with drawing chances for White. Black has now

accomplished a good deal, because White is reduced to two losing possibilities: (a) either he employs his Queen to menace the Queenside Pawns, in which case Black's King and KNP can advance fearlessly; (b) he keeps his Queen at home, in which case Black's Queenside Pawns are in no danger, and Black can proceed comfortably with his plans on the King-side.

55	Q–N7	Q–K6ch
56	K–N2	Q–Q7ch
57	K–N3	Q–Q6ch
58	K–B2	Q–Q3!
59	K–N3	K–N4

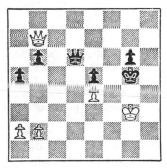

Black's retreat of the Queen was for the purpose of guarding against Q–K7ch at this point. Black's Queen will soon force a new entry, bringing us to the final stage of the ending.

60	K–B3	Q–Q1
61	K–N3	Q–B3
62	Q–Q5	Q–B5ch
63	K–N2	K–R5

White's stubborn resistance is crumbling at last.

64	Q–B6	Q–N6ch
65	K–B1	Q–B6ch
66	K–K1	Q–K6ch
67	K–B1	P–KN4
68	K–N2	Q–Q7ch
	Resigns	

White resigns, for if 69 K–B3, P–

N5 mate; or if 69 K–B1, K–N6 and
he must exchange Queens. An un-
usually interesting endgame.

37.

BOGOLYUBOV–RESHEVSKY

Nottingham, 1936

NIMZOINDIAN DEFENSE

E. Bogolyubov	Reshevsky
WHITE	BLACK
1 P–Q4	N–KB3
2 P–QB4	P–K3
3 N–QB3	B–N5
4 P–QR3	. . . .

The most aggressive continuation, played with the idea of compelling Black to surrender his
Bishop immediately, with the result that White obtains two Bishops and a strong central Pawn formation. Black must play alertly if
he is to avoid a permanent disadvantage.

4	BxNch
5 PxB	O–O
6 P–K3	. . . .

A frequently seen alternative is
6 P–B3, aiming for P–K4.

6	P–Q4
7 B–Q3	P–B4

Black must counter energetically
before his opponent's position in
the center becomes too powerful.

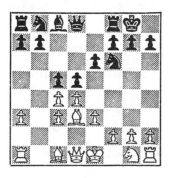

8 BPxP	. . . .

After 8 N–K2, Black would have
a good continuation in 8 . . . QPxP;
9 BxP, Q–B2.

8	QxP

An unusual but playable alternative to the more frequently played
alternatives . . . NxP and . . . KPxP.

9 Q–B3	. . . .

An interesting innovation. Bogolyubov courts the exchange of
Queens because his Bishops would
be powerful in the resulting
ending.

9	Q–Q1

Naturally avoiding the exchange.
Black is angling for . . . P–K4 in
order to free his game, although it
will also give the hostile Bishops
additional scope.

10 Q–K2	. . . .

After N–K2 Black could play . . .
N–B3 intending . . . P–K4.

10	Q–B2

Gaining time for . . . P–K4 because of the threat of . . . PxP etc.

11 B–N2	. . . .

The Bishop has a miserable position only for the time being.

11	P–K4
12 PxKP	QxP
13 P–QB4	. . . .

See the previous note.

13	Q–K2
14 N–B3	N–B3
15 Q–B2	R–K1!

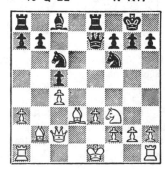

White's Bishops have become very troublesome, and Black must play with great care. The text is played to enable Black to continue with ... N–K5, breaking the KB's diagonal.

16 P–R3   . . . .

And not 16 BxN, QxB; 17 BxP ch?, K–R1 winning a piece.

16 . . . .   N–K5

17 O–O–O!?   . . . .

A great deal of thought must have gone into this move. It is by no means risky, as Black has no attacking chances; it also has the virtue of placing White's King in the vicinity of Black's Queen-side majority. In addition, White is now free to pursue his own attacking aims.

It should be noted that White had a strong alternative here in 17 P–N4, preventing the development of Black's Bishop; but the idea of attacking the Bishop once it plays to B4 also has its attractions.

17 . . . .   B–B4

18 P–N4   B–N3

19 P–KR4   . . . .

The game has taken a new and unpleasant turn for Black. 19 ... P–KR3 or ... P–KR4 would be answered by QR–N1 with a dangerous attack.

19 . . . .   N–B3!

Best under the circumstances.

20 BxB   BPxB!?

This makes possible Black's later counterplay on the KB file, but has the drawback of allowing White a passed KP.

21 P–R5   Q–K5!

Whereas Black evaded the exchange of Queens at an earlier stage, he now seeks simplification because of White's threatening advance.

22 QxQ   . . . .

The exchange is unavoidable (22 Q–K2, N–R4; 23 N–Q2, QxNP; 24 P–B3, Q–K3 and White has nothing for the sacrificed Pawn.

22 . . . .   NxQ

23 PxP!?   . . . .

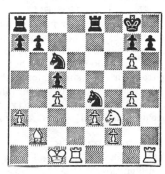

23 . . . .   PxP!?

Black spurns the draw which he could virtually force with 23 ... NxP, leading to these likely continuations:

I   24 R–Q7, R–K2; 25 RxR, Nx R(7); 26 RxP (26 PxPch, K–R1; 27 R–R5 should offer Black no trouble), N–Q6ch etc.

II 24 RxP, R–K2; 25 R–B1, NxP (if 25 ... N–Q6ch; 26 K–B2, NxB; 27 QR–KR1 and wins); 26 QR–R1, N–R3; 27 QRxN! and wins. However, after 24 ... NxR! White must take a draw.

24 R–R2   QR–Q1

Not 24 ... R–KB1?; 25 R–Q7, R–B2; 26 R–R8ch! with a winning position.

25 QR–R1   . . . .

White has no choice but to play for attack; if 25 N–Q2, N–R4! 26 NxN, RxRch; 27 KxR, RxN wins a Pawn.

25 . . . .   K–B2

26 R–R7   R–KN1

27 K–B2!   . . . .

A good move. The main idea is

that after 27 ... NxP?; 28 R–KB1,
Black would be unable to save him-
self with ...N–Q6ch and conse-
quently the Knight would be lost.
The text also helps to advance the
King to the center and protect the
QBP in case of need.

       27 . . . .   QR–KB1!?

This move has been praised and
condemned by the annotators, and
it is not easy to strike a proper
balance. Its good side is that it
prepares for pressure along the
KB file, where White is vulnerable.
On the other hand, the entry of
White's King will soon become
feasible.

      28 R(1)–R2   K–K3?

But this should have led to serious difficulties.

      29 R(7)–R3?   . . . .

White in turn misses his chance.
Correct was 29 K–Q3!, RxN; 30
KxN, R–B2; 31 B–B3! with a very
strong game for White.

      29 . . . .   R–Q1!

Preventing K–Q3.

      30 R–R7   KR–B1!

Black has been able to improve
his position as a result of White's
inexactitude.

      31 R(2)–R3   R–Q2!

31 ... NxP; 32 N–N5ch followed
by R–N3 would be too dangerous

for Black. The text threatens ...
QR–KB2 and therefore forces
White to simplify.

      32 RxP   RxR
      33 BxR   R–B2
      34 B–B3   NxP
      35 N–N5ch   K–Q2!

But not 35 ... K–K2?; 36 R–R6,
R–B1; 37 R–R7ch with a winning
position.

      36 R–R6?   . . . .

A time pressure move which
proves fatal. Either 36 NxR or 36
R–N3 would have given White better chances.

      36 . . . .   R–K2
      37 RxP   NxP
      38 P–K4   N(5)–K4

Thus Black comes out of the complications with the win of the BP.

      39 R–N8   NxP
      40 B–B6   R–K1
      41 RxR   . . . .

Or 41 R–N7ch, K–B1; 42 P–R4,
N–Q3 winning the KP.

      41 . . . .   KxR
      42 P–R4   K–Q2
      43 K–B3   N(5)–K4
      44 K–N3   K–K1
      45 K–B3   P–R3

The reasoning behind this ending is interesting. The Pawns are
so reduced that White has legiti-
mate hopes of drawing the game.
Black's winning chance resides in

getting two passed Pawns, but this involves further simplification, and therefore (theoretically, at least) enhances White's drawing chances. White also has a drawing chance in the hope that if he can rid himself of his Pawns, he can sacrifice a piece for each remaining Black Pawn and draw against the two Knights, which, as is well known, cannot effect checkmate. Thus, although the ending appears easy for Black, it has to be managed with the greatest care.

46	B–N7	K–K2
47	N–R3	P–N4
48	PxP	PxP

Black has completed the first step; he has two connected passed Pawns, but he has to be very solicitous about their welfare.

49	N–B4	N–Q2
50	N–Q5ch	K–Q3
51	N–K3	N(3)–K4

Black intends to bring his King to QR5 where it will be safe from attack and in a position to support the ultimate advance of the passed Pawns.

52	N–B5ch	K–B3
53	N–K7ch	K–N3
54	N–Q5ch	K–R4
55	K–N3	P–N5
56	N–K3	....

NxP would not suffice to draw. But B–R6, intending to return the Bishop to Q2, might have offered better chances.

56	....	K–N4
57	N–Q5	P–B5ch
58	K–B2	K–R5
59	B–R6	....

If 59 K–N2, N–B4! drives the King away from N2.

| 59 | .... | N–B4 |
| 60 | B–Q2 | .... |

Desperation; if 60 B–N7, N(B4)–Q6; 61 N–N6ch, K–N4; 62 N–Q5,

K–B4 followed by ... K–Q5 and wins.

60	....	P–N6ch
61	K–N1	NxP
62	N–B3ch	....

If 62 B–K1, N–Q6 wins.

62	....	NxNch
63	BxN	N–Q6
64	B–N7	N–B4
65	B–N2	....

After 65 B–B8, the same reply wins.

65	....	N–K5
66	B–R1	P–B6
67	K–B1	K–N5

Since Black's King cannot be kept out of Q6, White should have resigned.

68	K–N1	K–B5
69	K–B1	K–Q6
70	K–N1	K–Q7
71	B–N2	PxB
72	KxP	N–B4
	Resigns	

38.

THOMAS–RESHEVSKY
Nottingham, 1936

RUY LOPEZ

Sir G. A. Thomas	Reshevsky
WHITE	BLACK
1 P–K4	P–K4
2 N–KB3	N–QB3
3 B–N5	P–QR3
4 B–R4	N–B3
5 O–O	B–K2
6 P–B3?	....

This gives Black an easy game. The best moves here are 6 R–K1, 6 Q–K2 and 6 N–B3.

| 6 | .... | NxP |
| 7 | Q–K2 | N–B4 |

Now we see what is wrong with 6 P–B3? Not only does Black obtain the two Bishops through this forced exchange, but he will even have the better development!

8 BxN	QPxB
9 NxP	O-O
10 P-Q4	N-Q2

...N-K3 would only impede Black's development. The text either leads to the removal of White's well-posted Knight, or else to an exchange which will only accentuate the strength of Black's Bishops.

| 11 N-Q2 | .... |

Too slow. 11 P-KB4 would have been effectively answered by ... P-QB4, but 11 B-B4 would have permitted White to complete his development in normal fashion and therefore given him better prospects of equality.

| 11 .... | NxN |
| 12 QxN | .... |

If instead 12 PxN, B-KB4 (threatening ...B-Q6); 13 R-Q1 (if 13 N-K4?, Q-Q4 winning some material), Q-Q6! forcing a favorable ending.

| 12 .... | B-K3 |
| 13 N-B3 | B-Q3 |

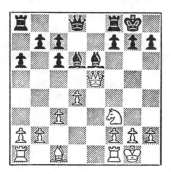

14 Q-KR5? ....

This turns out badly. The discreet withdrawal to K2 would have been preferable.

| 14 .... | P-B3! |

An important move which restricts the action of White's Knight. Black now turns his atten-

tion to exploiting the exposed position of the hostile Queen.

| 15 P-QN3 | .... |

This mysterious-looking move is explained by the fact that after B-Q2, White would not be able to move his QR because of the unprotected state of his QRP.

| 15 .... | Q-Q2 |
| 16 P-KR3 | P-QN4! |

Continuing the constriction of White's pieces.

17 R-K1	KR-K1
18 B-Q2	P-N3
19 Q-R4	....

Somewhat better would have been 19 Q-R6 and if 19 ... Q-B2 (intending ...P-N4); 20 P-KR4; but in any event the outlook for White's game would not have been promising.

| 19 .... | Q-B2 |

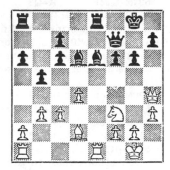

Black threatens 20 ... P-N4 and if 21 Q-R6, B-KB1 with a decisive gain of material.

| 20 Q-K4 | BxNP |
| 21 QxRch | .... |

He has no choice, for if 21 QxP, RxRch; 22 RxR, B-Q4 and the Queen is lost.

21	RxQ
22 RxRch	QxR
23 PxB	P-N5!

The quickest way, as it eliminates the technical difficulties resulting from 23 ... Q–QB1; 24 P–QN4 etc.

    24 RxP   . . . .

Or 24 PxP, Q–K7 and Black soon regains the Pawn.

    24 . . . .   **PxP**

    25 BxP   **Q–K7**

    26 RxP   . . . .

If 26 R–R1, Q–B7 followed by ... QxP and the double advance of the QBPs, giving Black a passed Pawn which would win easily. The winning plan is most instructive.

    26 . . . .   **Q–N4**

    27 RxB   . . . .

Desperation; if 27 R–B4, QxP; 28 N–Q2 (or 28 R–B6, Q–N4; 29 P–Q5, QxP and wins), Q–Q8ch; 29 N–B1, Q–B8; 30 P–Q5, Q–Q8 followed by the capture of the QP with an easy victory.

    27 . . . .   **PxR**

    28 P–QN4   **Q–Q6**

Because of the considerable disparity in material, White cannot stave off defeat. Nevertheless, the way in which his downfall is engineered is extremely interesting.

    29 B–Q2   **P–N4**

    30 B–K3   **Q–N8ch**

    31 K–R2   **QxP**

    32 P–N4   **Q–N2**

    33 N–Q2   **Q–Q4**

    34 N–B1   **K–B2**

The following excursion of the King will decide the issue.

    35 N–N3   **K–K3**

    36 N–B5   **Q–B6**

    37 N–R6   **K–Q4**

    38 N–N8   **K–B5**

    39 N–K7   **P–Q4**

    40 N–N8   **K–B6!**

A finesse: if 40 ... K–Q6; 41 N–K7, K–K7; 42 N–B5, K–B8; 43 N–N3ch.

    41 N–K7   **K–Q6**

    42 K–N1   . . . .

Black was threatening to force mate with ... K–K7–B8. 42 N–B5 would not do because of ... P–R4.

    42 . . . .   **QxP**

    Resigns

39.

RESHEVSKY–BOTVINNIK
Nottingham, 1936

DUTCH DEFENSE

Reshevsky	M. Botvinnik
WHITE	BLACK
1 P–Q4	P–K3
2 N–KB3	. . . .

As Botvinnik is famous for his virtuosity in handling the French Defense, I prefer to play against the Dutch Defense.

    2 . . . .   **P–KB4**

    3 P–KN3   . . . .

This is the line of play favored by most modern masters. It gives White a solid position and good prospects of exploiting the weaknesses with which Black is burdened in every variation of this defense.

    3 . . . .   **N–KB3**

    4 B–N2   . . . .

White defers P–B4 so that Black cannot simplify with ..B–N5ch.

    4 . . . .   **B–K2**

    5 O–O   **O–O**

    6 P–B4   **P–Q4**

Botvinnik is one of the few masters who are fond of this "Stonewall" Variation, which creates weaknesses on the black squares and makes a tardy development of the QB inevitable. The alternatives are ...P–Q3 or ...N–K5.

7	N–B3	P–B3
8	R–N1	....

An experimental move which is not quite so good as the more logical course P–N3, B–N2 followed by N–K1–Q3 and P–B3, intending an eventual P–K4.

| 8 | .... | Q–K1 |

The best way of getting the Queen into play.

| 9 | P–B5 | .... |

This explains White's previous move. The unorthodox text is the beginning of a plan to undertake an immediate onslaught against the Queen-side Pawns and it takes all of Black's ingenuity to parry his opponent's threats.

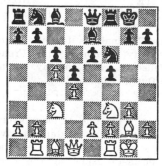

| 9 | .... | Q–R4 |

Playing for counterattack on the King-side. However, the move turns out to be loss of time, and it would have been more straightforward to play ...N–K5 followed by ...B–B3, ...N–Q2 and ...P–K4, taking advantage of the fact that White's last move has removed the tension in the center.

10	P–QN4	N–K5
11	Q–B2	N–Q2
12	P–N5	B–B3
13	B–B4!	Q–K1!

13 ... QNxP would not do because of 14 N–Q1!, N–Q2; 15 PxP, PxP; 16 QxP and wins. Botvinnik realizes that his chances on the King-side are too slow, and consequently he returns the Queen to the defense of his menaced Queen-side. The text also serves the object of freeing Black's position somewhat with ...P–K4.

| 14 | B–B7! | .... |

At B4 the Bishop was subject to attack by ...P–N4; hence White brings the Bishop to a more favorable square by means of a novel maneuver.

14	....	R–B2
15	B–R5	P–K4

At last Black has freed his game somewhat, but White still retains the initiative.

16	P–K3	NxN
17	BxN	P–K5
18	N–Q2	N–B1

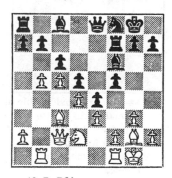

| 19 | P–B3! | .... |

A highly interesting positional sacrifice which leads to difficult play, and is certainly more aggressive than the routine 19 P–QR4, B–Q2; 20 Q–N3, P–N4 etc.

| 19 | .... | BPxP |

If instead 19 ... KPxP; 20 RxP,
PxP; 21 Q–N3, B–Q2; 22 N–B1 (if
22 QxQP?, B–B3), P–KN3; 23 R–
B2 regaining the Pawn advantageously. Or if 22 ... B–KN4; 23 R–
B2!, BxP; 24 NxB, QxN; 25 R–K1
followed by BxP and wins.

20 PxP   QPxP

Or 20 ... BPxP; 21 Q–N3 and
White regains the Pawn with a
good game.

21 P–Q5!   . . . .

This is the underlying idea of
White's Pawn sacrifice. His center
Pawns are very strong, and the
splendid square Q4 beckons to his
Knight.

21 . . . .   BxB
22 QxB   B–Q2
23 N–N3   R–B1

White was threatening N–Q4
followed by P–B6.

24 P–N4!   . . . .

Continuing to complicate matters.
The Tournament Book suggests
the promising alternative 24 KR–
B1, Q–K2; 25 N–Q4 threatening Nx
NP as well as P–QR4.

24 . . . .   P–KN3

Best, for if 24 ... PxP; 25 RxR,
KxR; 26 R–B1ch, K–N1; 27 N–Q2
winning the KP and obtaining an
overwhelming position in the center with two connected passed
Pawns.

25 Q–Q4   Q–K2
26 QR–B1   B–K1
27 R–KB4   R–Q1

In view of the strong pressure on
the KB file, Black must seek counterplay in the center.

28 QR–B1!   . . . .

White welcomes the possibility
of 28 ... N–K3; 29 PxN!, RxQ; 30
PxRch, BxP; 31 NxR and White
has a decisive material as well as
positional advantage.

28 . . . .   Q–Q2
29 PxP   PxP
30 B–R3   . . . .

But not 30 P–Q6? N–K3 etc.

30 . . . .   QxP

31 RxBP?   . . . .

A serious error in time pressure.
The correct move was 31 BxP! enabling White to win the important
KP, remaining with a much superior position.

| 31 . . . . | QxQ |
| 32 NxQ | . . . . |

White at least has the satisfaction of getting his Knight to this magnificent square — something that he has had in mind since his nineteenth move!

| 32 . . . . | R–N2ch |
| 33 K–R1 | B–Q2! |

This was the important move I had overlooked; White's valuable Bishop disappears and Black has time to consolidate his position.

34 R–R5	BxB
35 RxB	R–N4
36 N–B5	R–Q2

White threatened to win the exchange with N–R6ch–B7.

| 37 R–R4 | R–QB2! |

As White can hardly afford to lose the QBP, the following drawing maneuver is indicated.

| 38 N–R6ch | K–N2 |
| 39 N–B5ch | K–N1 |

But not 39 ... K–R1; 40 N–Q6, R–N1; 41 N–B7ch, K–N2; 42 RxP, RxP; 43 R–K7 and Black's position is uncomfortable.

| 40 N–R6ch | . . . . |

White would not have accomplished anything with 40 RxKP, RxP; 41 N–K7ch, K–N2; 42 R(4)–KB4, N–N3; 43 R–B7ch, K–R1 and the position is even.

| 40 . . . . | K–N2 |
| 41 N–B5ch | Drawn |

40.

LASKER–RESHEVSKY
Nottingham, 1936

QUEEN'S GAMBIT ACCEPTED

Dr. E. Lasker	Reshevsky
WHITE	BLACK
1 P–Q4	P–Q4
2 P–QB4	PxP

One of my favorite defenses. Although the acceptance of the gambit has been somewhat discredited of late, I am still convinced that it is one of the best defenses at Black's disposal.

| 3 N–KB3 | N–KB3 |
| 4 P–K3 | . . . . |

Q–R4ch is occasionally played here in order to get off the beaten track.

| 4 . . . . | P–K3 |
| 5 BxP | P–B4 |

| 6 N–B3 | . . . . |

Although I have played this move with the White pieces in Game 41, I am inclined to think that O–O followed by Q–K2 and R–Q1 is a preferable course for White.

| 6 . . . . | P–QR3 |
| 7 O–O | . . . . |

White can prevent ... P–QN4 by playing 7 P–QR4, but after 7 ... N–B3, Black's QN would have an unassailable post at QN5.

| 7 . . . . | P–QN4 |
| 8 B–Q3 | . . . . |

This retreat is inferior to B–N3 (as I played in the game previously referred to) because at N3 the Bishop has some prospect of supporting a later thrust to Q5, and also because the KB is more useful at N3 in the event that White's QP becomes isolated.

8 . . . .   PxP

A good alternative course was . . .
B–N2 followed by . . . QN–Q2.

The text frees White's QB for
action, but only at the cost of an
isolated QP and a strong point for
Black's pieces at Q4. True, White's
development is somewhat more rapid, but it does not take long for
Black to catch up.

9 PxP   . . . .

NxQP would surrender control of
the important squares K5 and QB5.

9 . . . .   B–N2
10 B–N5   B–K2
11 Q–K2   . . . .

The simplest way to avoid the
ensuing difficulties, as the Tournament Book points out, would have
been 11 BxN, BxB; 12 B–K4.

11 . . . .   O–O
12 QR–Q1   QN–Q2
13 N–K5   N–Q4!

Black must simplify before his
opponent can obtain a strong attacking position with P–B4.

14 B–B1?   . . . .

Highly questionable. L a s k e r
wishes to avoid too many exchanges, because of his desire to
build up an attacking formation.
However, since the Bishop's retreat
turns out to be a costly loss of
time, it would have been wiser to
play 14 BxB, QxB; 15 QNxN, BxN;

16 B–K4. The position does not jus-
tify a more ambitious effort on
White's part.

14 . . . .   KNxN
15 PxN   N–B3
16 P–QR4!?   . . . .

Although this move is part of a
conception that ultimately fails, it
shows Lasker's greatness. He must
have had this thrust in mind when
he played his fourteenth move, reasoning along the following lines:
once Black exchanges Knights,
White's QP is no longer isolated.
True, the new QBP is backward,
but 16 P–QR4 will practically force
. . . PxP. Then P–QB4 can be played, giving White control of Q5 with
strong play for his pieces, while
the temporarily sacrificed Pawn
can be regained at leisure later on.

16 . . . .   Q–Q4!

The flaw in Lasker's reasoning
is that, all appearances to the contrary, Black need not play . . . PxP.
The clash of ideas here is highly
dramatic.

17 N–B3   . . . .

A sorry retreat, but the seemingly aggressive 17 P–KB4 could be
effectively answered by . . . P–N5!

17 . . . .   KR–B1!

Hitting at the weak spot. In comparison to what White now plays,
his best course was 18 PxP, PxP;
19 BxP, RxP but his game would
still remain inferior.

18 B–N2   . . . .

A miserable square for the Bishop; hence the move can only be
explained by White's stubborn hope
of being able to play P–B4 eventually.

18 . . . .   N–K5!

Another well-timed stroke which
leaves White only a choice among
several disagreeable alternatives.
Thus a double exchange at K4

would leave Black with a strategically won game; and the same is true of 19 PxP, PxP; 20 BxP (if 20 BxN, QxB; 21 QxP, B–R3), Nx QBP; 21 BxN, RxB.

19 R–B1   ....

The fact that White must use two pieces for the unproductive task of guarding the QBP highlights the unsatisfactory state of his game.

19 ....   N–N4!

Decisive!

20 PxP   ....

After 20 N–K1 Black could simply play 20 ... PxP and if 21 P–QB4, N–R6ch; 22 K–R1, Q–KN4 threatening ... N–B5 as well as ... P–R6. Or else Black could play ... N–R6ch as in the following note.

20 ....   PxP

21 BxP?   ....

Losing outright, but there was no good move. If 21 N–K1, N–R6ch; 22 K–R1, N–B5; 23 Q–B3 (or 23 Q–N4, B–N4!; 24 R–B2, P–R4; 25 Q–N3, P–R5; 26 Q–N4, P–R6! and wins), QxQ; 24 PxQ, BxPch; 25 NxB, NxB; 26 R–B2, NxB; 27 RxN, RxP followed by ... P–N5 winning easily.

21 ....   NxNch

22 PxN   Q–N4ch

Resigns

White resigns, for after 23 K–R1,

Q–N5 wins the Queen. The moral: It is dangerous to try to force matters in fairly level positions.

41.

RESHEVSKY–VIDMAR
Nottingham, 1936

QUEEN'S GAMBIT ACCEPTED
(in effect)

Reshevsky	Dr. M. Vidmar
WHITE	BLACK
1 P–Q4	P–Q4
2 P–QB4	P–QB3
3 N–KB3	N–B3
4 P–K3	P–K3
5 B–Q3	PxP
6 BxP	P–B4

The opening has now transposed into the Queen's Gambit Accepted.

7 O–O	P–QR3
8 N–B3	P–QN4
9 B–N3	....

Reserving the option of a later P–Q5.

9	B–N2
10 Q–K2	N–B3

... QN–Q2 gives Black an easier game. The text leads to more complicated play.

11 R–Q1	Q–N3
12 P–Q5!	PxP

13 P–K4!   ....

This gives White an overwhelming game in exchange for a Pawn;

he gets all his pieces into rapid action, whilst Black is unable to castle King-side without damaging loss of material.

13 . . . .   **PxP**

Permitting White to secure a devastating attack along the K file; but if 13...P–Q5; 14 P–K5, N–KN1 (if 14...N–Q2; 15 P–K6 is decisive); 15 N–Q5, Q–Q1; 16 N–N5 threatening 17 N–B6ch!

13...O–O–O is Black's best chance.

14 NxP   **. . . .**

Stronger than 14 B–N5, N–Q5!; 15 NxN, PxN; 16 BxN, QxB; 17 Nx KP, Q–K4; 18 RxP, B–K2.

14 . . . .   **NxN**

15 QxNch   **B–K2**

If 15...N–K2; 16 Q–KB4 (stronger than 16 N–K5?!, P–B5; 17 N–QB7, RxQ etc.), O–KB3; 17 Q–B7, B–B3; 18 N–K5! and wins, for if 18...P–B5; 19 B–N5!

16 B–Q5   **. . . .**

Preventing Black from castling.

16 . . . .   **R–Q1**

A quick finish would result from 16...N–Q1; 17 B–N5, P–B3; 18 Bx B, NxB (not 18...QxB?; 19 RxN ch); 19 R–K1, Q–B2; 20 B–B4, Q–Q2; 21 QR–Q1. This is a good example of the rapidity with which White is able to marshall his forces as a result of the Pawn sacrifice.

17 B–N5   **RxB**

The best practical chance; if 17 ...P–B3; 18 B–KB4 and Black's helpless King cannot flee from the center.

18 RxR   **O–O**

19 R–Q7   **. . . .**

A very strong move which takes advantage of the rather clumsy way in which Black's pieces are bunched together on the Queen-side.

19 . . . .   **B–Q1**

19...BxB; 20 NxB would be even worse for Black because it would leave his position fatally exposed to attack.

20 R–QB1   **. . . .**

Even more forcing is the Tournament Book's suggestion 20 P–QN4, after which the QNP cannot be captured either way!

20 . . . .   **B–B2**

21 Q–K3   **N–N1**

22 R–K7   **. . . .**

22 . . . .   **BxN**

The alternatives are no better:

I 22...N–B3; 23 R–K8, B–Q3; 24 RxRch; 25 BxR; 26 Q–K8 with a terrific bind.

II 22...Q–Q3; 23 R–K8, BxN; 24 RxRch, KxR; 25 PxB, P–B5 (if 25...QxPch; 26 K–B1 with an easy win); 26 R–K1 and wins.

23 QxB   **P–R3**

Black would last somewhat longer with 23...N–B3, but after 24 R–Q7, N–Q5; 25 Q–K3 there could be little doubt about the outcome (if for example 25...P–B3; 26 Q–K7, N–B4; 27 QxQBP etc.).

24 B–B4   **B–Q3?**

Loses at once, but the end was already in sight.

25 R–N7!   **Q–Q1**

26 R–Q1   **Resigns**

42.

ALEKHINE–RESHEVSKY
Nottingham, 1936

COLLE SYSTEM

Dr. A. Alekhine | Reshevsky
WHITE | BLACK

1 N–KB3	P–Q4
2 P–Q4	N–KB3
3 P–K3	P–B4

By avoiding the routine ... P–K3, Black reserves the possibility of ... P–KN3, taking the game out of the usual channels where White frequently secures an easy initiative. 3 ... B–B4 is still another way to draw the sting from Colle's famous system.

4 P–B3	QN–Q2
5 QN–Q2	Q–B2
6 Q–R4	. . . .

This novel development of the Queen is intended to prevent Black from freeing his game with an early ... P–K4.

6	P–KN3
7 P–B4!	. . . .

A strong move which leaves Black with a difficult game.

7	B–N2
8 BPxP	NxP
9 Q–N3?	. . . .

But this is rather weak. The right way was 9 P–K4!, KN–N3; 10 Q–B2, Q–Q3; 11 P–QR4! (Colle-Rubinstein, Rotterdam, 1931) with a markedly superior position for White.

9	N(4)–N3
10 P–QR4	PxP!

Black does not fear 11 P–R5 because of 11 ... PxP; 12 PxP, N–B4; 13 PxN, NxQ; 14 PxQ, NxR; 15 B–Q3, O–O; 16 K–K2, B–K3 and White has no compensation for the exchange.

11 PxP	P–QR4

12 B–N5	O–O
13 O–O	N–B3

Intending to post one of his Knights at the splendid post Q4.

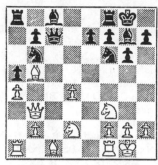

14 R–K1	B–B4

14 ... B–K3 would be refuted by 15 RxB, PxR; 16 N–N5!; but not 16 QxPch, K–R1; 17 N–K5, B–R3; 18 N–B7ch, RxN!; 19 QxR, N–N5; 20 P–KN3, Q–B7!; 21 Q–K6, Q–Q8ch and wins (Sidney Bernstein).

15 N–B1	Q–Q3

Bernstein recommends the more complicated but stronger line 15 ... N–K5 and if 16 N–N3 (16 P–N4?, B–K3 etc. or 16 N–K3, B–K3; 17 P–Q5, N–B4; 18 Q–R2, B–Q2 and Black has the advantage), B–K3; 17 Q–K3, N–Q3; 18 N–N5, B–Q4 (not 18 ... B–R3?; 19 NxB); 19 Qx P, QxQ; 20 RxQ, NxB; 21 PxN, Bx QP with much the better game.

16 Q–R3	. . . .

The alternative was 16 N–N3, B–K3; 17 Q–Q3. In playing the text, White hopes that the pressure exerted by his Rooks will offset his isolated QP.

16	QxQ
17 RxQ	N(B3)–Q4

The play which follows is extremely difficult, for, as has been indicated in the previous note, both players have chances and counterchances.

| 18 N-N3 | B-Q2 |
| 19 R-N3 | . . . . |

The simpler 19 BxB, NxB; 20 R-N3 would have given White better chances.

19	KR-Q1
20 B-Q2	NxP
21 R-R1	. . . .

Much stronger than 21 BxN?, Bx B; 22 RxP, B-QB3; 23 R-N3, P-R5; 24 R-R3, QR-N1 etc.

| 21 . . . . | N(R5)-N3 |

Not 21...N(Q4)-N3?; 22 BxB, RxB; 23 R-N5 and Black is helpless against P-N3.

After the text, 22 BxP, BxB; 23 RxB, N-QB5; 24 P-N3, NxB; 25 R(5)xN(R5), RxR; 26 RxR, P-K3 leads to equality.

| 22 RxP | BxB |
| 23 R(3)xB | P-K3 |

Intending ... N-QB5; hence White's reply.

24 P-N3	R-Q2
25 N-K4	RxR
26 BxR	N-B1
27 N-K5	. . . .

A tricky position, despite its surface simplicity. On 27 N-B5, N-Q3! would be in Black's favor. The simplest course was 27 R-B5, N (1)-K2; 28 B-Q2 (if instead 28 N-K5, BxN; 29 PxB, P-N3; 30 BxP, NxB; 31 N-B6ch, K-B1; 32 NxRch, NxN; 33 R-N5, N-Q4 and the position is very unclear).

| 27 . . . . | BxN |
| 28 PxB | N-B2! |

An effective reply to the threat of RxN followed by N-B6ch.

| 29 N-B6ch | . . . . |

This and the following exchange are compulsory because of Black's mating threat.

29	K-N2
30 NxR	NxR
31 B-Q2	N-K2

Black has a slight initiative, but the game should end in a draw with proper play.

32 K-B1	N-Q5
33 P-QN4	N-Q4
34 N-B5	P-QN4
35 N-Q3	P-B3

If instead 35...P-R3 (intending ...P-N4 followed by ...K-N3); 36 P-R4 etc.

| 36 B-B1? | . . . . |

A blunder, although not necessarily a fatal one. The proper course was 36 PxPch, KxP; 37 P-B3 etc.

| 36 . . . . | PxP |
| 37 NxP | N-B7! |

Simpler than 37...NxP; 38 B-N2, N(Q5)-B7; 39 K-K2, N-Q4; 40 K-Q3, N(B7)-N5ch; 41 K-Q4, N-R3! which was also playable.

| 38 B-N2 | N(7)xP |
| 39 K-K2 | . . . . |

He can accomplish nothing with a discovered check.

| 39 . . . . | K-N1 |
| 40 P-N3 | . . . . |

The Tournament Book suggests P-N4-5 as a good alternative.

40	N-K2
41 N-B3	N(2)-Q4
42 N-N5	N-B2

Because of the excellent position of White's pieces, it is far from easy for Black to formulate a plan for utilizing his extra Pawn. For some time to come, a waiting policy will be in order.

43 K-K3	N-B3
44 P-B4	P-R3
45 N-B3	K-B2
46 K-Q3	N-Q4
47 B-B1	N-B3
48 B-N2	N-Q2
49 B-R3?	. . . .

A second blunder after which White is apparently irretrievably lost. 49 B-Q4 should have been played, after which it would have been more difficult for Black to make progress.

49 . . . .   P–K4!

This important advance makes it possible for Black's King to take a hand in the proceedings, with results that soon make themselves felt.

50 K–K3   K–K3
51 B–N2   K–Q4!
52 N–R4   . . . .

An attempt at counterplay which proves inadequate, but likewise after 52 PxP White could hardly hold the game.

52 . . . .   N–N3!

The play that follows is a good example of the strength of the Knights. If now 53 BxP, NxB; 54 PxN, N–B5ch followed by . . . NxP and wins.

53 B–B1   N–B5ch
54 K–B2   . . . .

If 54 K–Q3, P–K5ch and White cannot stop the speedily onrushing Pawns. Or if 54 K–K2, N–Q5ch; 55

K–Q1, P–K5; 56 NxP, P–K6 followed by . . . K–K5 and wins.

54 . . . .   N–N5!

It is fascinating to observe the powerful cooperation of the Knights.

55 K–K2   N–R7
56 B–Q2   P–N5!

Black's candidate for queening honors! If now 57 NxP, P–N6; 58 K–Q1, P–K5 and wins.

57 PxP   P–N6
58 K–Q1   NxP!

White's last hope was 58 . . . P–N7?; 59 K–B2, NxB; 60 KxP, N–N5; 61 K–B3 and Black cannot avoid the draw!

59 N–N2   . . . .

The Tournament Book points out that if 59 NxP, NxN; 60 BxP, N–K4; 61 B–B1, NxB; 62 KxN, N–B5; 63 P–R4, K–Q5; 64 P–R5, K–B6; 65 P–R6, P–N7ch; 66 K–N1, K–N6 and mate follows.

59 . . . .   K–K5
60 P–R4   . . . .

Or 60 BxP, N–B6ch; 61 K–B1, N–Q6ch; 62 K–Q2, P–N7 and the Pawn queens.

60 . . . .   N–Q6!
61 B–R5   . . . .

Black threatened 61 . . . N–B7ch followed by . . . P–N7.

61 . . . .   N–N7ch!
Resigns

White resigns, for after 62 K–K1, N–B5 the QNP can no longer be stopped.

INTERNATIONAL TOURNAMENTS OF 1937

M Y MOST active chess year was 1937. I participated in three individual tournaments and one team event. After this extended tour, I realized that a master cannot do his best in ceaseless competition and resolved never to do it again.

At Kemeri, contrary to my general practice in tournament play, I began by winning. Usually I have to play myself into form. Often I have so many adjourned games that I do not stand among the leaders during the early stages. Here I took an early lead and held it throughout the tournament only to weaken at the finish. I lost my final game but still shared first place with Flohr and Petrov.

The international team tournament at Stockholm gave me my first opportunity to play on the United States team. Our masters had first won the championship at Prague in 1931 and then had successfully defended it at Folkestone in 1933, Warsaw in 1935—and was destined to retain it once again at Stockholm. While the United States had won by the narrowest possible margin at Prague, in each succeeding tournament, it won by a larger and larger margin. One reason for this outstanding series of victories was that the United States could count not only on outstanding players for first and second boards (which many other countries could supply) but also had players of international caliber all down the line. At this time United States players were judged to be among the best in the world.

Semmering, 1937, was an attempt to recapture the glories of the great Semmering tournament of 1926. A sobering feature was the presence of Rudolph Spielmann, winner of the 1926 event, as tournament director. The eight players who were selected to play in this tournament may well have wondered what they would be doing eleven years from then, when their successes as grandmasters had faded!

43.

KERES–RESHEVSKY
Kemeri, 1937

QUEEN'S PAWN OPENING

P. Keres	Reshevsky
WHITE	BLACK
1 P–Q4	P–Q4
2 N–KB3	N–KB3
3 B–B4	. . . .

A welcome relief from the routine 3 P–B4, although the text places no difficulties in the way of Black's achieving equality.

3	P–B4
4 P–K3	N–B3
5 P–B3	B–N5

The combination of Black's last three moves definitely gives him the initiative in the center (if 6 PxP?, P–K4). Since his QB's prospects are none too bright, he plays to exchange this piece against the more active KN.

| 6 QN–Q2 | P–K3 |
| 7 Q–R4 | . . . . |

Angling for N–K5. The alternative was 7 Q–N3, Q–N3 (but not 7 ... BxN?; 8 QxNP, N–QR4; 9 B–N5ch etc.); 8 N–K5.

| 7 . . . . | BxN |

Avoiding a possible N–K5.

| 8 NxB | Q–N3 |
| 9 QR–N1 | . . . . |

Since the Queen is now idle, it would have been more accurate to play Q–B2 at once.

9	B–K2
10 B–Q3	O–O
11 O–O	KR–Q1

The position is approximately even. Black has good prospects of effective Queen-side operations, while White hopes to use his two Bishops and command of K5 to build up an attack on the other wing.

| 12 B–N3 | . . . . |

Loss of time. The right move was 12 P–KR3, planning to retreat the QB in order to play N–K5 followed by P–KB4. If then 12 ... B–Q3; 13 B–KN5 (not 13 N–K5? BxN; 14 PxB, N–Q2) and Black has nothing better than ... B–K2.

| 12 . . . . | QR–B1 |
| 13 N–K5 | N–KR4! |

An excellent move which effectively disposes of White's hopes of attack.

| 14 Q–B2 | P–N3! |

This move is better than ... P–KR3, as it prepares for the resulting general advance of Black's Pawns. However, the consequences of the text had to be calculated with some care, in view of the sacrificial possibilities at White's disposal.

| 15 NxN | . . . . |

After 15 NxNP, RPxN; 16 BxP, PxB; 17 QxPch, N–Q2; 18 P–KR4, R–B1; 19 P–R5, R–B3 White would be at a loss for a continuation of the attack.

| 15 . . . . | QxN |
| 16 B–K5 | P–B3 |

| 17 B–N3 | . . . . |

Originally Keres must have intended 17 BxNP, PxB; 18 QxPch, N–N2; 19 BxP, BxB; 20 QxB, R–B1, with a position which would

have been difficult to appraise. On
the whole, Black would have been
better off; but the indecisiveness
of White's play has a bad psychological effect on his conduct of
the game.

    17 . . . .   **NxB**
    18 RPxN   **K–N2**

Banishing once for all the possibility of a sacrifice. Black's chances
are excellent, despite the Bishops
of opposite colors and White's possibilities on the KR file.

    19 P–KN4?   **. . . .**

Possibly played with a view to
P–KN3, K–N2 and R–KR1. 19 P–
KB4 would also be ineffectual be-
cause of the interesting reply . . .
P–K4! Best would have been 19 Px
P followed by P–K4.

    19 . . . .   **P–K4!**

Black takes the initiative in the
center. It is now quite difficult for
White to formulate a good plan.

    20 Q–K2   **Q–K3!**

It is important to avoid any premature action in the center. Thus
if 20 . . . KPxP; 21 KPxP, and White
gains whatever advantage there is
in the open file as Black cannot
play 21 . . . R–K1 on account of 22
B–N5, or else 20 . . . BPxP; 21 KPx
P, P–K5; 22 B–B2 followed by P–
B3 with even chances.

    21 QR–K1   **R–B2!**

A useful move which solidifies
Black's game by giving the Bishop
additional protection and making
possible the doubling of the Rooks
in certain eventualities.

    22 P–B3?   **. . . .**

Creating a new weakness on the
King-side. White should have tried
22 PxKP, PxP; 23 P–QB4, P–K5 (if
23 . . . P–Q5; 24 PxP, RxP; 25 P–
QN3); 24 B–N1, PxP; 25 P–B3, Px
P; 26 RxP and although White is
a Pawn down, he has good drawing

chances because of his control of
the KB file and the fact that his
Rooks can operate effectively.

    22 . . . .   **R–KR1!**

A good move which threatens
. . . P–KR4.

    23 B–B2?   **. . . .**

Giving Black a chance to make
immediate progress. But White's
game had become rather bleak in
any event.

    23 . . . .   **Q–N3!**

The simultaneous attack on two
Pawns practically forces the following exchange, which greatly
improves Black's position.

    24 PxKP   **. . . .**

The only alternative was 24 B–
N3, P–B5; 26 B–Q1, B–Q3 leaving
White with an exceedingly cramp-
ed game.

    24 . . . .   **PxP**
    25 P–QN3?   **. . . .**

This soon proves fatal because
of the resulting weakness of the
QBP. 25 B–N1 was the only chance.

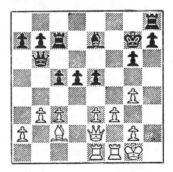

    25 . . . .   **P–B5!**

Decisive, for if 26 P–N4, P–Q5!
with a winning position; or if 26
PxP, RxP; 27 B–N3, RxP; 28 BxP,
RxP!

    26 Q–Q2   **R–Q1!**

Threatening . . . P–Q5. Black's
chances are now definitely on the
Queen's wing.

27 K–R1	PxP
28 BxQNP	. . . .

Or 28 PxP, Q–B4 winning the QBP.

28	Q–R4!
29 R–B1	P–Q5!

Black's last two moves have forced the win of a Pawn. White's position crumbles very rapidly now.

30 KPxP	PxP
31 KR–Q1	PxP
32 Q–K3	RxRch
33 RxR	Q–KN4!

The exchange of Queens is the easiest way. If now 34 QxQ, BxQ; 35 B–B2, R–K2 and wins.

34 Q–Q4ch   . . . .

But not 34 Q–K6?, Q–R5ch; 35 K–N1, B–B4ch; 36 K–B1, Q–B7 mate.

34 . . . .   K–R3

This is quicker than 34 . . . B–B3; 35 Q–K4, B–K4; 36 K–N1 etc.

35 Q–B2   . . . .

Black was threatening to win the Queen with . . . Q–R5ch and . . . B–B4.

35	Q–R5ch
36 QxQ	BxQ
37 K–R2	. . . .

Or 37 K–N1, B–N6; 38 B–B2, R–K2; 39 K–B1, R–K6 followed by the centralization of Black's King.

The Bishops of opposite colors would be of no importance in the ending.

37	B–N4
38 B–B2	R–K2
39 R–Q3	B–Q7
40 K–N3	R–K7

White resigns, for if 41 B–Q1, P–B7; 42 BxP, B–K8ch is followed by . . . RxB. A victory of which I am very proud.

44.

FINE–RESHEVSKY
Kemeri, 1937

KING'S INDIAN DEFENSE

R. Fine	Reshevsky
WHITE	BLACK
1 N–KB3	P–Q4
2 P–KN3	. . . .

Rather unusual at this stage; Black decides to counter with a similar development.

2	N–KB3
3 B–N2	P–KN3
4 P–Q4	B–N2
5 P–B4	P–B3

Black can also castle.

6 PxP   NxP!

This "surrender" of the center leads to far more interesting play than the obvious 6 . . . PxP. In addition, the text provokes the following weakening reply.

7 P–K4?   . . . .

Highly questionable, as the following play will demonstrate. 7 O–O, O–O; 8 N–B3 would have been better.

7 . . . .   N–N3

Naturally, he does not retreat to KB3, as the diagonal of the KB is left open so that Black can exert pressure on the QP. Even at this early stage, it is White who must fight for equality.

8 O–O   . . . .

After 8 P–KR3 (to prevent the pin) Black intended to strike at the center with 8 . . , P–QB4!; 9 P–Q5 (if 9 PxP, QxQch; 10 KxQ, N–R5 regaining the Pawn with a superior position), O–O; 10 O–O, P–K3 and White is embarrassed for good moves.

8 . . . .   B–N5

The Tournament Book suggests the promising alternative 8 . . . B–K3; 9 P–KR3, Q–Q2; 10 K–R2, and eventually . . . R–Q1 with strong pressure on the QP. The move actually made accomplishes the same purpose in a different way.

9 B–K3   . . . .

Against 9 P–K5, Black could proceed with 9 . . . Q–Q2 followed by . . . N–R3–B2, planting a Knight firmly at Q4.

9 . . . .   P–QB4!

Just at the right moment.

10 P–K5   . . . .

This turns out so badly that White should have tried 10 PxP, QxQ; 11 RxQ, N–R5; 12 B–Q4, P–K4; 13 B–B3, NxBP—although here too Black would have had the initiative.

10 . . . .   N–B3

The threat of . . . PxP at last forces a clearing of the situation in the center.

11 PxP   QxQ

12 RxQ   N–B5
13 QN–Q2   . . . .

Best under the circumstances. After 13 B–B1, QNxKP; 14 NxN, NxN, White would be in an even worse predicament because of his backward development.

13 . . . .   NxB!

Black is in no hurry to regain his Pawn, and prefers to create an irremediable weakness in White's Pawn position, obtaining two Bishops at the same time. Inferior would be 13 . . . NxNP; 14 KR–N1, NxP; 15 B–Q4, NxNch; 16 NxN, BxB; 17 NxB, N–B5; because of 18 BxP and White's QBP would be very dangerous.

14 PxN   O–O–O

As will be seen, castling on this wing gains time by leaving the King in the center. Black is content to regain the Pawn at his leisure.

15 N–B4   B–K3!

The Pawn could have been regained at once with . . . BxN, but true to his policy, Black prefers to increase the pressure.

16 B–B1   B–Q4
17 B–K2   . . . .

17 N–Q6ch? would have been refuted by 17 . . . RxN! but 17 N–Q4, NxP; 18 NxN, BxN; 19 QR–B1 (threatening P–B6) would have

been preferable.

17 . . . .   K–B2

Now that White's KN is protected, the other Knight must not be allowed to reach Q6 with a check.

18 K–B2   KR–B1

The position of the King on the KB file gives Black the idea of playing ... P–B3 in the hope of opening the KB file.

19 N–Q6?   . . . .

He should have tried 19 N–Q4 and if 19...NxP; 20 NxN, BxN; 21 P–QN4 with a position not wholly devoid of chances.

19 . . . .   BxN
20 N–N5ch   K–N1
21 BxB   NxP
22 B–K2   . . . .

The alternative 22 N–Q4, NxB; 23 KxN, P–QR3; 24 QR–B1, K–B2 followed by the doubling of the Rooks on the Q file would also be in Black's favor.

22 . . . .   N–B3!

This simple move poses White an insoluble problem, as there is no satisfactory method of protecting the QNP. Thus if 23 RxRch, RxR; 24 R–QN1, R–Q7 and White must lose some material. Or (as pointed out by Ragozin) 23 QR–N1, RxR; 24 BxR, R–Q1; 25 K–K1 (if 25 K–K2, R–Q4; 26 P–QN4, P–QR3; 27 N–R3, B–B6), P–QR3; 26

N–R3, R–Q4; 27 P–QN4, NxP etc.

23 N–B3   BxN!

Another move which is obvious but very strong. Black gets rid of the Bishops of opposite colors and smashes White's Pawn position at the same time.

24 PxB   . . . .

White's disastrous Pawn position suffices to lose the game for him.

24 . . . .   K–B2
25 P–K4   N–K4
26 R–Q5   N–Q2
27 B–N5   N–B3
28 RxR   RxR
29 K–K3   N–Q2!

Much more straightforward than 29...N–N5ch; 30 K–B4, NxP; 31 P–N4, R–Q7; 32 K–N3 (threatening to win the Knight with R–R1), P–KR4; 33 PxP, PxP; 34 R–R1, N–N5; 35 RxP and White has drawing chances.

The text forces further favorable simplification, for if 30 K–Q4, P–QR3; 31 B–K2 (or 31 BxN, RxBch; 32 K–B4, R–Q7 and wins), N–N3ch; 32 K–K3, N–R5 and wins.

30 BxN   RxB
31 R–KB1   P–K3
32 P–N4   K–B3
33 P–N5   KxP

The first booty; there is more to come.

34 R–B4   . . . .

Or 34 K-B4, K-Q3; 35 R-Q1ch, K-K2; 36 RxRch, KxR; 37 K-K5, K-K2; 38 P-B4, P-N3; 39 P-QR3, P-QR3; 40 P-QR4, P-QR4; 41 P-R3, P-R3! and wins (Flohr).

| 34 | . . . . | K-Q3 |

Another way was 34 ... K-B5; 35 R-R4, KxP; 36 RxP, P-N4 winning easily.

35	R-R4	P-B3!
36	PxP	K-K4
37	R-B4	R-KB2
38	R-B1	RxP
39	R-QN1	R-B2
40	R-N5ch	. . . .

White will soon run out of aggressive moves, after which the pressure on his weaknesses will be resumed.

40	. . . .	K-Q3
41	P-QR4	P-QR3
42	R-N5	R-B8
	Resigns	

White resigns, as he must lose another Pawn. For example: 43 P-R5, R-KR8; 44 R-N2, R-R8; 45 R-N5, P-K4. Or 43 P-R4, R-KR8; 44 R-N4, K-K4; 45 P-QR5, K-B3 winning easily.

45.

LANDAU–RESHEVSKY
Kemeri, 1937

QUEEN'S GAMBIT ACCEPTED

S. Landau	Reshevsky
WHITE	BLACK
1 P-Q4	P-Q4
2 P-QB4	PxP
3 N-KB3	P-QR3
4 P-K3	N-KB3

4 ... B-N5; 5 BxP, P-K3; 6 Q-N3, BxN; 7 PxB, P-QN4; 8 B-K2, N-KB3; 9 P-QR4, P-N5; 10 Q-B4 followed by P-R5 is in White's favor because Black has difficulty in playing ... P-QB4.

5	BxP	P-K3
6	O-O	P-B4
7	Q-K2	P-QN4
8	B-Q3	PxP

The same plan as in Game 40. Here, however, the text is not quite so satisfactory, for White has not yet developed his QN. The result is that after provoking ... P-N5, White can bring his QN to QB4 without any loss of time.

| 9 | PxP | . . . . |

Giving himself an isolated QP, but by way of compensation he is able to develop his pieces rapidly.

| 9 | . . . . | B-N2 |
| 10 | P-QR4! | . . . . |

See the note to move 8.

10	. . . .	P-N5
11	QN-Q2	B-K2
12	N-B4	. . . .

Even more exact would have been P-R5! in order to isolate Black's Queen-side Pawns.

| 12 | . . . . | P-QR4 |

Preventing the further advance of White's QRP, but Black's position remains quite difficult.

13	B-B4	O-O
14	KR-Q1	N-B3
15	B-K5!	N-Q4

After 15 ... NxB; 16 PxN, N-Q4; 17 Q-K4, P-N3; 18 P-R4 or 18 Q-N4 White would have splendid attacking chances.

16 Q–K4   P–N3

Some weakening of the King-side was unavoidable. ...P–B4 would have the drawback of weakening the KP irreparably.

17 Q–N4   N–B3
18 Q–B4   ....

Best. If 18 Q–R3, N–R4; 19 P–N4? (trying to force the issue), NxB; 20 N(4)xN (if 20 PxQN, N–B5 followed by ...NxB with a good game), N–B5; 21 Q–R6, NxB; 22 RxN, B–KB3 with a superior position.

18 ....   N–R4

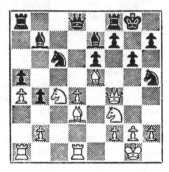

19 Q–K3!   ....

A judicious retreat. After 19 Q–R6, NxB, Black would get the better game:

I 20 N(4)xN, R–B1 and Black's position is preferable; his two Bishops are now free to operate effectively, while White's expectations of attack have failed.

II 20 PxN?, BxN; 21 BxP (if 21 PxB?, B–N4 wins the Queen!), BPxB; 22 RxQ, QRxR; 23 PxB (if 23 Q–K3, B–Q4 and Black should win with three pieces for the Queen), N–B5; 24 K–R1 (Black was threatening to win the Queen with ...B–N4), R–B4; 25 R–KN1, R–Q5! winning because of the double threat of ...RxN and ...R–R4.

19 ....   R–B1
20 QR–B1   NxB
21 PxN   B–B4

The excitement mounts steadily as both players succeed in posting their pieces more aggressively.

22 Q–R6   Q–K2?!

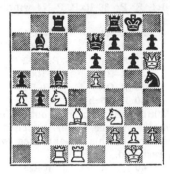

23 N–N5   ....

A very difficult position! If 23 NxP, BxN; 24 PxB, Q–R2; 25 N–B4, QxP or ...BxPch.

Or 23 N–Q6, KBxN; 24 PxB, Rx R!; 25 QxR (if 25 PxQ, RxRch; 26 B–B1, R–K1; 27 N–N5, N–B3 and Black should win), Q–B3; 26 Q–K3 (Black was threatening ...BxN and ...N–B5), BxN; 27 QxB, QxQ; 28 PxQ, R–Q1; 29 B–N5, N–B3; 30 B–B6, K–B1; 31 K–B1, R–B1; 32 B–N5, N–Q4 and Black has a slight edge.

23 B–K2 has been strongly recommended here, but Black has a convincing reply in 23 ...BxN; 24 BxB, Q–R5! etc.

23 ....   P–B3
24 PxP   ....

This leads to a quick debacle, but the following variations given by the Tournament Book demonstrate the seriousness of White's plight:

I 24 N–K4, PxP; 25 NxKP (or 25 N(B4)–Q6, KBxN; 26 NxB, RxR; 27 QxR, QxN; 28 BxP, Q–N3! and

wins), BxN; 26 BxB, BxPch; 27
K–R1, Q–R5! and wins.

II 24 BxP, PxN (also good
enough is 24 ... PxB; 25 QxPch, Q–
N2); 25 BxN, BxPch; 26 K–R1, Bx
Pch!; 27 KxB, Q–N2ch; 28 K–B1,
Q–R8ch; 29 K–K2, Q–K5ch forcing
mate.

24 . . . .   BxPch!!

Black has turned the tables completely.

25 KxB   . . . .

Loses very quickly, but if 25 K–
R1, RxP and White dare not play
26 NxQRP? because of 26 ... RxR;
27 RxR, B–K6! 28 R–K1, BxN; 29
QxB, R–B8ch winning the Queen.

25 . . . .   QxPch
26 N–B3   . . . .

Any King move allows a quick
mate.

26 . . . .   BxN
27 PxB   QxPch
28 K–N1   R–B5!

29 QxR   . . . .

Black was threatening ... R–N5
mate. If 29 P–R3, Q–N6ch; 30 K–
R1, QxPch; 31 K–N1, Q–N6ch; 32
K–R1, R–R5 mate. Or 29 N–K5, Q–
K6ch; 30 K–R1, RxR etc.

29 . . . .   NxQ

With a two-fold threat of mate.

30 B–B1   R–B4
31 R–Q8ch   K–N2

32 R–Q7ch   K–R3
    Resigns

White resigns, as he has no defense against the threat of ... R–
N4ch.

46.

RESHEVSKY–STAHLBERG
Kemeri, 1937

QUEEN'S GAMBIT DECLINED

Reshevsky	G. Stahlberg
WHITE	BLACK
1 P–Q4	N–KB3
2 P–QB4	P–K3
3 N–KB3	P–Q4
4 N–B3	B–K2
5 B–N5	QN–Q2
6 PxP	. . . .

Once more my favorite system
in this opening.

6	PxP
7 P–K3	P–B3
8 Q–B2	N–B1

An interesting novelty, branch-
ing off from the routine ... O–O.
Black's idea, as developed in the
next few moves, is to make possible the development of his QB to
B4.

| 9 B–Q3 | N–K3 |
| 10 B–R4 | P–KN3 |

So that if 11 O–O, N–N2; 12 KR–
N1, B–KB4! and Black rids himself
of the QB (usually a liability in this
variation) and has good chances of
getting a firm grip on K5. Under
the circumstances, White decides
to discard his positional plans,
heading for a wild game.

| 11 O–O–O!? | O–O |
| 12 K–N1? | . . . . |

An inaccuracy which has serious
consequences. Correct was 12 P–
KR3!, N–N2; 13 P–KN4 keeping
Black's pieces out of KB4 and preparing a promising King-side attack.

12 . . . .   N–N2
13 P–KR3   . . . .

Now this comes too late to be effective.

13 . . . .   B–KB4
14 BxN   . . . .

If instead 14 P–KN4, BxB; 15 Qx B, N–K5 and White must exchange his QB after all, leaving a powerfully posted Black Knight at K5. He therefore prefers to remove this Knight.

14 . . . .   KBxB
15 P–KN4   BxB
16 QxB   N–K3
17 P–KR4   P–B4!

It is not in Stahlberg's nature to sit by passively and await the coming attack. By sacrificing a Pawn, he secures a lasting initiative and compels White to play with the greatest care.

18 PxP   BxN
19 QxB   . . . .

At first sight there does not seem to be much sting in Black's Pawn sacrifice because of the weakness of his QP. But the depth of Stahlberg's calculations will become apparent later on.

19 . . . .   R–B1

So that if 20 P–N4, P–QR4!; 21 P–R3, PxP; 22 PxP, P–N3; 23 P–B6, Q–Q3; 24 P–QN5, R–R1 (threatening . . . R–R4) with a decisive at-

tack. For example, 25 P–K4?? would be refuted by . . . R–R6.

20 P–K4!   RxP
21 Q–R3!   Q–Q3!

But not 21. . . P–Q5? 22 NxP.

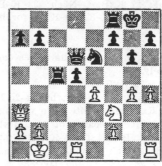

22 PxP   . . . .

The Tournament Book points out that 22 QxP would not be good because of 22 . . . Q–B5! and if 23 PxP, QxN; 24 PxN, R–Q4!; 25 Px Pch, RxP; 26 R–QB1, R–Q7. Not only would White's position be precarious, but his material advantage could not be maintained.

22 . . . .   R–Q1!

A valuable gain of time which enables Black to recapture on Q4. Since his King-side Pawns are so weak, he decides to seek compensation on the other wing. Needless to say, Black's Knight cannot be captured.

23 QxP   RxP
24 RxR   QxR
25 Q–K3   . . . .

White seems to have consolidated his position satisfactorily; thus if 25 . . . Q–Q6ch; 26 QxQ, Rx Q; 27 N–K5, R–Q7; 28 R–KB1 and while White's position is uncomfortable, Black does not seem to have adequate compensation for the Pawn.

25 . . . .   P–KR4!

A powerful thrust which makes

White's position extremely difficult; if 26 PxP? Q–B4ch; 27 K–R1, R–Q6 and wins—or 26 R–N1?, PxP; 27 RxP? Q–Q8ch again winning a piece.

26 R–K1! . . . .

Best under the circumstances. In the play that follows, both players give of their best.

26 . . . . PxP
27 N–K5 . . . .

Threatening to capture either of the KNPs.

27 . . . . N–N2!

An adequate defense to both threats, for if 28 NxP(4)?, Q–B4ch; 29 Q–K4, R–Q8ch winning outright.

28 Q–K4! . . . .

The best chance, difficult though the following ending will be.

28 . . . . QxQch
29 RxQ P–B4

Not 29 ... R–K1 because of 30 NxP(4)!

30 R–QB4! . . . .

30 R–N4 would be answered by ... R–Q7! and wins.

30 . . . . K–R2
31 K–B2! . . . .

White guards against ... R–Q7, thus freeing his Rook for action.

31 . . . . R–K1
32 N–Q3 N–K3

Preventing the inroad of White's Rook to B7.

33 P–R4! . . . .

Foreseeing that Black's coming attack on the KRP can only be countered by energetic action on the other wing.

33 . . . . K–R3
34 R–N4 R–K2

34 ... K–R4; 35 RxQNP, KxP; 36 R–R7ch, K–N4; 37 P–R5 would give White strong counterchances.

35 R–N6! P–B5!

... K–R4?? would be met by 36 RxN!

36 R–N4! . . . .

An important move which forces Black's reply, leading to the disappearance of the weak KRP.

36 . . . . P–KN4
37 PxPch KxP
38 R–N5ch K–R5
39 R–K5! . . . .

This powerful pinning move saves the day for White.

39 . . . . N–Q5ch
40 K–B3 RxR
41 NxR N–K3
42 N–Q3 P–B6

If 42 ... P–N6 White can draw by 43 PxPch, PxP; 44 N–K1 or by 43 NxP!, PxP (if 43 ... NxN; 44 PxPch, KxP; 45 K–N4 etc.); 44 N–N2ch followed by 45 N–K3 and the advance of the Queen-side Pawns.

43 P–N4 P–N6
44 PxPch KxP
45 P–R5 N–B5

46 N–B5!   . . . .

So that if 46...P–B7; 47 N–K4
ch, K–N7; 48 NxBP etc.

46	K–N7
47 N–K4	N–Q4ch

The draw is now clear, but the
remaining play is still interesting.

48 K–N3	N–B2
49 K–B4	N–K3
50 P–N5	N–N4!
51 N–Q2	P–B7
52 P–R6	N–K5
53 PxP	NxNch
54 K–B3	P–B8(Q)
55 P–N8(Q)	Q–B8ch
56 K–Q3	Drawn

47.

RESHEVSKY–FEIGIN
Kemeri, 1937

QUEEN'S GAMBIT DECLINED
Reshevsky   M. Feigin
WHITE   BLACK

1	P–Q4	P–Q4
2	N–KB3	N–KB3
3	P–B4	P–K3
4	N–B3	B–K2
5	P–K3	. . . .

T h i s apparently conservative
move is old enough to be a novelty.

5	. . . .	O–O
6	P–QN3	. . . .

Possibly premature, in view of
the pinning move ..B–N5.

6 . . . .   P–B4

Black prefers to be orthodox. It
is difficult to say whether he would
have fared better with 6...B–N5;
7 B–Q2, BxN; 8 BxB, N–K5; 9 Q–B2
(not 9 B–N4, P–QB4!; 10 QPxP, N–
QB3 and Black has the better
game), N–Q2; 10 B–Q3, P–KB4 and
the absence of Black's KB renders
him weak on the black squares.

7	B–Q3	P–QN3
8	O–O	B–N2

9 B–N2   . . . .

The almost complete symmetry
of the position is deceptive. The
fact that White's KB is more aggressively posted means that White
will be able to play his Queen to
K2—a maneuver which Black cannot imitate. This in turn means
that White will have good attacking chances, while Black will be on
the defensive.

9 . . . .   QN–Q2

Too passive. This Knight should
go to B3, where it will exert greater pressure on White's Pawns;
then, after the following exchanges,
the QN can be brought with good
effect to QR4 or QN5.

10	Q–K2	QPxP
11	NPxP	PxP
12	PxP	. . . .

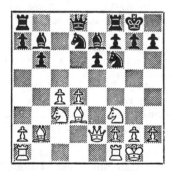

Black has played to give his opponent hanging Pawns, which are
generally considered a serious strategical drawback. In the present
position, however, this weakness is
reduced to a minimum, because
Black will be unable to attack the
Pawns effectively. This is due to
the fact that his QN was played to
Q2 instead of to QB3.

12 . . . .   R–B1

Black's chances lie in the endgame; but White has complete control of the center and the excellent

posting of his pieces gives him good chances of a strong King-side attack.

13 N-K5   P-QR3

In order to guard the Queen against attack by N-N5 after ... Q-B2. 13 ... NxN would not have been good because of 14 PxN, N-Q2 (14 ... N-N5 would lead to the loss of a Pawn after 15 BxPch, KxB; 16 QxN, Q-B2; 17 N-K4, QxBP; 18 Q-R5ch, K-N1; 19 N-B6ch, PxN; 20 PxP, R-B4; 21 Q-R6, Q-KN5; 22 P-B3 etc.); 15 QR-Q1, Q-B2; 16 P-B4 with a strong attack in the offing.

14 QR-Q1   Q-B2
15 P-B4   KR-K1
16 N-N1!   ....

To transfer the Knight to the King-side where it can be usefully employed

16 ....   P-N3?

In his anxiety to prevent P-KB5, Black weakens his castled position irreparably. It would have been better not to disturb his Pawn position, playing ... Q-N1-R1 instead.

17 N-Q2   N-R4
18 QR-K1   B-B1

19 P-N4!   ....

Driving away the a n n o y i n g Knight and preparing to storm the hostile position. The weakening of

the long diagonal is of little importance.

19 ....   KN-B3
20 P-KR3   ....

White could have saved a move with the more forceful P-KR4.

20 ....   QR-Q1
21 N(2)-B3   B-N5

In order to answer N-N5 with ... R-KB1.

22 R-Q1   R-KB1

Black is limited to passive defense and marking time.

23 N-N5   QR-K1

Sooner or later the KP will require additional protection against the latent threat N(K5)xBP.

24 P-KR4   B-R1

Black hopes to utilize the long diagonal for counterplay.

25 P-R5   ....

Rightly disregarding the threat and going ahead with his own attack.

25 ....   Q-N2
26 K-R2   ....

This disposes of all threats on the long diagonal.

26 ....   B-Q3
27 K-R3   R-K2
28 P-R3   ....

White wants to strengthen his position for the final assault. Before playing P-KB5 he wishes to post his KR at KN1 and his QR at K1; the text is played to prevent ... B-N5 in reply to QR-K1.

28 ....   PxP?

This exposes Black to a crushing attack by making the open KN file available to White's Rooks.

29 PxP   P-R3
30 N(N5)-B3   NxP

Black has won a Pawn, but at what a cost!

31 N-R2   N(2)-B3

But not 31 ... N(4)-B3 because of 32 R-N1ch, K-R1; 33 P-Q5! PxP;

34 NxN! QxNch (but not 34 ... Rx
Q; 35 BxN mate); 35 Q–N4! and
wins.

32 P–Q5!   ....

The decisive breakthrough, which
enables the QB to strike along the
diagonal.

32 ....   **N–N2**

32 ... PxP would allow a neat
sacrifice of the Queen by means
of 33 QxN!, NxQ; 34 R–N1ch, N–
N2 (if 34 ... K–R1; 35 NxP mate);
35 RxNch, KxR (if 35 ... K–R1;
36 R–R7ch, K–N1; 37 R–N1 mate);
36 R–N1ch, K–B3; 37 N–Q7ch, K–
K3; 38 NxR mate!

33 R–KN1   **N–K1**
34 N–B6   ....

This forces the win of the ex-
change, for if 34 ... R–Q2; 35 PxP,
PxP, 36 QxPch; or 34 ... R–B2; 35
RxNch, NxR; 36 R–KN1, P–B3; 37
QxPch etc.

Even stronger appears 34 N(2)–
N4; e. g. 34 ... PxP; 35 NxPch, K–
R1; 36 N(6)xPch, either RxN; 37
Q–R5 ch!!, NxQ; 38 NxR mate.

34 ....   **PxP**
35 NxRch   **QxN**
36 QxQ   **BxQ**
37 PxP   **BxQP**

The Tournament Book suggests
37 ... B–Q3 or ... B–KB3 here. However, after 37 ... B–Q3; 38 N–N4,
BxBP; 39 N–B6ch, NxN; 40 BxN,

B–N4; 41 BxB, PxB; 42 BxP or
37 ... B–KB3; 38 BxB, NxB; 39 P–
Q6, P–N4; 40 N–N4, NxN; 41 RxN
White wins easily in either event.

38 N–N4!   **B–K3**

If instead 38 ... P–KR4; 39 N–
R6ch, K–R1; 40 RxN! NxR; 41
N–B5 winning easily.

39 P–B5!   **B–B1**

The BP cannot be captured.

40 NxPch   **K–R2**
41 N–N4   **NxP?**

This hastens the end by losing
a piece, but his position was hopeless in any event.

42 N–K3   **Resigns**

48.

TARTAKOVER–RESHEVSKY
International Team Tourney
Stockholm, 1937

CENTER GAME

Dr. S. Tartakover	Reshevsky
WHITE	BLACK
1 P–K4	P–K4
2 P–Q4	PxP
3 QxP	N–QB3

The tempo gained by this obvious move gives Black a lasting initiative. That is why this opening
has disappeared from master play.

4 Q–K3	N–B3
5 N–QB3	B–N5
6 B–Q2	O–O
7 O–O–O	....

Almost obligatory, as White's
King must be removed from the K
file. The castling on opposite wings
foreshadows an exciting game.

7	R–K1
8 B–B4?!	P–Q3

Simple and good. 8 ... N–QR4! is
an excellent alternative, as it
forces an early ... P–Q4. The continuation 8 ... BxN; 9 BxB, NxP
(not 9 ... RxP??; 10 BxN winning

a piece) is somewhat questionable, however, for after 10 Q–B4 White has attacking chances.

9 N–B3   . . . .

Or 9 P–B3, N–K4; 10 B–N3, B–K3 and Black has a good game.

9 . . . .   B–K3
10 BxB   RxB

This exchange has eliminated White's most aggressively posted piece.

11 N–KN5   R–K1
12 P–B4   P–KR3

Should the advanced Knight retreat now, Black can win the KP. Hence Tartakover embarks on a characteristically risky attack.

13 P–KR4?!   Q–B1

But not 13 . . . PxN; 14 RPxP, N–Q2 (if 14 . . . N–R2; 15 Q–R3 regains the piece with a winning game); 15 Q–R3, K–B1; 16 N–Q5 and Black is lost.

Another possibility is 13 . . . PxN; 14 RPxP, BxN; 15 BxB, NxP; 16 Q–R3, K–B1; 17 BxPch!, K–K2; 18 KR–K1 winning easily.

14 Q–B3   K–B1!

This forces White's hand, since Black now threatens to play 15 . . . PxN followed by . . . N–KN1 leaving White with no compensation for the sacrificed piece.

15 N–Q5?!   . . . .

Again Tartakover invites complications.

15 . . . .   NxN!

Simple and effective. In the Russian magazine "64" Blumenfeld gives the following possibilities after 15 . . . BxBch; 16 KxB (not 16 RxB because in some variations the QR has to switch to the KR file), PxN and now:

I 17 RPxP, NxN (not 17 . . . Nx Pch?; 18 QxN!); 18 R–R8ch, K–K2; 19 RxRch, KxR; 20 R–KR1, N–Q5; 21 Q–B2, Q–N5! 22 R–R8ch, K–Q2; 23 RxR, NxKBP! and Black wins, for if 24 QxQN, QxPch is immediately decisive.

II 17 NxN!, PxN; 18 RPxP, PxP (or 18 . . . Q–K3; 19 R–R6 with a strong attack, for example 19 . . . N–Q5; 20 PxP! NxQch; 21 PxN and wins!); 19 PxP, Q–K3; 20 Q–B6!, QxQ; 21 PxQ, K–N1; 22 R–R3, N–K4; 23 QR–KR1, N–N3; 24 R–R7, R–R2; 25 R–R7ch, K–B1; 26 RxN! and White has a draw.

16 PxN   N–Q5!

Black is beginning to wrest the initiative from his opponent.

17 Q–Q3   . . . .

17 Q–R5 would be futile because of 17 . . . PxN; 18 RPxP, Q–B4 and White is lost; or if 17 Q–B2?, B–B4 and wins.

17 . . . .   N–K7ch
18 K–N1   BxB
19 RxB   . . . .

The loss of the Pawn is unavoidable, for if 19 QxB, PxN; 20 RPxP, Q–N5; 21 R–K1, K–N1 and wins.

19 . . . .   NxP
20 N–R7ch   K–N1
21 N–B6ch   PxN
22 Q–N3ch   N–N3
23 P–R5   . . . .

White regains the sacrificed piece, but in the process Black's Pawns are straightened out and White winds up a Pawn minus.

23	Q–B4
24 PxN	PxP
25 R–B2	Q–N4
26 Q–QB3	Q–K4!

Forcing the exchange of Queens, for if 27 Q–Q2 (not 27 Q–Q3??, Q–K8ch!), P–KR4 with two Pawns ahead.

| 27 RxBP | QxQ |
| 28 PxQ | K–N2 |

Black has a won ending, but the following play still presents some interesting technical difficulties.

29 R–B2	R–KB1
30 R–K2	QR–K1
31 KR–K1	RxR
32 RxR	R–B8ch!

If instead 32 . . . K–B2; 33 R–B2ch, K–K2; 34 R–K2ch, K–Q2; 35 R–K6, R–KN1; 36 R–B6 and Black is not making appreciable headway.

| 33 K–N2 | K–B2 |

The inroad of White's Rook is prevented and White's Pawns are kept subject to attack. But Tartakover manages to find some interesting counterchances.

| 34 P–B4 | P–KR4 |
| 35 K–B3 | P–KN4 |

Black is naturally intent on getting a passed Pawn on the Kingside.

| 36 P–B5!? | PxP |
| 37 K–B4 | P–N5! |

Best. 37 . . . P–N3 would allow White's King to penetrate to QB6.

38 KxP	P–N6
39 K–Q4	P–R5
40 P–B4	P–N3

Threatening 41 . . . R–B7 and if 42 K–K3, RxRch; 43 KxR, K–B3; 44 K–B3, K–B4 and wins.

| 41 P–R4 | R–B7 |
| 42 R–K4 | RxP |

Much better than 42 . . . P–R6; 43 PxP, P–N7; 44 R–N4 when the outcome would not be clear.

| 43 RxP | R–QR7 |
| 44 R–N4 | P–N7 |

White is now at a loss for a good move: if 45 K–K3, RxP can be played, and if 45 K–Q3 or 45 R–N3, K–B3 followed by the further advance of the King.

| 45 P–R5 | PxP |

Good enough, but 45 . . . P–N4! would have won more rapidly. If then 46 K–B3 (not 46 PxP??, R–R5ch), PxP; 47 K–Q4, R–QB7 winning easily.

46 K–B3	P–R5
47 P–B5	K–B3
48 R–N8	K–K4
49 R–N5ch	K–B3

49 . . . K–B5 would be answered by 50 P–Q6.

| 50 R–N8 | K–B2 |

Being pressed for time, Black has been repeating moves to gain time.

51 R–N4	P–R4
52 P–B6	K–K2
53 R–N6	K–B2
54 R–N4	. . . .

| 54 . . . . | R–B7! |

Black has carefully calculated the following forced win.

55 P–Q6	P–R6!
56 PxP	P–R7
57 P–B8(Q)	P–R8(Q)ch
58 K–B4	R–B7ch
59 K–N5	. . . .

If 59 K-Q5, Q-Q8ch; 60 K-K5, R-B4ch; 61 K-B4, R-B5ch winning the Rook.

| 59 . . . . | Q-B8ch |
| 60 K-R4 | . . . . |

If 60 KxP, R-B4ch; 61 K-N6 (if 61 K-N4, Q-N4ch; 62 K-R3, R-B6ch; 63 K-R2, Q-N6ch; 64 K-R1, R-B8 mate), Q-N4ch; 62 K-R7, Q-R4ch; 63 Q-R6, Q-B2ch; 64 K-R8, R-QR4 and wins.

60	R-R7ch
61 K-N3	Q-N8ch
62 K-B3	R-B7ch
63 K-Q4	P-N8(Q)ch
Resigns	

49.

RESHEVSKY-GAUFFIN
International Team Tourney
Stockholm, 1937

QUEEN'S GAMBIT DECLINED

Reshevsky	T. Gauffin
WHITE	BLACK
1 P-Q4	P-Q4
2 N-KB3	N-KB3
3 P-B4	P-K3
4 N-B3	B-K2

It may well be that the best line for equalizing purposes is 4 ... P-B4; 5 BPxP, NxP; 6 P-K4, NxN; 7 PxN, PxP; 8 PxP, B-N5ch etc.

| 5 P-K3 | . . . . |

Regarding this deceptively conservative move, see Game 47.

5	O-O
6 B-Q3	P-B4
7 O-O	N-B3

An interesting alternative would be 7 ... QPxP, transposing into the Queen's Gambit Accepted.

8 P-QN3	P-QN3
9 B-N2	B-N2
10 Q-K2	BPxP
11 KPxP	PxP

| 12 PxP | . . . . |

With his last two moves, Black has played to give his opponent the "hanging Pawns," which can easily become serious weaknesses, especially in the ending. (Note, incidentally, how effectively Black's QN is posted for this purpose, and how useless the same piece would be at Q2.) White, on the other hand, has a much freer game and real attacking possibilities.

If Black is given time, he can play the highly embarrassing ... QR-B1 followed by ... N-QN5, taking advantage of the shaky state of the QBP.

It would be a serious mistake, however, to play to win a Pawn with 12 ... NxP?; 13 NxN, QxN. There would follow 14 N-Q5!, Q-B4; 15 BxN, BxB; 16 Q-K4 or 15 ...BxB, 16 Q-N1ch, K-R1; 17 Q-R4 and wins.

| 12 . . . . | Q-B2 |

More to the point was 12 .. R-B1, followed, perhaps, by ... N-QR4 or ... Q-B2-N1-R1.

| 13 P-QR3 | KR-Q1 |
| 14 KR-Q1 | B-KB1? |

This permits a powerful breakthrough in the center. 14 ... QR-B1 would have been better.

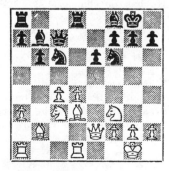

| 15 P-Q5! | . . . . |

The consequences of this sur-

prising thrust do not become fully
apparent until the 22nd move.

| 15 . . . . | PxP |

| 16 NxP! | . . . . |

Opening up the QB's diagonal
and exposing at one stroke the
deadly concentration of power directed against Black's almost de-
serted King-side. It would be
strange indeed if the position did
not offer scope for a striking combination!

| 16 . . . . | NxN |
| 17 PxN | N–K2 |

17 . . . RxP; 18 BxPch would lose
the exchange under even more unfavorable conditions than in the
text continuation.

The a l t e r n a t i v e 17 . . . N–R4
would have led to some pretty play
after 18 BxPch!, KxB; 19 N–N5ch:

I 19 . . . K–N1; 20 Q–R5, B–Q3; 21
R–K1 and Black has no defense a-
gainst Q–R7ch and Q–R8 mate.

II 19 . . . K–N3; 20 Q–K4ch, KxN;
21 R–Q3 and Black's King is helpless.

| 18 P–Q6! | . . . . |

But here 18 BxPch, KxB; 19 N–
N5ch, K–N3; 20 Q–K4ch, N–B4;
21 P–N4 would be unclear because
of 21 . . . Q–Q2.

| 18 . . . . | RxP |

He has no choice (18 . . . QxP?;
19 BxPch).

19 B–K5	BxN
20 QxB	RxB
21 BxQ	RxQ
22 PxR	. . . .

White has emerged with the exchange for a Pawn. His King-side
Pawns are ragged, but the superior
mobility of his Rooks is more than
enough compensation.

22	N–B4
23 P–QR4	R–K1
24 K–B1	B–B4
25 R–Q7	P–N3

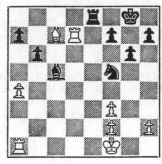

| 26 R–K1 | . . . . |

Practically forcing the exchange
of Rooks, since Black cannot afford to surrender control of both
open files. The exchange, however,
is a blow to Black, because a Rook
and minor piece can make more
headway against two minor pieces
than can two Rooks against a Rook
and minor piece.

26	K–B1
27 RxRch	KxR
28 R–Q8ch	K–K2
29 R–QR8	. . . .

This move proves the point made
in the previous note, for Black
must already lose a Pawn.

| 29 . . . . | K–Q2 |

If 29 . . . P–QR4; 30 R–R6 winning the QNP and the QRP as well.

30 RxP	K–B3
31 B–N3	B–K2
32 K–K2	P–R4

Beginning a series of "aggressive" moves which only hasten the
end.

33 K–Q3	P–B3
34 B–B4	P–N4
35 B–Q2	B–Q3
36 R–B7	B–K4

Or 36 . . . BxP; 37 RxPch, N–Q3;
38 BxP.

| 37 B–B3 | N–Q3 |
| 38 R–KR7 | N–N2 |

If 38 . . . BxB; 39 KxB, P–R5; 40
R–R6, N–K1; 41 P–B4 and Black's

King-side Pawns are untenable.

39	BxB	PxB
40	RxP	N–B4ch
41	K–B2	NxP
42	RxP	Resigns

He cannot stop the advance of White's RP.

50.

FINE–RESHEVSKY
Semmering, 1937

RUY LOPEZ

R. Fine	Reshevsky
WHITE	BLACK
1 P–K4	P–K4
2 N–KB3	N–QB3
3 B–N5	P–QR3
4 B–R4	N–B3
5 O–O	P–Q3
6 Q–K2	....

An unusual move at this point, hardly as promising as the familiar continuation 6 BxNch, PxB; 7 P–Q4.

6	....	P–QN4
7	B–N3	N–QR4
8	P–Q4	NxB
9	RPxN	N–Q2

Black has obtained the Bishop-pair, but in return his opponent has a lead in development and a somewhat freer game.

10	N–B3	B–N2
11	PxP	PxP
12	R–Q1	B–Q3
13	B–N5	P–KB3
14	B–K3	O–O

14 ... P–N5 (hoping to win the KP) would be very superficial, for after 15 N–Q5! the plausible 15 ... P–B3 could be answered effectively with 16 N–N6!

15	N–KR4	P–N3
16	Q–N4	K–R1
17	Q–N3	Q–K1
18	N–Q5	Q–B2

White has achieved nothing on the King-side, and Black is gradually freeing his game.

19 N–KB3	N–B4
20 BxN	....

Forced in order to avoid the loss of a Pawn. According to all orthodox notions, Black ought to have an overwhelming positional superiority, but as the game actually goes, the Knights give a highly creditable account of themselves.

20	....	BxB
21	N–K1	KR–Q1
22	N–Q3	B–KB1
23	P–QB4	P–B3
24	N–K3	R–Q5

Now Black is in a position to dispute the Q file. The coming exchange of all the Rooks is clearly indicated, but the real fight is only beginning!

25	Q–B3	Q–K3
26	N–K1	QR–Q1
27	N(1)–B2	R(5)–Q2
28	RxR	RxR
29	R–Q1	K–N2

Black begins to bring his King to the center, anticipating that his Bishops will soon command the board; but he is due for a rude surprise!

30	Q–K2	K–B2
31	P–R3	B–B1

Intending to post this Bishop more effectively at K3; but the project is never carried out.

32	R–Q2	B–K2
33	Q–K1	RxR
34	QxR	Q–Q3
35	Q–B3	P–N5

This does not turn out well.... B–K3 should have been tried.

36	Q–K1	Q–Q6

If instead 36 ... P–QR4; 37 Q–K2 and Black's Queen is shut out of Q6. Nevertheless, this would have been preferable to the text.

37	NxP	QxKP

The opening up of the position ought to favor the Bishops; but Fine's clever handling of the Knights nullifies this possibility.

| 38 Q–B3 | B–N2 |
| 39 N(4)–B2 | P–QB4?! |

A natural move, as Black wants to clear the long diagonal for his QB; but it gives White the chance to get a strong passed Pawn.

| 40 P–QN4! | PxP |
| 41 NxP | P–B4 |

Now Black actually threatens to win a piece with 42 ... BxN; 43 QxB, P–B5.

| 42 N–Q3 | K–K3 |

After this move, it is uphill work for Black all the way; ... B–Q3 would have been preferable.

| 43 Q–N3! | P–B5 |

Apparently very strong; yet White has an effective continuation.

| 44 P–B5ch | . . . . |

| 44 . . . . | B–Q4 |

The alternatives are even more unfavorable:

I 44 ... K–B3; 45 N–N4ch, K–N2; 46 P–B3, Q–Q5ch; 47 K–R2, B–Q4; 48 Q–B2, B–KB3; 49 P–B6 etc.

II 44 ... K–Q2; 45 NxPch, K–Q1; 46 Q–N6ch, K–K1; 47 Q–K6, B–B3; 48 Q–N8ch, B–B1; 49 Q–B7ch etc.

| 45 NxB | QxN(4) |
| 46 Q–N6ch | K–B4 |

Best; if 46 : .. K–Q2? 47 P–B6ch! wins; if 46 ... K–B2; 47 QxP, BxP; 48 Q–B4! and White should win.

| 47 QxP | P–K5! |

A very important move, as will be seen.

| 48 Q–B8ch | K–N4 |

Again best, for if 48 ... K–B3; 49 NxP, QxP; 50 Q–K6ch etc.

49 Q–N4ch	K–R3
50 QxPch	K–N2
51 Q–K5ch	QxQ
52 NxQ	BxP

With an outside passed Pawn to the good, White's theoretical winning chances are excellent. Black's hope of salvation lies in the fact that White's King is awkwardly situated and cannot approach the center.

53 P–QN3	B–Q5
54 N–B6	B–N3
55 N–N4	K–B2

Black's King is able to play an active role in the coming struggle.

56 N–Q5	B–Q5
57 K–B1	K–K3
58 N–K3	B–B4
59 K–K2	P–R4
60 N–B2	P–N4

In such situations, the weaker side must try to exchange as many Pawns as possible.

61 P–QN4	B–Q3
62 P–N3	K–K4
63 P–N5	. . . .

White hopes to pin down his opponent's pieces to the task of holding back the free Pawn, allowing White to proceed unhindered on the King-side. This is exactly what happens, but it does not prove to be good enough.

63	B–B4
64 N–K3	K–Q5
65 N–B5ch	K–K4
66 N–N7!	P–R5
67 P–N4	. . . .

Black's situation has become more desperate than ever, for with his King-side Pawns on black squares, his Bishop can be tied down to the defense of these Pawns.

67	. . . .	B–N3
68	N–B5	B–B4
69	N–K3	K–Q5

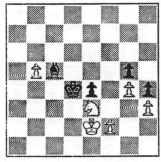

In "Basic Chess Endings," Fine claims a win by 70 P–B3!, B–N3 (if 70...PxPch; 71 KxP, K–K4; 72 P–N6!); 71 N–B1!, K–K4 (if 71 ...PxPch; 72 KxP, K–B5; 73 K–K4, KxP; 74 K–B5, B–Q1; 75 N–Q2 wins); 72 N–Q2, PxPch; 73 KxP, K–B3; 74 N–B4, B–B2; 75 P–N6, B–B5; 76 P–N7, K–K3 (or 76...B–B2; 77 N–R5 and wins); 77 K–K4, K–Q2; 78 K–B5 and the Pawns fall.

This analysis is highly interesting and beautifully worked out. However, there is a flaw in the parenthetical variation based on 71...PxPch. Thus, referring to the diagram, we get the following play: 70 P–B3, B–N3; 71 N–B1, Px Pch; 72 KxP and now 72...K–Q6!! (instead of Fine's materialistic move 72...K–B5?); 73 N–R2, B–K6; 74 K–N2, K–B5 and White still cannot win.

| 70 | N–B5ch | K–B5 |
| 71 | N–R6 | KxP |

| 72 | N–B7 | K–B5! |

And not 72...B–K2? 73 K–K3 and wins.

| 73 | NxP | K–Q4 |
| 74 | P–B3 | . . . . |

If instead 74 N–R7, K–K4; 75 P–N5, K–B4; 76 N–B6, B–K2 etc.

| 74 | . . . . | PxPch |
| 75 | NxP | K–K5!! |

But not 75...B–K2? 76 K–K3 and wins!

| 76 | NxP | K–B5 |
| 77 | N–B5 | B–N3 |

Despite his seemingly crushing material superiority, White can make no headway. Thus if 78 K–B1, K–B6! 79 P–N5, B–R4; 80 P–N6, B–B6; 81 P–N7, BxP; 82 NxB, K–N6 etc.

78	K–Q3	B–Q1
79	K–Q4	B–B3ch
80	K–Q5	. . . .

White is bringing his King to KB7 in the hope of being able to support the advance of his Pawns. This is the last attempt, and it will be repulsed.

80	. . . .	B–R1
81	K–Q6	B–K4ch
82	K–K6	B–R8
83	K–K7	B–N7
84	K–B7	K–N4!

Given up as a draw. This is one of my most difficult games.

51.

KERES–RESHEVSKY
Semmering, 1937

QUEEN'S GAMBIT ACCEPTED

P. Keres	Reshevsky
WHITE	BLACK
1 N–KB3	P–Q4
2 P–Q4	N–KB3
3 P–B4	PxP
4 P–K3	P–K3
5 BxP	P–B4
6 O–O	P–QR3
7 Q–K2	....

Compare the opening with the initial moves of my game with Lasker (Game 40). As in my game with Vidmar (Game 41), I had the opportunity of playing 7 P–QR4 here. If then 7 ... N–B3; 8 Q–K2, B–K2 (or 8 ... PxP; 9 R–Q1 regaining the Pawn with a good game); 9 R–Q1, Q–B2; 10 N–B3, O–O; 11 P–R3, R–Q1; 12 P–Q5!, PxP; 13 BxQP (Reshevsky-Fine, Semmering 1937) and Black can equalize only with considerable difficulty.

7	P–QN4
8 B–N3	B–N2
9 R–Q1	QN–Q2
10 P–QR4	....

White plays to disarrange his opponent's Queen-side Pawns, partly to weaken them and partly with a view to gaining a good square for his QN at QB4.

10	P–N5

Black can keep his Pawn position intact with 10 ... Q–N3; 11 PxP, PxP; 12 RxRch, BxR; 13 N–B3, B–B3 with about even chances. Also possible is the surprising 10 ... B–K2, for if then 11 RPxP, RPxP; 12 RxR, QxR; 13 QxP?, BxN etc.

11 QN–Q2	Q–B2
12 N–B4	....

Keres has achieved his object-ive; but his position has the draw-back that his QB cannot be developed effectively.

12	B–K2
13 KN–K5	O–O
14 B–Q2	QR–B1
15 QR–B1	....

Since White intends to fix the QRP with P–R5, he might have advanced the QRP at once while it still had the protection of the QR.

15	KR–Q1
16 P–R5!?	....

Threatening to secure control of QN6 with B–R4. But Black has an effective reply.

16	B–Q4!

A good move, which induces White to avoid further complications and seek safety in simplification.

17 NxN	NxN
18 P–K4	BxN
19 BxB	QxP
20 R–R1	Q–B2
21 PxP?	....

An astonishingly careless blunder for a master like Keres. The proper course was 21 BxRP, R–R1; 22 B–K3 with equal chances.

21	P–QR4

Winning a Pawn, as the QBP falls at once.

22 B–K3	NxP
23 BxN	....

Relying on the resulting Bishops of opposite colors, but, as will be seen, this proves to be a vain hope.

| 23 . . . . | BxB |
| 24 P–QN3 | . . . . |

Black is not yet threatening ... BxPch, but White's Bishop will eventually require protection.

| 24 . . . . | B–Q5 |
| 25 QR–B1 | . . . . |

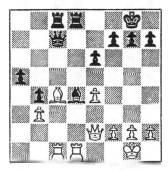

25 . . . .   P–R5!

Very strong. He returns the extra material in order to acquire a formidable passed Pawn which will tie up White's pieces.

| 26 PxP | P–N6! |
| 27 P–N3 | . . . . |

If instead 27 BxNP, QxR; 28 Rx Q, RxRch; 29 B–Q1, RxBch; 30 Qx R, BxPch and wins.

| 27 . . . . | P–N7 |
| 28 R–B2 | BxPch! |

Another unpleasant surprise for White. If now 29 KxB, RxR; 30 Qx R, Q–N3ch and the terrible Pawn Queens.

29 K–N2	B–Q5
30 B–N3	B–B6
31 R–KB1	Q–N2
32 B–R2	R–Q5!

Forcing the win of further material since it is impossible for White to defend both isolated Pawns simultaneously.

33 R–B3   RxRP

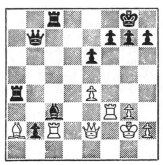

| 34 B–N1 | . . . . |

If 34 R(3)xB, RxR; 35 RxR, RxB and White must resign, for example 36 Q–QB2, P–N8(Q); 37 R–B8ch, QxR and White cannot recapture!

34	RxP
35 Q–Q3	R–Q5
36 Q–K3	R(5)–QB5
37 K–R3	B–Q5
38 Q–Q3	RxR
39 BxR	RxB!

The finishing touch.

40 QxB	R–B1
41 R–Q3	P–R3
Resigns	

52.

RESHEVSKY–A. THOMAS
Hastings, 1937-38

CATALAN SYSTEM

Reshevsky	A. R. B. Thomas
WHITE	BLACK
1 P–Q4	N–KB3
2 P–QB4	P–K3
3 P–KN3	. . . .

A comparatively new system of development which generally leads to interesting and complicated positions. The basic idea is to exert pressure along the long diagonal with the fianchettoed Bishop. Black's main difficulty as a rule is the development of his QB.

3 . . . .   P–Q4

4 B–N2   P–B4

Best is 4 ... PxP; 5 Q–R4ch, QN–Q2 as in Game 63, although White might try the following line, used with good results by one of the Russian masters: 6 N–Q2, P–B4; 7 NxP, B–K2; 8 PxP, BxP; 9 N–B3, O–O; 10 O–O, etc.

5 BPxP   KPxP

Turning the opening into the Tarrasch Defense, which is inferior for Black. Correct was 5 ... NxP; 6 N–KB3, N–QB3; 7 O–O, N–B3! with a satisfactory game.

6 N–KB3   QN–Q2

Another poor move, instead of the natural 6 ... N–B3, which gives Black more control of the center and does not impede the development of his QB.

7 O–O   B–K2
8 N–B3   O–O
9 B–B4   P–QR3

Black's position is very difficult; 9 ... P–B5, for example, could be answered effectively with 10 N–K5.

10 N–K5   . . . .

The Knight is, of course, well placed here, but 10 PxP, NxP; 11 N–Q4 would also have been very promising because of White's control of the center squares.

10 . . . .   PxP
11 QxP   B–B4
12 Q–Q3   N–N3
13 KR–Q1   B–K3
14 B–K3!   . . . .

Black's KB is impeding White's progress because it commands an important diagonal. The following exchange can hardly be avoided (if 14 ... B–Q3; 15 B–Q4 with a magnificent position), so that Black's lack of control of the black squares is accentuated.

14 . . . .   Q–K2
15 BxB   QxB
16 QR–B1   . . . .

White continues to gain ground by steadily increasing the concentration of his forces on the vital lines; Black, on the other hand, is handicapped by having to consider the welfare of his QP.

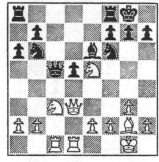

16 . . . .   Q–K2

White was threatening to win a Pawn by 17 NxQP, even in the event of 16 ... N–B5. Relatively best was 16 ... QR–B1, after which 17 Q–Q4 would have confronted Black with the sorry choice of exchanging Queens and leaving White with a superior ending, or else of retreating to Q3 and increasing White's command of the board.

17 Q–Q4   N–B5
18 N–Q3!   . . . .

18 NxQP would have led to no more than equality after 18 ... Bx N; 19 NxN, BxB; 20 KxB, QxP etc. 18 NxN would only have enabled Black to rid himself of the weak QP.

18 . . . .   QR–Q1
19 P–N3   N–QR4
20 Q–B5   . . . .

In this type of position, simplification almost always helps the stronger side.

20 . . . .   N–B3
21 QxQ   NxQ
22 N–B5   B–B1
23 N(3)–R4!   . . . .

Threatening to win a Pawn by means of N–N6 followed by NxB.

23	P–QN4

. . . R–Q3 would only make matters worse because of 24 P–K4! threatening P–K5.

24 N–N2!	. . . .

But now 24 N–N6 would have been out of place because of 24 . . . R–Q3; 25 NxB, RxN and Black has improved his position somewhat.

24	KR–K1
25 R–Q2	. . . .

In order to double Rooks against the hapless QP.

25	N–K5?

Black is under a false impression that by giving up the weak Pawn, he will obtain sufficient counterplay through posting his Rook on the seventh rank. It can safely be said that in such positions, where a player is constantly on the defensive, he is handicapped in a psychological sense. At one point or another, whenever the opportunity seems to present itself, he will snatch at a desperate freeing maneuver, no matter how little chance of success it may offer.

26 NxN	PxN
27 RxR	RxR
28 BxP	R–Q7
29 R–Q1	. . . .

R–B2 would also have been good enough, but the text simplifies the ending by forcing the exchange of Rooks.

29	RxRch

And not 29 . . . RxN?? 30 R–Q8 mate.

30 NxR	B–K3
31 N–B3	. . . .

Although White is a Pawn ahead, he must still play with care, as will be seen. In this connection, it is appropriate to remark that many players, including masters, are afflicted with the fault of relaxing upon gaining an advantage. A good maxim for such situations is "never relax for a moment."

31	P–B4
32 B–N7	P–N5
33 N–R4	P–QR4
34 N–B5	K–B2
35 P–B4	N–Q4

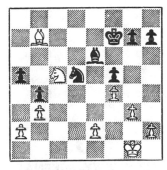

36 BxN!	. . . .

Had White been unduly eager to reach a King and Pawn ending, he would have lost the game: 36 NxB? KxN; 37 BxNch (Black threatens . . . N–B6 winning the important QRP), KxB; 38 K–B2, K–Q5; 39 K–B3, P–KR3; 40 P–KR3, P–R4; 41 P–KN4, RPxPch; 42 PxP, PxPch; 43 KxP, K–K6; 44 P–B5, KxP; 45 K–N5, K–B6; 46 K–N6, K–B5; 47 KxP, KxP; 48 K–B7, K–K5; 49 K–K6, K–Q6; 50 K–Q5, K–B6; 51 K–B5, K–N7; 52 K–N5, KxP; 53 KxP, KxP and wins.

36	BxB
37 K–B2	K–K2
38 K–K3	K–Q3
39 K–Q4!	. . . .

Just in time! Had White's King been unable to occupy this important square at just this moment, the winning process would have been much more difficult.

39	K–B3
40 N–N7!	. . . .

Wins another Pawn.

40	P–R5
41 N–R5ch	K–Q3
42 N–B4ch	K–B3
43 PxP	B–N1
44 N–R5ch	K–Q3
45 N–N3	B–Q4
46 P–R5	. . . .

This Pawn will advance with decisive effect.

46	B–N2
47 P–K3	B–R3
48 N–B5	B–K7
49 P–R6	B–B6
50 N–Q3	K–B2
51 K–B5	P–N6
52 PxP	B–Q8
53 N–B1	Resigns

53.

RESHEVSKY–MIKENAS
Hastings, 1937-38

G R U E N F E L D   D E F E N S E

Reshevsky	V. Mikenas
WHITE	BLACK
1 P–Q4	N–KB3
2 P–QB4	P–KN3
3 N–QB3	P–Q4

One of the strongest defenses at Black's disposal.

4 Q–N3	P–B3
5 B–B4	PxP
6 QxBP	B–K3

The best move is 6 . . . Q–N3! when 7 R–N1 will not do because of 7 . . . B–B4.

7 Q–Q3	N–Q4

Even here . . . Q–N3 would be more promising. If, however, 7 . . . B–N2; 8 P–K4, O–O; 9 N–B3, QN–Q2; 10 B–K2, N–N3; 11 O–O and White has a splendid position in the center while Black cannot develop his pieces effectively.

8 NxN	PxN

If 8 . . . QxN; 9 P–K4, Q–R4ch;

10 B–Q2, Q–N3; 11 B–B3 and White has a fine position.

9 Q–N5ch!	Q–Q2
10 P–K3	QxQ

Black can hardly avoid the exchange of Queens, for after 10 . . . N–B3 White's Queen would exert an extremely irritating pressure on Black's Queen-side. Thus . . . P–QR3 could always be answered by Q–N6.

11 BxQch	B–Q2
12 B–Q3	. . . .

Since White's KB will be more active than Black's QB, White naturally avoids the exchange.

12	N–B3
13 N–K2!	. . . .

Kt–B3 is more obvious, but the Knight will be more useful at QB3.

13 . . . .   P–B3?

Black is naturally reluctant to shut in his QB with . . . P–K3, but the text initiates a plan which turns out to be faulty. If instead 13 . . . N–N5; 14 B–N1, B–N4; 15 K–Q2! followed by P–QR3 and N–B3 forcing Black's pieces to retreat.

Relatively best was 13 . . . P–K3; 14 N–B3, P–QR3 (preventing the annoying N–N5) and White is momentarily unable to play N–R4 because of . . . N–N5.

14 N–B3	P–K4
15 PxP	PxP
16 B–N3	B–QN5

Black's idea of exchanging this Bishop for the Knight turns out to be weak. ... B–K3 would have offered sterner resistance.

17 O–O	BxN
18 PxB	P–K5
19 B–K2	N–R4

Black seems to have done well; his center Pawns are aggressively posted and the QBP looks weak. It will soon be clear, however, that Black's center Pawns are feeble, while White's QBP is in no real danger.

The text turns out to be pointless, as the Knight is much more usefully posted at B3. ... O–O was in order.

20 P–B3	. . . .

Beginning the pressure on the center Pawns.

20	O–O
21 KR–Q1	B–K3

Another mistake. ... B–B3 would have given the Pawns better protection.

22 PxP	PxP
23 R–Q4	. . . .

Had Black's Knight remained at B3, this square would not have been accessible to White's Rook.

23	QR–B1

Losing a Pawn outright with very little compensation. His position had already become untenable, however, for if 23 ... B–B4; 24 B–Q6, KR–K1; 25 P–N4 forcing the Bishop to B1 (not 25 ... B–Q2??; 26 B–B7 winning a piece).

24 RxP	B–B4
25 R–K5	N–B5
26 R–N5	. . . .

After 26 R–K7, R–KB2 Black would have had better fighting chances than after the text.

26	P–N3
27 B–B4	KR–Q1
28 R–Q1	N–R6

29 R–N3	RxRch
30 BxR	N–B5
31 R–N4	. . . .

White is gradually consolidating his position.

31	N–R4

31 ... P–QR4 would only have weakened Black's Pawns. The continuation would have been 32 R–N5, B–Q2; 33 R–N5.

32 B–K5	B–K3

Or 32 ... N–B3; 33 B–N3ch, K–B1; 34 B–Q6ch, K–K1; 35 B–R4 and White has greatly improved his position.

33 B–N4!	. . . .

Very important. The remaining Bishop is much stronger than Black's Knight.

33	BxB
34 RxB	R–K1
35 B–Q4	N–B5
36 K–B2	P–QN4
37 R–N5	. . . .

37 BxP, R–R1 would only have improved Black's chances, as he would have regained the Pawn with a more favorable position for his Rook.

37	R–N1
38 R–QB5!	R–N2

He cannot allow R–B7.

39 K–B3	K–B2
40 P–QR4!	P–QR3

Losing a Pawn, but after 40 ...

N–Q3; 41 P–R5! White would have had an easy win.

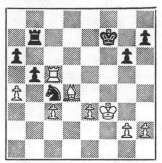

41	R–B6	N–N7
42	P–R5	N–R5
43	RxRP	R–B2
44	R–B6ch	K–K2
45	P–R6	Resigns

For if 45 ... NxP; 46 P–R7, RxP (if 46 ... R–B1; 47 BxN wins); 47 BxR, KxR; 48 B–Q4ch winning the Knight. A highly instructive game.

54.

RESHEVSKY–G. THOMAS
Hastings, 1937-38

QUEEN'S INDIAN DEFENSE

Reshevsky	Sir G. A. Thomas
WHITE	BLACK
1 P–Q4	N–KB3
2 P–QB4	P–K3
3 N–KB3	P–QN3

As already indicated in my notes to Game 14, this is not a defense to which I am very partial; it leads to a cramped position and it offers Black few fighting chances.

4 P–KN3	B–N2
5 B–N2	B–N5ch

Experience has shown that Black is better off with 5 ... B–K2, which leads to a more complicated and more promising middle game.

6 B–Q2	BxBch
7 QxB	....

Regarding this move, see Games 14 and 18.

7	P–Q3
8 O–O	QN–Q2
9 Q–B2	Q–B1

Black has played rather passively, and the text is an indication that he intends to continue in that vein. ... Q–K2 would place the Queen more effectively and would facilitate the development of the QR. Aside from these considerations, 9 ... B–K5 would put up more of a fight against White's contemplated seizure of the center.

10 N–B3	O–O
11 P–K4	....

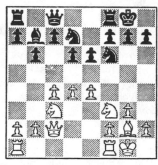

What have been the consequences of the opening play? White has established a powerful Pawn formation in the center, and he can develop his pieces effectively at his leisure; Black, on the other hand, is exceedingly cramped and he must be content with waiting moves.

11	P–QR3
12 KR–K1	P–R3
13 P–N3	N–R2

The natural ... P–K4 would only provoke a strong reaction in the form of N–Q5. Black therefore continues to mark time.

14 QR–Q1	R–N1
15 N–KR4	Q–Q1

Whereas White has steadily strengthened his position, Black has maneuvered aimlessly, condemned to await the eventual onslaught.

16 P–B4   P–KN4?

There comes a time when even the most timid player can no longer endure his cramped position and decides to strike out blindly, whatever the cost. The drawback to the text is that it creates a fatal weakness on the King-side, thus adding to Black's woes.

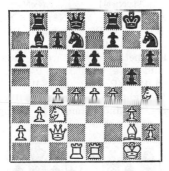

17 PxP   PxP
18 N–B3   Q–B3

After the headlong advance of the KNP, the Queen must be utilized to guard the King-side. But this leaves the Queen-side in a virtually defenseless state!

19 P–K5!   . . . .

This serves the double purpose of action against both wings.

19 . . . .   Q–R3

19 ... PxP; 20 PxP, Q–K2; 21 N–K4 would have been even worse, for then White's QR would be cooperating in the attack, while Black's Queen would be unable to guard the exposed King-side.

20 PxP   PxP
21 N–K4   P–Q4

No better would be 21 ... BxN; 22 QxB (threatening Q–B6), KR–

B1; 23 P–KR4 followed by a crushing attack on the KR file.

22 N–Q6   B–R1

23 N–K5!   NxN

If instead 23 ... QR–Q1; 24 PxP followed by Q–B7 leaving Black with a hopeless poition. If 23 ... KN–B3; 24 PxP, PxP; 25 NxN, Nx N; 26 Q–B7, QR–Q1; 27 R–K7 with telling effect.

24 PxN   PxP
25 QxP   . . . .

The powerful position of White's Knight renders Black's Rooks ineffectual as fighting pieces. Note also that Black's Queen and Knight are virtually out of play.

25 . . . .   BxB
26 KxB   P–B4?!

A suicidal advance, but Black had little choice. Thus if 26 ... P–N4; 27 Q–B6, R–R1; 28 R–Q4! (threatening to win the Queen with 29 N–B5, Q–R4; 30 P–KN4) followed by P–KR4 with a devastating attack.

27 PxP e.p.   RxP
28 N–B5!   . . . .

Bringing the game to a quick conclusion. Since Black must lose at least the KP, he tries a desperate resource.

28 . . . .   RxN
29 RxP   R–B7ch

Any Queen move would lose the

Queen by a discovered check.

30 KxR	QxPch
31 K-B3	Resigns

If 31 ... R-B1ch; 32 R-B6ch, K-N2; 33 RxR winning easily. Or 31 ... Q-R4ch; 32 K-N2 and Black's game is quite hopeless. Black never recovered from his poor opening.

55.

RESHEVSKY–TYLOR
Hastings, 1937-38

QUEEN'S GAMBIT DECLINED

Reshevsky	T. H. Tylor
WHITE	BLACK
1 P-Q4	P-Q4
2 P-QB4	P-K3
3 N-QB3	N-KB3
4 B-N5	B-K2
5 P-K3	QN-Q2
6 PxP	....

Once again my favorite Exchange Variation. It gives White an almost impenetrable position, and at the same time he has excellent chances of breaking through on the Queen-side by advancing his Pawns on that sector.

| 6 .... | NxP |

Not relishing the type of game just described, Tylor tries a rather novel alternative.

| 7 BxB | QxB |
| 8 R-B1 | .... |

Threatening to win a Pawn by NxN. Dr. Euwe recommends ... P-QB3 in reply, followed in due course by ... NxN and ... P-K4, with a position very much like that of the main line of the Orthodox Defense.

| 8 .... | QN-B3? |

This is inferior because it gives White a free hand in the control of K5.

| 9 N-B3 | O-O |
| 10 P-QR3! | .... |

A useful move which guards against ... N-N5 or ... Q-N5 in some variations.

| 10 .... | P-QN3? |

Black's chief difficulty, as in so many variations of this opening, is the problem of how to develop his Bishop. Since the text creates a number of serious weaknesses in his position, there was apparently nothing better than ... P-B3 followed by ... B-Q2. In that event, Black's game would have remained in a badly cramped state.

| 11 NxN! | NxN |

And not 11 ... PxN?; 12 Q-B2, N-K1; 13 Q-B6 winning a Pawn.

| 12 B-N5! | B-N2? |

For better or for worse, Black should have tried 12 ... P-QB4. If then 13 PxP, PxP; 14 Q-B2, R-N1 with fighting chances. As Black plays, he finds himself in a hopeless predicament.

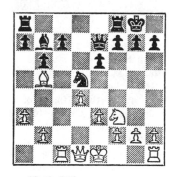

| 13 B-B6! | .... |

Permanently preventing the advance of Black's QBP, which becomes a helpless target on an open file.

| 13 .... | BxB |
| 14 RxB | KR-B1 |

Black does not play economically. Better was ... KR-Q1-Q3 in the hope of dislodging the powerfully posted Rook.

15 O-O N-B3

In order to guard the QBP with his Knight, which, however, is thus condemned to eternal passivity. The alternative would have been 15 ... Q-Q1 followed by ... N-K2 and ... P-QB3; this would have relaxed the pressure on Black's game a bit, but hardly enough to matter in the long run.

16 N-K5	N-K1
17 Q-B3	Q-B3
18 Q-K2!	....

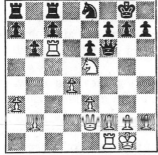

This involves no loss of time, as the powerful thrust Q-R6 must be prevented. In this way, White gains time for his next move.

18 .... P-QR4

Parrying the threat, but at the cost of weakening his Queen-side still further.

19 P-B4 ....

Gaining time by the threat of P-B5 to bring his Queen to the strong post KB3.

19 .... R-Q1

So that if 20 P-B5, R-Q3; 21 PxP, QxP; 22 RxR, NxR with some improvement in Black's position.

20 Q-B3! ....

Continuing with his plan. Note that ... R-Q3?? would now lose a Rook.

20	QR-B1
21 KR-B1	R-Q3
22 R(6)-B3	....

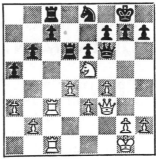

White must now win a Pawn by force, for if 22 ... R(3)-Q1 (the threat was 23 N-B4 followed by 24 NxNP); 23 N-B6, R-Q2; 24 N-R7, R-N1; 25 N-N5 etc. Similarly, if 22 ... R(1)-Q1; 23 N-B6, R-B1; 24 N-R7 etc.

22 .... P-B4

Black reasons that since he must lose a Pawn, he would like to do it in a manner which will give him some freedom of action. But this proves unavailing.

23 PxP	PxP
24 RxP	RxR
25 RxR	Q-Q1

Black has a little play on the Q file, but this is very far from being adequate compensation.

26 P-R3	P-B3
27 N-B4	R-Q8ch
28 K-R2	R-QB8

T h i s loses quickly. ... R-Q4 would have held out longer.

29 Q-B6! ....

A deadly reply. If 29 ... Q-K2; 30 RxP; or 29 ... K-B2; 30 N-K5ch.

29	P-N4
30 QxPch	K-N2
31 R-Q5	Q-N1
32 R-Q7ch	Resigns

If 32 ... K-R3; 33 Q-B7, PxP; 34 QxRPch, K-N4; 35 P-R4ch, K-N5; 36 Q-N6ch, KxP; 37 R-R7 mate. Black's poor opening left him with a permanent disadvantage.

SECOND U. S. CHAMPIONSHIP TOURNAMENT NEW YORK, 1938

THE manner in which I had won the first United States championship in 1936 was probably dramatic enough to satisfy any critic; but it may not have been sufficiently convincing for some. Moreover, many of the leading players of the United States had gained so notably in stature that it was a question whether I could successfully defend my title.

The field included many players who at one time or another had held the United States Open Championship, various State championships, and even some who had distinguished themselves in international play. It was clear that the winner would have his work cut out for him.

The score reveals that I won ten games and drew six. Nevertheless, the fact that I did not lose a game should not mislead anyone into supposing that I had an easy time. Not only did I have to fight every inch of the way in every one of the games that I won — to say nothing of some of those which I drew — but also the issue was in doubt to the very end.

In Game 59 I once again encountered George Treystman whose success in the 1936 United States Championship had been so unexpected. So far as I know, Treystman had never played in a tournament before; and yet he succeeded in tying for third place. This is the more remarkable when it is considered that at the end he was only half a point behind the leader. As a substitute for tournament experience, Treystman had developed his skill in countless offhand games. "Coffeehouse" chess, although much maligned, is a prime developer of chess ability. The player whose almost daily practice it is to play a half a dozen games which he can ill afford to lose, speedily learns that pessimism does not pay. No matter how bad his position may be in theory, he knows that he must win the game. The player who is consistently successful under these conditions is a living proof that will power is not a negligible factor in success at the chess table. (I might add that some observers have attributed a good part of my own success to this same factor.)

56.

MORTON–RESHEVSKY
U. S. Championship, 1938

KING'S INDIAN DEFENSE

H. Morton	Reshevsky
WHITE	BLACK
1 P–Q4	N–KB3
2 N–KB3	P–KN3
3 B–B4	B–N2
4 N–B3	. . . .

An unusual continuation, occasionally adopted by Capablanca, Marshall and Torre. The idea is to play for a quick advance of the KP, but the move has certain drawbacks.

     4 . . . .   P–Q4

Black prevents P–K4, but at the same time Black weakens his black squares somewhat.

     5 Q–B1   . . . .

Planning an exchange which turns out to be nothing more than an elaborate waste of time. In the game Capablanca — Yates, N e w York, 1924, White continued in more interesting and effective fashion: 5 P–K3, O–O; 6 P–KR3, P–B4; 7 PxP! (the surrender of the center is more wisely motivated than in the present game), Q–R4; 8 N–Q2!, QxBP; 9 N–N3, Q–N3; 10 B–K5!, P–K3; 11 N–N5, N–K1; 12 BxB, NxB; 13 P–KR4 and White has a promising game.

     5 . . . .   O–O
     6 B–R6   P–B4!

While White wastes time with his exchanging maneuver, Black counter-attacks in the center.

     7 BxB   KxB
     8 P–K3   N–B3
     9 B–N5   . . . .

White hopes to curb Black's initiative in the center. If instead 9 Q–Q1, B–N5 with all sorts of promising possibilities for Black, such as ... Q–R4 or ... Q–N3 or ... N–K5 or ... P–K4.

     9 . . . .   B–N5!

A troublesome move to meet.

     10 BxN   . . . .

White is already in difficulties and the text is practically forced. For example, 10 N–K5 leads to disaster after 10 ... PxP!; 11 BxN, PxN; 12 BxNP, QR–N1; 13 N–B6, PxP; 14 QxP, Q–B2; 15 NxR, RxN; 16 QR–N1, B–B1 gaining two pieces for the Rook.

If 10 PxP, BxN; 11 PxB, N–K4; 12 B–K2, Q–R4 and Black regains the Pawn with a much superior position.

     10 . . . .   BxN!
     11 PxB   . . . .

If 11 BxNP, BxP; 12 KR–N1, QR–N1; 13 RxB, RxB and White's King is dangerously insecure.

11	PxB
12 PxP	Q–R4
13 Q–Q2	QxBP
14 N–K2	P–K4
15 P–B3	QR–N1
16 P–N3	Q–K2

The position thus arrived at is decidedly in Black's favor: strong center Pawns and aggressive development as against White's ineffectual development and the insecure position of his King.

17 QR–B1   . . . .

This begins a policy of aimless maneuvering which must inevitably lead to White's downfall. Here and later on, he could have put up a better resistance by castling on the King-side.

17 . . . .   QR–Q1

Having in mind the eventual thrust of his QP.

18 Q–N2   . . . .

Since White has no constructive plan at his disposal, he adopts "come and get me" tactics.

18 . . . .   Q–K3!

Black accepts the invitation.

19 N–N3   . . . .

The alternative 19 P–KR4, Q–B4 is hardly attractive.

19 . . . .   Q–R6
20 Q–K2   P–KR4
21 Q–B1   Q–K3

As Black is playing for the attack and preparing to concentrate his forces for a quick, decisive blow, he naturally avoids the exchange of Queens.

22 Q–R6   P–R5
23 N–K2   . . . .

Equally uninviting would be 23 N–B1, Q–R6; 24 N–Q2, Q–N7; 25 K–K2, P–Q5 with a winning attack.

23 . . . .   Q–R6
24 QxBP   . . . .

White has nothing left but Pawn-hunting, for on 24 P–KB4, N–N5 would be decisive.

24 . . . .   QxBP
25 R–B1   N–N5
26 Q–B7   KR–K1

Since White can no longer avoid the fatal loss of his KRP, he resigns himself to the inevitable.

27 QxP   P–Q5!

After a thoroughgoing preparation, the final breakthrough is at last in order.

28 BPxP   PxP

29 NxP   . . . .

29 . . . .   NxKP!

A pretty finish. Black could also have won with 29 . . . RxPch; 30 PxR, QxPch; 31 K–Q1, RxNch; and White must part with his Queen. The text method, however, is more pleasing.

30 PxN   . . . .

30 NxQ would allow mate on the move.

30 . . . .   RxPch
31 K–Q2   Q–K7 mate

57.

RESHEVSKY–SHAINSWIT
U. S. Championship, 1938

CATALAN SYSTEM

Reshevsky	G. Shainswit
WHITE	BLACK
1 P–Q4	P–Q4
2 P–QB4	P–K3
3 N–KB3	N–KB3
4 P–KN3	. . . .

The move from which the opening gets its name. The basic idea is to transpose into a favorable variation of Reti's Opening in which Black is unable to develop his QB to KB4, because of his early . . . P–K3.

4 . . . .   QN–Q2

This is questionable because it leads to a cramped game for Black.

The best defensive system is 4 ...
PxP; 5 Q–R4ch, QN–Q2; 6 B–N2,
P–QR3 followed by a general advance of the Queen-side Pawns as
in Game 63.

| 5 B–N2 | P–B3 |

There was still time for ... PxP.

6 Q–B2	B–Q3
7 QN–Q2	O–O
8 O–O	Q–K2

Striving for ... P–K4. After 8 ...
P–K4; 9 BPxP, Black would have
to resign himself to an isolated
QP, for if 9 ... NxP; 10 N–B4!
would assure White a clear advantage.

| 9 N–R4 | P–KN3 |

Black is obviously intent on freeing himself with ... P–K4; hence
his last move, which prevents N–
B5. However, the text creates a
weakness which White will be able
to exploit later on. Black's great
difficulty is the problem of developing his QB. Thus if 9 ... P–QN3; 10
PxP, BPxP; 11 P–K4! and Black's
game is most uncomfortable.

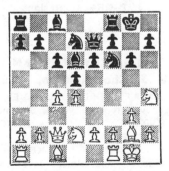

| 10 P–K4! | .... |

Since White's position is freer,
he will profit by the opening up of
new lines.

10	PxKP
11 NxKP	NxN
12 QxN	P–QB4

This eventually turns out to be

unsatisfactory because of the resulting striking power of White's
KB, but the natural 12 ... P–K4
also has its drawbacks: 13 PxP, Nx
P; 14 R–K1 (threatening P–B4),
R–K1; 15 B–Q2 followed by B–QB3
and Black's position is very awkward.

| 13 N–B3 | .... |

The Knight has completed his
task of provoking a weakness in the
hostile game and is now returned
to a centralized position.

| 13 .... | P–B4 |

If instead 13 ... PxP (or 13 ... N–
B3, 14 Q R1 with the nasty threat
of B–N5); 14 QxP, P–K4; 15 Q–B3
followed by R–K1 with considerable pressure.

| 14 Q–K2 | P–K4 |

This immediately leads to trouble, but if 14 ... PxP; 15 NxP, N–
N3; 16 N–N5 and Black is likewise
in difficulties.

15 B–N5!   ....

An important gain of time. It is
instructive to see how White gains
a clear advantage by perfectly
simple moves.

15	Q–N2
16 PxKP	NxP
17 NxN	BxN

Or 17 ... QxN; 18 QxQ, BxQ; 19
B–K7, R–K1; 20 BxBP, BxQNP; 21
QR–N1 and Black must resign him-

self to the loss of a valuable Pawn, for if 21 ... R–K7?; 22 B–Q5ch, K–N2; 23 RxB! etc.

18 B–R6!   . . . .

By forcing the exchange of Bishops, White is left with the **magnificent** fianchettoed KB **against** Black's undeveloped QB. Add **to** this White's pressure against **the** Queen-side Pawns, the ease with which his Rooks can be brought into play and Black's vulnerability on the black squares, and the **sum** total is a won game for White.

18	QxB
19 QxB	Q–N2
20 Q–Q6!	. . . .

Even stronger than 20 QxQBP, B–K3 (not 20 ... QxP??; 21 B–Q5 ch, K–N2; 22 Q–K7ch etc.) after which Black would have more play than in the text continuation.

20	P–B5
21 B–Q5ch	K–R1
22 QR–K1	B–B4

Black has finally succeeded in developing his Bishop, but meanwhile White, thanks to his surprising 20th move, has gained time for obtaining control of the all-important seventh rank.

| 23 R–K7 | Q–Q5 |
| 24 Q–K5ch! | . . . . |

The apparently powerful 24 Q–B7 is answered by ... P–KN4. The

text, on the other hand, leads to an easily won ending: White has complete control of the K file and cannot be kept off the seventh rank, with a devastating attack o n Black's Queen-side Pawns.

24	QxQ
25 RxQ	PxP
26 RPxP	QR–N1
27 KR–K1	P–QN4

This desperate attempt at counterplay leaves a weak QBP.

28 P–N3	PxP
29 BxP	KR–B1
30 R–K7	P–QR4
31 R–R7	R–R1
32 R(1)–K7	RxR

The loss of a Pawn is unavoidable, for if 32 ... P–N4 (not 32 ... P–R4??; 33 R–R7 mate); 33 RxR, RxR; 34 R–K5 winning easily.

33 RxR	B–K5
34 RxP	R–Q1
35 K–B1	R–Q8ch

If 35 ... B–B6 (threatening mate); 36 B–K2 and Black has nothing.

| 36 K–K2 | R–QR8 |
| 37 P–QR4 | Resigns |

58.

RESHEVSKY–SUESMAN
U. S. Championship, 1938

DUTCH DEFENSE

Reshevsky   W. B. Suesman
WHITE   BLACK

| 1 P–Q4 | P–K3 |
| 2 N–KB3 | P–KB4 |

This defense almost invariably creates a serious weakness in Black's Pawn structure.

3 P–KN3	N–KB3
4 B–N2	B–K2
5 O–O	O–O
6 P–B4	N–K5

For the Stonewall Variation, see Game 39. The text allows White to take the initiative in the center, leaving Black's Pawn position in a permanently compromised state.

7 P-Q5!   . . . .

Taking immediate advantage of Black's inferior move. Had the correct move 6 ... P-Q3 been played, 7 P-Q5 could have been answered by ... P-K4.

7 . . . .   B-B3

He has nothing better. If 7 ... PxP; 8 PxP, P-Q3; 9 N-Q4 and Black's terrible weakness at K3 gives him a positionally lost game. Or if 7 ... P-Q3; 8 PxP, BxP; 9 N-Q4! and Black is in serious difficulties.

8 Q-B2   P-QR4

Unfortunately, the plausible 8 ... P-K4 would not do because of 9 N-K4! N-Q2; 10 P-B5 winning a Pawn.

9 QN-Q2!   . . . .

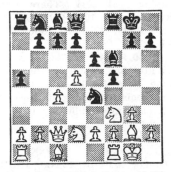

A useful gain of time; if Black exchanges, the QB retakes, with a considerable lead in development for White.

9 . . . .   N-B4

Avoiding the exchange, but still losing time.

10 P-K4!   . . . .

Intensifying his command of the center and opening up new lines for his pieces. Black is given no chance for a breathing spell.

10	**NxP**
11 NxN	**PxN**
12 QxP	**PxP**
13 QxQPch	**K-R1**
14 N-N5	**Q-K1**
15 B-B4!	**. . . .**

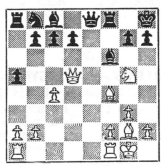

With Black's Queen-side immobilized and with White's pieces in such powerful play, it is clear that Black's game must crumble in short order. Thus if 15 ... P-Q3; 16 KR-K1, Q-N3; 17 N-B7ch! and wins (17 ... QxN; 18 QxQ, RxQ; 19 R-K8ch and mate follows.)

15	**BxN**
16 QxB	**N-B3**

There is no time to save the Pawn, for example 16 ... P-Q3; 17 KR-K1, Q-N3; 18 Q-K7 and Black's position collapses.

17 KR-K1	**Q-N3**
18 QxQ	**PxQ**
19 BxP	**N-Q5**
20 KR-Q1	**N-B4**

Of course not 20 ... N-K7ch?; 21 K-B1 and the Knight is lost. However, with White in full control of all important lines and Black's Queen-side blockaded, resignation cannot be staved off much longer.

21 P-QR4	**R-R3**
22 P-B5	**R-K3**
23 BxRP	**R-K7**
24 B-QB3	**N-K2**

25 R–K1	KRxBP
26 B–B1!	Resigns

For if 26 . . . RxR; 27 RxR, R–B2; 28 B–B4 winning a piece. This game demonstrates in a highly instructive manner how indifferent handling of the opening can lead to ruinous consequences.

59.

RESHEVSKY–TREYSTMAN
U. S. Championship, 1938

C A T A L A N   S Y S T E M

Reshevsky	G. Treystman
WHITE	BLACK
1 P–Q4	N–KB3
2 P–QB4	P–K3
3 P–KN3	. . . .

As in Game 57, White hopes to exert pressure on the long diagonal. The course of the present game is a good example of such strategy.

| 3 . . . . | B–N5ch |

Regarding the alternative . . . P–Q4, see the game just quoted.

| 4 B–Q2 | Q–K2 |

The simplest line is 4 . . . BxBch; 5 NxB, P–Q3; 6 B–N2, Q–K2; 7 KN–B3, P–K4 and Black stands well; or 5 QxB, P–Q4! 6 Q–B2, N–B3! and Black has good chances of seizing the initiative.

| 5 B–N2 | O–O |
| 6 N–KB3 | . . . . |

If 6 P–K4, P–Q4; 7 P–K5, N–K5 and White's center is precarious.

| 6 . . . . | P–Q4 |

After this Black must play carefully to avoid a disadvantage, because after the disappearance of his KB he will tend to be weak on the black squares. A promising alternative is 6 . . . BxBch; 7 QxB, N–K5; 8 Q–B2, P–KB4 and Black has a form of the Dutch Defense which

is more favorable than the general run of positions in that opening.

| 7 Q–B2 | N–K5 |

This move is plausible but bad, as it loses valuable time and only develops White's game with the ensuing exchanges. Black's main problem is to develop his QB effectively; hence he might have proceeded with 7 . . . P–B3; 8 O–O, BxB; 9 QNxB, P–QN3; 10 P–K4, PxKP; 11 NxP, B–N2. However, after 12 NxNch, QxN; 13 N–K5! followed by P–B5, Black's position would still have been very difficult.

| 8 O–O | NxB |

If 8 . . . BxB, White can play 9 KNxB, P–KB4; 10 P–B3 followed in due course by P–K4 with a very strong game.

| 9 QNxN | P–QB3 |

It would have been futile for Black to attempt to stop P–K4 by playing . . . P–KB4. There would have followed 10 P–QR3, BxN; 11 NxB, P–B3; 12 P–B3 followed by P–K4.

| 10 P–K4 | . . . . |

White has definitely the better game now, for he has so much more mobility for his pieces. Black will have great difficulty in developing his QB.

| 10 . . . . | BxN |
| 11 NxB | PxKP |

Or 11 . . . . PxBP; 12 NxP, P–QB4; 13 P–Q5!, PxP; 14 PxP, N–Q2; 15 KR–K1, Q–B3; 16 P–Q6 and White's advantage is quite marked.

| 12 NxP | N–Q2 |
| 13 P–B5! | . . . . |

This advance enables White to establish a lasting bind on the position because of the coming occupation of Q6.

| 13 . . . . | P–K4? |

In his anxiety to free his game, Black makes the mistake of open-

ing up lines which can be utilized
only by White. Treystman should
have relied on purely defensive
measures, for example 13 ... N–B3;
14 N–Q6, N–K1 or 14 ... N–Q4 followed by ... P–QN3 and ... B–Q2
or ... B–R3 and Black's position is
by no means hopeless.

14 PxP   NxKP

14 ... QxKP would be equally
disagreeable, for example 15 KR–
K1, N–B3; 16 N–Q6, Q–N4; 17 QR–
Q1 with a magnificent position.

15 KR–K1!   . . . .

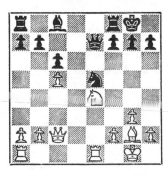

15 . . . .   N–N3

Black is already in a bad way,
as the following variations prove:

I 15 ... B–B4; 16 Q–B3!, P–B3
(not 16 ... BxN?; 17 RxB, P–B3; 18
P–B4 winning a piece); 17 N–Q6,
Q–Q2; 18 Q–N3ch, K–R1; 19 QxP,
QxQ; 20 NxQ, QR–N1; 21 P–B4,
RxN; 22 PxN, PxP; 23 RxP and
wins (if 23 ... RxP?; 24 R–KB1
winning a piece.)

II 15 ... B–B4; 16 Q–B3, N–N3;
17 N–Q6, Q–Q2; 18 QR–Q1 with
many threats.

III 15 ... B–K3; 16 N–Q6, N–N3;
17 P–B4 and Black must lose some
material.

IV 15 ... B–N5; 16 P–B4, N–N3
(if 16 ... N–B6ch; 17 BxN, BxB;
18 N–N5 and wins); 17 N–Q6, Q–
Q2 (or 17 ... Q–B3; 18 P–B5 and

Black cannot avoid material loss);
18 P–B5, N–K2; 19 Q–K4 and wins.

16 N–Q6   Q–B2
17 P–B4   B–Q2

After this, the unfortunate
Knight remains out of play for the
rest of the game; but 17 ... R–Q1;
18 P–B5, N–B1; 19 R–K3 (also good
is 19 Q–B3! threatening N–K8!)
followed by the doubling of the
Rooks on the K file, was hardly
any better.

Likewise after 17 ... N–K2; 18
P–B5 Black's game would be badly
tied up.

18 P–B5   N–R1

Out of play for the duration! A
degrading spot for the Knight.

19 R–K7   P–QN3
20 P–QN4!   . . . .

White's last two moves have
enormously strengthened the pressure, and now P–N5 is threatened.

20 . . . .   PxP
21 QxP   QR–Q1
22 P–N5   Q–N1

The only move, but it does not
help the situation much.

23 P–QR4!   . . . .

23 PxP would be less effective
because of the reply ... BxQBP.

23 . . . .   PxP
24 PxP   B–B1

Black's position is hopeless, as
he is in effect fighting on with a
piece down against White's effectively posted forces.

25 R–B7!   . . . .

Now the loss of a Pawn is unavoidable.

25 . . . .   Q–N3
26 QxQ   PxQ
27 R–B6   P–N3
28 P–N4   . . . .

28 P–B6 would be premature because of ... P–N4, permitting the
Knight to escape after all by means
of ... N–N3.

28 . . . .   P–R4

This desperate attempt to obtain freedom leads to some droll variations later on. However, Black is helpless against the coming advance of White's QNP.

29 P–R3   RPxP
30 RPxP   K–N2

Or 30 ... PxP; 31 PxP, B–Q2; 32 RxP, R–N1; 33 RxR, RxR; 34 R–R8, RxR; 35 BxR and Black must play ... BxNP, leaving White with an easy win.

31 K–B2   B–Q2
32 RxP   R–QN1

He could have put up a bit more resistance with 32 ... PxP; 33 PxP, R–QN1; 34 RxR, RxR; but after 35 K–K3 etc., White would make steady progress.

33 P–B6ch!   K–R3

Of course if 33 ... KxP; 34 N–K8ch wins the exchange.

34 K–N3!   . . . .

White threatens 35 R–R1ch, K–N4; 36 N–K4 mate! If 34 ... P–N4; 35 B–K4, N–N3; 36 RxR, RxR; 37 R–R1ch, N–R5; 38 NxP mate!

34 . . . .   K–R2
35 RxR   RxR
36 P–N5   . . . .

Now Black's King is nailed down for good, in addition to the Knight. A remarkable position!

36 . . . .   R–N3

36 ... BxP? would of course lose

a piece after 37 R–QN1.

37 R–R6   R–N1
38 B–B6   B–B4
39 R–R8   RxR

If 39 ... R–N3; 40 N–B4 wins.

40 BxR   B–Q6
41 P–N6   B–R3
42 B–N7!   Resigns

The fianchettoed Bishop has followed the basic theme of the opening right down to the very last move! If 42 ... B–Q6 or 42 ... B–K7; 43 B–B8! forces the queening of the Pawn. One of my best games.

60.

DAKE–RESHEVSKY
U. S. Championship, 1938

RUY LOPEZ

A. W. Dake	Reshevsky
WHITE	BLACK
1 P–K4	P–K4
2 N–KB3	N–QB3
3 B–N5	P–QR3
4 B–R4	N–B3
5 O–O	P–Q3

An old favorite with Tchigorin, Janowski and Rubinstein, this defense has been the subject of some clever analysis by Soviet masters in recent years.

6 BxNch   . . . .

Generally considered the least promising continuation for White, but it leads to very tricky play in which Black can easily go wrong.

6 . . . .   PxB
7 P–Q4   NxP

I do not care for Tchigorin's move 7 ... N–Q2, since Black is left with a miserable Pawn position after 8 PxP etc.

8 Q–K2   . . . .

A critical line here is 8 R–K1, P–KB4; 9 PxP, P–Q4; 10 N–Q4, B–B4! (10 ... P–B4? is bad, for after

11 N–K2 Black's advanced Knight is in rather a precarious position); 11 P–QB3, Q–R5! with good attacking chances, for example 12 P–B3, N–B7!; 13 P–KN3, Q–R4!; 14 Q–K2, N–R6ch; 15 K–N2, P–B5! etc.

8 . . . .   P–KB4

9 PxP   . . . .

Routine play. In the Hastings Christmas Tournament of 1937–38, Alexander tried an interesting line against me: 9 QN–Q2!, NxN; 10 NxN, B–K2 (if 10 . . . P–K5; 11 P–KB3, P–Q4; 12 PxP, QPxP; 13 NxP!, PxN; 14 QxPch, B–K2; 15 B–N5 with a winning attack); 11 PxP, PxP; 12 N–B4 and White regains his Pawn with a good game.

9 . . . .   P–Q4
10 QN–Q2   B–B4!

An important move: the Bishop prevents N–Q4 and is posted more aggressively here than at K2. The move is timed just right, as White was just on the point of playing N–N3, necessitating the modest development . . . B–K2.

11 N–N3   B–N3

An interesting position. White really has no potentialities for constructive action, and his apparently strong KP is of little value. Black, on the other hand, with his open QN file and two Bishops, has really dynamic possibilities.

12 B–K3   P–B4

Rather a daring move, as the KB will be blockaded for some time to come. However, Black has faith in the future of this Bishop.

13 KN–Q2   . . . .

This at least succeeds in removing the enemy's well-posted Knight.

13 . . . .   NxN
14 NxN   O–O
15 P–KB4   P–QR4!

Creating a splendid diagonal for the QB.

16 R–B3   B–R3
17 P–B4   . . . .

Best under the circumstances, as it restrains Black's Pawns for some time, despite the fact that the QP becomes passed. If instead 17 Q–K1, P–Q5; 18 P–B2, P–B5 with catastrophic effects for White.

17 . . . .   P–R5!

This move has a double object: it prepares for pressure on the QN file, as White will soon be compelled to play P–QN3; and it also creates a square for the KB at R4.

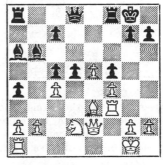

18 R–QB1   Q–K1
19 Q–K1   P–Q5
20 B–B2   B–R4

The KB comes into active play, and at the same time the QN file is made available to Black's Rooks.

21 Q–Q1   R–N1
22 P–QN3   . . . .

Creating a target for Black's Rooks; but the move can always be forced by ... Q–K3.

22 . . . .   B–N2

The QB is now more effective on the long diagonal.

23 R–N3   B–B3
24 B–K1   R–R1

This maneuvering phase is difficult for both players; at this point the QR file has replaced the QN file as a promising base of operations.

25 N–B3   . . . .

Since his pieces have so little scope, White is glad to exchange Bishops. However, his Knight proves no match for Black's QB in the ensuing play.

25 . . . .   BxB
26 NxB   PxP

27 QxNP   . . . .

After 27 PxP the game would proceed along much the same lines, except that White would have a weak QNP instead of a weak QRP.

27 . . . .   B–K5
28 N–Q3   . . . .

A fine post for the Knight: it blockades the passed Pawn and attacks Black's weak QBP. Black's task is now to combine attack on the QRP with defense of his QBP.

28 . . . .   R–R4
29 P–QR3   Q–K2

30 R–K1	Q–K3
31 N–B2	B–B3
32 Q–R2	P–R3
33 R–QB1	K–R2
34 N–Q3	KR–QR1

Before Black can undertake decisive action, he needs to rearrange his pieces. He intends to bring his Bishop to K3, where it will keep the hostile QBP under observation; meanwhile the Queen will be shifted to the Queen-side.

35 Q–K2	B–K5
36 N–B2	B–B3
37 N–Q3	R–QN1
38 Q–R5	B–K1
39 Q–Q1	R–N3
40 Q–Q2	R(3)–R3
41 Q–QB2	B–Q2
42 Q–N2	Q–QN3
43 Q–K2	Q–K3
44 Q–N2	Q–K2!

Now that the QBP is guarded a second time, ... RxP is threatened. Black has the proper formation sketched out, and the decisive phase is at hand.

45 R–R1   B–K3!
46 Q–B1   . . . .

White's Queen has been reduced to the lowly function of guarding two weak Pawns.

46 . . . .   Q–B1!
47 N–N2   Q–QR1!
48 P–QR4   . . . .

Now Black can attack both weak Pawns simultaneously with ...R–N3–N5. However, if 48 N–Q1, R–R5 wins: or 48 N–Q3, R–R5; 49 NxP?, RxBP etc.

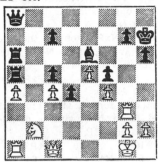

48	R–N3!
49 Q–B2	R–N5

White is now powerless against the coming ...Q–K5 or ...B–Q2.

| 50 R–N9 | Q–K5! |

This formidable centralizing move forces the following exchanges, with the result that Black secures three passed Pawns. The final winning process is extremely interesting.

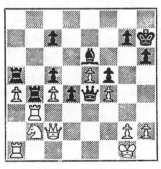

51 QxQ	PxQ
52 RxR	PxR
53 P–R3	P–R4
54 R–K1	P–K6
55 K–B1	P–N4!
56 R–Q1	P–B4
57 PxP	K–N3

White has to return the Pawn, and meanwhile Black's King comes into play advantageously.

58 K–K2	KxP
59 R–KB1	. . . .

Trying to keep Black's King from the center; but this exposes him to a stunning surprise.

59	RxP!!

This and the moves that follow, had to be calculated accurately.

60 P–R4ch!	K–N5!
61 NxR	BxPch
62 K–K1	. . . .

If now 62...BxR?; 63 KxB!, K–B4; 64 NxP, KxP; 65 P–N4!, PxP; 66 P–R5, K–B4; 67 K–K2 and White can draw! This variation shows the value of White's 60 P–R4ch! However, Black avoids this variation with:

62	P–Q6!!

The devastating threat of ...P–Q7ch leaves White little choice.

63 R–R1	P–Q7ch
64 K–Q1	B–N6ch
65 K–K2	BxN
66 P–K6	. . . .

Is the KP to become dangerous at last?!

66	K–B4
67 P–K7	K–K5!

Much clearer than 67...K–K3; 68 P–K8(Q)ch, BxQ; 69 KxP.

68 R–QN1	B–N4ch

69 K–Q1   K–Q5!
         Resigns

White resigns, as he has no defense against ... K–B6. If 70 R–N2, B–R5ch; 71 K–K2, P–Q8(Q) mate; or 70 R–R1, K–Q6 etc.

61.

HANAUER–RESHEVSKY
U. S. Championship, 1938

ENGLISH OPENING

M. Hanauer   Reshevsky
WHITE   BLACK

1 P–QB4   P–K4
2 N–QB3   N–QB3
3 N–B3   . . . .

Stronger is 3 P–KN3, P–KN3; 4 B–N2 followed by P–K3 and KN–K2.

3 . . . .   N–B3
4 P–KN3   B–N5!?

This is something of a novelty, the usual course being 4 ... P–Q4; 5 PxP, NxP; 6 B–N2, N–N3; 7 P–Q3, B–K2; 8 O–O, O–O; 9 B–K3, B–K3; 10 R–B1, P–B4 with chances for both sides (somewhat along the lines of Game 73.).

5 B–N2   . . . .

If there is any possibility of refuting Black's last move, it must consist in playing N–Q5 at this or a later point. As White plays, he gives his opponent no trouble.

5 . . . .   O–O
6 O–O   R–K1

6 ... P–Q4 looks good here, but it would not do because of 7 PxP, NxP; 8 NxP, KNxN; 9 NPxN and White emerges with a Pawn ahead.

7 P–Q3   . . . .

N–Q5 was still possible.

7 . . . .   BxN

This and the following move give Black a marked advantage.

8 PxB   P–K5!

Very strong. Black has conceded his opponent the advantage of two Bishops against a Bishop and Knight, but Black's demolition of White's Pawn structure is more than enough compensation.

9 N–N5   . . . .

9 PxP?, NxP is out of the question for White, but 9 N–Q4 might have been ventured.

9 . . . .   PxP
10 PxP   . . . .

Virtually forced, since 10 QxP? would leave him with a doubled and isolated QBP.

10 . . . .   P–KR3
11 N–K4   P–Q3
12 R–K1   . . . .

A very natural move, which, however, has serious consequences. R–N1 would have been better.

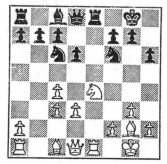

12 . . . .   B–N5!

This important move is the key to Black's plan.

13 P–B3   . . . .

Practically forced, but he has no good alternative. Thus if 13 NxN ch, QxN; 14 RxRch, RxR; 15 QxB (if 15 Q–Q2, N–K4 with an overwhelming game), QxP; 16 ·R–N1, QxQP! with the double threat of ... R–K8ch as well as ... QxR.

Other possibilities are: 13 Q–B2, N–K4; 14 N–Q2, B–B4 with a fine game for Black; or 13 B–B3, NxN;

14 RxN, RxR; 15 PxR, BxB; 16
QxB, Q–K2 and Black has practically a won endgame.

13	NxN!
14 QPxN	. . . .

White has had to submit to this
horrible weakening of his Pawns
after all; he had no choice.

14	B–K3
15 B–B1	. . . .

As will be seen, the effort to
guard the feeble QBPs is futile.

15	Q–B3

Decisive; if now 16 B–Q2, N–K4
wins a Pawn.

16 R–N1	P–QN3
17 P–B4	N–R4!

17 . . . QxQBP was also feasible,
but after 18 B–N2, Q–R4 the Queen
would be out of play and White
would have some attacking chances.
Since Black must win a Pawn in
any event, he is in no hurry and
prefers to increase the pressure
until the Pawn can be annexed in
the most advantageous manner.

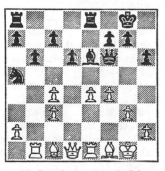

18 R–N5	P–R3
19 R–R5	. . . .

Realizing that his Pawn weaknesses must cost him the game,
White throws caution to the wind
and goes in for a desperate attack
which is easily repulsed.

19	QxQBP
20 B–K3	P–QB4

To prevent B–Q4.

21 P–B5	BxQBP
22 B–N2	P–Q4
23 BxRP	. . . .

A final attempt which is repulsed
easily enough.

23	PxB
24 Q–N4ch	K–B1
25 R–N1	Q–K6ch
26 K–R1	B–K7
27 Q–R4	BxR
28 Q–B6	N–B5
29 P–N4	BxP
Resigns	

62.

RESHEVSKY–SANTASIERE
U. S. Championship, 1938

GRUENFELD DEFENSE

Reshevsky	A. E. Santasiere
WHITE	BLACK
1 P–Q4	N–KB3
2 P–QB4	P–KN3
3 N–QB3	P–Q4
4 B–B4	. . . .

Beginning a plan of development
which is intended to cramp Black's
game. However, as in most variations of this defense, Black can
hold his own by alert counterplay.

4	B–N2
5 P–K3	O–O

Offering the sacrifice of a Pawn
by means of 6 PxP, NxP; 7 NxN,
QxN; 8 BxP. After 8 . . . N–B3; 9
N–K2 (stronger than 9 N–B3, B–B4
threatening . . . N–N5 with strong
attacking possibilities), B–N5; 10
P–B3, BxP; 11 PxB, QxBP; 12 KR–
N1, QxP, Black has three Pawns
and attacking chances for the piece.
So far all the games in which this
variation has been played have ended in victory for Black, and while
these results are not conclusive,
they show he has good prospects.

6 Q–N3   . . . .

In order to force Black's hand. For 6 R–B1 see Game 68.

6 . . . .   PxP
7 KBxP   QN–Q2
8 N–B3   N–N3
9 B–K2   B–K3
10 Q–B2   KN–Q4

Simpler is 10 ... QN–Q4; 11 B–K5, P–QB4! ; 12 PxP, Q–R4 winning back the Pawn with a level position.

11 B–K5   . . . .

B–N3 is often played here, but the text has the merit of neutralizing any pressure by Black's fianchettoed Bishop.

11 . . . .   R–B1!

A good move; Black wants to free his game with ... P–QB4, the thematic move of this variation.

12 NxN   . . . .

12 O–O would of course be answered by ... P–QB4.

12 . . . .   QxN

Simpler and better than 12 ... NxN; 13 BxB, KxB; 14 P–K4, with marked advantage for White.

13 BxB   KxB?

13 ... Q–R4ch! would have given Black equality. The inaccurate text lands Black in difficulties.

14 P–QN4!   . . . .

Establishing a powerful bind on QB5 and thus preventing ... P–QB4. White's position is now superior.

14 . . . .   B–B4

Necessary, for if 14 ... N–B5?; 15 P–K4! Q–QN4 (if 15 ... N–R6; 16 Q–Q3 wins a piece); 16 Q–B3 forcing the win of a piece as there is no defense against the threatened advance of the QP.

15 Q–N2   N–B5
16 Q–N3   N–N3

16 ... P–QN4? would be a serious blunder, because eventually White would exchange or drive back the advanced Knight, leaving the critical weaknesses on the QB file exposed to crushing pressure.

17 Q–B3   Q–Q3

Threatening to win a Pawn by ... N–Q4.

18 P–QR3   N–Q4
19 Q–N2   B–N5

The attempt to free himself with 19 ... P–N3; 20 O–O, K–N1; 21 KR–Q1, P–QB4 would turn out badly after 22 QPxP etc.

20 O–O   . . . .

White has fully consolidated his position and is now ready for action on the Queen-side.

20 . . . .   P–QB3

This is inevitable, but it has the drawback of inviting an advance of White's Pawns on the Queen's wing.

21 KR–B1   P–B3
22 R–B5   P–K3
23 QR–QB1   . . . .

White steadily strengthens his position.

23 . . . .   P–QR3
24 P–QR4   Q–N1

In order to take the sting out of P–N5. But White has other plans.

25 P–R3!   . . . .

Forcing the following exchange.

25 . . . .   BxN
26 BxB   KR–Q1
27 Q–N3   P–B4

In order to safeguard the Knight against P–K4. But this move does not achieve the desired result.

28 P–N3   K–B3
29 K–N2   P–R3
30 P–R4   . . . .

Realizing that Black cannot improve his position and may easily go wrong, White is content to strengthen his game and await new developments.

30 . . . .   P–KN4?

A mistake which gives White just the opportunity he was waiting for.

31 P–K4!   . . . ..

This breaks the position wide open for an effective exploitation of Black's many weaknesses and the exposed state of his King.

01	BPxP
32 PxPch	PxP
33 BxP	. . . .

Threatening to win quickly with 34 Q–B3ch, K–K2; 35 Q–N4, R–N1; 36 R–K1 etc.

33	K–K2
34 R–K1	K–Q3
35 BxN!	KPxB

If 35...BPxB; 36 Q–K3 wins in short order.

36 R–K5!	R–N1

Black cannot afford to lose the valuable KNP, but ...

37 R(B5)xQPch! PxR

38 QxPch	K–B2
39 Q–B5ch	. . . .

But not 39 R–K7ch?, K–N3 and Black's King escapes.

39	K–Q2
40 Q–K7ch	K–B3
41 Q–K6ch	Resigns

For after 41...Q–Q3; 42 R–B5ch he loses the Queen, while 41...K–B2; 42 R–B5ch, K–Q1; 43 R–Q5ch leads to mate.

63.

KASHDAN–RESHEVSKY
U. S. Championship, 1938

CATALAN SYSTEM

I. Kashdan	Reshevsky
WHITE	BLACK
1 N–KB3	P–Q4
2 P–Q4	N–KB3
3 P–B4	P–K3
4 P–KN3	PxP

This undoubtedly constitutes the best system of defense for Black.

5 Q–R4ch	QN–Q2
6 B–N2	P–QR3
7 QxBP	P–B4

A good alternative is 7...P–QN4, as in my Nottingham game with Capablanca: 8 Q–B6 (the immediate retreat is preferable), R–R2!; 9 B–B4, B–N2; 10 Q–B1 (if 10 QxP??, QxQ; 11 BxQ, BxN wins a piece), P–B4 etc.

8 O–O	. . . .

Even after 8 P–QR4 Black could still reply ...P–QN4!

8	P–QN4
9 Q–Q3	. . . .

The Queen is exposed here; hence Q–B2 was preferable.

9	B–N2
10 P–QR4	. . . .

The familiar maneuver to weaken Black's Pawn structure.

10	P–N5

11 QN–Q2   . . . .

White has a fine square for his QN at B4, but Black also has excellent possibilities. It must be admitted that Black has come out of the opening very well.

11 . . . .   PxP

This move, obvious and played as a matter of course, is nevertheless valuable since it gains time.

12 QxQP   . . . .

And not 12 NxP?, N–K4; 13 Q–K3, KN–N5; 14 Q–B4, P–N4! and White's Queen is trapped!

12 . . . .   B–B4
13 Q–R4   . . . .

Apparently looking forward to the exchange of Queens, which will, however, be somewhat in Black's favor.

13 . . . .   O–O
14 P–N3   . . . .

This creates a permanent weakness at QB3 which plagues White for the remainder of the game. However, Kashdan's desire to complete his development is readily understandable.

14 . . . .   N–Q4!
15 QxQ   KRxQ
16 B–N2   N–B6

The Knight's invasion is very annoying for White, but capturing it is out of the question.

17 KR–K1   QR–B1
18 QR–B1   N–B3
19 P–K3   . . . .

At last threatening to capture twice on B3, now that . . . BxPch is prevented.

19 . . . .   B–R2
20 N–B4   . . . .

Thus far Kashdan has defended himself ably in a trying situation. Black cannot support the advanced Knight by 20 . . . N(3)–K5, for then 21 N–N5 is difficult to meet.

20 . . . .   N(6)–K5
21 N–N5   B–Q4!
22 NxN   NxN
23 KR–Q1   . . . .

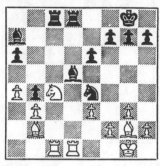

23 . . . .   P–B3

23 . . . BxN looks attractive here, but it turns out poorly: 24 RxRch, RxR; 25 RxB, R–Q8ch; 26 B–B1, RxBch; 27 KxR, N–Q7ch; 28 K–K2, NxR; 29 PxN, P–QR4 (else P–R5); 30 B–K5, B–N3; 31 B–Q6 wins.

24 K–B1   K–B1

And here 24 . . . BxNch; 25 PxB is less promising than it seems:

I 25 . . . N–Q7ch; 26 K–K2, NxP?; 27 RxRch followed by 28 RxN.

II 25 . . . RxRch; 26 RxR, RxP?; 27 BxN, RxB; 28 R–Q8ch, K–B2; 29 R–Q7ch winning a piece.

III 25 . . . N–B4; 26 B–Q4 and White forces Bishops of opposite colors with a very likely draw.

25 B–Q4   BxB
26 RxB   . . . .

On 26 PxB? N–B6 would be a crushing reply.

26 . . . .   N–Q7ch!

On 26 . . . BxNch White would have replied 27 QRxB with a satisfactory game — but not 27 PxB?, RxR; 28 PxR, N–Q7ch; 29 K–K2, N–N6!; 30 R–QN1, NxPch; 31 K–Q3, R–Q1! etc.

27 RxN   BxBch
28 K–K1   RxR

29 KxR	B–Q4

Threatening to capture on QB5 followed by ... P–QR4. The strongly protected passed Pawn would then give Black very promising winning chances.

30 K–Q3	P–K4
31 P–K4	B–K3

Hereabouts the time pressure had already become very acute!

32 R–B2	K–K2
33 N–Q2	RxR
34 KxR	....

White must now play with great care—for which, alas! he has no time. Black's Bishop is stronger than the Knight, and has a fine target in the weak QNP. In addition, Black's King will try to force an entry via Q5.

34	K–Q3
35 K–Q3	K–B4
36 K–K3	P–N3
37 K–Q3	P–B4

38 P–B3? ....

The time pressure proves White's undoing. Correct was 38 P–B4! and White draws.

38	P–B5!

This wins. White's King no longer has access to K3 and must therefore permit the entry of Black's King at Q5.

39 PxP	PxP

In addition to his other advantages, Black will now be able to force a distant passed Pawn on the King-side.

40 P–KR4	....

Else Black plays ... P–N4 followed by ... P–KR4.

40	P–R3
41 P–QR5	B–Q2
42 K–B2	....

White's King must give way. If 42 N–B4, B–N4; 43 P–K5, K–Q4; 44 K–B2, BxN; 45 PxBch, KxKP; 46 K–N3, P–N4; 47 PxP, PxP; 48 KxP, P–N5 and wins.

42	K–Q5
43 N–B4	B–K3
44 N–Q2	K–K6
45 K–Q1	K–B7
46 K–B2	K–K7

White's position is quite hopeless.

47 K–B1	P–R4!
48 P–K5	P–N4
49 N–K4	PxP
50 N–N5	P–R6
51 NxB	P–R7
52 NxPch	KxP
Resigns	

Perhaps it was a consolation to Kashdan to be beaten by a Bishop!

64.

RESHEVSKY–SIMONSON
U. S. Championship, 1938

Brilliancy Prize Game

QUEEN'S GAMBIT DECLINED

Reshevsky	A. C. Simonson
WHITE	BLACK
1 P–Q4	P–Q4
2 P–QB4	P–QB3
3 N–KB3	N–B3
4 N–B3	PxP
5 P–K3	....

5 P–QR4 is the customary move here, but I prefer the text because it gains a move for White and

avoids creating a weakness at QN4.
The idea behind P–QR4 is to prevent ... P–QN4, but, as the next
note indicates, this is not abso-
lutely necessary.

    5 . . . .   B–B4

For 5 ... P–QN4 see Game 101.

    6 BxP   P–K3
    7 O–O   QN–Q2
    8 P–KR3   . . . .

In order to prevent ... B–KN5 as
a possible reply to an eventual
P–K4.

    8 . . . .   B–Q3

In order to be able to play ... P–
K4 later on; but the subsequent
course of the game demonstrates
that this advance will either be impossible or disadvantageous. Hence
it would have been wiser to play
... B–K2.

    9 Q–K2   N–K5

White was threatening to win a
piece with P–K4–5.

If 9 ... P–K4; 10 P–K4, B–N3; 11
PxP, NxP; 12 NxN, BxN; 13 P–B4!
and if 13 ... BxN; 14 PxB with the
double threat of P–B5 and B–R3.

    10 N–Q2!   . . . .

Beginning a struggle for control
of K4 which must end in White's
favor.

    10 . . . .   QN–B3
    11 KNxN   NxN

    12 B–Q3   NxN

Black has no choice.

    13 PxN   BxB
    14 QxB   O–O

Or 14 ... P–K4; 15 P–K4, O–O;
16 P–KB4! with a very strong
game.

    15 R–N1   Q–K2
    16 P–KB4   . . . .

To prevent ... P–K4 once for all.

    16 . . . .   KR–Q1

If instead 16 .. P–KB4; 17 P–K4
and Black's KP is a permanent
weakness.

    17 P–K4   Q–Q2

... P–B3 should have been tried
here in an effort to stem the advance of White's KP.

    18 P–K5   . . . .

Now White has secured a formidable position, as he will be able
to concentrate his forces against
the hostile King.

    18 . . . .   B–B1
    19 P–B5   . . . .

Forcing the opening of the KB
file, which gives White a lasting
attack.

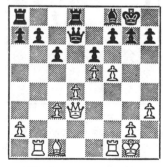

    19 . . . .   PxP
    20 RxP   P–QN3

After 20 ... P–B4 White would
have a strong continuation in 21
B–N5, B–K2; 22 BxB, QxB; 23 Q–
K4! followed by P–Q5.

    21 B–N5   B–K2

22 QR–KB1	BxB
23 RxB	R–K1
24 Q–N3!	. . . .

An important move which forces a serious weakness in Black's King-side. Despite the considerable amount of simplification which has already taken place, White is still able to exert far from negligible pressure.

24	P–N3
25 R(5)–B5	R–K2
26 R(5)–B4	R–Q1
27 Q–N5	Q–K1

Black finds himself in an extremely unpleasant position. The awkward text is the only parry to the nasty threat of Q–R6 and R–R4.

28 R–R4	Q–B1
29 R(1)–B4	R(1)–Q2
30 R–B6	R–K3
31 R(4)–B4	Q–R6?

True to his enterprising style, Simonson loses patience and strikes out aggressively. He undoubtedly underestimated the possibilities in the position.

32 K–R2!	. . . .

The value of this move will be seen later: after an eventual P–Q5, it prevents Black's Queen from (a) returning to B4 with a check, or else (b) from pinning White's QR should it go to Q4. This note can only be properly understood after a study of the remaining play.

32	RxR

32 . . . QxRP would not do because of 33 P–Q5!

33 QxR	QxRP

Apparently overlooking White's crushing reply; but he could not defend himself against the double threat of P–K6 and QxP.

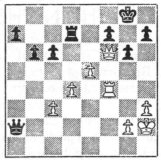

34 P–Q5!!	. . . .

A problem-like move: the Pawn is offered in three ways, and each mode of capture would be disastrous: 34 . . . RxP?; 35 QxBPch and mate next move; 34 . . . PxP; 35 P–K6 and wins; 34 . . . QxP; 35 R–Q4 and wins (see the note to White's thirty-second move!)

34	R–N2

There was no satisfactory defense.

35 PxP	. . . .

Another way was 35 P–K6, QxP; 36 R–Q4 and wins.

35	R–N1
36 P–B4	. . . .

Cutting off Black's Queen and thus putting an end to all resistance.

36	Q–K7

Or 36 . . . R–KB1; 37 P–K6 winning quickly.

37 QxBPch	K–R1
38 P–B7	R–QB1
39 Q–B6ch	Resigns

The play with the "heavy" pieces has been very interesting.

AVRO TOURNAMENT, THE NETHERLANDS, 1938

THE AVRO Tournament was conducted by the General Dutch Broadcasting Company (the letters A.V.R.O. stand for the name of this Company, in Dutch) on the assumption that the player other than Alekhine who placed highest in this tournament could claim the right to play for the world championship title. The eight players who participated — Alekhine, Botvinnik, Capablanca, Euwe, Fine, Flohr, Keres, and the writer — were, in the judgment of the tournament committee, the leading players of the world.

When the tournament began, however, Alekhine announced that there had been a misunderstanding and that while he was willing to encounter any of his fellow contestants who would comply with his known conditions, he would feel under no obligation to play the winner of this tournament in a title match.

At that time, the chess championship of the world was considered the personal property of the titleholder. There was no international chess body with sufficient authority to hold a championship tournament or to put the championship at stake in any other manner. The world's champion put his title into competition only when a challenger was able and willing to put up a sufficiently large purse. It will be remembered that this was the condition which obtained in the United States prior to 1936.

In a "mixed" tournament one occasionally encounters a comparatively weak player and then gets a much needed breathing spell. In the AVRO Tournament, however, there were no weak spots: every player was of world championship calibre and each was out to do his best.

The world championship matches of 1935 and 1936 between Alekhine and Euwe had been played in many different towns. Similarly, the AVRO Tournament was so arranged that we played for three weeks with little rest, and each round in a different town. Some of the older masters found the physical strain more than they could contend with.

65.

EUWE–RESHEVSKY
Avro Tournament, 1938

KING'S INDIAN DEFENSE

Dr. M. Euwe	Reshevsky
WHITE	BLACK
1 P–Q4	N–KB3
2 P–QB4	P–KN3
3 P–B3	. . . .

A fighting move despite its modest appearance. White avoids the Gruenfeld Defense and at the same time he intends to build up a strong center formation; thus if 3 . . . B–N2; 4 P–K4, P–Q3; 5 B–K3, O–O; 6 N–K2 etc.

| 3 . . . . | P–Q4 |

Black accepts the challenge. He provokes the following aggressive occupation of the center in order to loosen up White's Pawn structure. Whether this policy should succeed is not certain; but at any rate, it leads to interesting chess.

4 PxP	NxP
5 P–K4	N–N3
6 N–B3	B–N2
7 B–K3	O–O
8 P–Q4	. . . .

White must continue to play aggressively; the text prevents . . . P–K4.

| 8 . . . . | N–B3 |

Practically forcing the following advance, since 9 N–B3 would be answered by 9 . . . B–N5.

| 9 P–Q5 | N–N1 |
| 10 N–B3 | . . . . |

Not the best. Black is now ready to attack the center with . . . P–QB3 or . . . P–K3. White should therefore continue to try to force the play with 10 B–Q4 and if 10 . . . P–QB3; 11 BxB, KxB; 12 Q–Q4ch, P–B3; 13 O–O–O, PxP; 14 PxP with fighting chances for both players. As the game goes, Euwe soon has cause to regret his failure to eliminate the hostile KB.

| 10 . . . . | P–QB3 |
| 11 Q–N3 | . . . . |

The play which results from this move is anything but favorable to White; it would therefore have been better to simplify with 11 PxP etc.

11	PxP
12 NxP	NxN
13 PxN	N–Q2

One can see that Euwe's treatment of the opening has turned out to be a fiasco; his lead in development has disappeared, and his QP and general situation in the center are deplorably shaky.

| 14 B–K2 | . . . . |

| 14 . . . . | Q–R4ch! |

This well timed check comes just at the right moment, for White was on the point of castling. If 15 N–Q2, N–N3 is a troublesome move to meet, while if 15 K–B2, N–B3 attacks the QP and threatens . . . N–N5ch at the same time.

| 15 B–Q2 | Q–N3! |

This powerful move prevents White from castling King-side and also threatens to win a Pawn at once. Nor would White be too happy after 16 O–O–O, N–B4 followed by . . . B–B4 with withering pressure against his exposed King.

16 B–B3   BxBch

Again forcing White's hand, for if 17 QxB, N–B3; 18 R–Q1, R–Q1; 19 B–B4, B–N5 followed by ... QR–B1 with a winning position.

17 PxB   Q–K6!
18 P–B4   . . . .

He has no choice, for if 18 P–N3, N–B4; 19 Q–B2, B–B4 and wins.

18 . . . .   QxP
19 O–O   Q–B2
20 K–R1   N–B3
21 Q–K3   . . . .

As he has no compensation for the Pawn, Euwe strives to build up an attack.

21 . . . .   B–N5!

Black exchanges this Bishop, for it has no good square.

22 Q–R6   BxN
23 RxB   P–QN4!

Taking advantage of the momentary disorganization of White's forces, Black breaks up the hostile Pawn formation.

24 PxP   Q–K4!
25 R–K1   NxP
26 R–KR3   Q–N2
27 Q–Q2   P–K3
28 R–Q3   . . . .

28 B–B3, KR–K1 would leave White's KR out of play.

28 . . . .   QR–N1

In order to take the sting out of B–B3.

29 P–QR4   N–N3
30 Q–N4   . . . .

Too slow; he should have tried 30 P–R5, N–Q4; 31 R–QN3 and the Queen-side majority would still create technical difficulties for Black.

30 . . . .   QR–B1
31 P–R5   N–Q4
32 Q–N3   R–B4

Black is now in a much better position to handle the hostile Pawns; and White's next move

gives him an opportunity to banish all further danger.

33 B–B3   R–N1
34 BxN   R(4)xP!

But not 34 ... R(1)xP! which would give White a chance for a fine "swindle" with 35 BxP!

35 Q–R2   PxB
36 RxP   Q–B6
37 R–KB1   R–N7

Now Black has the initiative well in hand and he can work out the final winning process at his leisure.

38 Q–R4   R–N8
39 R(5)–Q1   RxR
40 RxR   P–QR3!
41 P–R3   R–N4
42 R–R1   K–N2
43 Q–R2   Q–N7
44 Q–R4   . . . .

The exchange offers White no prospect of drawing; his Rook would be tied to the defense of the QRP.

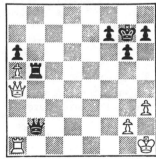

44 . . . .   R–N4!

The winning idea. White is hampered in his defense of the King by the need for guarding the QRP.

45 R–R2   Q–B6
46 R–R1   P–R4
47 Q–R2   R–KB4
48 K–R2   P–N4!

The advance of the King-side Pawns will expose White's King to an overwhelming attack.

49 Q–R4   R–B5

50	Q–R2	P–N5
51	PxP	Q–K4!
52	P–N3	. . . .

To retreat the King would not be good enough, as Black would win with ... PxP and ... P–N6.

52	. . . .	R–K5
53	Q–N1	R–K7ch
54	K–R3	. . . .

If the King goes to the first rank, Black mates in short order.

54	. . . .	PxPch
55	K–R4	. . . .

Or 55 KxP, R–K5ch; 56 K–R3 (if 56 K–B3, R–K6ch), Q–R4ch etc.

55	. . . .	R–R7ch
56	KxP	Q–K7ch
	Resigns	

White resigns, as mate is unavoidable. Once more inferior opening play has proved disastrous.

66.

RESHEVSKY–FLOHR
Avro Tournament, 1938

G R U E N F E L D   D E F E N S E

Reshevsky	S. Flohr
WHITE	BLACK
1 P–Q4	N–KB3
2 P–QB4	P–KN3
3 N–QB3	P–Q4

A favorite defense with Flohr.

4 Q–N3	P–B3
5 N–B3	B–N2
6 P–K3	. . . .

This move is less conservative than it seems! For the alternative B–B4, see Game 68.

6	O–O
7 B–Q2	P–K3
8 B–Q3	. . . .

R–B1 is usually played here, but the text indicates that White is angling for an early P–K4.

8	P–N3

9 O–O	B–N2
10 QR–Q1	QN–Q2
11 PxP	KPxP

The recapture with the BP would prevent P–K4, but after 12 N–QN5, threatening B–N4 in conjunction with N–Q6, Black's game would be extremely uncomfortable.

12 P–K4	PxP

Here or on the next move, Black could introduce almost unforeseeable complications with ... P–B4.

13 NxP	NxN
14 BxN	N–B3
15 B–B2	N–Q4

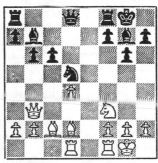

Black seems to have profited by the advance of the KP, for he has an unassailable Knight at Q4, and White's QP is isolated. A closer examination of the position indicates, however, that there are also advantageous factors for White: he has a strong point for his pieces at K5 and Black's QB remains sadly out of play.

16 KR–K1	R–K1
17 B–Q3	Q–Q2
18 Q–R4	RxRch
19 RxR	P–QR3?

Seriously weakening his position. ... R–Q1 should have been tried, although after 20 N–K5 (not 20 QxRP??, R–R1) White's prospects would have remained promising.

20 R–QB1	Q–Q3

21 Q–N3	R–QB1
22 P–QR4	P–R3?

Altogether too passive. . . . P–QB4 could have been ventured here or on the next move.

23 B–K4	R–K1?
24 BxN!	. . . .

There is no harm in letting Black have the two Bishops, as his QB will be worthless for the rest of the game.

24	PxB
25 N–K5!	. . . .

This unexpected move gives White a strong initiative.

25	R–QB1

25 . . . BxN; 26 PxB, QxP (if 26 . . . RxP; 27 B–B4); 27 QxNP would lose a Pawn for Black and leave him with a dreadful weakness on his black squares.

26 R–K1	R–K1
27 P–R3	. . . .

In such positions, it is always useful to create a flight square for one's King, so as to assure freedom of action for the Rook.

27	R–K3

Again . . . BxN would lead to the loss of a Pawn because of the resulting unprotected state of the KRP.

28 P–B4	Q–K2
29 R–QB1	K–R2

Preparing to drive off the Knight with . . . P–B3. But now White forces the pace.

30 B–N4!	. . . .

In this way White seizes control of the seventh rank.

30	Q–R5

So that if 31 R–B7, QxBP; 32 RxB, QxPch etc.

31 Q–KB3	BxN

The threat of R–B7 leaves Black little choice; if 31 . . . P–B3??; 32 B–K1, Q–R4; 33 P–KN4 wins the Queen!

32 BPxB!!	. . . .

This move (instead of the prosaic 32 QPxB, which would have been answered by . . . R–QB3) must have taken White by surprise. If now 32 . . . QxPch; 33 K–R1, K–N1; 34 R–B7, P–B4; 35 B–B3 and wins.

32	P–B4
33 R–B7ch	K–N1
34 Q–B3	. . . .

Another winning method was 34 Q–B2 forcing a won ending.

34	R–QB3

Either this or . . . B–B3 is forced. Black cannot avoid a decisive loss of material.

35 RxR	BxR
36 K–R1!	Q–B7

If instead 36 . . . BxP; 37 Q–B8ch, K–R2; 38 Q–B7ch, K–N1; 39 P–K6, Q–B3; 40 Q–B8ch, K–R2; 41 P–Q6 and wins; or 36 . . . B–N2; 37 Q–B7, Q–B7; 38 Q–N8ch! winning the Bishop with a check.

37 QxB	Q–B8ch

It is true that White must now return the Bishop to avoid a draw, but he still has an easy win.

38 K–R2	Q–B5ch
39 K–N1	QxPch
40 K–R1	QxB

Black is actually a Pawn ahead! But this is at once reversed.

41 QxNPch	K–R1
42 QxPch	K–N1

43 Q–N6ch   K–R1
44 Q–B6ch   Resigns

For after 44 ... K–N1; 45 QxP
White has an easy win.

67.

FINE–RESHEVSKY
Avro Tournament, 1938

RUY LOPEZ

R. Fine   Reshevsky
WHITE   BLACK

1	P–K4	P–K4
2	N–KB3	N–QB3
3	B–N5	P–QR3
4	B–R4	N–B3
5	O–O	B–K2
6	R–K1	P–QN4
7	B–N3	P–Q3
8	P–B3	N–QR4
9	B–B2	P–B4
10	P–Q4	Q–B2
11	P–KR3	....

If White wants to advance the
QRP, he should proceed with 11 P–
QR4. In that event 11 ... QR–N1 or
11 ... P–N5 is virtually forced, for
if 11 ... O–O?; 12 RPxP, RPxP; 13
P–QN4 wins.

11 . . . .   O–O
12 P–QR4   B–QB1

Now that Black has castled, this
excellent developing move protects
him from the threat mentioned
above.

13 QN–Q2?   . . . .

Black has no trouble in demon-
strating the inferior character of
this move. There is apparently
nothing better than 13 RPxP or 13
P–Q5.

13 . . . .   BPxP!
14 BPxP   KR–B1!
15 B–Q3   . . . .

He decides to surrender the QRP
—a plausible idea, for Black's QRP
does not give the impression of be-

ing very strong, while the alternative 15 RPxP, QxB; 16 QxQ, RxQ;
17 RxN, BxP, as in my match with
Kashdan, is very promising for
Black and allows White only drawing chances at best.

15 . . . .   NPxP

Contrary to White's expectations,
both QRPs play a useful role
throughout the game!

16 Q–K2   N–R4!

A strong move which gives
White little choice. Thus if 17
BxP?, KN–B5; 18 Q–B1, RxB!; 19
QxR, R–N1! and White is helpless
against the threat of ... B–QN4. If
17 N–B1, N–QN6 is a powerful re-
ply; while 17 NxP? is refuted by
... N–KB5.

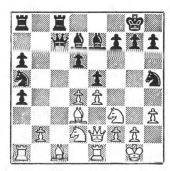

17 P–KN3   KR–N1

Black wants to exert pressure on
the QN file so as to make it difficult for White to develop his QB.
At the same time, the text guards
the QRP indirectly, since 18 BxP??,
RxB; 19 QxR, B–QN4 would be
fatal for White.

17 ... BxP would be weak, as
White would reply 18 BxP followed
by RxP.

18 K–N2   P–N3
19 R–R3   PxP

Opening up the position advantageously, as the KB will be
formidable on the long diagonal.

20 NxP	B–KB3
21 QN–B3	Q–N3
22 Q–Q2	N–B3

Maintaining the pressure; 22...
BxN; 23 NxB, QxN; 24 QxN would
greatly improve White's prospects,
in view of the weakening of Black's
black squares. If instead 22...N–
N6; 23 NxN, PxN; 24 B–B4 and
the QNP falls.

| 23 N–B2 | .... |

Since 23 NxN, BxN would give
Black too comfortable a game, Fine
prefers to play for complications.

| 23 .... | Q–R4 |

Reducing the position to an ending is a much simpler course than
23...BxNP; 24 BxB, QxB; 25 P–
N4, N–B3; 26 Q–B4, N–K1; 27 B–B4,
B–K3; 28 R–R2 and the position is
rather unclear.

| 24 QxQ | NxQ |
| 25 P–K5 | .... |

Advancing desperately in order
to obtain more room for his pieces,
but this works both ways: Black
also benefits.

25	PxP
26 NxP	B–K1
27 P–KN4	N–KN2

Black is not troubled by this retreat, as the Knight will soon be
posted more advantageously.

| 28 N–Q4 | R–Q1 |
| 29 N(4)–B3 | .... |

After 29 B–Q2, N–N6! is a strong
reply.

29	B–K2
30 R–R2	N–K3
31 B–B1	....

The position of the Bishop was
beginning to get too precarious, but
the text is the first of a series of
moves which reduce White's mobility to the vanishing point.

| 31 .... | N–N6 |
| 32 B–K3 | B–N5 |

Now Black's Bishops begin to as-

sert themselves. If 33 R–K2, R–Q8
with the terrible threat of...B–N4.

| 33 R–N1 | P–QR4 |
| 34 K–N1 | .... |

White wants to play N–Q3, but
this cannot be done at once because of the reply 34...B–B3 with
a nasty pin. Hence the text.

34	K–N2
35 B–K2	P–B3
36 N–B4	....

The alternative 36 N–Q3 is an-
swered by 36...B–N4; 37 R–Q1,
QR–B1; 38 NxB, BxB; 39 RxR, Nx
R winning a piece.

36	B–N4
37 K–B1	QR–B1
38 N–N6	BxBch
39 KxB	R–B7ch
40 K–B1	P–R6!

| 41 PxP | .... |

If instead 41 N–B4, RxN; 42 PxP,
N–B8!; 43 BxN, R–Q8ch; 44 K–N2,
R(8)xB; 45 RxR, RxR; 46 PxB, Px
P; 47 R–N2, N–B5ch; 48 K–N3, N–
Q6 and wins. 44 K–K2 would be no
better in this variation.

| 41 .... | RxR |
| 42 PxB | R–Q6! |

Much stronger than 42...P–R5;
43 NxP etc.

| 43 PxP | .... |

43 N–K1? would be a blunder because of 43...RxB!; 44 PxR, N–
Q7ch.

43 . . . .   RxP

The straightforward winning course was 43 . . . N–N4! and if 44 BxN, RxN; 45 B–K3, RxB! or 44 NxN, RxB; 25 PxR, N–Q7ch and wins.

44 K–N2   R–R7
45 K–N3   N(3)–B4?

And here again Black misses a quick win with 45 . . . P–B4! If then 46 R–KB1, P–B5ch; 47 BxP, NxB; 48 KxN, R–R3; 49 N–B8, R–B3ch and wins.

46 R–K1   N–K5ch
47 K–N2   R–B7
48 N–QR4   P–B4
49 PxP   PxP
50 N–K5   R–Q4
51 N–KB3   K–B3

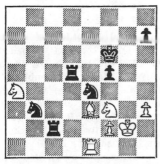

White's mobility is being steadily reduced.

52 R–QN1   R–R4?

52 . . . P–B5! was the move to win. If then 53 B–R7, R–QR4! wins; or 53 RxN, PxB; 54 RxP, RxPch; 55 K–N1, R–Q8ch; 56 N–K1 R–B5 and wins.

53 RxN   RxN
54 R–N6ch   K–K2
55 N–Q4   . . . .

Here White overstepped the time limit, in a drawn position. It is a pity that the final phase was ruined by acute time pressure. Despite the fact that neither player has been seen at his best, this game has its interesting qualities and instructive aspects.

68.

CAPABLANCA–RESHEVSKY
Avro Tournament, 1938

G R U E N F E L D D E F E N S E

J. R. Capablanca   Reshevsky
WHITE   BLACK

1 P–Q4   N–KB3
2 P–QB4   P–KN3
3 N–QB3   P–Q4
4 B–B4   . . . .

At present considered the most aggressive line of play.

4 . . . .   B–N2
5 P–K3   O–O
6 R–B1   . . . .

White's best move is 6 Q–N3, which forces Black to decide whether he wants to play defensively with . . . P–B3 or energetically with 6 . . . P–B4!? (see Game 96).

The win of a Pawn with 6 PxP, NxP; 7 NxN, QxN; 8 BxP is discussed in the notes to Game 62.

6 . . . .   P–B4!

This was just the move that 6 R–B1 was intended to prevent! It took me no less than fifty minutes to decide on this move, which leads to almost unfathomable complications.

7 QPxP   . . . .

If 7 BPxP, NxP; 8 PxP (if 8 NxN, QxN; 9 RxP, QxRP with a satisfactory position), NxN; 9 QxQ, RxQ; 10 PxN, N–B3 and Black has the better game for the following reasons: (a) he can regain his Pawn advantageously; (b) his development is definitely preferable; (c) White's Pawns are badly scattered.

Another good reply to 7 BPxP is ...PxP and if 8 QxP, NxP!

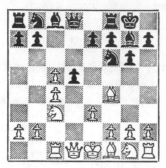

7 . . . .   Q–R4

The Russians have devoted a good deal of fascinating analysis to this defense; an example is the line of play adopted by Botvinnik in 1940 in his match with Ragozin: 7...B–K3!; 8 N–B3 (if 8 PxP; Nx P; 9 NxN, BxN; 10 P–QN3, Q–R4ch; 11 Q–Q2, QxQch; 12 KxQ, R–Q1, 13 K–K1, P–QR4! with a splendid game for Black), N–B3; 9 Q–R4, N–K5! with a very complicated game not unfavorable for Black.

8 PxP   R–Q1
9 Q–R4   . . . .

If 9 Q–Q2, NxP!; 10 B–B7?!, QxB; 11 NxN, RxN!; 12 QxR, B–K3; 13 Q–Q2, N–B3; 14 R–Q1, R–Q1; 15 Q–B1, Q–R4ch (Tolush—Botvinnik, USSR Championship, 1939) and Black's lead in development wins.

9 B–QB4 leads to unclear play, for example 9...B–K3; 10 PxB!?, RxQch; 11 RxR, PxP; 12 BxPch, K–B1.

9 . . . .   QxQ
10 NxQ   NxP
11 B–QN5   . . . .

There is no time to withdraw the QB, for if 11 B–N3, B–Q2!; 12 N–QB3, NxN; 13 PxN, B–QB3; 14 N–B3, N–Q2 regaining the Pawn with a vastly superior position.

11 . . . .   NxB
12 PxN   B–K3
13 P–QN3   B–Q4
14 N–KB3   . . . .

If 14 P–B3, N–B3; 15 N–QB3 (or 15 N–K2, N–N5), N–Q5; 16 NxB, NxB and if 17 NxPch, K–B1 winning the Knight.

14 . . . .   BxN

Black is in too much of a hurry to give his opponent a tripled Pawn. Further development with 14...N–B3 would have been excellent here, for if 15 O–O, BxN; 16 PxB, N–Q5 winning back the Pawn with a fine game.

15 PxB   N–B3

Here again...B–R3! would have won back the Pawn.

16 BxN   PxB
17 K–K2   B–R3

If instead 17...R–Q5; 18 KR–Q1, QR–Q1 (18...RxP is bad, for after 19 R–Q7 Black's QR is completely tied down; by doubling his Rooks on the Q file, White gets complete control of the seventh rank); 19 RxR, RxR; 20 R–Q1 and Black can hardly afford to take the Pawn because of 21 R–Q7.

Promising, however, was 17...P–K4; 18 PxP, BxP and White is unable to challenge the Q file immediately—for if 19 QR–Q1, RxR; 20 KxR (if 20 RxR, BxP; 21 R–Q7, B–B5 and the passed Pawn becomes very dangerous), R–Q1ch; 21 K–K2, B–B5 followed by 22... R–Q7 with a won game. Therefore, White is compelled to play 19 P–KR3 (instead of 19 QR–Q1), when Black continues simply 19...P–B4; 20 KR–Q1, K–B2. If White exchanges both Rooks, the position is in Black's favor — despite his Pawn down — because White's Knight is out of play.

18 R–B4 . . . .
Now this move is possible.
18 . . . . **P–K4**
Best under the circumstances.
19 PxP **R–Q7ch**
20 K–B1 **RxRP**
21 K–N2 . . . .
21 N–B3 would not be good because of 21 . . . R–N7 and if 22 P–N4?, R–B7 followed by . . . B–Q7 and wins.
21 . . . . **B–K6**
After this Black has an uphill game all the way and must play with great care. He should have played 21 . . . R–N1, for if 22 N–B3, R–N7 etc. or 22 R–B3, B–B5; 23 R–K1, R–K1 and Black regains the Pawn with the better ending.
22 R–KB1 **R–N1**
23 K–N3 **B–Q7**
24 N–B3 **BxN**
Practically forced, for if 24 . . . R–N7; 25 N–K4, R(1)xP; 26 R–QR1 with good prospects for White. If 24 . . . R–B7; 25 N–K4, RxR; 26 Px R, B–N5; 27 R–Q1, P–QR4; 28 R–Q7, P–R5; 29 P–K6, PxP; 30 N–B6 ch, K–B1; 31 NxPch, K–K1; 32 N–B6ch and White has at least a draw.
25 RxB **R–N7**
26 R–Q1 . . . .
26 R–QR1, R(7)xP; 27 RxR, Rx R; 28 R–R6 (better than 28 RxP, R–N4) would have led to the same ending.
26 . . . . **R(7)xP**
27 RxR **RxR**
28 R–Q6 **R–B6**
29 RxBP . . . .
Black must put forth his best efforts hereabouts, lest the advanced QBP become formidable. However, he has adequate counterplay.
29 . . . . **P–QR4**
30 K–B4 **K–B1**
31 R–B7 **P–R5**

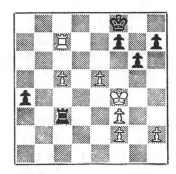

32 P–B6 . . . .
An attempt to force a win by marching the King to the support of the QBP would be extremely hazardous. Here are some possibilities: 32 K–K4, P–R6; 33 K–Q5, R–Q6ch.
I 34 K–B4, RxP; 35 R–R7, RxP; 36 RxP, RxP; 37 P–B6, R–B7ch; 38 K–Q5, P–R4; 39 K–Q6, R–Q7ch; 40 K–B7, P–N4 and Black has winning chances.
II 34 K–B6, RxP; 35 R–R7, RxP; 36 RxP, RxP; 37 R–QB3, K–K2; 38 K–B7, K–K3; 39 P–B6, R–R7; 40 K–N8, R–N7ch; 41 K–B8, R–QR7; 42 P–B7, R–R1ch; 43 K–N7, R–K1 and Black should not lose.
32 . . . . **P–R6**
Bringing about the liquidation of the Queen-side Pawns.
33 K–N3 **P–R7**
34 R–R7 **RxBP**
35 RxP **K–N2**
36 R–R7 **R–K3**
37 P–B4 **R–N3**
White has little chance to win, despite his "extra" Pawn.
38 P–R3 **R–QB3**
39 P–B5 . . . .
After this the game can be given up as a draw. However, better moves, such as 39 R–Q7, should give Black no real trouble.
39 . . . . **PxP**

40 K–B4	K–N3
41 R–Q7	R–B5ch
42 K–N3	Drawn

A hard-fought battle; the opening is of great theoretical importance.

69.

RESHEVSKY–BOTVINNIK
Avro Tournament, 1938

NIMZOINDIAN DEFENSE

Reshevsky	M. Botvinnik
WHITE	BLACK
1 P–Q4	N–KB3
2 P–QB4	P–K3
3 N–QB3	B–N5

The adoption of this complicated line is well in keeping with Botvinnik's aggressive style.

4 P–K3	O–O
5 N–K2	. . . .

Rubinstein's move, which avoids a doubled Pawn while preparing for P–QR3. However, it has the disadvantage of blocking the KB for some time, and may thus land White in difficulties if it is not handled carefully. 5 B–Q3 is certainly more energetic.

5	P–Q4

Also playable is 5 . . . P–QN3; 6 P–QR3, BxNch; 7 NxB, P–Q4 (if 7 . . . B–N2; 8 P–Q5); 8 B–Q3, B–N2; 9 O–O, P–B4 when Black's initiative in the center should compensate for the two Bishops.

6 P–QR3	B–K2

The alternative was 6 . . . BxN ch; 7 NxB, P–QN3 transposing into the previous note. But Botvinnik prefers to retain the KB.

7 PxP	NxP

More customary is 7 . . . PxP and if 8 N–N3, P–B4 giving Black a free game at the cost of an isolated Pawn (9 PxP, BxP; 10 P–QN4? P–Q5!, for example, gives Black a

clear initiative).

8 NxN	. . . .

After 8 P–K4, NxN followed by . . . P–QB4, or 8 . . . N–N3 followed by . . . P–QB4, Black would have a good game.

8	PxN
9 P–KN3	. . . .

A novel idea which is at least as promising as the more orthodox N–B3 followed by B–Q3.

9	N–Q2
10 B–N2	N–B3
11 O–O	B–Q3

Black loses time with the Bishop. Why not . . . R–K1 followed by . . . B–B1 at once, saving a useful tempo?

12 N–B3	P–B3
13 P–QN4	. . . .

Intending my favorite maneuver of the minority attack on the Queen-side, but this idea, thanks to Botvinnik's resourceful play, never comes to fruition.

13	P–QR3
14 R–K1	. . . .

Alatortsev queries this move, recommending in its stead 14 P–B3, R–K1; 15 P–K4, PxP; 16 PxP, B–N5; 17 Q–Q2, B–KB1; 18 P–K5 etc. The position is a difficult one, and its subtleties unfold very gradually.

14	R–K1
15 B–N2	B–B1
16 Q–Q3	B–K3
17 P–B3	. . . .

White is now ready to proceed with what is apparently an irresistible plan: the advance of the KP. But Botvinnik knows how to create difficulties for his opponent!

17	N–Q2!

A profound move: if now 18 P–K4, PxP; 19 PxP, N–N3 and Black's threatened occupation of QB5 is embarrassing.

18 N–R4   P–QN3!

Black threatens to free himself with ... P–QB4, and if 19 P–K4, PxP; 20 PxP, P–QN4 followed by ... B–B5 and ... P–QR4 w i t h strong counterplay on the Queenside.

In addition, the text involves a finesse which can only be appreciated later on.

19 QR–B1   P–QN4!

Black appears to have lost time, but actually he has gained it, for now that the QR is no longer on its original square, the eventual ... N–B5 will compel White to lose a move guarding the QRP.

20 N–B5   N–N3

Black is now on the point of obtaining a fine game with ... P–QR4; hence White's reply.

21 N–D2   R–B2!

The play hereabouts is a fine example of the depth of Botvinnik's handling of such complex positions.

22 P–K4   . . . .

The indicated move, but Black is fully prepared for it.

22 . . . .   N–B5

23 R–R1   BxN!

Few players would have been prepared to part with what is apparently Black's more effective Bishop.

24 QPxB   . . . .

Very tempting, for now the QB comes to life, whereas after NPxB, it would continue to have no scope.

24 . . . .   R–Q2!

Black has brought this Rook into play very cleverly.

25 Q–Q4   P–B3

26 P–B4?   . . . .

It was not easy to foresee that this move would lead to trouble, since Black's reply, which exposes his weak QBP to attack, is such an unlikely move. 26 B–B1, N–K4; 27

B–K2, PxP; 28 QxKP, B–Q4; 29 Q–KB4, QR–K2 would have left Black with an excellent game, but it would have been better than the text.

26 . . . .   PxP!

27 QxKP   R–Q6!

The inroad of this Rook should have been decisive.

28 QR–B1   RxB!

29 RxR   B–B2!

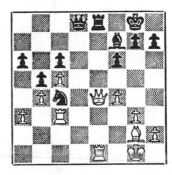

Apparently a hopeless situation for White, since 30 Q–N1 (what else?) is refuted by ... Q–Q5ch.

30 R–Q3!?   . . . .

The only chance.

30 . . . .   Q–N1?

Correct was 30 ... Q–B1!; 31 KR–Q1, RxQ; 32 BxR, B–Q4! (not 32 ... Q–K3; 33 R–Q8ch, B–K1; 34 R–K1!, K–B1; 35 K–B2!); 33 BxB ch, PxB; 34 RxP, Q–N5! and Black has warded off the attack.

Another possibility would have been 30 ... Q–B1!; 31 QxP, RxRch; 32 K–B2 R–K1; 33 QxQ, RxQ; 34 B–N7, R–N1 and Black wins.

31 R(1)–Q1!   . . . .

A delightful position: although White will have only two Rooks against Queen and Knight, he should win!

31 . . . .   RxQ

32 BxR   Q–KB1

If instead 32 ... B–Q4; 33 BxBch,

PxB; 34 RxP, K–B2; 35 R–Q8 winning the Queen!

   33 R–Q8   **B–K1**

If now 34 BxP, BxB; 35 RxQch,
KxR with two pieces for Rook and
Pawn. White naturally prefers to
utilize the enormous power of the
cooperating Rooks.

   34 R–K1!   **. . . .**

Threatening RxB! Black's position is fearfully difficult.

   34 . . . .   **K–B2**

   35 BxRP   **. . . .**

With the terrible threat 36 R(8)x
B, QxR; 37 B–N6ch.

   35 . . . .   **N–K4**

Black has no choice. If 35 . . .
Q–R1; 36 B–B5 (threatening B–
Q7), Q–R4; 37 P–N4 and wins.

   36 PxN   **Q–R1**

   37 B–B2?   **. . . .**

Missing a simple win with 37
PxP!, QxB; 38 PxP, QxP; 39 R(8)x
B. The united Rooks plus two
passed Pawns (not to mention the
weakness of Black's BP) would
have decided the game in White's
favor.

   37 . . . .   **K–K2**

   38 R–B8?   **. . . .**

Again White misses a win—this
time with R–N8 or R–R8.

   38 . . . .   **P–B4**

The terrible K file must be kept
closed.

   39 BxP   **Q–R4**

Had White played 38 R–N8 or 38
R–R8, he could now win with 40
R–N7ch (or 40 R–R7ch), K–Q1; 41
R–Q1ch—or 40 . . . K–B1; 41 B–K6!
and Black is helpless against R–
B1ch.

   40 P–N4?   **. . . .**

Now he misses his last winning
chance: 40 B–K4! and . . . QxP? is
refuted by 41 RxBch.

   40 . . . .   **Q–N4!**

   41 R–B7ch   **K–Q1**

   42 R–B8ch   **. . . .**

If 42 R–R7 Black can save himself with . . . Q–Q7!

   42 . . . .   **K–K2**

   43 P–K6   **. . . .**

A last winning attempt, against
which, however, Black has adequate resources.

   43 . . . .   **P–N3!**

   44 R–B7ch   **K–Q1**

   45 R–Q7ch!   **K–B1!**

Of course not 45 . . . BxR? 46 P–
K7ch, K–B2; 47 BxB and wins; or
46 . . . QxP; 47 RxQ, KxR; 48 BxB,
KxB; 49 K–B2 and White's extra
Pawn is decisive.

   46 P–K7   **PxB**

   47 R–Q8ch   **K–B2**

   48 RxB   **QxPch**

   49 K–R1   **Q–B6ch**

   50 K–N1   **Q–N5ch**

Drawn. Any attempt on White's
part to evade the perpetual check
would lose one of the Rooks.

SOVIET TRAINING TOURNAMENT, LENINGRAD-MOSCOW, 1939

THIS tournament gave me an opportunity to visit the USSR, where chess masters are lionized more than in any country of the world. As most people know, chess seems to be the national game of the Soviet Union. Like other countries, Russia publishes many books on chess and finds a ready market for magazines devoted to the game, but the USSR is alone in having made chess a spectator sport.

When a large tournament is held in the Soviet Union, the tournament committee finds it necessary to engage a large hall or theatre. Chess enthusiasts by the thousands queue up to buy admissions, and many are turned away disappointed when all available places are sold. The games themselves are played on the stage where the players can be easily seen.

Those who cannot manage to watch the actual games follow the play from wall boards, which are placed in such a position that many more thousands can watch them from the street than could crowd into the necessarily limited area devoted to the tournament itself. Daily bulletins are issued, containing not only the results but also the scores of all games played. These bulletins carry the news to all parts of the country. In addition, masters who are not participating in the tournament are often asked to appear on the radio to comment on the progress of the tournament and to analyze games.

This affords an interesting comparison with the publicity given to chess in the United States. Although matters have taken a turn for the better in recent years, we are far behind Russia in the amount of publicity given to tournaments both abroad and at home.

During a good part of the tournament I was so ill with a cold that I had to play many of the games in my hotel bedroom. Few realize how important a role physical condition plays in so sedentary a sport as chess, but actually it has helped decide many a championship. Fortunately for me, illness seemed not to affect my game too much in this tournament, since I finished second in a strong field.

70.

BONDAREVSKY–RESHEVSKY
Leningrad-Moscow, 1939
QUEEN'S INDIAN DEFENSE

I. Bondarevsky	Reshevsky
WHITE	BLACK
1 P–Q4	N–KB3
2 P–QB4	P–K3
3 N–KB3	P–QN3
4 P–KN3	B–N2
5 B–N2	B–K2
6 O–O	O–O
7 Q–B2	....

Preparing for N–B3. The immediate 7 N–B3 is best answered by ...N–K5 as in Game 79.

| 7 .... | B–K5 |

Black is playing for control of the vital square K5.

| 8 Q–R4 | .... |

Or 8 Q–N3, N–B3; 9 QN–Q2, P–Q4 and Black has a promising position.

| 8 .... | P–B4 |
| 9 PxP | PxP |

The result of the exchange is that Black gains a foothold on the important squares Q5 and QN5; White has pressure on the square Q6, or rather on Black's QP after it advances one square.

| 10 N–B3 | B–B3 |
| 11 Q–B2 | .... |

White's Queen has moved three

times without appreciable results.

| 11 .... | P–Q3 |

But not 11...P–Q4; 12 N–K5, B–N2; 13 R–Q1 and Black is subjected to an unpleasant pin.

| 12 B–B4 | .... |

Note that White scrupulously avoids P–K4 here or later on. There are two drawbacks to that move: it cedes Black command of White's Q4 (which would no longer be guarded by Pawns), and it prevents White from occupying K4 at a later date.

| 12 .... | P–QR3 |
| 13 KR–Q1 | Q–B2 |

Had Black omitted his 12th move, he would have to exchange his valuable QB after 14 N–QN5.

| 14 R–Q2 | R–Q1 |
| 15 QR–Q1 | B–N2 |

Making room for the development of the QN at B3, where it will control the important center square Q5.

| 16 N–KN5 | BxB |

If 16...N–B3; 17 QN–K4! (threatening NxQBP in addition to NxÑch) with a difficult position for Black.

| 17 KxB | P–R3 |
| 18 KN–K4 | N–K1 |

Threatening to win a piece with ...P–B4.

| 19 P–KN4?! | .... |

Aggressive and quite in keeping with the reputation of the Russian players for lively play. However, the merit of this move is questionable since it exposes White's King without adequate compensation. 19 P–B3 was preferable.

19	N–QB3
20 Q–R4	N–R4
21 P–B3	Q–N3
22 P–QR3	....

Black was threatening ...Q–N5.

22	QR–B1
23 B–N3	P–N3

Black is preparing for ... P–B4, gaining considerable terrain on the King-side.

24 B–B2	. . . .

Threatening P–N4 very strongly.

24	Q–B2
25 K–R1	K–R2
26 B–K3	P–B4
27 PxP	NPxP
28 N–B2	R–N1
29 N–R3	N–N6

In order to force the exchange of Queens, which will leave Black with a somewhat superior ending.

30 R–B2	Q–R4
31 N–B4	QxQ
32 NxQ	N–N2
33 N–Q3	B–B3
34 N–B1	. . . .

White is anxious to remove the troublesome Knight, which paralyzes any action of White's Rooks on the Q file.

34	N–QR4

Better than 34 ... N–Q5; 35 R(2)–Q2, P–K4 (else White plays P–N4 every strongly); 36 N–B3 followed by N–Q5.

35 B–Q2	N–B3
36 B–B3	P–K4!

Contrary to appearances, this move is quite good, as Black can easily defend the backward QP and need not worry about an attempt on White's part to occupy Q5.

The exchange of Bishops would have been inferior, as it would have given more freedom to White's pieces.

37 R(2)–Q2	B–K2
38 P–K3	N–K3
39 N–K2	N–N4
40 N–N1	N–B2
41 N–K2	R–N1
42 N–N3	P–B5

43 PxP	PxP
44 N–B5	. . . .

If 44 N–K4, R–KN3 followed by ... N(3)–K4. If 44 N–R5, N(3)–K4 winning a Pawn (White cannot play 45 NxKBP because of ... B–N4).

44	B–B1

45 NxQP?	. . . .

Energetic but faulty play, and apparently the intended sequel to White's 44th move.

45 NxBP? looks inviting but would also turn out to be unsound after 45 ... PxN; 46 R–Q7, N–Q1; 47 B–B6, K–N3; 48 BxN, RxB; 49 RxR, NxR; 50 N–R4ch, K–R4 and Black comes out a piece to the good.

White's best course was 45 R–Q5, R–KN4; 46 P–R4, R–R4 with a complicated position full of possibilities.

45	BxN
46 RxB	NxR
47 RxN	N–Q5!

A surprise for White. If now 48 BxN, PxB; 49 RxQP, QR–K1; 50 R–Q1, R–K7 and White's Pawns are no compensation for the deadly power of the Rooks.

48 NxP	N–K7
49 R–Q7ch	K–N3
50 B–K5	. . . .

White cannot very well permit the removal of his Bishop; but now he runs into new difficulties.

50	K–B4
51 B–N7	QR–Q1
52 RxR	RxR

White is now at a loss for a
move. If 53 BxP, R–KR1; 54 B–N7,
R–KN1 winning the Bishop. Or 53
K–N2 (if 53 NxP, R–KN1 wins), R–
KN1; 54 K–B2, RxB; 55 KxN, R–
N7ch etc.

| 53 P–KR4 | N–N6ch |
| 54 K–N2 | . . . . |

Loses a piece; however, after 54
K–R2, R–KN1; 55 BxP, N–B8ch;
56 K–R1, N–Q7 White can resign.

54	R–KN1
55 NxP	RxB
56 K–B2	R–K2
57 P–N4	R–K7ch
58 K–N1	K–K4
59 N–B5	K–Q5
60 P–R4	K–K6
61 N–K6	R–Q7
	Resigns

71.

ROMANOVSKY–RESHEVSKY
Leningrad-Moscow, 1939
R U Y   L O P E Z

P. Romanovsky	Reshevsky
WHITE	BLACK
1 P–K4	P–K4
2 N–KB3	N–QB3
3 B–N5	P–QR3
4 B–R4	N–B3
5 O–O	B–K2
6 R–K1	. . . .

For the kind of play which results
from 6 Q–K2, see Game 83.

6	P–QN4
7 B–N3	P–Q3
8 P–B3	N–QR4
9 B–B2	P–B4
10 P–Q3	. . . .

This conservative move, in place
of the customary 10 P–Q4, came as
a surprise to me.

10	O–O
11 QN–Q2	N–B3
12 P–QR4	B–K3

As a result of White's quiet
tenth move, Black has an easier
development than he usually gets
in this opening.

| 13 N–B1 | P–N5 |
| 14 P–Q4? | . . . . |

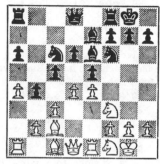

It frequently happens in this variation that the second advance of
the QP can be played with good
effect at some moment when Black
is caught off guard. This does not
happen to be the case here, so
White would have been wiser to
play P–R3 first in order to avoid
the troublesome pin.

| 14 . . . . | BPxP |
| 15 PxQP | B–N5! |

An embarrassing move for White.
The best reply was probably 16 B–
K3, although after 16 . . . PxP; 17
BxP, N–Q2 and if 18 N–K3, BxN;
19 PxB, B–B3; 20 BxB, QxB Black
would have the better game.

| 16 P–Q5 | N–Q5 |
| 17 B–Q3 | N–R4! |

Preparing to reinforce the irritating pin by advancing his BP. 17
. . . BxN; 18 PxB would have been
less clear (18 . . . N–R4; 19 P–B4,
NxP; 20 BxN, PxB; 21 BxP etc.).

| 18 B–K2 | . . . . |

A vain attempt to prevent the

shattering of his King-side.

18	NxBch
19 QxN	P–B4!

The initiative is now firmly in Black's possession.

20 P–R3	PxP
21 PxB	PxN
22 PxP	N–B5
23 BxN	RxB

Black has a clear advantage because of his command of the KB file, the exposed position of White's King and his weak QP.

24 N–N3	Q–Q2

Momentarily preventing N–K4, which would be answered by 25 . . . P–KR4; 26 PxP, Q–R6 with a winning game.

25 K–N2	QR–KB1
26 R–R1	. . . .

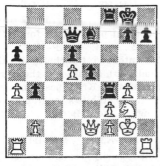

26	B–Q1!

A far from obvious move. Most players would automatically continue with 26 . . . RxBP, winning the Queen and a Pawn for the two Rooks. Black postpones this transaction, however, until he can follow up with . . . Q–B2ch winning the QP. In such positions, where victory seems assured, it is always well to pause and ascertain whether a careful examination of the position may not lead to a more convincing winning line than the most obvious continuation.

27 Q–Q3	. . . .

Or 27 KR–Q1, B–N3; 28 N–K4, B–Q5 and Black will win the QP after all.

27	P–N3
28 N–K4	RxBP

Now the exchange is in order.

29 QxR	RxQ
30 KxR	Q–B2ch
31 K–N2	QxP
32 P–B3	Q–N6
33 QR–QB1	. . . .

Likewise after 33 NxP, QxNPch; 34 K–R3, B–N4 Black would win easily.

33	P–Q4
34 R–B8	PxN
35 RxBch	K–N2

The two Rooks are no match for the Queen in this position. The Rooks cannot cooperate, and White's Pawns are too weak.

36 PxP	Q–N6

Even more convincing than . . . QxPch, for White will soon lose his KP and KNP.

37 R–Q7ch	K–B3
38 R–B1ch	K–N4
39 R(7)–KB7	QxPch
40 K–R2	Q–Q5

Naturally not 40 . . . KxP?? 41 R–N1ch, K–R5; 42 RxP mate.

41 R(7)–B2	KxP
42 R–N2ch	K–R4
43 R–B3	P–N4
44 R–K2	K–N3
45 R(3)–K3	. . . .

White's resistance is long drawn out but quite futile.

45	K–B4
46 R–B3ch	K–K3
47 R(3)–K3	K–Q4
48 P–N3	Q–B5ch
49 K–N2	P–K5
50 R–N3	P–N5
51 R–KB2	Q–N4
	Resigns

72.

RESHEVSKY–TOLUSH
Leningrad-Moscow, 1939
NIMZOINDIAN DEFENSE

Reshevsky	A. Tolush
WHITE	BLACK
1 P–Q4	N–KB3
2 P–QB4	P–K3
3 N–QB3	B–N5
4 P–K3	....

Aside from 4 P–QR3, no other move has the quality of the text of putting Black on his own resources, and calling forth his best efforts in the resulting mid-game complications.

4 ....   N–B3

Rather unusual, but this move has its points; Black's intention is to play ... P–K4 at an early stage. Other good moves at his disposal are 4 ... P–QN3, 4 ... P–Q4 and 4 ... O–O.

5 B–Q3   P–K4

Black has achieved his objective, but, as the following play demonstrates, his newly attained freedom may be deceptive if he does not continue aggressively.

6 N–K2   ....

After 6 P–Q5, BxNch; 7 PxB, N–QN1 the square QB4 would beckon invitingly to Black's QN.

6 ....   O–O

The first passive misstep. He should have played 6 ... PxP; 7 PxP, P–Q4 or else 6 ... P–Q4; 7 BPxP (if 7 P–QR3, QPxP; 8 BxP, B–Q3 with a satisfactory game), NxP; 8 P–QR3, NxN; 9 PxN, B–Q3 and Black stands well.

7 O–O   ....

More exact was P–Q5, in order to prevent ... P–Q4.

7 ....   R–K1

This is a double mistake, partly because Black misses his opportunity to free himself, and also because his KR will be useless at K1 in the ensuing play.

8 P–Q5!   ....

An advance which has a seriously cramping effect on Black's position, and should therefore have been avoided by him.

8 ....   N–N1

The first of a series of abject retreats which prove that Black has played the opening indifferently.

9 P–K4   P–QR4
10 P–QR3   B–B1

The upshot of the opening play is that White has a considerable lead in development and that his position in the center is far more promising.

11 N–N3   P–Q3
12 P–R3   ....

The usual preparation for B–K3.

12 ....   P–KN3

The intended fianchetto of the KB ends with a fiasco, as the weakening of the KN's position only strengthens White's contemplated opening of the KB file. ... N–R3–B4 was relatively best.

13 B–K3   P–B4?

Unnecessarily weakening his QP and also enabling White to obtain an excellent square for his QN at QN5. ... N–R3 or ... QN–Q2 followed by ... P–N3 and ... N–B4 was a better course.

14 Q–Q2   QN–Q2
15 B–R6!   ....

Before opening the KB file, White desires to eliminate the hostile KB, weakening Black's black squares and his QP as well.

15 ....   B–K2

Or 15 ... B–N2; 16 Q–N5, N–B1; 17 P–B4 and White has greatly strengthened his position.

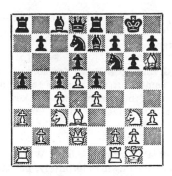

16 N–B5! . . . .

A little surprise which enables White to achieve his goal of removing the black-squared Bishop.

16 . . . . **N–R4?**

Of course 16 ... PxN?? would allow mate in two, but the feeble text accentuates the weakness of his black squares by allowing White's QB to remain on the board. Black should have played 16 ... B–B1.

17 NxBch **QxN**
18 B–K2 . . . .

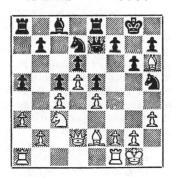

18 . . . . **N–N2**

On 18 .. QN–B3 would have come 19 B–N5 (threatening KBxN) and Black would be unable to play 19 ... Q–B1? because of 20 P–KN4 winning a piece.

If 18 ... KN–B3; 19 P–B4, PxP; 20 QxP and the outlook for Black's game is very bad, for example 20 ... Q–K4 (there seems nothing better); 21 QxQ, PxQ (if 21 ... RxQ; 22 B–B4, R–K1; 23 B–Q3, R–R3; 24 N–N5 and Black has no adequate defense against the double threat of NxP and N–B7); 22 N–N5, R–N1; 23 N–Q6, R–K2; 24 P–KN4 followed by P–N5 and Black's position is as good as hopeless.

19 P–B4 **PxP**

If 19 ... P–B3; 20 P–B5 followed by P–KN4 and Black's position is untenable.

20 QxP **R–B1**
21 N–N5 **R–R3**

Or 21 ... N–K4; 22 B–N5 with decisive effect.

22 B–N4! **N–K4**

This leads to a quick debacle, but if 22 ... P–B3; 23 N–B7 followed by QBxN and N–K6 winning the exchange. Or if 22 ... P–R4; 23 PxP, PxP; 24 BxN, KxB; 25 BxP, N–K4; 26 Q–N3ch, K–R1; 27 BxB, RxB; 28 QR–K1 (threatening NxP) with an easy win.

23 B–N5 **P–B3**

After 23 ... Q–K1 White would have played 24 N–B7 winning the exchange or else 24 B–B6 threatening 25 Q–R6.

24 BxP **RxB**

The loss of the exchange is unavoidable.

25 QxR **QxQ**
26 RxQ **BxB**
27 PxB **NxBP**
28 N–B7 **R–N3**
29 N–K6! . . . .

The quickest way. **The British Chess Magazine** comments: "The Knight has made a pleasant and profitable tour of the board."

29 . . . . **NxN**
30 PxN **Resigns**

The KP must queen.

73.

GOGLIDZE–RESHEVSKY
Leningrad-Moscow, 1939
ENGLISH OPENING

V. Goglidze	Reshevsky
WHITE	BLACK
1 P–QB4	P–K4
2 N–QB3	N–KB3
3 P–KN3	P–Q4
4 PxP	NxP
5 B–N2	N–N3

Now generally a c c e p t e d a s
Black's best move at this stage.

6 N–B3	N–B3
7 P–Q3	B–K2
8 O–O	O–O

Black has adopted one of the best
defenses to this opening. He has
better control of the center and
more freedom of action for his
pieces. White in turn is using the
hypermodern strategy of control-
ling the center with a fianchettoed
Bishop, and he has prospects of occupying the important square QB5
by means of a later R–QB1 coupled
with N–K4 or N–QR4. Black must
meet this threat and in addition he
must provide for the protection of
his QNP, which is indirectly menaced by the fianchettoed Bishop.

9 P–N3? ....

A serious misconception of the
strategical requirements of the position. The logical course was B–
K3 followed by R–B1 and N–K4 or
N–QR4, with fighting chances for
both sides.

9	B–K3
10 B–N2	P–B3

Protecting the KP in order to
free his QN for action.

11 R–B1	P–QR4
12 N–Q2	....

In order to assert the striking
power of the KB along the diagonal; but the text has the drawback
of permitting the occupation of Q4
later on.

12	P–R5!

Giving up a Pawn for some time
to come, but the results (bringing
the QR into action and weakening
White's Queen's wing) are well
worth it.

13 NxP ....

13 PxP would allow White to
hold the Pawn indefinitely, but the
extra Pawn would be worthless,
and White's QN would have to remain at QB3 to hold the Pawn,
thus blocking the action of his QB.
13 N–B4 seems relatively best.

13	NxN
14 PxN	Q–Q2!

Black is in no hurry to regain
the Pawn, for after 14 ... BxP; 15
N–B4, he would have to exchange
off his QB sooner or later. As he
plays, he recovers the Pawn eventually and retains the useful QB.

15 N–K4 ....

15 BxN, despite the weakening of
Black's Pawns, would be a mistake: 15 ... PxB; 16 Q–B2, KR–N1;
17 B–R1, R–N3 18 N–B4, R(3)–R3.
The weakening of Black's Pawns
could be less important than the
splendid placement of B l a c k's
pieces, the power of his Bishops,
and the weakening of White's King-
side.

15	R–R4
16 B–QB3	R–R3
17 B–Q2	N–Q5

Black is still in no hurry to regain his Pawn, and prefers to
strengthen his position. The text
completes a maneuver which will
consolidate the Queen-side and remove the QNP from the jurisdic-
tion of White's KB.

18 N–B5	BxN

19 RxB	P–QN3
20 R–B3	P–QB4

Although White has the two Bishops, his position is definitely inferior because of the deterioration of his Pawn structure and his lack of mobility.

21 P–K3	. . . .

Creating a weakness which was unavoidable, because the Knight was too powerfully posted and hampered the movements of White's pieces.

21	N–B4
22 P–B4	PxP
23 RxKBP	. . . .

NPxP would have exposed White's King, while KPxP was out of the question because of the resulting isolation of the QP.

23	N–K2
24 B–K1	B–Q4!

Provoking White's reply (which weakens his Pawns still more), since he cannot afford to part with the KB.

25 P–K4	. . . .

Black has achieved the desired result. White's KB is out of play and his Q4 is once more accessible to Black's pieces.

25	BxRP

At last!

26 R–KB2	B–K3
27 R–N2	. . . .

White has finally obtained some compensating pressure on the QN file, but he is still at a considerable disadvantage.

27	N–B3

If 27 ... RxP; 28 RxNP and White's position has improved considerably, as he has rid himself of his weak Pawn and at the same time produced an isolated Pawn for Black.

28 K–R1	R–Q1
29 Q–N1	Q–R2

The plausible 29 ... N–N5 would be inferior because of 30 P–Q4! PxP (not 30 ... QxP? 31 R–Q2 etc.); 31 R–B1, N–B3; 32 RxP, RxR; 33 QxR, R–B1; 34 P–R5 and White has slightly the better of it.

30 R–B1	Q–QB2
31 B–QB3	P–R3
32 B–B1	N–Q5
33 P–R5!	. . . .

Since this Pawn has to fall sooner or later, White loses patience and decides to simplify while he can still get a Pawn in return.

33	PxP
34 BxN	RxB
35 R–N5	R–B3
36 R–N7	Q–Q3

Black will soon have to return the extra Pawn, but he will retain a winning advantage.

37 R–R7	R–N5
38 Q–R1	R–R3

Black prefers to give up the QBP and to retain the QRP; the latter, as a passed Pawn, is much more valuable.

39 RxR	QxR
40 P–Q4	. . . .

40 RxP, P–R5; 41 P–Q4, Q–R2 would not be much better, as it would be difficult to stop the QRP and White's center Pawns would be too weak to produce results.

40	P–B5
41 P–Q5	B–N5
42 Q–Q4	Q–Q3

Not only stopping the passed QP, but also preparing to use the Queen for attacking purposes as well.

| 43 BxP | . . . . |

If 43 RxP, R–N8; 44 K–N2, Q–R6 with a winning attack.

43	P–R4
44 K–N1	P–QR5
45 R–B2	B–R6
46 K–B2	P–R6

The envelopment of White's position proceeds apace. The dangerous passed Pawn requires White's attention on one wing, while the danger to his King steadily grows on the other wing.

| 47 Q–B3 | . . . . |

Unfortunately, White has no counterplay. Thus if 47 Q–R7, R–N7; 48 B–Q3, Q–N5 and White's position is untenable.

| 47 . . . . | R–N8 |
| 48 B–K2 | Q–N3ch |

Curiously enough, the game ends with a combination of direct attack on White's King and the queening of the QRP!

| 49 Q–K3 | Q–N5 |
| 50 Q–Q3 | . . . . |

Or 50 Q–Q2, QxP; 51 P–Q6, Q–B4ch; 52 K–K3, R–N6ch; 53 K–Q4, Q–K4ch; 54 K–B4, B–K3ch etc. (if 53 R–B3, Q–N4ch; 54 K–Q3, B–B4ch etc.)

50	Q–K8ch
51 K–K3	P–R7!
52 P–Q6	. . . .

If 52 RxP, Q–N8ch; 53 K–B3 (if 53 K–Q2, Q–B8 mate), B–N5ch; 54 K–B4, P–N4 mate.

52	P–R8(Q)
53 Q–Q5ch	K–B1
Resigns	

White resigns; there are no more checks. A good example of consistent positional chess.

NORTH AMERICAN CHAMPIONSHIP NEW YORK, 1939

T HIS tournament was the last held under the auspices of the American Chess Federation which was soon to merge with the National Chess Federation. Jointly they became the United States Chess Federation, the sole governing chess organization in the United States. Under this unified leadership, it was possible for chess to make bigger advances than ever before.

The sad lesson I learned in this tournament was that sometimes drawing two games, even while winning nine, is one too many! Normally a score of 10-1 is good for first prize in any tournament. Surprisingly enough this time was the exception and I had to be content with second. Reuben Fine was in top form for this event and he allowed only one draw to edge me by half a point.

Perhaps this is not without a certain justice. I was favored by good fortune in two of my games, one of which I won and the other I drew. Of the first, one critic remarked that " luck is more valuable than a license to steal." And I might add that it is a lot more surprising. It must not be forgotten, however, that alertness is part of chess. The player who is led astray in a complicated position, who thinks along pre-formulated lines, can easily be a greater danger to himself than his opponent is. "Attention," the late Frank Marshall was fond of saying," is more important than concentration in chess." By being always on the alert, a resourceful player, can frequently turn defeat into victory, often save an apparently "hopeless" game. This, I repeat, is as much a part of chess as the most refined technique.

74.

RESHEVSKY–ADAMS
U. S. Open Championship
New York, 1939

R U Y   L O P E Z

Reshevsky	W. W. Adams
WHITE	BLACK
1 P–K4	P–K4
2 N–KB3	N–QB3
3 B–N5	P–QR3
4 B–R4	N–B3
5 O–O	B–K2
6 R–K1	P–QN4
7 B–N3	P–Q3
8 P–B3	O–O

I have played against this variation so often that I was curious to see how it felt to play on the other side! The text is quite feasible although less frequently adopted than 8 ... N–QR4; 9 B–B2, P–B4; 10 P–Q4, Q–B2; 11 P–QR4 etc.

9 P–KR3 ....

In order to avoid the pin on his KN. The alternative 9 P–Q4, B–N5; 10 P–Q5! N–QR4; 11 B–B2, P–B4; 12 PxP e. p.! also gives White a good game.

9	N–QR4
10 B–B2	P–B4
11 P–Q4	Q–B2

12 QN–Q2 ....

12 P–QR4? B–Q2! 13 QN–Q2, BPxP! 14 BPxP, KR–B1! 15 B–Q3,

NPxP is distinctly in Black's favor (see Game 67). If, however, 12 ... P–N5; 13 BPxP, PxNP; 14 QN–Q2, B–K3; 15 N–B1, KR–B1; 16 N–K3 followed by P–QN3 and B–N2 with a very promising position for White.

12 .... N–B3

Preferable is 12 ... BPxP; 13 PxP, N–B3; 14 N–N3 (if 14 P–Q5, N–QN5; 15 B–N1, P–QR4; 16 P–QR3, N–R3; 17 N–B1, N–B4 and I prefer Black's chances), P–QR4; 15 B–K3, P–R5; 16 QN–Q2, B–Q2. The results are thus far inconclusive, but I believe that Black's position is satisfactory.

13 PxBP! ....

The idea of this move, made fashionable by the younger Soviet masters, is of course a later attempt to occupy Q5.

13	PxP
14 N–B1	R–Q1
15 Q–K2	B–K3
16 N–K3	P–N5?

Badly timed; if Black considered this move useful, he should have prefaced it with ... P–R3, in order to prevent White's next move. An interesting alternative was 16 ... P–B5 threatening ... N–Q5!

17 N–N5 P–QR4

Hoping to drive back White's KB once it switches to the important diagonal—but this proves to be a futile hope. However, if 17 ... B–Q2; 18 B–N3, B–K1; 19 N–Q5 with a splendid position for White.

18 NxB	PxN
19 B–N3	Q–B1
20 Q–B4	K–B2

The necessity for such a move indicates how Black's position has deteriorated.

21 P–QR4! ....

Preventing ... P–R5.

21 .... P–N3

This prevents N–B5, but it weakens the black squares.

22 N–N4!   **NxN**

White was threatening to win a Pawn with 23 N–R6ch or 23 QxPch.

23 PxN   **N–N1**

Foreseeing the coming attack on the KB file, Adams plays for the exchange of Queens. But even this proves inadequate.

24 P–B4   ....

Opening the KB file so that the KR can join in the attack. Incidentally, White threatens P–B5!

24 ....   **KPxP**

25 BxP   **Q–R3**

If instead 25 ... N–R3; 26 R–KB1, K–N2; 27 B–K5ch, K–R3; 28 Q–K2 followed by Q–K3ch wins.

26 R–KB1   **QxQ**

27 BxQ   **K–N2**

28 B–K5ch   **K–R3**

If 28 ... K–N1? 29 BxP mate!

29 R–B7   ....

29 ....   **B–Q3**

There was no saving move:

I 29 ... R–K1; 30 B–N5 or 30 K–B2 etc.

II 29 ... R–Q2; 30 BxP (or 30 K–B2 etc.), R(2)–R2; 31 B–Q5.

III 29 ... B–B1; 30 B–B6, R–K1; 31 P–N5ch, K–R4; 32 B–K2ch, K–R5; 33 K–B2 etc.

IV 29 ... N–B3; 30 P–N5ch! KxP (if 30 ... BxP; 31 B–N7ch, K–R4;

32 B–K2ch, K–R5; 33 K–R2, B–K2; 34 RxB, NxR; 35 B–B6ch, P–N4; 36 P–N3 mate); 31 B–B4ch, K–R5; 32 P–N3ch, K–R6; 33 RxPch, K–N5; 34 B–K2 mate.

30 B–N7ch   **Resigns**

For if 30 ... K–N4; 31 B–B6cb etc.

75.

SEIDMAN–RESHEVSKY
U. S. Open Championship
New York, 1939

BIRD'S OPENING

H. Seidman   Reshevsky
WHITE   BLACK

1 P–KB4   ....

This opening is rarely encountered in tournament play. It has at most surprise value, as Black can equalize readily in a number of variations.

1 ....   **P–Q4**

2 P–K3   **P–KN3**

One of the most popular systems of development for Black. It gives the game the character of a Dutch Defense with colors reversed.

3 N–KB3   **B–N2**

4 P–B4?   ....

Of dubious value, as it leaves lasting weaknesses in the center. A better plan is P–KN3 followed by B–N2, Q–K2 and P–Q3, intending an eventual P–K4.

4 ....   **N–KB3**

5 N–B3   **O–O**

6 P–QN3   ....

This is bound to lead to trouble on the long diagonal, but the alternative 6 PxP, NxP; 7 B–B4, N–N3 followed by ...P–QB4 is also in Black's favor.

6 ....   **P–B4**

...N–K5 was also playable, but the text keeps more threats in reserve. Thus if now 7 B–N2, N–N3;

8 B–K2, P–Q5; 9 PxP, PxP; 10 N–QN5, N–K1 followed by . . . P–QR3 with much the better game.

7 P–Q4 . . . .

This prevents . . . P–Q5 and apparently removes all danger on the long diagonal; but Black has other possibilities at his disposal.

7 . . . . N–K5!

Seizing the initiative. Naturally White cannot play 8 NxP?? P–K3 nor can he exchange Knights.

8 B–N2 Q–R4
9 R–B1 B–N5

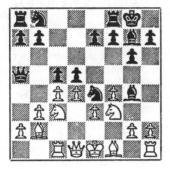

After only nine moves, the initiative rests completely with Black!

10 B–K2 BPxP
11 NxP . . . .

Or 11 PxP, PxP; 12 PxP, R–Q1 and Black wins a Pawn (13 Q–R4, Q–N3).

11 . . . . BxB
12 QxB . . . .

Or 12 NxB, PxP; 13 PxP, R–Q1; 14 Q–B2, N–Q3 (or . . N–B4) leaving White with a wretched position.

12 . . . . N–QB3
13 PxP . . . .

13 NxN, PxN would also be unfavorable for White, for example 14 Q–QB2, NxN; 15 BxN, BxBch; 16 QxB, QxP safely winning a Pawn.

13 . . . . QNxN
14 PxN NxN
15 BxN QxQP

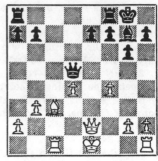

16 O–O . . . .

White decides to give up a Pawn without protracted suffering, realizing that after 16 R–Q1, QR–B1; 17 B–R1, Q–R4ch; 18 Q–Q2, Q–KB4 he would have a lost game because of the threat of . . . R–B7; or 16 Q–Q2, QR–B1; 17 R–Q1 (not 17 O–O? RxB! 18 RxR, QxQPch! and wins) Q–K5ch and White's game is untenable.

16 . . . . BxPch
17 K–R1 BxB
18 RxB P–K3
19 R–Q3 Q–QN4
20 P–QR4 Q–N3
21 Q–K1 . . . .

A despairing attempt at attack on the KR file which is easily foiled.

21 . . . . KR–Q1
22 R–R3 R–Q4!

Preparing to double on the Q file and at the same time meeting the attack on the KR file, for if 23 Q–R4, R–KR4; 24 Q–N4, RxR; 25 QxR, R–Q1 with an easy win.

23 R(3)–KB3 QR–Q1
24 Q–K2 R–Q7
25 Q–B4 Q–Q5
26 Q–N5 . . . .

The exchange of Queens would be hopeless for White.

26 . . . . Q–Q4
27 Q–N4 R–QB1
28 K–N1 P–N3!
29 P–R3 R(1)–B7

30 R(3)–B2	RxR
31 RxR	Q–Q8ch
32 R–B1	Q–K7
Resigns	

Note that if Black's QNP were still at N2, White could now stop the mate by QxP. This explains Black's 28th move.

76.

ULVESTAD–RESHEVSKY
U. S. Open Championship
New York, 1939

KING'S INDIAN DEFENSE

O. Ulvestad	Reshevsky
WHITE	BLACK
1 P–Q4	N–KB3
2 N–KB3	P–KN3
3 P–KN3	B–N2
4 B–N2	O–O
5 QN–Q2	....

5 P–B4 followed by N–B3 is the natural course, but White is content with a quiet and somewhat bizarre system of development.

| 5 .... | P–Q3 |

After White's last move, the advance of the QP one square offers more chances of interesting play than 5...P–Q4; 6 P–B4 etc.

| 6 P–B3 | N–B3 |
| 7 N–B4 | P–K3 |

After this Black's development is rather slow. 7...N–Q2 followed by ...P–K4 would have been a promising alternative.

| 8 B–B4 | P–QN4 |

Driving away the well-posted Knight.

9 N–R3	R–N1
10 N–B2	Q–K2
11 N–N4	B–N2

A good alternative was 11...Nx N; 12 PxN, N–Q4; 13 B–Q2, P–K4 etc. In the play that follows, Black disregards the possibility of ad-

vancing the KP, and steers the game into more complicated lines.

| 12 O–O | P–QR4 |
| 13 N–Q3 | .... |

The many moves of this piece constitute a novel Knight's tour; but it has finally reached a good post.

| 13 .... | P–KR3 |
| 14 P–QR4 | PxP |

The beginning of some risky but fascinating play on the Queen-side. From this point on, the excitement mounts steadily.

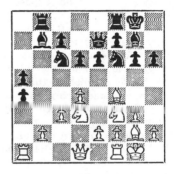

| 15 QxP | N–Q4 |
| 16 P–K4 | N–N3! |

Far better than the obvious 16... NxB; 17 NxN when Black would have two Bishops, to be sure, but a very difficult game as well, after 17...R–R1; 18 P–Q5!

| 17 Q–B2 | P–R5 |
| 18 KR–K1 | .... |

18 P–N3 would have been safer, but an aggressive player like Ulvestad is not interested in safety.

18	N–R4
19 R–K2	Q–Q2
20 QR–K1	Q–N4
21 P–K5	....

While Black strengthens his position on the Queen-side, White builds up counterplay in the center.

| 21 .... | N(3)–B5 |

Not 21 ... P–Q4; 22 N–B5, after
which Black's position contains
serious weaknesses and his Bishops have very little play.

    22 P–R4   **N–N6**

Black hopes to open up the position with ... P–R6, but this will
turn out to be very dangerous.

    23 N–R2   **BxB**
    24 KxB   **P–R6**
    25 NPxP   **NxRP**
    26 Q–Q1   **Q–B3ch**
    27 N–B3?   **. . . .**

K–N1 was much stronger, f o r
then this Knight is not exposed to
attack later on.

    27 . . . .   **KR–Q1?!**

"Reshevsky had to make the remaining fourteen moves in a frac-
tion of a minute or thereabouts.
How he accomplished this task,
and how he made such good moves
while he was about it, will forever
remain something of a mystery.
The text leads to great difficulty, as
will be seen. 27 ... N–R4 should
have been played." (Reinfeld in the
Tournament Book)

    28 R–R2!   **Q–R1!**

Very uncomfortable, but compulsory nevertheless, for if 28 ... N–
B5? 29 N–N4 wins.

    29 N–N4   **. . . .**

At first glance, it seems that
there must be some way of cap-

turing the trapped Knights, but
Black's defenses are adequate: for
instance 29 B–B1, NxB; 30 QxN,
R–N6; 31 N–N4 (or 31 Q–R1, KR–
N1; 32 N–B1, R–N8!), P–QB4! 32
N–B2, RxP; 33 R–K3, RxN! etc.
Or 29 PxP, PxP; 30 N–B1, P–K4;
31 B–K3, PxP; 32 PxP (if 32 BxQP,
BxB; 33 PxB; NxN; 34 QxN, R–
N6; 35 R–K3, RxR; 36 QxR, N–
B5), Q–R5; 33 K–N1, R–N5.

    29 . . . .   **NxP!**
    30 PxN   **. . . .**

Or 30 QxN, PxP regaining the
piece advantageously.

    30 . . . .   **RxN**
    31 Q–Q3   **R–R5**

If now 32 PxP, PxP; 33 R(1)–
QR1, BxP!! saves Black!

    32 R(1)–QR1   **. . . .**

Even this formidable move can
be refuted.

    32 . . . .   **PxP!**
    33 RxN   **. . . .**

Obviously Black has nothing to
fear from 33 BxKP, BxB; 34 RxN,
RxR; 35 RxR, Q–Q4 etc.

    33 . . . .   **RxR**
    34 RxR   **Q–Q4**

Miraculously enough, everything
clicks, since a retreat of White's
Bishop would be answered by ...
P–K5.

    35 Q–B3   **PxB**
    36 QxP   **PxP**
    37 R–R5   **. . . .**

Despair; if 37 PxP or QxP, BxP
wins easily.

    37 . . . .   **Q–Q3**
    38 Q–B4   **PxP**
    39 R–R4   **P–B8(Q)ch**
    40 KxQ   **Q–Q4**
    Resigns

White resigns, as his opponent's
troubles with the clock are over.
This is probably my most remarkable time pressure game!

77.

RESHEVSKY–SANTASIERE
U. S. Open Championship
New York, 1939

QUEEN'S GAMBIT DECLINED

	Reshevsky	A. E. Santasiere
	WHITE	BLACK
1	P–Q4	P–Q4
2	P–QB4	P–QB3
3	N–KB3	N–B3
4	N–B3	PxP
5	P–QR4	B–B4
6	P–K3	P–K3
7	BxP	B–QN5
8	O–O	O–O
9	Q–K2	B–N5

In this and similar positions, Black generally plays ...N–K5 (as in Game 64) to prevent P–K4. However, Santasiere realizes that the advance is inevitable and therefore tries a different method.

After 9...N–K5, White has the enterprising continuation 10 B–Q3! (if 10 NxN, BxN; 11 R–Q1, N–Q2; 12 B–Q3, BxB; 13 QxB, Q–R4 and the position is about even), BxN (after 10...NxN; 11 PxN, BxP; 12 R–N1, Q–B2; 13 BxB, PxB; 14 Q–B2 White regains the Pawn advantageously); 11 PxB, NxQBP; 12 Q–B2, BxB; 13 QxB, N–Q4; 14 B–R3, R–K1; 15 QR–N1, P–QN3; 16 P–K4 with a strong position for the Pawn.

10	P–R3	B–KR4
11	R–Q1	QN–Q2
12	P–K4	Q–K2
13	P–K5	....

On other moves Black can play ...P–K4.

| 13 | .... | N–Q4 |
| 14 | N–K4 | .... |

All standard play up to this point. White has secured a strong center formation, and his KP ex-erts powerful pressure. However, his QP is weak, and Black's pieces are well posted. This is a position which gives considerable scope for maneuvering possibilities, requiring the utmost alertness on the part of both players.

| 14 | .... | P–KR3 |

Recommended as best by the writer.

| 15 | N–N3 | B–N3 |

It may well be that 15...BxN; 16 QxB, P–B3 offers better chances.

| 16 | N–K1 | .... |

In order to dislodge Black's KB.

| 16 | .... | P–B3!? |

The crucial move in this variation. Black exposes a weak KP to White's attack and gives White's pieces a mighty square at K5 — while Black in turn hopes for play on the KB file.

| 17 | PxP | QxP |

Losing an important tempo, as will soon become clear. Preferable therefore was 17...QNxP; 18 N–Q3, B–Q3; 19 N–K5, B–R2.

| 18 | N–Q3 | B–Q3 |

...B–QR4 was better, as it would have avoided the need for parting with one of the Bishops.

| 19 | N–K4 | Q–K2 |

19...BxN; 20 QxB, QR–K1 followed by ...Q–B4 looks better.

| 20 | NxB | QxN |

Up to this point the game has proceeded move for move as my encounter with Flohr at Semmering-Baden, 1937 (in which I had Black!). There the continuation was 21 B–Q2, QR–K1; 22 B–N3, P–K4 and Black has equalized. But in the present game I found a far better continuation for White.

| 21 | R–R3! | .... |

The effects of this powerful move will be noticeable in short order.

21 . . . .   QR–K1
22 N–K5   . . . .

22 . . . .   B–R2?

Santasiere later remarked, "The
kind of move which makes one
marvel at how profoundly stupid
one can be. It is as bad a move as
Black has at his command; of
course, I overlooked the neat combination which follows, to win a
Pawn."

And Reinfeld comments interest-
ingly in the Tournament Book:
"This frank criticism is too harsh,
as the position is more difficult
than surface appearances would
indicate. For example, Santasiere
recommends instead of the text
22 . . . NxN; 23 PxN, Q–B4; 24 R–
KN3, K–R2 etc. But then White
has a win with 25 P–N4!, for example:

I 25 . . . QxP; 26 Q–N4, N–K2;
27 B–R3 etc. etc.

II 25 . . . NxP; 26 RxB!, KxR; 27
Q–K4ch, K–B2 (if 27 . . . R–B4; 28
B–B4! and Black is helpless against
P–N4, as 28 . . . K–B2? is answered
by 29 QxRch); 28 R–Q7ch, R–K2;
29 B–K3!, Q–R4; 30 Q–B5ch, K–K1
(or 30 . . . K–N1; 31 BxPch and
wins); 31 RxRch, KxR; 32 QxPch,
K–Q1; 33 Q–Q6ch and wins.

Because of the presence of such
complicated variations, Black must

not be criticized too vigorously for
missing his way.

However, Santasiere's other suggestion 22 . . . B–B4; 23 R–KN3, K–
R2 seems feasible, although Black's
position would be somewhat uncomfortable."

A third variation should be added
to those given above: if 25 . . . Q–K2
(instead of 25 . . . QxP or 25 . . . Nx
P); 26 RxB!, KxR; 27 B–Q3ch, K–
B2; 28 Q–R5ch, K–N1; 29 Q–N6
wins.

23 R–KN3!   K–R1

The loss of a Pawn had become
unavoidable, for if 23 . . . R–B3; 24
N–N4 or 23 . . . N–B5; 24 Q–N4 etc.

24 BxN!   BPxB

If 24 . . . KPxB (the natural
move); 25 N–B7ch wins the exchange. If 24 . . . QxB; 25 BxP! Px
B; 26 NxN and wins.

25 BxP!   R–K2

Again, if 25 . . . PxB; 26 NxN, Qx
N? 27 Q–K5ch and mate follows.

26 B–Q2   NxN

Else R–N3! wins at least a Pawn.

27 PxN   Q–N3
28 B–K3   Q–R4

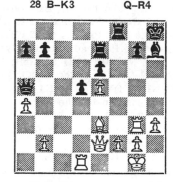

29 R–Q4   . . . .

White is building up a powerful
attack which will win very quickly.

29 . . . .   R–B4

Or 29 . . . B–B4; 30 Q–R5ch, K–
N1; 31 R–R4 winning easily.

30 R–R4	Q–B2
31 Q–N4	....

Threatening Q–N6.

31	K–N1
32 B–N5!	R(2)–B2
33 B–B6	P–R3

If 33...P–KN3? 34 QxPch! etc.
Or 33...R(4)xB; 34 PxR, RxP; 35
Q–R5 and wins.

34 P–R5	Q–Q2

Black is out of moves. If 34...
K–B1; 35 RxB, PxB; 36 Q–N8ch
etc. Or 34...R–Q2; 35 K–R2!, P–
Q5; 36 R–R6, P–Q6; 37 Q–R4 and
wins.

35 R–R6	K–R1

If 35...Q–B2; 36 Q–R4, Q–B8ch;
37 K–R2 and wins.

36 Q–N6	Resigns

The triple pin in the final position is curious!

78.

HOROWITZ–RESHEVSKY
U. S. Open Championship
New York, 1939

GRUENFELD DEFENSE

I. A. Horowitz	Reshevsky
WHITE	BLACK
1 N–KB3	N–KB3
2 P–B4	P–KN3
3 P–KN3	B–N2
4 B–N2	O–O
5 O–O	P–Q4

Black has a great variety of
moves here, for example: (A) 5...
P–B3 followed by ...P–Q4; (B)
5...P–Q3 intending ...QN–Q2 or
...N–B3 and ultimately ...P–K4;
(C) the symmetrical 5...P–B4.

The text is the most interesting
and riskiest of all—Black follows
the same policy as in Game 44,
allowing his opponent to build up
a strong—or apparently strong!—
central Pawn formation.

6 PxP	NxP
7 P–Q4	N–R3

Intending a thrust at the center
with ...P–QB4 in due course.

8 P–K4	....

As will be seen, White's center
is less formidable than it appears.
At all events, its strength or weakness will be the key to the bitter
struggle which soon begins to rage.

8	N–N3
9 N–B3	....

If 9 P–KR3, P–QB4; 10 P–Q5, P–
K3; 11 PxP (practically forced),
BxP and Black has already secured
an appreciable positional advantage.

9	B–N5!

10 B–K3	....

More energetic would have been
10 P–Q5!? Q–Q2 (10...P–K3? 11
P–KR3! is in White's favor); 11
Q–K2, KR–K1! (11...B–R6; 12 B–
B4, BxB; 13 KxB, P–K3; 14 QR–Q1,
KR–K1; 15 P–Q6! is good for
White, while if 11...P–K3; 12 P–
KR3, BxN; 13 QxB!); 12 KR–Q1
with a real fighting game in pros-
pect. The text eases Black's prob-
lems.

10	Q–Q2

10...N–B5; 11 Q–N3, NxB; 12
PxN is not so good as it looks, as
Black's position on the Queen-side
is very poor.

11 N–K2   . . . .
Over-protecting the QP. Now his
Queen is freed for action.

11 . . . .   QR–B1

Horowitz's suggestion of 11 . . .
N–B5; 12 Q–N3, NxB has merit
here, for 13 PxN can be answered
by . . . P–QB4.

12 Q–B2   P–QB4!

At last the long-awaited thrust!
White cannot very well reply 13
P–Q5 for then 13 . . . P–K3 would
be very strong.

13 PxP   N–R5
14 KR–Q1   Q–K1
15 B–Q4!   . . . .

Leaving Black little choice, for
if 15 . . . P–K4; 16 B–K3 (not 16 Bx
P? BxB; 17 NxB, QxN; 18 QxN,
BxN winning a piece), N(5)xBP;
17 N–B3 threatening the occupation of Q5.

15 . . . .   BxB
16 N(2)xB   N(5)xBP

If 16 . . . N(3)xP; 17 P–N3, N–N3
and the Knight is poorly placed at
N3. Or 16 . . . RxP; 17 Q–N3 and
again Black's Knights are poorly
posted and he has to lose time
guarding the QNP.

17 P–KR3   BxN

If instead 17 . . . B–Q2; 18 Q–K2
(Black threatened to win the ex-
change with . . . B–R5), P–K4; 19
N–B2, B–N4; 20 Q–K3, N–R5; 21
N–R3! NxP; 22 R–Q5 regaining the
Pawn and leading to a highly com-
plicated position.

18 NxB   Q–N4
19 N–Q4   Q–N3
20 Q–K2   KR–Q1
21 P–K5!   . . . .

Now his Bishop comes to life,
and P–K6 is threatened in certain
eventualities. It is up to Black to
create complications.

21 . . . .   N–N5!

22 P–R3   N(5)–Q6!
23 P–QN4!   . . . .

Expecting 23 . . . RxN; 24 PxN
and Black is in difficulties.

23 . . . .   N–R5!!

So that if 24 QxN, N–N7; 25 Q–
Q2, NxR; 26 RxN, R–B5 and wins.

24 RxN   RxN
25 RxR   . . . .

Simpler was 25 QR–Q1, N–B6;
26 Q–K3, RxR; 27 RxR, QxQ; 28
RxQ, P–N3; 29 R–Q3, R–B2 with
an approximately even ending.

25 . . . .   QxR
26 R–K1   . . . .

But not 26 R–Q1?? N–B6! winning a Rook.

26 . . . .   P–N3?

An inexact move which gives
White good chances. Better was 26
. . . N–B6 and if 27 Q–N2, R–B2.

27 Q–R6?   . . . .

Correct was 27 P–K6! R–B1
(practically forced; if 27 . . . P–B4?
28 Q–N5, N–B6; 29 Q–Q7 wins—or
if 27 . . . Q–B3; 28 B–Q5!); 28
PxPch, RxP and White has nothing
to fear.

27 . . . .   R–B7!
28 R–KB1   N–B6
29 QxRP??   . . . .

Losing immediately; but after 29
B–B3, N–N8! 30 Q–N7, N–Q7; 31
R–Q1, QxKP Black should win.

29 ....   RxP!
The move that White overlooked.
30 Q-R8ch   ....
If 30 RxR, N-K7ch!! (not 30 ...

N-Q8? 31 Q-R8ch, K-N2; 32 Q-B3); 31 K-B1, Q-Q8 mate or 31 K-R2, QxR and mate follows.

    30 ....   K-N2
    31 K-R1   ....
If 31 K-R2, N-K7; 32 R-K1, Q-K6 wins.

    31 ....   N-K7
    32 K-R2   ....
Or 32 R-K1, NxPch; 33 K-R2, Q-KB5; 34 K-N1, N-K7ch; 35 K-R1, Q-N6; 36 R-Q1, N-B5; 37 R-KN1, NxB; 38 RxN, R-B8ch etc.

    32 ....   RxR
    33 BxR   Q-N8 mate

THIRD U. S. CHAMPIONSHIP TOURNAMENT NEW YORK, 1940

OCCASIONALLY a tournament becomes a personal duel between two masters. This is more apt to be the case in a "mixed" event where three or four players overshadow all the rest. The Third U. S. Championship was such an event. Almost from the beginning, it was clear that first honors, rested between Reuben Fine and myself.

By chance we two were paired in the last round. As it turned out, this game was to decide the championship of the United States. Judge for yourself under what strain two players labor when the result of more than two weeks work hinges on a single game. To make matters more difficult I had been ill during much of the tournament and, in addition, had several adjourned games prior to this fateful encounter.

Fine established a strong edge by leading the opening into a line I did not know. By shrewd middle-game play, he turned this into an "overwhelming" advantage. Already spectators were saying the game was a "win" for Fine. With so much at stake, I was determined to be shown. Then the miracle happened! Fine miscalculated and with a surprising resource I was able to equalize the position. Nothing remained but a draw — good enough to give me the title by a half-point.

79.

POLLAND–RESHEVSKY
U. S. Championship, 1940
QUEEN'S INDIAN DEFENSE

D. Polland	Reshevsky
WHITE	BLACK
1 P–Q4	N–KB3
2 P–QB4	P–K3
3 N–KB3	P–QN3
4 P–KN3	B–N2
5 B–N2	B–K2

More promising than ... B–N5ch, which generally simplifies to a dreary position for Black in which he has drawing prospects at best (see for example Game 18).The text leads to a fuller game with more possibilities for both sides.

6 O–O	O–O
7 N–B3	N–K5

Virtually imperative, since White is planning to continue Q–B2 followed by P–K4, with a strong center.

8 Q–B2	NxN

8 ... P–KB4 would be disadvantageous because of 9 N–K5! P–Q4 (not 9 ... P–Q3? 10 NxN! winning some material); 10 PxP, PxP and Black's QB is inactive and his position on the QB file is weak.

However 8 ... P–Q4 and if 9 N–K5, NxN; 10 PxN, N–Q2 seems quite playable.

9 QxN	P–KB4
10 P–N3	B–KB3
11 B–N2	P–Q3

Black is developing quite satisfactorily.

12 QR–Q1	Q–K2
13 N–K1	N–B3

Better than 13 ... BxB; 14 NxB followed by N–B4 where the Knight is favorably placed.

14 Q–B1	....

Black was threatening 14 ...

NxP; 15 RxN (if 15 BxB? NxPch), BxB; 16 NxB, P–B4 winning the exchange. But 14 Q–K3 would have been more to the point.

14	K–R1
15 N–B2	....

The Knight has no future here. White should have endeavored to get it to KB4 where it would have exerted more pressure. Hence Q–K3 was still in order, with a view to playing N–Q3–B4.

Another plausible continuation was 15 P–K4, PxP; 16 BxP followed by N–N2.

15	QR–K1
16 KR–K1	N–Q1
17 BxB	NxB
18 P–K4	....

This looks promising, and yet, contrary to appearances, White is advancing at an inopportune moment; most of his pieces are on the Queen-side, so that Black can concentrate effectively on the other wing. It would have been more prudent to play N–K3–N2, enabling the Knight to play a useful defensive role.

18	PxP
19 RxP	Q–Q2
20 R(4)–K1	N–Q1

Intending to i m p r o v e t h e Knight's position by playing ... N–B2–N4 or ... N–B2–R3.

21 P–Q5	BxB
22 QxB	P–K4
23 P–KR4	....

White can hardly avoid this weakening of his King-side, as it is essential to prevent the hostile Knight from reaching KN4 with the formidable threats of ... N–B6ch or ... N–R6ch.

23	N–B2
24 K–N2	N–R3
25 N–K3	Q–B2
26 Q–K2	Q–N3

Black is steadily gaining ground.

27	P–R5?	. . . .

White has become desperate, since he sees that his opponent is ready to strengthen the pressure unobtrusively by doubling t h e Rooks on the KB file. The text, however, is rather pointless, since it weakens the KRP and gives Black's Queen the valuable square KN4. White's best hope was to pursue a quiet waiting policy, hoping to be able to hold the position.

27	. . . .	Q–N4
28	R–KR1	R–B5
29	R–R3	R(1)–KB1
30	R(1)–KR1	. . . .

Polland permits the following transaction in the realization that after 30 R–KB1, P–K5 followed by . . . N–B2–K4 the outlook for him would be grim indeed.

30	. . . .	RxPch!

In the present position, this exchange is favorable to Black, as his Queen is very active and able to harry White's King and Pawns. The Rooks, on the other hand, are curiously ineffective.

31	QxR	RxQch
32	KxR	N–B4!

Offering an exchange which White cannot decline, with the result that Black's Queen is now free to display its enormous mobility.

33	NxN	QxNch
34	K–K3	Q–N4ch
35	K–Q3	P–KR3

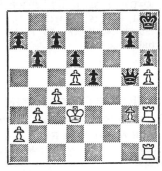

36	R–R4	. . . .

Surprising at first sight, but the loss of the KNP was really unavoidable, for example 36 R(1)–R2, Q–N5; 37 K–K3 (if 37 R–R1, Q–B6ch; 38 K–B2, Q–K7ch; 39 K–N1, P–K6 and White's position is hopeless), P–QN4! 38 PxP, Q–Q8ch, 39 K–K2, QxP. The QNP falls, and Black has two connected passed Pawns which cannot be stopped.

36	. . . .	QxNPch
37	K–K4	. . . .

If 37 K–K2 (or K–Q2), P–K5 and White is unable to capture the KP because of . . . Q–N7ch.

37	. . . .	K–N1
38	R(1)–R2	P–QN4!

This decides quickly.

39	PxP	Q–K8ch
40	K–B3	. . . .

Or 40 K–B5, Q–B8ch winning easily.

40	. . . .	Q–Q8ch
41	K–N3	QxQP
42	R–QB4	P–K5
43	RxBP	Q–K4ch
44	K–N2	P–K6
45	R–R1	Q–K5ch
46	K–R2	Q–R5ch
	Resigns	

White resigns. The conclusion

might have been: 47 K–N2, Q–
N5ch; 48 K–R2, QxPch; 49 K–N2,
Q–N5ch; 50 K–R2, Q–R5ch; 51 K–
N2, Q–B7ch; 52 K–R3, P–K7; 53
R(7)–B1, P–KR4; 54 R(R1)–N1, K–
R2; 55 P–R4, K–R3; 56 P–R5, P–
N4 and wins.

80.

RESHEVSKY–WOLISTON
U. S. Championship, 1940

FRENCH DEFENSE

Reshevsky	P. Woliston
WHITE	BLACK
1 P–K4	P–K3

Here is one of the few occasions
on which I have played 1 P–K4, and
my opponent is not even curious to
see how I would continue after 1 . . .
P–K4.

2 P–Q4	P–Q4
3 N–QB3	PxP

Rarely played nowadays, because
it is rather passive and gives White
too great a command of the board.
3 . . . B–N5 and 3 . . . N–KB3 are
fighting defenses.

4 NxP	QN–Q2
5 N–KB3	KN–B3
6 NxNch	. . . .

6 B–KN5, B–K2; 7 NxNch, BxN;
8 BxB, NxB; 9 B–Q3, O–O; 10 Q–
K2, P–QN3 leads to about an even
game. The text avoids excessive
simplification.

6	NxN
7 B–Q3	P–B4

This early advance frees Black's
game appreciably, but White will
be the first to seize the open Q file.

8 PxP	BxP
9 O–O	O–O
10 B–KN5	P–QN3

The most effective way to develop the Bishop, as 10 . . . B–Q2; 11
N–K5 looks rather unpromising.

11 Q–K2	. . . .

11 N–K5 is aggressive but not
too formidable; thus if 11 . . . B–N2;
12 BxN, QxB! 13 N–Q7, Q–N4
threatening mate.

11	B–N2
12 QR–Q1	Q–B2

Permitting a troublesome weakening of his Pawn structure, but
after 12 . . . Q–K2; 13 N–K5 (threatening N–N4) White would have
good attacking chances.

13 BxN	PxB

This is a far from easy situation
to appraise properly. Black's King
is exposed, and yet it is difficult
to find a clear-cut continuation
which holds out promise of decisive
action. The principal reason for
this is that Black can always shut
out the hostile Bishop with . . . P–
B4! and no attack can amount to
much with this Bishop not taking
part in the attack. An instance: 14
N–Q2, P–B4; 15 Q–R5, K–R1; 16
N–B3, P–B3; 17 N–R4, R–KN1 and
Black's prospects are better. Or 14
N–R4, P–B4; 15 Q–R5, Q–KB5.

This reasoning explains White's
choice of his next move, which
leaves him with a somewhat preferable position for the endgame.

14 B–K4!	QR–Q1
15 BxB	QxB
16 N–Q2	. . . .

Intending to occupy the central square K4.

16	B–K2
17 N–K4	RxR
18 RxR	R–Q1
19 RxRch	BxR
20 Q–Q3	. . . .

This is the kind of position White had in mind when he played his thirteenth and f o u r t e e n t h moves. He has two well-defined advantages in the endgame. One is the nature of the Pawn position, which (a) makes it possible for White to obtain a distant passed Pawn, while the best that Black can do is to obtain a passed KP; and (b) leaves Black's doubled KBP's at the mercy of the kind of attack to which they are later subjected. White's other advantage is that his King has more effective centralizing possibilities, with the result that he will soon be threatening a decisive penetration into Black's position.

20	B–K2
21 P–KR3	Q–B2

Inviting the exchange of Queens, which was inevitable in any event.

22 Q–N3ch	QxQ
23 NxQ	K–B1
24 K–B1	K–K1
25 K–K2	K–Q2

26 K–Q3   . . . .

26 K–B3 (intending to go after the KRP) would be futile because of . . . P–B4.

26	K–B3
27 N–K2!	B–B4
28 P–KB4	P–N4?

This move was best omitted. **The player with the Pawn minority should avoid moving his Pawns when that will facilitate the creation of a hostile passed Pawn.**

29 P–KN4!   . . . .

Gaining a hold on the square KB5, so that his King can occupy the vital post K4; the text also has another object.

29 . . . .   P–QR3

Black is only marking time; he has nothing better available.

30 K–K4!   . . . .

Now there is a standing threat of P–B5, in addition to which the King is poised menacingly for aggressive action.

30	B–B1
31 N–Q4ch	K–Q3
32 N–N3	B–K2
33 N–Q2	B–B1
34 P–B4!	. . . .

Utilizing his Queen-side Pawn majority; by threatening to get a passed Pawn on the Queen-side and at the same time preparing a breakthrough on the other wing, White

creates a double threat against
which Black is powerless.

    34 . . . .   **K–B4**

Black is putting up stout resistance, but his defensive resources
shrink steadily.

    35 PxP   **PxP**
    36 N–N3ch   **K–Q3**

Or 36 . . . K–B5; 37 P–B5! P–K4;
38 N–Q2ch, K–B4; 39 N–B3 followed by P–N5.

    37 N–Q4!   **K–B4**
    38 P–B5!   **P–K4**

If 38 . . . PxP; 39 NxP, K–B3; 40
P–R3! K–B4; 41 P–N3! K–B3; 42
P–N4! K moves; 43 K–Q5 and wins.

After the text Black has a passed
KP, but it is worthless. The threatened advance of White's KNP now
becomes a decisive factor.

    39 N–B3   **P–KR3**

To prevent P–N5.

    40 P–KR4   **B–K2**

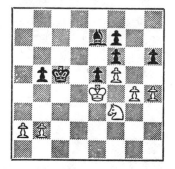

    41 P–R5!   **. . . .**

41 P–N5 is inadequate because of
41 . . . BPxP; 42 PxP, PxP; 43 Nx
KP, P–B3 and Black's KNP is too
dangerous.

    41 . . . .   **B–Q3**
    42 P–R3   **P–N5**

Not good, but Black's position
was already lost. If 42 . . . K–B5; 43
N–Q2ch, K–B4; 44 P–N4ch, K–B3;
45 N–B3, B–B1 (King moves are
answered by K–Q5); 46 P–N5!

RPxP; 47 N–R2! B–N2; 48 N–N4,
K–Q3; 49 P–R6, B–R1; 50 P–R7, B–
N2; 51 N–R6, K–K2; 52 K–Q5 winning the QNP and Black can resign. This shows the underlying
idea of the variation.

    43 P–R4   **P–N6**
    44 N–Q2   **K–N5**
    45 P–R5   **KxP**
    46 N–B4ch   **Resigns**

81.

RESHEVSKY–HANAUER
U. S. Championship, 1940

NIMZOINDIAN DEFENSE

Reshevsky   M. Hanauer
WHITE   BLACK

    1 P–Q4   N–KB3
    2 P–QB4   P–K3
    3 N–QB3   B–N5
    4 P–K3   . . . .

This quiet move gives Black
plenty of leeway and thus holds
out the likely prospect of interesting middle game play.

    4 . . . .   **P–QN3**

For equalizing purposes, 4 . . . P–
Q4 followed by . . . P–B4 is the
simplest course.

    5 N–B3   **B–N2**
    6 B–Q3   **O–O**
    7 P–QR3   **. . . .**

More exact is 7 O–O, P–Q4; 8
PxP, PxP; 9 P–QR3. The text is
superfluous if Black intends . . . P–
Q3, which will virtually force . . .
KBxN in any event, as the KB
would have no retreat.

    7 . . . .   **BxN**
    8 PxB   **P–Q3**

This is more promising than 8
. . . P–Q4, with the likely continuation 9 PxP, PxP; 10 P–B4; P–B4;
11 BPxP, QxP; 12 O–O and White's
position is preferable.

    9 O–O   **Q–K2**

10 R–K1 . . . .

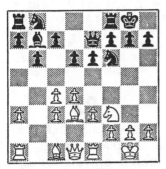

10 . . . . N–K5?

A superficial move which allows White to obtain a definitely superior position. He should either restrain P–K4 by means of 10 ... P–Q4 (despite the loss of time involved) or else play 10 ... P–K4; 11 P–K4, P–B4 followed by ... N–B3, trying to force P–Q5 with an unwieldy Pawn position for White.

However, the method of preventing P–K4 by occupation of K5 will prove unsatisfactory; even after 10 ... B–K5 this would be true (11 B–B1! followed by N–Q2 and P–K4).

11 BxN . . . .

A good alternative was 11 N–Q2, NxN (not 11 ... NxQBP?? 12 Q–B2 winning the Knight); 12 BxN, N–Q2; 13 P–K4, P–K4; 14 P–B4 with an excellent position.

11 . . . . BxB
12 N–Q2 B–N2

... B–N3; 13 Q–B3, P–B3; 14 P–K4 would leave Black with a very poor game.

13 P–K4 . . . .

Despite the Bishops of opposite colors, White has an appreciable advantage because of his strong center and the more promising outlook for his pieces.

13 . . . . P–K4
14 N–B1 . . . .

The Knight is headed for Q5 or KB5 via K3.

14 . . . . N–B3

Black hopes to obtain counterplay by exerting pressure on the QBP.

15 N–K3 PxP?

Undoubling the Pawns is a serious strategic lapse. ... N–R4 was in order.

16 N–Q5 Q–R5

And the wisdom of this move is also questionable. Sooner or later the Queen will have to retreat from this advanced post.

17 PxP QR–K1
18 B–B4! . . . .

This simple developing move puts an end to Black's demonstration of aggressive play.

18 . . . . R–K3
19 B–N3 Q–Q1
20 Q–Q3 N–R4
21 N–N4! . . . .

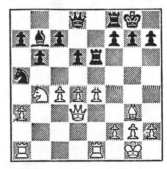

An important move. It prevents ... B–R3 and at the same time prepares the centralized thrust P–Q5 followed by P–B4 and P–K5.

21 . . . . P–QB4

Practically forced in order to secure some counterplay by getting the Bishop to R3; but at the same time he weakens the QP irreparably.

22 P–Q5 R(3)–K1

23 N–B2	B–R3
24 N–K3	Q–B3
25 KR–Q1	R–Q1
26 QR–B1	. . . .

As one of the by-products of
Black's inferior fifteenth move,
White is able to guard his QBP
with the QR, thus freeing his
Knight for action.

| 26 . . . . | R–Q2? |

It was essential to play . . . B–B1
in order to keep the Knight out of
B5. But then White would have an
effective continuation in P–B4 followed by P–K5.

| 27 N–B5 | R–K1 |

And now . . . Q–Q1 had to be
tried, although the advance of
White's center Pawns would still
have been decisive.

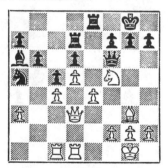

| 28 NxQP! | RxN |
| 29 P–K5 | RxQP |

29 . . . RxKP?? would have been
immediately disastrous because of
30 BxR, QxB; 31 R–K1 and Black's
Queen is lost.

30 PxR	BxQ
31 PxQ	P–B5
32 P–Q6	PxP

. . . R–Q1 would have held out
somewhat longer.

| 33 P–Q7 | R–Q1 |
| 34 RxB! | PxR |

Black's QP looks formidable, but
the danger is slight indeed.

| 35 R–B8! | P–Q7 |

Or 35 . . . N–N2; 36 K–B1, K–N2
(if 36 . . . K–B1; 37 RxRch, NxR; 38
B–Q6ch!); 37 RxR, NxR; 38 B–B7
and wins.

| 36 RxRch | K–N2 |
| 37 R–N8ch | Resigns |

82.

RESHEVSKY–DENKER
U. S. Championship, 1940

QUEEN'S GAMBIT DECLINED
Reshevsky   A. S. Denker
WHITE   BLACK

1 P–Q4	P–Q4
2 N–KB3	N–KB3
3 P–B4	P–K3
4 B–N5	B–K2
5 N–B3	O–O
6 P–K3	N–K5

Lasker's variation, which, despite
its clear violation of opening principles (moving the same piece twice
early in the opening) remains one
of the most satisfactory lines at
Black's disposal. However, the interpolation of 6 . . . P–KR3 has generally proved useful, and the consequences of this omission will be
glaringly noticeable later on.

7 BxB	QxB
8 Q–B2	P–QB3
9 NxN	. . . .

B–Q3 offers somewhat better
chances of securing a slight opening advantage; whereas after the
text, Black has little difficulty in
obtaining a good game.

| 9 . . . . | PxN |
| 10 N–Q2 | . . . . |

After 10 QxP, Q–N5ch; 11 N–Q2,
QxNP; 12 Q–N1, QxQch etc., the
game takes on too drawish a character to suit my taste.

| 10 . . . . | P–KB4 |
| 11 P–B5 | . . . . |

It is important to give White's pieces access to QB4. Against other moves, Black has an easy game (characterized by an early ... P–K4) while White's development is too passive.

| 11 . . . . | N–Q2 |
| 12 B–B4 | N–B3 |

The alternative was ... K–R1 intending an immediate ... P–K4.

| 13 O–O | K–R1 |
| 14 P–B3 | P–K4!? |

The natural move was ... PxP, but true to his style, Denker aims for interesting complications.

| 15 BPxP | N–N5! |

This clever stroke explains his previous move and requires close calculation.

| 16 Q–B3 | . . . . |

But not 16 QR–K1, P–B5! 17 KPxP, PxQP! 18 Q–Q3, QxBP with a good game for Black. However, the immediate Q–Q3 would have saved important time for White.

| 16 . . . . | P–B5! |
| 17 KPxP | PxQP |

Now we see the point of Black's clever fourteenth move: if 18 QxP? R–Q1; 19 Q–B3, QxPch; 20 K–R1 and Black has a choice of winning with 20 ... N–B7ch or 20 ... RxN.

| 18 Q–Q3 | N–K6 |
| 19 R–B2 | QxBP |

Black has regained his Pawn and

in the meantime has posted his Knight favorably and secured a formidable Queen-side m a j o r i t y. White has to play his best from now on to hold his own.

20 P–QR3	P–QN4
21 B–R2	Q–N3
22 N–B3!?	. . . .

The inviting P–QN4 would be effectively answered by ... P–QR4.

White prefers to remove the troublesome QP, for example 22 ... RxP; 23 QxQP! (much better than 23 NxP? RxR; 24 KxR, N–N5ch), QxQ; 24 NxQ, RxR; 25 KxR, N–N5ch; 26 K–N3, N–K4; 27 R–QB1 with annoying pressure on the QBP.

| 22 . . . . | P–B4! |

Denker pluckily continues to seek complications.

| 23 P–QN4! | . . . . |

The situation calls for energetic measures.

| 23 . . . . | P–B5! |

A clever parry. Black gets a strong passed Pawn and immobilizes White's Bishop.

| 24 QxQP | RxP |
| 25 P–R3! | . . . . |

Cutting off the Knight's retreat. The position has become very critical.

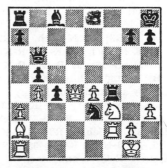

| 25 . . . . | BxP?! |

A very fine conception, which

just barely falls short of success.

26 QxQ!   . . . .

The acceptance of the Bishop would be ruinous: 26 PxB? Q–N3ch; 27 K–R2, RxN! and White is lost.

26 . . . .   PxQ
27 N–N5!!   . . . .

The key to the defense. White wins a piece, but on his terms! 28 PxB? would be wrong because of 28 . . . QR–KB1.

27 . . . .   RxR
28 KxR   . . . .

An extremely difficult situation, especially in time pressure!

28 . . . .   RxP

Some critics have suggested that Black had better practical chances here with . . . BxP or . . . N–N5ch, although White would have won all the same!

I   28 . . . BxP; 29 KxN, RxPch; 30 K–Q4! P–R3; 31 N–B7ch, K–R2; 32 N–Q6, R–Q6ch; 33 K–K5, R–K6; 34 R–Q1, P–B6; 35 B–N1, R–K7; 36 B–Q3 and White wins fairly easily by advancing his KP.

II 28 . . . N–N5ch; 29 K–N3! RxPch; 30 K–B4, BxP; 31 KxN, P–R3; 32 N–B7ch, K–R2; 33 P–K5, R–K6; 34 B–N1ch, K–N1; 35 B–N6, B–Q4; 36 R–Q1!! and wins.

29 PxB   P–R3
30 N–B7ch   K–N1

Or 30 . . . K–R2;   31 R–KN1! RxBch (or 31 . . . P–N3; 32 B–N1 with a winning position); 32 KxN and White wins by advancing the KP.

31 N–Q6   N–Q8ch

If 31 . . . K–B1; 32 NxNP, R–Q6; 33 R–K1 and the KP decides the game. Or 31 . . . N–B7; 32 NxNP, RxP; 33 BxPch and Black can resign.

32 RxN   RxBch
33 K–K3   R–QN7

The game is over.

34 NxNP   RxP
35 N–B3   R–N7
36 R–QN1   R–KR7
37 RxP   Resigns

The win is only a matter of time.

83.

KASHDAN–RESHEVSKY
U. S. Championship, 1940

R U Y   L O P E Z

I. Kashdan	Reshevsky
WHITE	BLACK
1 P–K4	P–K4
2 N–KB3	N–QB3
3 B–N5	P–QR3
4 B–R4	N–B3
5 O–O	B–K2
6 Q–K2	. . . .

This seems to me to give better prospects than 6 R–K1; the Queen move is more aggressive and compels Black to proceed with great care. Its primary purpose is to play R–Q1 followed by P–B3 and P–Q4, creating a strong center and exerting pressure on the Q file—at the same time presenting Black with the troublesome problem of finding a good square for his Queen. In many cases, R–Q1 may be postponed to a later stage.

6 . . . .   P–QN4

7 B–N3	P–Q3
8 P–QR4	B–N5

... QR–N1 is too passive: White plays 9 PxP, PxP; 10 P–R3, O–O; 11 P–B3 followed by P–Q4 and White's control of the QR file is a substantial point in his favor. 8... R–R2 is playable but hardly inviting.

9 P–B3	....

...N–Q5 must be prevented.

9	O–O
10 P–R3	B–R4

A fateful decision. 10...B–Q2 would give the QB better prospects, for as the game goes, the Bishop is eventually driven to KN3, where it plays rather a passive role.

11 P–Q3	....

Kashdan intends to play P–N4 soon; hence he avoids the somewhat loose position which would ensue after R–Q1 and P–Q4 in combination with P–N4.

11	N–R4

Gaining time to round out his Pawn position with ...P–B4.

12 B–B2	P–B4
13 PxP	PxP
14 P–KN4	B–N3
15 QN–Q2	Q–B2
16 N–R4	....

A plausible idea which, however, allows a powerful counterstroke. If however 16 R–Q1 (intending to bring the QN to K3) there might follow 16...N–Q2 (permanently preventing N–R4); 17 N–B1, N–N3 and Black stands well.

16	P–Q4!
17 QN–B3	....

17 PxP would only free Black's game, while if 17 P–N5, N–R4; 18 QN–B3, PxP; 19 PxP, P–B3! with a fine game for Black.

17	PxP

...P–Q5 was a good alternative, with the likely continuation 18 N–B5, PxP; 19 PxP, P–N5 etc.

18 PxP	P–B5

In order to post a Knight at QB4 and eventually at Q6.

19 N–B5	N–N2
20 RxR	....

B–N5 was a promising alternative to the simplifying text. However, Kashdan is indulging in his favorite strategy of obtaining Bishops for Knights.

20	RxR
21 NxBch	QxN
22 N–R4	N–B4

Both players proceed consistently with their respective plans.

23 N–B5	BxN

Permitting White to achieve his ambition and leading to play of great delicacy and complexity.

24 KPxB	....

If 24 NPxB, R–Q1 intending ... N–Q6. If then 25 R–Q1?, RxRch; 26 QxR, KNxP; 27 BxN, NxB; 28 Q–Q5, N–Q3 and Black is a Pawn to the good.

After the text, however, the diagonal of White's KB has been lengthened and P–N5 seems to be a formidable threat. Black's problem of how to employ the short-stepping Knights to good advantage has become very serious.

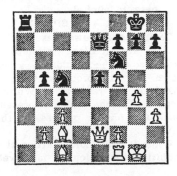

24 ....   P–K5!

Strengthening his command of Q6, at the risk of creating an apparently weak KP. As will be seen, the move requires very thorough consideration of the resulting possibilities.

25 R–Q1   ....

Better was 25 P–B3, leaving Black nothing better than the defensive ...R–K1; if 25...N–Q6; 26 P–N5, N–R4; 27 QxP, QxQ; 28 PxQ, N–N6; 29 BxN!, PxB; 30 R–Q1, R–R8; 31 RxP, RxBch; 32 K–N2 regaining the piece because of the mating threat.

25 P–N5 would have been satisfactorily answered by ...N–Q4; 26 R–Q1, N–Q6; 27 BxN, BPxB; 28 Q–N4, R–R8 or 26 P–B3, P–K6!; 27 P–R4, R–R8—in either event with a splendid game for Black.

25 ....   R–K1

To strengthen the exposed KP.

26 R–Q4   ....

This assures the Rook some freedom before it can be blocked by ...N–Q6.

26 ....   P–R3

Ruling out the possibility of B–N5 or P–N5.

27 B–K3   N–Q6
28 BxN   ....

The capture is inevitable, as the Knight is too strongly posted to be left here indefinitely.

28 ....   BPxB!?

Beginning a new phase which centers around Black's attempt to capitalize on the formidable passed Pawn. Any such procedure must be based on the removal of White's Rook and Bishop, which at present block the further progress of the Pawn.

While it is difficult to arrive at a definitive conclusion, it may well

be that 28...KPxB may have been stronger than the text, which allows White some counter-chances

29 Q–Q1   N–Q2

The Knight is headed for QB5, with a view to exchanging off White's Bishop.

30 K–N2   N–N3
31 Q–N3   ....

This is one of the counterchances allowed by Black's 28th move. The QNP cannot be held.

31 ....   N–B5
32 QxP   NxBch
33 PxN   P–R4?

An inexactitude: Black should have played 33...R–Q1, which would have led to the same kind of ending as actually arises, except that Black's King would have had more secure shelter.

34 P–B6!   ....

Alertly played.

34 ....   NPxP
35 QxP   R–Q1
36 Q–R5   ....

Black was threatening ...P–Q7.

36 ....   RxR
37 BPxR   ....

Forced, as 37 KPxR?? P–K6 would lose in a few moves.

37 ....   Q–N2

Beginning an extraordinarily difficult and exciting struggle. The question is whether Black can support the advance of his passed Pawn and at the same time repulse White's efforts to secure a perpetual check.

38 Q–Q8ch!   ....

Passive defense would never do: if 38 Q–Q2, Q–B2! and the threat of ... Q–B7 is deadly (if 39 K–B2?, Q–R7ch wins at once). If 38 Q–B3, Q–R1! and Black forces an entry via ... Q–R5 or ... Q–R8.

38 ....   **K–N2**

39 P–N5!   ....

The consistent continuation.

39 ....   **P–B4!**

After 39 ... PxP the game would at once be drawn: 40 QxPch, K–R2; 41 Q–R5ch, K–N2; 42 Q–N5ch, K–B1; 43 Q–Q8ch etc.

40 K–B2   ....

In effect, White is marking time. If 40 Q–B6ch, K–N1; 41 P–N6 (or 41 QxP, P–Q7; 42 Q–B1, Q–N6 and the QP queens), P–Q7; 42 PxPch, QxP; 43 Q–Q8ch, K–R2; 44 Q–R4ch, K–N2; 45 Q–N3ch, Q–N3 and wins.

40 ....   **QxPch**

41 K–N3   **Q–N2**

Black has no choice: to play 41 ... P–Q7 would allow White to draw by 42 Q–B6ch etc.

42 K–B2   ....

But not 43 Q–B6ch, K–N1; 44 Q–Q8ch, K–R2; 45 Q–B6, P–Q7; 46

QxP(5)ch, K–N1 and the Pawn must queen.

42 ....   **K–R2**

A new attempt.

43 P–R4?   ....

To prevent Black's next move, White should have played 43 Q–B6. Black would then have no convincing continuation, for if 43 ... P–Q7; 44 K–K2 or 43 ... Q–N7ch; 44 K–N3 and Black's Queen must retreat; or 43 ... Q–B2; 44 Qx P(5)ch, K–N2, 45 QxP etc.

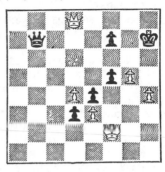

43 ....   **P–B5!!?**

Creating two passed Pawns — and a severe headache for White! A good alternative method was 43 ... Q–N7ch; 44 K–N3, Q–K7 (taking advantage of the momentary freedom allowed by White's last faulty move); 45 P–N6ch, K–N2; 46 PxP, QxPch; 47 K–N2, Q–B6ch; 48 K–R2, KxP and Black has excellent winning chances.

It must be borne in mind that both players were in terrific time pressure hereabouts.

44 PxP   ....

Black was threatening 44 ... Q–N7ch; 45 K–N1, Q–B8ch; 46 K–N2, Q–Q7ch; 47 K–R1, Q–K8ch; 48 K–N2, Q–N6ch and at last Black picks up the Pawns with check.

44 ....   **P–Q7**

45 K–K2   **P–K6**

Threatening an immediate catastrophe with ... Q-N4ch.

46	Q-B6	K-N1
47	Q-Q8ch	K-R2
48	Q-B6	Q-B2!

But not 48...Q-N4ch; 49 KxP, P-Q8(Q); 50 QxPch and White draws with a Queen down! After the text Black threatens 49 ...Q-B5ch (preventing the perpetual check!); 50 KxP, P-Q8(Q) and wins.

| 49 | P-N6ch! | PxP |
| 50 | P-R5! | .... |

Simpler than 50 P-Q5?!, Q-B5ch; 51 KxP, P-Q8(N)ch! (not 51...P-Q8(Q)? 52 Q-K7ch and White draws); 52 K-Q2!, QxPch; 53 K-K1, N-N7!; 54 QxN, Q-R8ch and Black wins both remaining White Pawns and remains with some winning chances.

50	....	Q-B5ch
51	KxP	P-Q8(Q)
52	Q-K7ch	K-R3

After 52...K-N1 White draws with 53 Q-K8ch, K-N2; 54 Q-K7ch!, Q-B2; 55 P-R6ch!, K-N1; 56 P-R7ch!!, QxP; 57 Q-K8ch, K-N2; 58 Q-K7ch, K-R1; 59 Q-B8ch, Q-N1; 60 Q-R6ch etc. or 58...K-R3; 59 Q-R4ch etc.

| 53 | Q-N5ch | K-N2 |

54 QxPch??   ....
Throwing away the draw—very

excusable, after what White has gone through. Correct was 54 Q-K7ch, Q-B2; 55 P-R6ch transposing into the drawing line indicated above.

54	....	K-B1
55	Q-Q6ch	K-K1
	Resigns	

Had Kashdan found the right method on move 54, it would have confirmed the correctness of his intuitive judgment on move 43, although the latter move would still deserve censure because of the practical difficulties which it involved. The lesson which this game drives home is that in difficult situations, one should always select the clearest line (43 Q-B6!) in order to simplify one's problems.

84.

RESHEVSKY-PINKUS
U. S. Championship, 1940
GRUENFELD DEFENSE
Reshevsky   A. S. Pinkus
WHITE   BLACK

1	P-Q4	N-KB3
2	P-QB4	P-KN3
3	N-QB3	P-Q4
4	B-B4	B-N2
5	Q-N3	P-B3
6	P-K3	O-O

More energetic, perhaps, is 6... Q-R4 intending a Queen-side counterattack, similar to that of the Cambridge Springs Defense.

7	N-B3	PxP
8	BxP	QN-Q2
9	O-O	....

The more exact 9 P-K4! would make Black's development more difficult.

9	....	N-N3
10	B-K2	B-K3
11	Q-B2	QN-Q4

Better than 11...KN–Q4, **for** after 12 B–N3 or B–K5, Black need not fear a possible P–K4.

12 B–K5	**B–B4**
13 Q–Q2!	....

An improvement on 13 Q–N3, Q–N3 as played in the game Capablanca–Flohr, Semmering, 1937.

13	**R–B1**

14 KR–B1!	....

Discouraging the contemplated 14...P–B4, for then there would follow 15 NxN, QxN; 16 B–QB4, Q–Q2; 17 PxP, RxP? 18 BxPch etc.

14	**Q–Q2**
15 P–KR3	**KR–Q1**
16 NxN	**NxN**

After 16...PxN; 17 Q–R5 White would have a considerable initiative on the Queen-side.

17 P–QN4!	....

The "good old" minority attack!

17	**P–B3**

This implies that Black intends to utilize another diagonal for his KB; not a bad idea if he had followed it up consistently.

18 B–N3	**B–R3**
19 Q–N2	**P–R3**
20 K–R2	**B–K3**
21 P–QR4	**B–B2**

Black is limited to a patient, waiting policy; he does not know whether White intends a Queen-side advance or a push in the center with P–K4. The latter requires preparation until all of White's forces are posted to the best advantage.

22 N–K1!	**R–R1**
23 N–Q3	....

With the double objective of occupying QB5 and also being able to play P–K4 without allowing... N–B5.

23	**P–N3**

He cannot permit N–B5.

24 R–B2	....

Now he is almost ready for P–K4.

24	**P–K3**
25 R–Q1	....

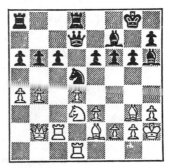

25	**B–B1?**

In view of this cramped position, it is not strange that Black has difficulty in making up his mind to play 25...BxP; 26 PxB, NxKP which was doubtless his best chance; although White's Bishops would eventually assert themselves very strongly. After the text, Black is crushed in short order.

26 P–K4	**N–K2**
27 P–R5!	**QxP**

If 27...PxP; 28 N–B5 with overwhelming positional superiority.

28 QxQ	**RxQ**
29 PxP	**P–K4**

Black apparently relied on this move, as it seems to shut out White's QB.

30 NxP!   RxNP

If 30 . . . RxR (or 30 . . . PxN; 31 RxR, PxR; 32 P–N7 and wins); 31 BxR, PxN; 32 BxP and there is no defense against P–N7.

31 N–Q7!   B–N6

The threat was B–B7 followed by N–B5.

32 R–QN1   BxR

32 . . . P–QR4 would be futile because of 33 R(2)–N2, P–R5; 34 B–Q6 and wins.

33 RxR   N–Q4
34 P–N7   Resigns

85.

BERNSTEIN–RESHEVSKY
U. S. Championship, 1940

G I U O C O   P I A N O

S. N. Bernstein   Reshevsky
WHITE   BLACK
1 P–K4   P–K4
2 N–KB3   N–QB3
3 B–B4   N–B3
4 P–Q3   . . . .

The ancient move 4 N–N5 has once more become contemporary (see for example my memorable game with Fine in the same tournament). In the present encounter, however, White has different intentions.

4 . . . .   B–B4
5 N–B3   P–KR3

Unusual at this point, but I preferred to avoid the Canal Variation (5 . . . P–Q3; 6 B–KN5, P–KR3; 7 BxN, QxB; 8 N–Q5) because of its tricky character and possibilities of prepared analysis.

6 B–K3   B–N5

Here again I avoid the customary line. The text is played in preference to the standard . . . B–N3 in order to avoid drawish positions and routine play.

7 O–O   BxN
8 PxB   O–O

Black's QP has been held back with a vague idea of possibly advancing it two squares; however, 8 . . . P–Q4? would be a mistake because of 9 PxP, NxP; 10 B–B5 and Black is unable to castle.

9 R–K1   P–Q3

Deciding against the advance after all, for if 9 . . . P–Q4; 10 PxP, NxP; 11 B–Q2, R–K1; 12 P–KR3 and while Black's KP can be defended without too much difficulty, the opening up of the position has given White's Bishops good prospects.

10 R–N1   . . . .

P–QR3 or P–QR4 would have preserved the KB against the exchange which follows. The text was played with the idea of shifting the QR to the King-side, but, as will be seen, Black has nothing to fear from this maneuver.

10 . . . .   N–QR4

Removing the KB makes it possible for Black to free his game later on with . . . P–KB4. He does not mind the Bishops of opposite colors, as there is still plenty of play left in the position.

11 B–N3   NxB
12 RxN   . . . .

Still faithful to the plan outlined in the note to his tenth move;

the recapture with the RP would
have strengthened his Pawn position.

12	P–QN3
13 P–B4	B–K3
14 N–Q2	. . . .

Preparing for P–Q4 or P–B4 according to circumstances. If instead
14 P–KR3 (to prevent Black's next
move), ...N–Q2 followed by ...
P–KB4 and Black still manages to
seize the initiative.

14	N–N5

With this move, Black accomplishes three worthwhile object-
ives: he gets rid of the Bishops of
opposite colors, he prepares for ...
P–KB4 and he leaves himself with
a strong Bishop against a rather
weak Knight.

15 P–Q4?	. . . .

White would have been much
better off to avoid this move, which
leads to a lasting weakness in his
Pawn position. But he is still angling for the shift of his QR to the
King-side.

15	NxB

15 ... PxP would leave White
with a terrible Pawn position, it is
true; but after 16 BxQP White
would have good attacking chances.

16 PxN	P–KB4
17 P–Q5	. . . .

This move was inevitable, as the
BP cannot indefinitely be left exposed to attack. However, White's
Pawns fixed on white squares are
bound to succumb to the Bishop in
an endgame.

17	B–Q2

Black's position is now quite
promising. His pieces can be developed effectively and his Pawn
structure shows no weaknesses.

18 PxP	RxP
19 R–B1	. . . .

Too slow. The immediate P–K4
was preferable.

19	RxRch
20 NxR	Q–R5

Seizing the initiative, which he
now maintains.

21 Q–K2	R–KB1
22 N–N3	B–K1!

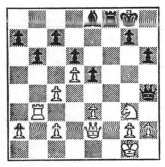

23 P–K4	. . . .

That Bernstein was well aware
of the difficulties of his position is
indicated by the following note in
Chess Review: "Played very reluc-
tantly, since it creates a terrible
weakness at KB4. But otherwise
Black simply plays ...B–N3, ...
Q–N4, ...P–KR4–5 followed by ...
B–K5 with an overwhelming position. An attempt by White to prevent this maneuver would be futile: 23 R–N1, B–N3; 24 R–KB1,
RxRch!; 25 NxR forced, B–R4; 26

Q–Q3 forced, Q–K8; 27 Q–Q2, Q–
N8! 28 P–B3, B–N3 with a winning
game."

From now on, the superiority of
the Bishop over the Knight plays
a vital role.

23	B–N3
24 R–R3	P–QR4
25 R–KB3	R–B5!

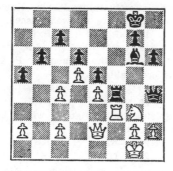

Black's last move has established
a powerful bind on the position, as
shown in the following variations:

I 26 RxR, QxR; 27 Q–K1, P–R4
followed by . . . P–KR5 with decisive effect.

II 26 N–B5, BxN; 27 PxB, RxR;
28 QxR, QxP and wins—or 28 . . . Q–
K8ch; 29 Q–B1, QxQch; 30 KxQ,
K–B2; 31 K–B2, K–B3; 32 P–N4,
P–R4; 33 P–KR3, PxP; 34 PxP, K–
N4; 35 K–B3, P–K5ch and wins.

26 Q–B1   . . . .

A clever defense which serves
for the time being: if 26 . . . BxP?,
27 RxR wins a piece.

26 . . . .   Q–N4

The duly prepared advance of
Black's KRP will eventually shatter White's defensive system.

27 Q–B1	Q–N5
28 P–KR3	Q–R5
29 K–R2	P–R4
30 P–R3	Q–B3
31 Q–B1	Q–N4
32 Q–B1	Q–R3!

A strong move; now that the
Queen is protected, Black threat-
ens 33 . . . P–KR5, for if 34 N–B5,
BxN; 35 RxR (if 35 PxB, RxQBP
—or else 35 . . . RxR; 36 QxQ, PxQ;
37 PxR, K–B2; 38 K–N2, K–B3
etc.), QxRch; 36 QxQ, PxQ; 37
PxB, K–B2; 38 K–N1, K–B3; 39 K–
B2, KxP; 40 K–B3, P–R5; 41 P–B3,
P–KN4 and wins.

33 K–N1   P–KR5

Forcing a won ending.

34 RxR	QxR
35 QxQ	PxQ
36 N–K2	BxP

37 N–Q4   . . . .

Now the ending proves hopeless
for White. On 37 NxP, BxBP;
38 N–K6, B–N6; 39 NxBP, BxP; 40
N–R8, P–QN4; 41 N–N6, K–B2; 42
N–B8, K–B3; 43 NxP, K–K4 and
Black wins easily with his Queen-
side Pawns.

37 . . . .   K–B2

38 N–N5   . . . .

If 38 P–B3, B–Q6 wins.

38	BxBP
39 NxBP	B–Q6
40 N–R8	P–QN4
41 PxP	BxP
42 K–B2	K–B3
43 N–N6	B–R3

To prevent N–B8. White is steadily forced to give ground.

44 K–B3   K–B4

45	N–R8	B–Q6!
46	N–N6	P–N4
47	P–R4	....

Putting another Pawn on the fatal color; however, if the Knight moves, ...B–K5ch wins; or if 47 K–B2, K–K5 etc.

| 47 | .... | B–R3 |

48	N–R8	B–B5
49	N–N6	B–N6!

Zugzwang! White's King must give way.

50	K–B2	K–K5
	Resigns	

White resigns. T h e vulnerable Pawns must soon fall.

U. S. CHAMPIONSHIP MATCH, 1940

MY MATCH with I. A. Horowitz, one of America's most popular masters, was one of those affairs which make certain critics tear their hair. Of sixteen games, only three were decisive. This, the critics insist, shows that chess suffers from the "death of the draw." The elusive fallacy of this argument is revealed by the answer to the simple question "why were the games drawn?" If they were the consequence of perfect play by both sides, the critics might be justified but when, as frequently happens, they are the result of mutual blunders (in time pressure and otherwise), the argument falls flat. The games in my match with Horowitz were exceptionally hard-fought. We had to play them at the rate of one a day so that toward the finish it became a matter of endurance rather than chess generalship. Both of us missed opportunities to score; in this respect my opponent was quite unfortunate. A study of all of the games gives quite a different picture from the bald recitation of three wins, thirteen draws.

Amusing confirmation of the curious way in which draws come about can be found in my game with Fine from the New York State tournament at Hamilton. This can be most charitably termed a comedy of errors authored by the severe time pressure into which we got ourselves.

86.

RESHEVSKY–HOROWITZ
5th Match Game, 1941

KING'S INDIAN DEFENSE

Reshevsky	I. A. Horowitz
WHITE	BLACK
1 P–Q4	N–KB3
2 P–QB4	P–KN3
3 N–QB3	B–N2

As time goes on, this line of play (in which White is permitted to play P–K4) is steadily losing popularity in favor of 3 . . . P–Q4. The text gives White too much leeway.

4 P–K4	P–Q3
5 P–KN3	O–O
6 B–N2	P–K4
7 P–Q5	....

White could also postpone committing himself in the center by simply continuing his development with KN–K2.

| 7 . . . . | P–QR4 |

In order to post his QN at QB4 and secure it from attack by P–QN4 — a maneuver frequently encountered in this type of Pawn position.

| 8 KN–K2 | .... |

Superior to N–B3; now White will be able to advance his KBP quickly.

8	N–R3
9 O–O	N–B4
10 P–KR3	....

Preventing . . . N–N5 in reply to B–K3.

| 10 . . . . | N–K1 |

He prepares for . . . P–B4 — the only plausible form of counterplay available to him.

| 11 B–K3 | P–B4 |
| 12 PxP | BxP |

Despite the fact that Black gains time for development by this mode of recapture, it would have

been more logical to play 12 . . . PxP. Then, after 13 P–B4, Q–K2 (in order to be able to answer PxP with . . . PxP), Black would still have fighting chances. Inferior, however, would be . . . P–K5, which would allow White to proceed by occupying the important square Q4 and later driving away the QN with P–R3 and P–QN4.

| 13 P–B4! | P–N3 |

This creates a serious weakness at Black's QB3 which will be effectively exploited later on.

. . . N–Q6? would have been even worse because of 14 P–KN4, NxNP; 15 Q–N3 winning a piece. And 13 . . . B–Q6? would have been refuted by 14 BxN, BxN; 15 QxB, PxB; 16 PxP etc.

But 13 . . . Q–K2 would have been relatively better.

| 14 PxP | BxKP |

Allowing White to occupy t h e valuable center square Q4 with unpleasant consequences for his opponent. However, the alternative 14 . . . PxP; 15 BxN, PxB; 16 P–KN4, B–Q2; 17 N–K4 was even less inviting; White's Knight would have been posted unassailably at K4, with the loss of the QBP inevitable.

| 15 P–KN4! | .... |

The necessary preliminary to a

maneuver which will soon set off
White's superiority convincingly.

15 . . . .   B–Q2

After the apparently more aggressive 15 . . . B–Q6 White could
continue 16 RxRch, KxR; 17 N–B4!
(not 17 BxN, QBxN; 18 BxPch, Qx
B; 19 QxB, BxN; 20 PxB, N–B3
and White's win of a Pawn is nul-
lified by his worthless Pawn position), BxP (if 17 . . . BxKN; 18 Bx
B, BxP? 19 Q–Q4 with a winning attack); 18 N–K6ch, NxN; 19 PxN,
R–N1; 20 B–Q5 with a strong
attack.

For example, if 20 . . . BxN; 21
BxB, BxP; 22 B–R6ch, B–N2; 23
Q–B3ch, Q–B3; 24 R–KB1, QxQ; 25
RxQch, K–N1; 26 P–K7ch, K–R1;
27 R–B8ch and mate next move.

16 RxRch   KxR
17 Q–Q2   K–N1
18 N–Q4   R–B1

The Rook must be removed from
the terrible diagonal; White was
threatening N–K6 with overwhelming effect.

19 QN–N5!   N–B3

Black is equally p o w e r l e s s
against the following formidable
Knight maneuver. If 19 . . . Q–R5;
20 N–KB3, Q–N6; 21 NxB, QxN; 22
B–Q4 and White's mastery of the
black squares leaves t h e hostile
King in a precarious position.

20 N–R7   R–R1
21 N(7)–B6   Q–K1
22 NxB   . . . .

22 R–KB1, KN–K5; 23 Q–QB2,
B–N2; 24 R–K1 was an attractive
alternative, but the removal of the
valuable Bishop was too tempting
a consideration.

22 . . . .   QxN

. . . PxN would leave Black with
a shattered Pawn position.

23 N–B6   BxN

Black must have parted with his
remaining Bishop only with the
greatest reluctance, but 23 . . . Q–
K1; 24 B–Q4 (or R–K1 or R–KB1)
would have lost even more rapidly.

24 B–Q4!   KN–K5
25 Q–K3   Q–N6

In view of the many weaknesses
in Black's position, forcing the exchange of Queens seems his best
course. But, as will soon be apparent, the ending is extremely unfavorable for him.

26 PxB!   . . . .

The seemingly crushing 26 Q–R6
is met by 26 . . . N–K3!! 27 PxN,
N–B3!

26 . . . .   QxQch
27 BxQ   R–K1

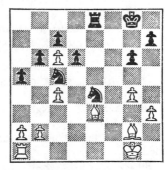

The ending is very much against
Black. The Bishops have considerable range, whereas the Knights
can accomplish very little. In addi-

tion, the advanced QBP is a constant menace, and White has concrete possibilities of invasion via the KB file.

28 R–K1   K–B1

White was threatening to win a piece with QBxN.

29 B–Q4   . . . .

P–KR4 (preventing Black's next move) would be even stronger.

29 . . . .   P–KN4
30 R–K3   R–K2
31 P–N3   P–R3
32 K–B1   R–B2ch

Or 32 ... N–Q7ch; 33 K–K2, N(7)–K5; 34 K–Q1 followed by K–B2, P–R3 and P–N4.

33 K–K1   R–K2

Black is condemned to passivity.

34 K–Q1   K–B2
35 P–R3   N–B3

White was threatening to win a piece with 36 P–N4.

36 R–B3   . . . .

Preferring to retain this Rook because it is more active than its adversary.

36 . . . .   N–K5
37 R–B5   K–N3

White was again threatening to win a piece—this time with 38 KBxN. 37 ... K–K3?? would have led to a lovely finish: 38 QBxN, NxB; 39 B–Q5ch!, NxB; 40 PxN mate!

38 K–B2   P–R4

Or 38 ... R–B2; 39 K–Q3 and Black is helpless.

39 KBxN!   NxB
40 R–B3!   . . . .

The decisive inroad into Black's position.

40 . . . .   PxP
41 PxP   R–R2

This offers little hope, as the Rook must guard the QBP and the Knight has no prospects.

42 P–N4   P–R5

Or 42 ... PxP; 43 PxP, R–R7ch; 44 K–Q3, N–Q7; 45 R–N8ch, K–B2; 46 R–N7ch, K–K3; 47 RxBP and Black can resign.

43 K–Q3   R–K2
44 R–N8ch   K–R3

44 ... K–B2; 45 R–N7ch wins a piece for White.

45 R–Q8!   N–N6
46 R–Q7   R–K8

Or 46 .. R–R2; 47 RxRch, KxR; 48 BxP! and wins.

47 BxP!   R–QR8

If 47 ... PxB; 48 P–B7, R–K1; 49 R–Q8 etc.

48 RxPch!   Resigns

87.

RESHEVSKY–HOROWITZ
11th Match Game, 1941

QUEEN'S GAMBIT DECLINED
Reshevsky   I. A. Horowitz
WHITE   BLACK

1 P–Q4   P–Q4
2 P–QB4   P–QB3
3 N–KB3   N–B3
4 N–B3   PxP
5 P–QR4   . . . .

An excellent alternative is 5 P–K3, P–QN4; 6 P–QR4, P–N5; 7 N–R2, P–K3; 8 BxP etc. as in Game 101.

5	B–B4
6 P–K3	P–K3
7 BxP	QN–Q2
8 O–O	B–K2

...B–QN5 is usually played in order to restrain an eventual P–K4 and also to make room for Black's Queen at K2. The text, although more passive, should lead to a reasonably satisfactory position.

| 9 P–R3 | . . . . |

A conservative move which gives Black time to obtain a fair game. Q–K2 was in order.

| 9 . . . . | O–O |
| 10 B–Q3 | . . . . |

And here again Q–K2 would have been more promising, for instance 10 . . . N–K5; 11 N–Q2, QN–B3; 12 KNxN, NxN; 13 B–Q3, NxN; 14 PxN, BxB; 15 QxB and White's Pawn position given him a promising game (see Game 64 for an instance of the utilization of such a position).

| 10 . . . . | BxB |
| 11 QxB | Q–B2 |

This quiet move makes room for the QR, which should be quite effective on the Q file after White's next move. However, 11 . . . P–B4 was also playable.

| 12 P–K4 | . . . . |

This leaves White's center in a somewhat shaky state, but he has no choice, as Black is gaining freedom too rapidly.

| 12 . . . . | P–K4 |
| 13 B–N5 | . . . . |

Too ambitious; he should have been content with 13 B–K3.

| 13 . . . . | QR–Q1 |
| 14 Q–K2 | . . . . |

Hardly an ideal square for the Queen because Black is about to play his KR to K1. Other things being equal, the proper square for the Queen would have been QB2,

but White did not care for 14 Q–B2, PxP; 15 NxP, N–N5; 16 PxN (forced), BxB and White has a King-side weakness which will prove troublesome.

14	PxP
15 NxP	KR–K1
16 Q–B2	. . . .

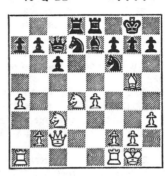

| 16 . . . . | B–Q3? |

Weak, after his excellent play to this point, Horowitz misses the far superior move 16 . . . N–N5! which would have assured him at least equality.

| 17 QR–Q1 | P–KR3 |
| 18 B–R4 | B–K4 |

18 . . . P–KN4?; 19 B–N3, BxB; 20 PxB, QxP would be poor policy because of 21 N–B5 followed by 22 NxPch with a winning attack.

| 19 KN–K2 | N–B1 |

At the moment Black appears to have a promising position, but White quickly demonstrates that this is not the case.

| 20 RxR! | QxR |

20 . . . RxR; 21 P–B4 would also leave Black with a difficult position.

21 P–B4	B–Q5ch
22 NxB	QxNch
23 B–B2	Q–N5
24 P–K5	. . . .

This advance may be reckoned as virtually decisive, for White now has access to the important square Q6 and a general advance of his King-side Pawns—with devastating effect for Black.

    24 ....   **N–Q4**

    25 N–K4!   **....**

White naturally avoids the exchange as he prefers to preserve his pieces for attacking purposes

    25 ....   **N–K3**

But not 25 ... NxP? 26 B–B5 winning a piece.

    26 P–KN3   **....**

P–B5 would not do because of ... N–Q5.

    26 ....   **N–Q5**

    27 Q–Q3   **N–B4**

This attempt to prevent the occupation of his Q3 is bound to be inadequate.

    28 P–N3   **P–KN3**

Black has to protect his Knight on B4 before N–B6ch becomes a serious threat.

    29 B–B5   **Q–R4**

    30 P–KN4   **N–N2**

    31 B–Q6   **....**

At last the stage has been set for P–B5.

    31 ....   **Q–N3ch**

    32 K–R1   **....**

    32 ....   **P–QR4**

White's attack has attained overwhelming proportions. If 32 ... N–K3; 33 P–B5, N(3)–B5; 34 PxP!, NxNP (if 34 ... PxP; 35 N–B6ch,

K–R1; 36 Q–K4, NxN; 37 Qx N and wins. Or 34 ... NxQ?; 35 PxPch and wins); 35 Q–KB3, and Black can resign.

    33 P–B5   **PxP**

White was threatening 34 PxP, PxP; 34 N–B6ch, NxN; 36 PxN and the game is over.

If 33 ... Q–K6; 34 N–B6ch, K–R1; 35 QxQ, NxQ; 36 R–B3 wins.

    34 PxP   **K–R1**

    35 P–K6!   **P–B3**

Or 35 ... PxP; 36 P–B6, N–B4; 37 P–B7 winning the Rook.

    36 B–B5!   **Q–R3**

What to do?! if 36 ... Q–Q1; 37 N–Q6 wins easily. If 36 ... Q–B2; 37 Q–Q2, K–R2; 38 Q–KN2, N–B5; 39 Q–N4 wins.

    37 Q–KB3   **R–KN1**

    38 R–KN1   **N–K1**

Or 38 ... P–N3; 39 R–N6!, K–R2; 40 Q–N2!, PxB; 41 RxPch!, KxR; 42 Q–N6 mate!

    39 Q–R5   **RxRch**

    40 KxR   **N–N2**

    41 QxPch   **K–N1**

    42 B–B8!   **Resigns**

Black is helpless: if 42 ... KxB (or 42 ... Q–R2ch; 43 K–R1, P–N3; 44 P–K7 wins); 43 Q–R8ch, K–K2; 44 QxNch, K–K1; 45 Q–B7ch, K–Q1; 46 Q–Q7 mate. If 42 ... NxBP; 43 Q–N6ch decides the issue.

88.

RESHEVSKY–FINE
N. Y. State Championship
Hamilton, 1941

NIMZOINDIAN DEFENSE

Reshevsky	R. Fine
WHITE	BLACK
1 P–Q4	N–KB3
2 P–QB4	P–K3
3 N–QB3	B–N5
4 P–K3	P–Q4
5 P–QR3	. . . .

White's best continuation: the two Bishops and solid center assure him attacking chances, while the resulting doubled Pawn can be liquidated at will.

5	BxNch
6 PxB	P–B4
7 BPxP	KPxP

Judging from the further course of this game, Black might be better off with 7 ... QxP, as in Game No. 90.

8 B–Q3	O–O
9 N–K2	P–QN3
10 O–O	B–R3
11 BxB	. . . .

Both sides gain from this exchange: Black rids himself of the dangerous attacking Bishop, while White brings about the placement of the hostile QN on rather a poor square. 11 B–B2 would preserve the Bishop as the spark plug of White's attacking chances, but at the same time Black's Bishop would be left with a superb diagonal.

11	NxB
12 Q–Q3	. . . .

Hoping for ... P–B5, which would stabilize the center and lead to a powerful reaction later on with P–B3 and P–K4.

12	Q–B1
13 B–N2	. . . .

The only drawback to White's potentially powerful position is the fact that this Bishop has to operate behind his own Pawn structure.

13	PxP

Realizing that the consequences of 13 ... P–B5 are likely to prove unsatisfactory, Fine hopes to obtain counterplay on the QB file. In this he is doomed to disappointment.

14 BPxP	N–B2

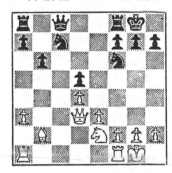

15 KR–B1!	. . . .

Fine had hoped for 15 P–B3 (White's logical continuation), R–K1; 16 N–N3, Q–R3; 17 Q–Q2, N–N4; 18 KR–K1, N–Q3. Not only is P–K4 prevented, but Black is on the point of playing ... N–B5 ...

15	Q–Q2

... Whereas if now 15 ... Q–R3; 16 QxQ, NxQ; 17 R–B6, QR–B1; 18 QR–QB1, RxR; 19 RxR and White's control of the QB file gives him a vastly superior game.

16 P–B3	KR–K1
17 N–N3	N–K3

So that if 18 P–K4? PxP; 19 PxP, N–B4 winning the KP. However, the advance of the KP cannot be held back much longer.

18 R–K1	QR–B1
19 QR–Q1	. . . .

It is important to give the Queen additional protection, for if 19 P–K4?, PxP; 20 PxP, N–B4; 21 Q–

KB3, N–R5 with good counterplay.

| 19 . . . . | Q–R5 |

And now 20 P–K4 would be answered by . . . Q–B7. One must admire the resourcefulness w i t h which Fine makes the most of an inferior position.

| 20 R–Q2 | Q–B5 |
| 21 Q–N1 | Q–N6 |

Consistently carrying out his plan by aiming at the occupation of White's QB2. However, this plan proves inadequate; hence Fine subsequently recommended . . . KR–Q1 —still with the idea of impeding the advance of the KP.

| 22 N–B5 | R–B2 |
| 23 P–K4 | . . . . |

At last this Pawn advances.

| 23 . . . . | KR–QB1 |
| 24 R–Q3 | . . . . |

Well-timed, as 24 . . . Q–B7? would cost the exchange after 25 QxQ, RxQ; 26 N–K7ch.

24	Q–R5
25 P–K5	N–K1
26 N–K3	Q–N4
27 R–Q2	Q–N6

He does not care to allow Q–R2.

| 28 R–Q3 | Q–N4 |
| 29 R–Q2 | Q–R4 |

There is not much point in returning to N6, as White could simply continue his King-side activities with P–N3 and P–B4, with a formidable attacking formation.

| 30 Q–Q1 | Q–N4 |
| 31 P–N3 | P–N3 |

This weakening advance is unavoidable if Black is to defend himself against the threatened advance of the BP.

| 32 P–B4 | P–B4 |
| 33 Q–B3 | . . . . |

To capture in passing would be poor play, as it would enable Black to land a Knight on K5.

| 33 . . . . | R–Q1 |

| 34 P–N4 | N(1)–N2 |
| 35 PxP | N(2)xP |

Black has little choice: after 35 . . . PxP the maneuvering scope of his pieces would be drastically restricted, and he could hardly hope to meet an attack based on the doubling of the Rooks on the KN file supplemented by the advance of White's KRP right down to KR6.

| 36 N–N4 | . . . . |

After 36 NxN, PxN; 37 R–N2ch, R–N2 Black would be much better off than in the previous note.

36	R–B2
37 N–B6ch	K–R1
38 R–QB1	RxN!?

Fine felt that the sacrifice of the exchange was his best chance, for passive defense would leave him permanently cramped.

| 39 PxR | R–KB1 |
| 40 R–K1 | RxP |

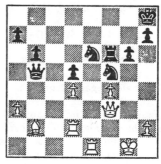

White's task is now to activate his Rooks and get a good diagonal for his Bishop.

| 41 P–QR4! | . . . . |

A strong and unexpected sealed move!

| 41 . . . . | Q–Q2 |

41 . . . QxP?; 42 QxP is obviously bad for Black, as the eventual opening of the long diagonal by means of the advance of the passed QP would soon have fatal consequences.

42 R–KB2	N–B2

It is clear that the capture of the QP would be suicidal.

43 R–B2	R–B2
44 R(1)–QB1	N–K1
45 B–R3!	....

At long last the Bishop becomes an active participant in the game.

45	N–B3?

This should have been fatal. Correct was 45...K–N2; 46 R–B8, R–B3 followed by...R–K3; or 46 Q–K2, N–B3; 47 Q–K5, N–R5 — and in either event Black seems to have an adequate defense.

46 R–B8ch	K–N2
47 B–B8ch!	....

With proper play, this should have been the winning move. Capture of the Bishop would lose the Queen.

47	K–N1

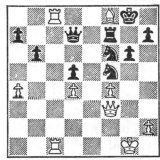

48 B–Q6ch?	....

There was a clear win with 48 QxP!! (48 B–R6ch, N–K1; 49 QxP! would also do the trick, for if 49 ...NxB; 50 QxQ, RxQ; 51 RxNch and wins). After 48 QxP!! Black would have no good move:

I 48...QxQ? or 48...NxQ; 49 B–R6ch and mate follows.

II 48...QxR? 49 RxQ, NxQ; 50 B–R6ch and mate follows.

III 48...N–N2; 49 QxQ, RxQ; 50 BxNch, KxB; 51 R(1)–B7 with a technically easy win.

48	N–K1
49 B–K5	N–K2
50 R–R8?	....

And here there was a much more forceful line in 50 R(1)–B7! QxP (or 50...NxR; 51 RxQ, RxR; 52 Q–N4 and wins); 51 R–R8, P–QR4; 52 R–N7 with a winning game. The text allows Black to remove the formidable B i s h o p. White's inexactitudes are due to shortage of time (the next ten moves had to be made in four minutes).

50	N–B3
51 P–R3	NxB
52 QPxN	QxQRP
53 R(1)–B8	R–B1
54 P–K6	K–N2

What a position to have to play in time pressure!

55 P–K7?	....

55 Q–K1! would have won for

I 55...RxP; 56 RxN, Q–Q8ch; 57 K–N2, Q–B8ch; 58 K–N3, R–K5 (if 58...P–N4; 59 P–K7 wins); 59 R–N8ch and wins.

II 55...P–Q5; 56 Q–K1!, RxP; 57 RxN, R–B4; 58 R–N8ch, K–R3; 59 R(R8)–KB8 and wins.

55	RxP
56 Q–Q3	R–B4
57 R–B2	....

But not 57 RxN?, Q–R8ch; 58 K–N2 (if 58 K–R2, R–B7ch; 59 K–N3, Q–N8ch; 60 K–R4, R–B5 mate), R–N4ch; 59 K–B3 (if 59 K–B2, Q–N8ch), Q–B3ch; 60 K–K2 (if 60 K–K3, R–N6ch; 61 K–K2, Q–N7ch; 62 Q–Q2, R–N7ch etc.), R–N7ch; 61 K–K1, Q–R8ch or...Q–B7ch winning.

57	Q–R5?!

A swindle which should not have succeeded. The right course was 57 ...Q–R8ch; 58 K–R2, Q–K4ch followed by...QxP and White must fight for a draw.

58 R–K2? . . . .

A final mistake: 58 RxN would have won, as the following analysis demonstrates:

I 58 ... Q–N4ch; 59 K–R1 and Black has no more checks.

II 58 ... Q–K8ch; 59 K–R2, Q–K4ch; 60 Q–N3 with the same result.

III 58 ... Q–K8ch; 59 K–R2, R–B7ch; 60 RxR, QxRch; 61 K–R1, Q–K8ch; 62 K–N2 and again the checks are over.

IV 58 ... R–N4ch; 59 K–R2, Q–B5ch; 60 K–R1 and despite the apparently exposed position of White's King, Black has no check!

| 58 . . . . | R–N4ch |
| 59 R–N2 | . . . . |

If 59 K–R1 (not 59 K–R2??, Q–B5ch followed by mate), R–N6 etc.

59	RxRch
60 KxR	QxP
61 QxP	Drawn

A wise decision: after 61 ... Q–K7ch; 62 K–N1!, Q–K8ch Black must be content with the perpetual check, and White must not try to evade it.

FOURTH U. S. CHAMPIONSHIP TOURNAMENT NEW YORK, 1942

SAVING a lost game in the final round of the U. S. championship seems to have become my specialty. That I should have to do it at all in the 1942 event shows how difficult it is to win a title. After scoring 8½-½ in my first nine games and coming into the last one with 12-2, I should have had a big lead. Yet my margin over Kashdan was only half a point. Playing some of the best chess of his career, he had dogged my steps every inch of the way. In the final session, he quickly defeated his opponent, while I faced a terrific battle with Horowitz. At adjournment, I was a Pawn behind and it seemed as if I were lost. The slim drawing chances lay in the fact that we had Bishops of opposite colors. At the crucial point, Horowitz faltered. Suddenly I was able to block the position. He could not win and I had saved the title.

89.

SEIDMAN–RESHEVSKY
U. S. Championship, 1942

R U Y   L O P E Z

H. Seidman	Reshevsky
WHITE	BLACK
1 P–K4	P–K4
2 N–KB3	N–QB3
3 B–N5	P–QR3
4 B–R4	N–B3
5 O–O	B–K2
6 Q–K2	. . . .

As I have already indicated, this is the continuation best calculated to create difficulties for Black.

6	P–QN4
7 B–N3	P–Q3
8 P–QR4	B–N5
9 P–B3	O–O
10 P–R3	. . . .

In order to compel a decision by the QB. 10 PxP, PxP; 11 RxR, QxR; 12 QxP, N–R2!; 13 Q–K2, QxP; 14 QxQ, NxQ is slightly in Black's favor.

10	B–R4
11 R–Q1	. . . .

In Game 83 Kashdan played the more solid 11 P–Q3, N–R4; 12 B–B2, P–B4; 13 PxP, PxP; 14 P–KN4. In the present game, Seidman contemplates a combination of P–Q4 and P–KN4 — perhaps an overambitious conception.

11	P–N5!

Beginning a counteraction whose consequences Seidman underestimates, else he would have replied 12 P–R5!

12 P–Q4	NPxP!
13 P–N4	. . . .

This leads to a crisis. White apparently thinks that he can either gain a piece or else secure an overwhelming position.

Somewhat better was 13 NPxP

with the likely continuation 13 . . . PxP; 14 PxP, P–Q4!; 15 P–K5, N–K5 with a satisfactory position for Black.

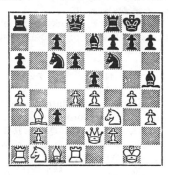

13	Q–N1!

After 13 . . . B–N3 White could play 14 QNxP with a fine game, or else, more aggressively, 14 QPxP, KNxP; 15 NxP (not 15 B–Q5, when Black saves himself with P–B7!).

The text had to be calculated very carefully, as White's reply seems to win a piece.

14 B–Q5?	. . . .

Snatching at the bait.

14	NxB!

To interpolate . . . BPxP? would be a serious blunder, for reasons that will soon be clear. **The QBP must be preserved.**

15 PxN	. . . .

How is Black to avoid the loss of a piece?!

15	B–N3!

This is the resource which White overlooked. If 16 PxN? P–B7! wins.

16 NPxP	. . . .

Or 16 QNxP, NxP; 17 NxN, PxN; 18 QxB, PxN; 19 PxP, Q–N6 and the outlook for White's game is poor.

16	N–R4

Now Black has the initiative. If 17 B–K3, N–N6; 18 R–R2, PxP; 19

PxP, BxN; 20 RxB, NxP! winning the exchange.

    17 QN–Q2   PxP!

Another pretty move.

    18 QxB   . . . .

After 18 NxP, Black could play either . . . . R–K1 or . . . B–B3 with marked advantage.

    18 . . . .   R–K1
    19 Q–N5   PxP
    20 N–R4   . . . .

An attempt to retain the piece would be disastrous, for example 20 N–B1, P–KB3; 21 Q–B4, R–K5; 22 Q–N3, P–B7; 23 R–K1, N–N6; 24 RxRch, BxR and wins.

    20 . . . .   P–KB3!

The most exact reply, for after 20 . . . PxN; 21 BxP, N–N6 (or 21 . . . N–B5; 22 B–B3); 22 NxB, RPx N; 23 QR–N1 the pin is troublesome for Black.

    21 Q–B4   B–B7!

The Knight will not run away.

    22 N–B5   . . . .

If instead 22 R–B1, B–Q6! 23 QN–B3, R–K5; 24 Q–N3, BxR; 25 KxB, N–N6; 26 R–N1, P–B7; 27 R–N2, Q–N5 winning easily.

    22 . . . .   BxR
    23 N–K4   . . . .

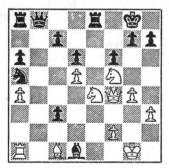

    23 . . . .   RxN!

By far the simplest. Thus if 23 . . . B–B7; 24 N–R6ch, PxN; 25 Nx Pch, K–R1; 26 NxR, QxN; 27 Q–

B6ch, K–N1; 28 QxBP with good prospects. Or if 23 . . . Q–N6; 24 N–R6ch, PxN; 25 NxPch, K–R1; 26 NxR, RxN; 27 Q–B7 and Black is in difficulties. Or, finally, 23 . . . N–N6; 24 NxNP! and the outcome is unclear.

    24 QxR   Q–K1!

Naturally White cannot go in for the exchange of Queens in view of his material inferiority.

    25 Q–N4   N–N6
    26 R–N1   NxB!

Best. 26 . . . Q–K8ch; 27 K–N2, NxB; 28 RxN, B–B6ch is tempting, but after 29 KxB, QxR; 30 Q–N7, R–K1; 31 QxBP Black still has a fight on his hands.

    27 RxN   P–B7

Nailing down White's Rook permanently.

    28 Q–N7   Q–Q1

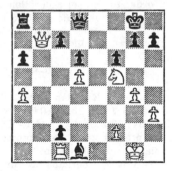

    29 Q–N3   . . . .

If 29 N–K3, R–N1 followed by . . . R–N8 wins easily.

If 29 N–K7ch, K–R1 (not 29 . . . QxN; 30 QxRch, K–B2; 31 Q–B6 and it is difficult for Black to make progress, for if 31 . . . Q–K8ch; 32 K–N2, Q–Q7; 33 Q–Q7ch, K–N3; 34 Q–B5ch, K–B2; 35 Q–Q7ch with perpetual check); 30 N–B6, Q–K1; 31 QxBP (or 31 N–Q4, R–N1; 32 QxBP, R–N8; 33 N–K6, Q–KN1 and wins), Q–K8ch; 32 K–N2, Q–Q7 and wins.

29 ....   R–N1
30 Q–R2   ....
Now the Queen is tied up as well.
30 ....   P–KR4!
Weakening the King-side, after
which the coming invasion of the
Queen will be decisive.
31 N–Q4   ....
If 31 PxP, Q–K1 and White cannot parry all the threats; or 31 N–
K3, PxP; 32 PxP, Q–Q2 and wins.
31 ....   PxP
32 PxP   Q–K1
Threatening ... Q–K8ch with fatal
effect.
33 NxP   ....
If 33 N–K6, Q–N3 is decisive.
White has finally succeeded in
removing the terrible Pawn, but he
has a lost game.
33 ....   Q–K7!
Now White cannot move a single
piece!

34 P–N5   PxP
35 Q–R3   BxN
36 Q–QB3   B–K5
37 QxP   Q–N5ch
Resigns

90.

RESHEVSKY–LEVIN
U. S. Championship, 1942
NIMZOINDIAN DEFENSE
Reshevsky   J. Levin
WHITE   BLACK
1 P–Q4   N–KB3
2 P–QB4   P–K3
3 N–QB3   B–N5
4 P–QR3   ....
The sharpest continuation, where-
by White takes into consideration
the weakening of his Queen-side
Pawns in return for the two Bishops and an aggressive position.
4 ....   BxNch
5 PxB   P–B4

Reserving the option of a later
... P–Q4 or ... P–Q3.
6 P–K3   O–O
7 B–Q3   P–Q4
The alternative was 7 ... P–Q3;
8 P–K4, N–B3; 9 N–K2, P–K4; 10
P–Q5, N–QR4 with a difficult game
for both sides: White plays for
King-side attack, while Black tries
to hammer away at the QBP.
8 BPxP   QxP
This is reminiscent of Game 37
in which Bogolyubov played 9 Q–B3
in a similar position. The alternative 8 ... KPxP; 9 N–K2, P–QN3;
10 O–O, B–R3; 11 BxB, NxB; 12
Q–Q3 (as in Game 88 against Fine)
gives White excellent attacking
chances by means of an eventual
advance in the center.
9 N–B3   P–QN3
10 Q–K2!   ....
Preparing for the following
thrust of the KP.
10 ....   B–N2?
An inexactitude which gets him
into serious trouble. He should
have played ... PxP first.

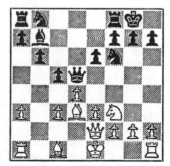

11 P–K4!   Q–R4
Black cannot find a wholly satis-
factory move. Thus if 11 ... NxP;
12 P–B4, Q–B3 (or 12 ... Q–B4; 13
N–N5, N–B6; 14 BxQ, NxQ; 15 Bx
Pch, K–R1; 16 KxN, P–N3; 17 P–
KR4, P–B3; 18 P–R5, PxN; 19

RPxP and wins); 13 N–K5, Q–Q3;
14 BxN, QxP; 15 BxB, Q–B6ch (if
15 . . . QxR; 16 O–O); 16 K–B1,
QxR; 17 Q–N2, QxQ; 18 BxQ and
wins.

If 11 . . . Q–Q1; 12 B–KN5 (threatening P–K5) is embarrassing for
Black.

    12 P–R3!   . . . .

Threatening P–K5 followed by P–
N4. Black must now take steps to
safeguard his Queen.

    12 . . . .   **PxP**
    13 PxP   **B–R3**

Eliminating White's KB and thus
establishing a flight square for his
Queen at KN3 in case of need.
However, after the ensuing exchange, Black will find himself
burdened with an exceedingly uncomfortable position.

    14 B–KN5!   . . . .

A very troublesome reply, which
blocks off Black's Queen from the
other wing.

If 14 BxB, Q–R4ch; 15 B–Q2,
QxB and Black has materially improved his chances.

    14 . . . .   **BxB**
    15 QxB   **QN–Q2**
    16 O–O   **KR–B1**

In the play that follows, Black
will be seriously handicapped by
the fact that his Queen will be out
of play for the duration. Note also
that Black's Knights have virtually
no play.

If, however, 16 . . . P–KR3 then
simply 17 BxN, NxB (17 . . . PxB;
18 Q–R6 is also very promising for
White); 18 N–K5, KR–Q1; 19 Q–
K3, N–Q2; 20 N–B6, etc. — or 19
. . . R–Q3; 20 KR–B1 with a con-
siderable positional advantage for
White.

    17 QR–B1   **Q–N3**
    18 KR–K1   **P–KR3**
    19 B–Q2   . . . .

Now BxN could be answered by
. . . QxB followed by . . . Q–Q1.

    19 . . . .   **RxR**
    20 BxR   **R–QB1**

Now Black has temporary control of the QB file, but he cannot
derive any tangible gain from it.

    21 B–Q2   **R–Q1**

Lacking a definite plan, Black
drifts. The text threatens . . . N–B4
followed by . . . QNxP. White disposes of the threat once for all.

    22 Q–K2   **N–N1**

Allowing N–K5 with fatal effect,
but it is difficult to suggest a satisfactory continuation.

    23 N–K5   **Q–R4**
    24 Q–B4   **N–K1**

He cannot allow the deadly Q–
B7; but now the position of Black's
Knights is pitiable.

    25 B–N4!   . . . .

Threatening B–K7. Black has little choice.

    25 . . . .   **Q–N4**

The awkward position of Black's
pieces allows a drastic finish.

    26 P–B4!   **Q–B3**

If 26 . . . QxP; 27 B–K7 and White
wins pretty much as he pleases.

    27 P–QR4   . . . .

A curious position: Black is practically in **Zugzwang**.

    27 . . . .   **N–Q2**
    28 N–B6   **R–R1**

Or 28 ... R–B1; 29 N–K7ch, QxN;
30 QxR, QxB; 31 QxNch and White
has won the exchange.

| 29 P–B5! | .... |

Threatening B–K7, winning the
Queen!

29	PxP
30 P–K5	Q–R5
31 P–K6!	....

Wins a piece.

31	PxP
32 QxPch	K–R1
33 QxN	N–B3

Black should resign, as he has
no compensation for the piece.

34 QxBP	P–QR4
35 B–B3	R–KB1
36 N–K7	Q–N6
37 N–N6ch	K–N1
38 Q–K6ch!	....

Stronger than 38 NxR, QxB and
White has two pieces en prise.

| 38 .... | R–D2 |
| 39 N–K5 | Resigns |

91.

PINKUS–RESHEVSKY
U. S. Championship, 1942
R U Y   L O P E Z

A. S. Pinkus   Reshevsky
WHITE   BLACK

1 P–K4	P–K4
2 N–KB3	N–QB3
3 B–N5	P–QR3
4 B–R4	N–B3
5 O–O	B–K2
6 R–K1	P–QN4
7 B–N3	P–Q3
8 P–B3	N–QR4
9 B–B2	P–B4
10 P–Q4	Q–B2
11 QN–Q2	BPxP

In this variation, it is White's
plan invariably to build up a King-
side attack; hence Black must open
the QB file. Otherwise, White may

block the position with P–Q5, limit-
ing Black to passive defense.

| 12 PxP | N–B3 |
| 13 P–KR3 | O–O |

After 13 ... PxP; 14 N–N3 would
regain the Pawn advantageously.

| 14 N–N3 | P–QR4 |
| 15 P–Q5 | .... |

Here we part company from
Game 103, in which White postponed this advance.

15	N–QN5
16 B–N1	P–R5
17 QN–Q2	....

This Knight has not much time,
and now prepares for the orthodox
journey to KN3 after all.

| 17 .... | B–Q2 |

17 ... P–R6; 18 PxP!, Q–B6? is
tempting but bad for Black; there
follows 19 PxN!, QxR; 20 Q–B2 and
21 N–N3 winning the Queen.

18 P–R3	N–R3
19 N–B1	KR–B1
20 B–Q2	P–N3

To keep White's QN out of B5.

| 21 N–N3 | .... |

White is well advised to avoid
the routine 21 P–KN4? which would
be answered by ... P–R4!

| 21 .... | B–K1 |

The KN is to be brought to QB4
eventually by way of Q2.

| 22 B–Q3 | N–B4 |
| 23 B–N4 | .... |

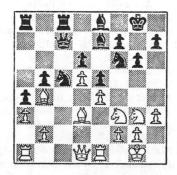

23 . . . .   Q–N2

23 . . . NxB; 24 QxN, Q–B7 is attractive but inferior because of 25 QxQ, RxQ; 26 B–B3 followed by N–B1 and N–K3.

Nor would 23 . . . N–N6 accomplish anything: 24 R–N1, QR–N1 (in order to play . . . N–Q2); 25 Q–K2, Q–N2; 26 B–B2 and the Knight must retreat.

The text, on the other hand, makes it possible to bring the KN at once to the Queen-side.

24 QR–B1	KN–Q2
25 Q–K2	QR–N1
26 R–B3	NxB

Black decides to exchange after all, for although the KB is not particularly useful, Black feels that his two Bishops will eventually become formidable when the position is finally opened up.

27 QxN	RxR
28 BxR	R–B1
29 Q–K3	N–B4

. . . . P–B4 might have been more energetic. White's next move eliminates this possibility by protecting the QP.

| 30 R–Q1 | N–R3 |
| 31 Q–R6 | P–B3 |

In order to prevent the exchange of his valuable KB by N–N5. The alternative was . . . B–B1.

| 32 Q–Q2 | R–B5 |
| 33 N–R2 | P–R4 |

Playing to hem in White's Knights. Another possibility was 33 . . . P–N5; 34 PxP, NxP.

34 Q–K2	N–B4
35 P–B3	N–N6
36 N(3)–B1	B–Q1!

At last the Bishop comes to life.

37 K–R1	B–N3
38 N–K3	R–B2
39 P–N4	. . . .

Black is threatening . . . B–Q5 very strongly: hence White must counter aggressively on the other wing.

39 . . . .   P–R5

Allowing White to parry ingeniously. . . . R–R2 would have been safer.

40 P–N5!   . . . .

Temporarily sacrificing a Pawn to activate his Knights.

| 40 . . . . | PxP |
| 41 N(2)–N4 | R–B1 |

Black was reluctant to part with his QB, but after 41 . . . K–N2; 42 Q–R2 would have been very strong (threat: NxP).

42 N–B6ch	K–N2
43 NxBch	RxN
44 QxP	R–KB1
45 N–B4?	. . . .

Too greedy. Correct was 45 R–KB1, Q–R2; 46 N–N4, B–B4 (or . . . B–Q5) with a difficult game.

45 . . . .   Q–B1!!

A subtle resource which Pinkus has failed to foresee. His position is now untenable.

46 K–N2   . . . .

46 . . . .   RxP!!

This perfectly sound sacrifice is the logical result of White's failure to guard his King adequately.

47 KxR	QxPch
48 K–K2	Q–N7ch
49 K–Q3	N–B4ch
50 K–K3	. . . .

50 QxN, BxQ would obviously be quite hopeless for White.

50 . . . .   QxPch
51 K–Q2   . . . .

Amusing would be 51 K–B2, N–Q6ch; 52 K–B1, Q–B6 mate.

51 . . . .   N–N6ch
52 QxN   Q–N7ch!

More exact than 52 . . . PxQ; 53 NxB etc.

White resigned after the text, for if 53 K–Q3, PxQ; 54 NxB, Q–B7ch; or 53 K–B1 (53 K–K1, Q–B7 mate), PxQ; 54 NxB, Q–B7 mate.

92.

RESHEVSKY–CHERNEV
U. S. Championship, 1942

NIMZOINDIAN DEFENSE

Reshevsky	I. Chernev
WHITE	BLACK
1 P–Q4	N–KB3
2 P–QB4	P–K3
3 N–QB3	B–N5
4 Q–B2	P–Q4
5 PxP	QxP

After this move White generally obtains two Bishops and a slight initiative. Perhaps Black can do better with the rather wild continuation 5 . . . PxP; 6 B–N5, P–B4!?

6 N–B3   P–B4
7 B–Q2   . . . .

Practically forcing Black to exchange his KB, if his Queen is to retain its commanding position.

7 . . . .   BxN
8 BxB   . . . .

As will be seen later on, this Bishop has great possibilities, even after being forced back to the modest square Q2.

8 . . . .   N–B3
9 PxP   . . . .

Kashdan has shown (Game 99) that after 9 R–Q1, O–O (9 . . . Qx

RP; 10 P–K4 is too risky for Black); 10 P–K3, QxRP; 11 PxP, N–Q4 is an eminently playable continuation for Black.

9 . . . .   QxBP
10 R–B1   B–Q2
11 Q–N1   Q–N3

As will be noted later on, the Queen is misplaced here. The centralizing move . . . Q–K2 was in order at this point.

12 P–K3   QR–B1
13 B–K2   . . . .

The more natural B–Q3 would be answered by . . . N–QN5. Besides, White wants to keep the Q file clear for his KR.

13 . . . .   O–O
14 O–O   N–Q4
15 B–Q2   . . . .

15 N–N5, P–B4 leads to nothing definite for White.

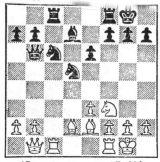

15 . . . .   P–K4

A two-edged move: Black gains more freedom, but he also exposes the KP to attack and weakens his Q4 somewhat.

16 KR–Q1   KN–K2

The Knight eventually gets into difficulties on this unfortunate square. . . . P–KR3 followed by . . . B–K3 would have been preferable.

17 P–QN4!   . . . .

Threatening to drive away the QN by P–N5, followed by B–N4 with overwhelming pressure on

Black's position.

17 . . . .   B–B4

Relatively best. 17 . . . P–QR3 would be answered by 18 P–QR4.

18 Q–N2   B–N5?

Somewhat better was 18 ... P–K5, although after 19 N–K5 (not 19 N–R4 because of ... B–K3 threatening . . . P–N4), Black's position would still be very uncomfortable and hardly tenable in the long run.

19 P–KR3!   . . . .

This highlights the weakness of Black's last move. He must exchange his remaining Bishop in order to save his KP, after which White's Bishops have a field day.

19 . . . .   BxN

20 BxB   . . . .

There follows an unequal struggle between the far-ranging Bishops and the sadly limited Knights.

20 . . . .   N–N3

Or 20 ... KR–Q1; 21 B–B3, N–N3 (if 21 ... P–B3; 22 P–N5, N–N1; 23 Q–R3 with a winning game); 22 P–N5 and wins.

21 B–B3   Q–B2

After this Black is driven back all along the line, but if 21 ... KR–K1; 22 P–N5, N–N1; 23 P–QR4 gives White a winning game.

22 P–N5   N(B3)–K2

23 B–QN4   Q–N1

Or 23 ... Q–N3; 24 BxN, NxB; 25 QxP winning easily.

24 R–Q7   . . . .

A murderous invasion against which Black has no resource.

24 . . . .   RxRch

25 QxR   R–K1

26 BxP!   . . . .

Even stronger than RxP, as Black's Queen is stalemated!

26 . . . .   N–KB1

Resigning himself to the inevitable; if 26 ... N–QB1; 27 Q–B4 wins easily, while 26 ... N–B4 is refuted by 27 P–N4.

27 B–Q6   NxR

28 BxQ   NxB

29 Q–B5   N–Q2

30 QxRP   Resigns

93.

RESHEVSKY–STEINER
U. S. Championship, 1942

QUEEN'S GAMBIT DECLINED

Reshevsky   H. Steiner

WHITE   BLACK

1 P–Q4	N–KB3
2 P–QB4	P–K3
3 N–QB3	P–Q4
4 B–N5	B–K2
5 P–K3	O–O
6 R–B1	. . . .

After the more usual 6 N–B3, Black might play 6 ... N–K5; 7 Bx B, QxB; 8 PxP, NxN; 9 PxP, PxP; 10 Q–N3, Q–Q3 with about even chances.

After the text, however, if 6 ... N–K5; 7 BxB, QxB; 8 PxP, NxN; 9 RxN, PxP; 10 Q–B2, P–QB3; 11 B–Q3, P–KR3; 12 N–K2, N–Q2; 13 O–O, N–B3; 14 R–N1 followed by the advance of the QNP and White has excellent chances to gain an advantage on the Queen-side by means of the "minority attack."

| 6 . . . . | QN–Q2 |
| 7 N–B3 | P–B4 |

7 ... P–B3 is the usual move. The impetuous text is not to be recommended.

    8 BPxP   . . . .

Also good is 8 QPxP, when 8 ... PxP is forced, allowing the strong reply 9 P–B6! leaving Black with a weak QBP.

    8 . . . .   **BPxP**

If 8 ... KPxP? 9 PxP, NxP; 10 BxN, BxB; 11 NxP and White has won a Pawn.

    9 NxP   . . . .

Inferior would be 9 QxP, NxP; 10 BxB (if 10 NxN, BxB and White has gained nothing), NxB and White's Queen is subject to attack at Q4.

    9 . . . .   **NxP**
    10 BxB   . . . .

If 10 NxN, BxB and Black has nothing to fear.

    10 . . . .   **NxB**

This leaves Black with a deplorably cramped game. He could have had freedom with 10 ... QxB; 11 NxN, PxN but after 12 B–K2 he would have had no compensation for the isolated QP.

    11 B–K2   **P–QR3**

Black's greatest difficulty in this opening is the problem of developing his Bishop. The way in which he goes about it in the present game involves him in lasting diffi-

culties, but it is not easy to suggest a preferable course.

    12 O–O   **P–QN4**
    13 Q–N3!   **R–N1**

Not 13 ... B–N2, when 14 P–QR4 would be troublesome.

    14 KR–Q1   . . . .

White has an ideal development: all his pieces are placed effectively, and his KR is particularly powerful.

    14 . . . .   **Q–N3**
    15 Q–N4!   . . . .

White already has his eye on the weak spot: Q6. In general, Black is seriously vulnerable on the black squares, which have been enfeebled by the exchange of his KB and the advance of the QRP and QNP.

    15 . . . .   **R–K1**

15 ... N–N3; 16 N–K4 (threatening R–B6 and N–Q6) would have been even worse for Black. If 15 ... Q–B4; 16 Q–R5 would have been a strong reply.

    16 N–N3   . . . .

Preventing Black from securing some freedom with 16 ... P–QR4; 17 QxNP, Q–R2 followed by ... RxP.

    16 . . . .   **N–K4**
    17 R–Q6   **Q–R2**

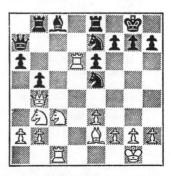

    18 Q–B5!   . . . .

Forcing the exchange of Queens with decisive effect, as Black's helplessness will become more and more marked as the game goes on.

18 ....   QxQ
19 NxQ   N–B4

Driving away the obstreperous Rook—but only for the time being.

20 R(6)–Q1   B–N2
21 P–K4   N–K2
22 P–B4   N(4)–B3

... N(4)–N3 would not help matters much, for after 25 P–KN3 Black would be tied up just as badly.

23 R–Q7   ....

The Rook asserts itself with more force than ever, now that Black's Knights have been driven back for good.

23 ....   B–B1
24 R–Q6   P–KR3
25 K–B2   R–Q1
26 QR–Q1   ....

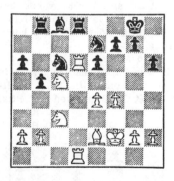

Black is in no position to dispute control of the Q file.

26 ....   RxR
27 RxR   P–N5

Tempting, but it only facilitates White's task.

28 N(3)–R4   P–QR4
29 P–K5   ....

Preparing for the posting of the Bishop on the long diagonal; this will lead to a quick decision.

29 ....   B–N2
30 B–B3   ....

The intervention of the Bishop is decisive. The immediate threat is NxB winning a piece.

30 ....   B–R1
31 N–Q7   R–Q1

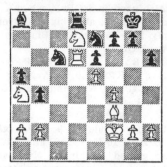

32 N(4)–N6!   ....

This forces the win of a piece, for if 32 ... B–N2; 33 N–B5! and a piece must fall. A curious position!

32 ....   N–B1
33 NxN   RxN
34 N–N6   Resigns

94.

LESSING–RESHEVSKY
U. S. Championship, 1942
RUY LOPEZ

N. Lessing	Reshevsky
WHITE	BLACK
1 P–K4	P–K4
2 N–KB3	N–QB3
3 B–N5	P–QR3
4 B–R4	N–B3
5 O–O	B–K2
6 R–K1	P–QN4
7 B–N3	P–Q3
8 P–B3	N–QR4
9 B–B2	P–B4
10 P–Q4	Q–B2
11 QN–Q2	BPxP

It may be noticed that the author has invariably resorted to this defense because he believes that it offers Black more opportunities than any other variation.

12 PxP	N–B3
13 P–Q5	. . . .

This immediate advance has the advantage for Black that it allows him to plan for the coming middle game play.

13	N–QN5
14 B–N1	P–QR4

Else P–QR3 wins a piece.

15 P–QR3	N–R3
16 B–Q3	. . . .

A plausible idea, but the QNP can be defended easily enough.

16	B–Q2
17 Q–K2	QR–N1
18 N–B1	. . . .

White originally must have intended 18 P–QR4 here, but Black parries with 18 ... N–QN5!; 19 PxP (not 19 BxP?, N–B7 and White loses the exchange), NxB; 20 QxN, BxP; 21 Q-K0, P R0 or N-Q1 and Black's two Bishops give him an edge.

18	N–B4

This confronts White with a difficult decision: he must allow his opponent the two Bishops, or else he must retreat his KB in the knowledge that this piece will be of no great value to him.

19 P–QN4	. . . .

He gives up the Bishop and succeeds in keeping Black's pieces out of QB4; however, the future is with the player who has the Bishop.

19	PxP
20 PxP	NxB
21 QxN	O–O
22 B–Q2	KR–B1
23 KR–B1	. . . .

A mass exchange of Rooks on the QB file is now indicated.

23	Q–N2
24 N–N3	. . . .

As White has no real prospects of King-side attack, it would have been advisable to keep this Knight in contact with the Queen-side. N–K3 would therefore have been more to the point although Black would have continued with ... P–N3, intending the eventual advance of his BP.

24	P–N3

Preventing any inroad by the QN and preparing for the strategically vital advance of the BP later on.

25 B–N5	K–N2
26 P–R3	N–N1
27 B–K3	. . . .

Not the best; 27 BxB, NxB; 28 N–Q2 would have offered White better chances.

27	RxRch
28 RxR	R–QB1
29 R–B2	. . . .

The struggle for the QB file will ultimately end in Black's favor.

29	R–Q1
30 N–Q2	RxR
31 QxR	Q–R3

Gaining control of the QR file. White's control of the QB file is meaningless, since the united Bishops prevent any invasion.

32 K–R2	N–K2
33 N–K2	P–B4!

34 P–B3	. . . .

Black was threatening to win a piece with ... P–B5.

If 34 P–B4, Q–R5; 35 Q–B3 (if 35

QxQ, PxQ with a strong passed
Pawn for Black. Or 35 Q–N1, BPxP;
36 QxP, B–B4; 37 Q–B3, QxP and
wins), BPxP; 36 PxP, NxP; 37 Q–
Q4, NxB; 38 QxN, QxP and Black's
advantage is clear.

34	P–B5
35 B–B2	N–B1
36 N–QB1	N–N3
37 BxN	. . . .

This turns out to be fatal, as it
enables Black to get a mating attack on the weakened b l a c k
squares. Better was 37 N(1)–N3,
N–B5; 38 NxN, PxN; 39 N–Q2, B–
QN4; 40 Q–B3 and White may still
be able to hold on.

| 37 . . . . | QxB |
| 38 N–Q3 | . . . . |

The Knights are sadly limited,
acting mainly as observers of the
tragedy that now unfolds.

| 38 . . . . | Q–K6 |
| 39 N–N3 | B–N3 |

Setting up a mating threat at
KN8 which will keep White's
Queen permanently occupied.

| 40 Q–Q1 | P–R4 |
| 41 N(N3)–B1 | P–N4 |

White's position is hopeless. He
is limited to meaningless waiting
moves.

| 42 Q–K1 | Q–Q5 |
| 43 Q–Q1 | P–N5 |

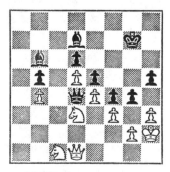

44 RPxP   . . . .

On other moves Black plays . . .
P–N6ch followed by . . . Q–B5 and
. . . B–K6, with a fatal tieup of
White's pieces which will lead to
at least the win of the QNP.

44	PxP
45 PxP	QxKP
Resigns	

Black threatens . . . Q–R2 mate. If
46 Q–B3, Q–R2ch; 47 Q–R3, BxP
wins.

95.

RESHEVSKY–BAKER
U. S. Championship, 1942
GRUENFELD DEFENSE

Reshevsky	H. Baker
WHITE	BLACK
1 P–Q4	N–KB3
2 P–QB4	P–KN3
3 N–QB3	P–Q4

As is well known, I like to play
this defense with the Black pieces,
and it is generally good psychology to adopt a player's favorite
opening lines against him.

4 B–B4	P–B3
5 P–K3	B–N2
6 N–B3	O–O
7 Q–N3	PxP

Regarding this line of play, see
also Game 84.

| 8 BxP | QN–Q2 |
| 9 O–O | . . . . |

9 P–K4 is much stronger here,
and would leave Black with a difficult game.

| 9 . . . . | N–N3 |
| 10 B–K2 | B–K3 |

10 . . . B–B4; 11 KR–Q1, P–QR4
is an interesting alternative.

| 11 Q–B2 | N–R4 |

The usual continuation is 11 . . .
QN–Q4; 12 B–N3, B–B4; 13 Q–N3,
Q–N3 with approximate equality.
The text has as its purpose the ex-
change of the KN for White's QB.

But this is of questionable value in view of the fact that in order to effect the exchange Black must play...P-B3, thereby considerably weakening his King-side Pawn position, and also putting his KB out of play — permanently, as the game actually goes.

    12 B-K5!   ....

Forcing...P-B3 if Black really wishes to go through with the exchange.

    12 ....   **P-B3**

12...BxB; 13 PxB! would be bad for Black, as his KN could not return to KB3 and would consequently be out of play for a long time to come.

    13 B-N3   **B-B2**
    14 N-K4   **NxB**
    15 RPxN   **N-Q2**

To prevent White from posting his QN powerfully at B5.

    16 KR-Q1   ....

Preventing the freeing move... P-K4.

    16 ....   **Q-N3**

Apparently the natural move for the Queen, but the following play does not come up to Black's expectations. Better was...Q-B2 followed by...QR-Q1 and (eventually) ...P-K4.

    17 B-B4!   ....

17...P-K4 would not be good because of 18 N-Q6 with a winning game.

Or if 17...BxB; 18 QxBch, K-R1; 19 N-B5! (but not 19 Q-K6, QR-Q1; 20 QxKP?, KR-K1 and White loses a piece), NxN (on 19 ...KR-Q1; 20 N-K6 would be powerful); 20 PxN, Q-B2 (if 20... QxNP; 21 QR-N1, Q-R6; 22 RxP with much the better game); 21 N-Q4 followed by N-K6 with considerable advantage for White.

    18 N-B5!   **KR-Q1**

Of course not 18...NxN?; 19 PxN, QxBP??; 20 BxBch winning the Queen. Or if 18...Q-B2; 19 P-K4, B-B2 (if 19...BxB; 20 QxBch, K-R1; 21 N-K6 winning the exchange); 20 BxBch, RxB; 21 N-K6, Q-Q3; 22 P-Q5 with marked advantage for White.

    19 P-K4   **BxB**

Not 19...B-B2?; 20 BxBch, KxB; 21 Q-B4ch and Black can resign.

    20 QxBch   **K-R1**
    21 N-K6   ....

White has achieved his objective: the occupation of this square has been made possible by the line of play inaugurated by his seventeenth move.

    21 ....   **R-K1**
    22 R-Q3!   **QxNP**

17 ....   B-Q4

Overlooking the strength of White's reply. There was nothing better than 22 ... QR–N1, although after 23 R–N3 Black's position would have been anything but inviting.

        23 R(3)–Q1!   N–N3

White was threatening QR–N1 as well as the win of the exchange by N–B7. If 23 ... Q–N3; 24 QR–N1, Q–R4; 25 RxP with a won game because of the threats of RxN and N–B7 and the shattering of Black's Pawn position.

        24 Q–Q3   . . . .

Now Black is worse off than ever, for in addition to the threatened N–B7, there is the terrible menace of KR–N1 winning the Queen!

24	. . . .	Q–N4
25	N–B7	Q–KR4
26	QR–B1	QR–Q1
27	NxR	RxN
28	Q–R3	N–B1
29	Q–N4	N–Q3

Or 29 ... N–N3; 30 P–R4 and wins.

        30 P–K5   Resigns

For if 30 ... N–N4; 31 P–R4, N–B2; 32 QxNP and the Queen-side Pawns must fall.

U. S. CHAMPIONSHIP MATCH, 1942

IT WAS clearly undesirable for the United States to have two chess champions at the same time. Kashdan and I agreed to play a fourteen game series to determine which of us would hold the title until the 1944 tournament.

The early games of this match created a sensation. After winning the first one, I lost the second. I defeated Kashdan in the third game but lost the fourth! These were my first defeats in U. S. championship play since my loss to Horowitz in the 1936 event. I had played seventy-five games without a loss! This inauspicious beginning was a shock to me and to the chess world. Chastened by these defeats, I settled down to work. I won four and drew three of the next seven games: the score stood 7½-3½. Realizing that play in the remaining three games was meaningless, Kashdan resigned the match.

It is interesting to note that of the eight decisive encounters in this series, *seven* were won by the player with the white pieces.

96.

RESHEVSKY–KASHDAN
1st Match Game, 1942
GRUENFELD DEFENSE

Reshevsky	I. Kashdan
WHITE	BLACK
1 P–Q4	N–KB3
2 P–QB4	P–KN3
3 N–QB3	P–Q4
4 B–B4	. . . .

It may well be that 4 Q–N3 (as in the next game) is preferable, as it avoids the complications that result from the text move.

4	B–N2
5 P–K3	O–O

Another example of the Pawn sacrifice discussed in the notes to Game 62.

| 6 Q–N3 | P–B4!? |

After this move, with its promise of endless complications, I realized that my suspicion of prepared analysis when I played my fourth move had been well founded.

| 7 QPxP | . . . . |

The win of a Pawn with 7 BPxP, PxP; 8 PxP, QN–Q2; 9 B–K2, N–N3; 10 B–B3 did not appeal to me greatly, for after 10 ... B–N5 Black must soon regain the Pawn with at least equality.

| 7 . . . . | N–K5! |

A difficult move to meet adequately; thus if 8 NxN (the most obvious), PxN; 9 N–K2, Q–R4ch; 10 N–B3, N–R3 and Black regains the Pawn in a highly advantageous manner, for his Pawn at K5 greatly restricts the development of White's pieces, while at the same time the KP supports Black's pressure on Q6.

Another possibility is 8 NxN, PxN; 9 Q–R3, P–K4; 10 B–N3, P–B4; 11 N–K2, B–K3 and again White has a difficult position.

| 8 PxP | . . . . |

Better than 8 NxP, which would be answered by ... Q–R4ch with devastating effect.

| 8 . . . . | Q–R4 |
| 9 N–K2 | . . . . |

Black's counter attack has assumed formidable dimensions and must be met with the greatest care.

| 9 . . . . | N–QB3 |

This is good, but 9 ... N–R3! bringing a new piece into play, was even better. Here are some possible continuations:

I 10 Q–R4, QxQ; 11 NxQ, B–Q2; 12 QN–B3, QNxP; 13 R–Q1, QR–B1 with excellent chances.

II 10 N–Q4 (If 10 P–B3, QNxP; 11 Q–B4, P–QN4; 12 QxP, QxQ; 13 NxQ, N–Q6ch etc.), QNxP; 11 Q–B4 (if 11 Q–B2, B–Q2 followed by ... QR–B1 with a powerful position), P–K4; 12 PxP e. p. (if 13 P–QN4, Q–R6), BxP; 13 NxB, NxN and White's position is difficult to defend in view of the threats of ... NxN, ... QR–B1 and ... NxB.

III 10 N–Q4, QNxP; 11 Q–N5 best, QxQ; 12 BxQ, P–QR3; 13 B–K2, R–Q1 with approximate equality.

| 10 Q–Q1 | . . . . |

Safer than Capablanca's move 10 Q–B4 against Flohr in their Avro encounter. After 10 Q–B4, Black has a powerful counter in

... P–K4!
10 . . . .   P–K4

An even stronger course would be steady development with ...QN–R3 followed by ... B–Q2, ... QR–B1 and ... KR–Q1.

11 B–N5   P–B3

Black could have gained time with the immediate 11 ... N–K5, for if 12 B–R4, P–KN4; 13 B–N3, P–B4 and Black is a move to the good as compared to the text continuation; or 12 B–K7, R–K1; 13 P–Q6, B–K3 and Black is developing very quickly, reinforced by the conviction that the QP has only been weakened by its advance.

12 P–QR3!   . . . .

An unexpected resource. Black must have been looking forward to 12 B–R4, P–KN4; 13 B–N3, B–B4 when White must content himself with the puny reply 14 N–B1.

12 . . . . .   N–K5

After 12 ... PxB; 13 P–QN4, Q–N3; 14 PxN, QxP; 15 N–K4 Black would have equality in material, but his weak Pawn position would tell against him subsequently.

13 B–R4   . . . .

13 P–QN4? would have been decidedly inferior because of 13 ... NxN; 14 NxN, Q–B2!; 15 N–N5, Q–N3; 16 B–R4, P–N4; 17 B–N3, P–B4; 18 P–R3 (White is unable

to play 18 P–B3 on account of ... QxPch), P–B5; 19 B–R2, PxP etc.

13 . . . .   P–KN4
14 B–N3   P–B4
15 P–B3   NxN

After 15 ... NxB; 16 PxN (better than 16 NxN, P–K5! 17 R–B1, PxP; 18 PxP, P–B5 with a strong game for Black), N–Q2; 17 P–QN4, Q–Q1; 19 R–B1, N–B3; 19 R–B2 White completes his development with N–B1 and B–B4.

16 NxN   P–B5
17 B–B2   . . . .

Forced, as 17 PxP? KPxP would be disastrous for White.

17 . . . .   P–K5

Kashdan's energetic efforts to force matters are certainly making for interesting chess!

18 R–B1   . . . .

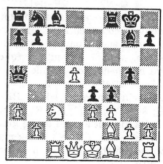

18 . . . .   B–B4

Fine recommends 18 ... KPxP; 19 NPxP, PxP; 20 BxP, R–K1; 21 K–B2, RxB!?; 22 KxR, Q–N3ch as Black's best chance. However, White can simply play 21 Q–Q2! (instead of 21 K–B2) and if 21 ... Q–N3; 22 N–K4, QxP; 23 QxQ, BxQ; 24 R–B2, B–N2; 25 K–B2 threatening N–Q6, NxP and BxNP.

19 B–K2   . . . .

At last White is within sight of castling!

19 . . . .   KPxP

20 NPxP	PxP
21 BxP	N-Q2
22 O-O	....

Having consumed considerable time, White prefers to give his King a safe haven rather than go in for the dubious complexities of 22 BxNP, QR-B1; 23 B-Q2, KR-K1 etc.

White is now safely a Pawn ahead and should be able to make continuous progress with careful play on his part.

22	QR-K1
23 B-Q4	....

Continuing to consolidate his position. 23 BxNP would be effectively answered by ... Q-N3ch.

23	N-K4
24 K-R1	....

White is now ready to fight for the initiative.

24	P-QR3

Else White might play N-N5 with threats of N-Q6 or P-N4.

25 P-Q6!	K-R1

To parry the threat of Q-N3ch. White's advance of the QP was rather daring, but he is confident that he can either retain it or secure compensation for its loss.

26 P-N4!	....

Playing for complications. The prosaic 26 N-K4 (chiefly threatening R-B5) was also good.

26	Q-Q1

According to Fine and the other annotators, Kashdan should have played 26 ... QxRP; 27 N-Q5 (threatening to win the Queen with R-R1), Q-R7; 28 B-B3, R-Q1 "and Black's Queen will not be lost."

However, on 27 ... Q-R7 I would have played 28 B-B4!, NxB; 29 BxBch, KxB; 30 Q-Q4ch, N-K4; 31 N-K7, Q-K3; 32 KR-K1 regaining the piece with a strong attack.

27 N-Q5!	P-N5?!

Kashdan continues to play with desperate ingenuity. If 27 ... QxP; 28 B-B5 wins the exchange.

In reply to 27 ... N-B3, Fine gives the following clever refutation: 28 B-N6, Q-Q2; 29 N-K7!, NxN; 30 R-B7, Q-K3; 31 PxN, R-B3 (if 31 ... R-B2; 32 B-R4 wins); 32 Q-Q8, Q-N1 (if 32 ... B-N3; 33 B-Q5 wins); 33 R-Q1, RxR; 34 QxR, QxQ; 35 R-Q8, B-N3; 36 R(7)-B8 and wins.

28 N-B7!	PxP
29 BxBP!	NxB
30 BxBch	KxB
31 NxRch	QxN

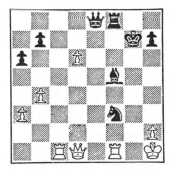

Or 31 ... RxN; 32 R-B7ch!, K-N3; 33 RxN!, B-K5; 34 Q-N1ch, K-R3; 35 Q-N7ch, K-R4; 36 R-B5ch, K-R5; 37 Q-N3 mate.

A pretty alternative is 31 ... RxN; 32 R-B7ch!, K-R3; 33 RxN!;

B–K5; 34 Q–Q2ch, Q–N4 (if 34 ...
K–N3; 35 Q–N2ch, Q–N4; 36 R–
N7ch or 34...K–R4; 35 RxPch!
etc.); 35 RxPch!, BxR; 36 R–R3ch,
K–N3; 37 R–KN3 etc.

32 R–B7ch   . . . .

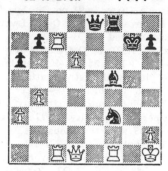

32 . . . .   K–N1

He had no good move, as the
following variations prove:

I 32...K–R3; 33 RxN, B–K5;
34 Q–Q2ch, K–R4; 35 R–B5ch, K–
N5; 36 Q–N2ch, K–R5; 37 Q–N3
mate.

II 32...K–N3; 33 RxN, B–K5;
34 Q–N1ch, K–R3 (if 34...K–R4;
35 RxPch!); 35 Q–N7ch, K–R4; 36
R–B5ch etc.

III 32...B–Q2; 33 RxN, RxR; 34
QxR, Q–K8ch; 35 K–N2, Q–Q7ch;
36 K–B1! and Black has no more
checks.

33 R–K7!   Q–N3

Or 33... Q–B3; 34 QxN!, QxQch
(if 34 ...B–K5; 35 R–N1ch, K–R1;
36 QxB); 35 RxQ, B–K5; 36 RxB,
RxR; 37 P–Q7, R–Q6; 38 R–K8ch
and the Pawn queens.

34 Q–Q5ch   K–R1

If 34...R–B2; 35 RxR, QxR; 36
QxN, B–K5; 37 R–N1ch! and wins
— or, more simply, 36 QxQch, Kx
Q; 37 RxN, K–N3; 38 RxB etc.

35 RxN   . . . .

But not 35 QxN??, B–K5! and
Black wins!

Black overstepped the time limit
here, but his position was quite
hopeless: if 35...B–K5; 36 QxB,
QxQ; 37 RxQ, RxR; 38 R–K8ch,
K–N2; 39 P–Q7 and wins.

97.

RESHEVSKY–KASHDAN
3rd Match Game, 1942
GRUENFELD DEFENSE

Reshevsky	I. Kashdan
WHITE	BLACK
1 P–Q4	N–KB3
2 P–QB4	P–KN3
3 N–QB3	P–Q4

Evidently Kashdan is well satisfied with his opening play in the
previous game and is ready to
have another try at it.

4 Q–N3   . . . .

This time I vary. The Queen
move is probably best, as it compels Black to come to a decision
regarding the center.

4 . . . .   PxP

The alternative 4... P–B3 is
theoretically sounder, as it does
not relinquish the center to White.
It has the drawback, however, of
renouncing the possibility of a freeing advance by... P–B4.

5 QxBP   B–K3
6 Q–Q3   . . . .

The excursion 6 Q–N5ch, N–B3
only wastes time; Black's development is helped along, and White's
Queen will be driven back later.

6 . . . .   B–N2

Black fails to fight for the center. Horowitz's suggestion 6...P–
B4!?; 7 PxP, N–B3 deserves a
thorough test in master play, for
it seems to be the only worthwhile attempt on Black's part to

dispute the center and fight for the initiative.

7 P–K4 　　**. . . .**

This gives White a considerable advantage in terrain, and it now requires all of Kashdan's skill to obtain a playable game.

7 . . . . 　　**P–B3**

The key to Kashdan's strategy. He wants to restrain the possible advance of White's center Pawns, thereby (1) assuring the stability of his own pieces in the center and (2) preparing for a later phase in which he hopes to stamp White's center Pawns as a weakness.

8 N–B3 　　**O–O**
9 B–K2 　　**N–K1**

It is difficult to appraise the ultimate value of the policy which is inaugurated with this move. Black has to shift his forces to the Queen-side, allowing White to concentrate on the other wing — with the result that the Black King is seriously menaced once White's attack sets in with real force.

10 O–O 　　**N–Q3**

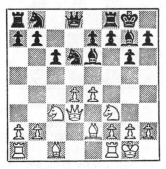

11 Q–B2 　　**. . . .**

In view of Black's cramped position, it seemed desirable to prevent the simplifying move which follows. However, after 11 P–QN3 Black would obtain just the kind of pressure on the long diagonal which is the basic theme of the defense: 11 ...P–QB4!; 12 P–K5, PxP!; or 12 PxP, NxP!; or 12 P–Q5, B–N5; 13 B–N2, N–Q2 etc.

11 . . . . 　　**B–B5**
12 B–B4 　　**BxB**

White was threatening to win a Pawn with 13 BxN, BxB; 14 BxP etc.

13 QxB 　　**Q–N3**

Even at this late date, the development of the QN would be premature because of 14 P–K5, N–KB4; 15 P–K6, PxP (if 15 ... N–B3; 16 PxPch and Black cannot recapture because of N–N5 winning the exchange); 16 QxPch, K–R1; 17 QR–Q1 and Black's center and King-side have been weakened.

14 QR–Q1 　　**Q–R3!**

Foreseeing White's reply and creating counterplay for himself.

15 N–Q3! 　　**. . .**

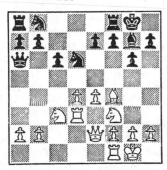

Accepting the challenge. White realizes that in some of the coming variations, this Rook may be in danger; but this momentary difficulty will be compensated for by the Rook's later participation in the eventual King-side attack.

15 . . . . 　　**N–Q2**
16 P–K5 　　**N–N4**

16 ... N–KB4? would be answered by 17 P–KN4!, N–R3; 18 P–KR3 and the unfortunate Knight is

stranded for the remainder of the game.

17 N–N5!   . . . .

Far superior to the impetuous 17 P–K6, NxN; 18 PxN, PxP; 19 Qx Pch, K–R1; 20 R–K3, RxB; 21 QxN, B–B3 when Black's prospects have improved considerably.

17 . . . .   NxN

M o m e n t a r i l y strengthening White's center but at the same time he prepares for the counter-thrust . . . P–QB4. Here or later . . . P–K3 would have a seriously weakening effect on Black's game, while if 17 . . . P–QB4?; 18 NxN, QxN; 19 NxRP! and Black dare not play 19 . . . KxN?? because of 20 R–R3ch.

18 PxN   P–R3

Weakening his King's position, but something must be done about the threat of 19 P–K6. If 18 . . . P–K3? White can continue with 19 NxRP!, KxN; 20 R–R3ch, K–N1; 21 Q–N4, KR–Q1; 22 Q–R4, N–B1; 23 B–N5 followed by 24 B–B6 and wins.

19 N–K4   P–QB4!

At last the position is ripe for this long-awaited thrust, which gives the game a dramatic turn: White prepares for a King-side attack, while Black tries to divert his attention as best he can by action in the center.

20 KR–Q1   . . . .

Before embarking on his attack, he first fortifies his position in the center. Note that 20 NxP, NxN; 21 PxN, Q–B5 would give Black exactly the kind of game that he is angling for.

20 . . . .   PxP
21 PxP   QR–B1

It must be admitted that, granted the limitations of his position, Black has played admirably hereabouts. If he can permanently restrain the advance of White's QP, it may yet become a target for attack.

22 Q–Q2!   . . . .

Black now seems to be in serious difficulties, for if 22 . . . K–R2; 23 BxP, BxB; 24 R–KR3 wins. However, Kashdan finds a clever reply.

22 . . . .   KR–Q1!

Adequately disposing of the threat of 23 BxP, which would be answered by 23 . . . NxP! with the following possibilities:

I 24 BxB?, QxR (but not 24 . . . NxR?; 25 Q–R6); 25 QxQ (if 25 BxN, QxN; 26 Q–R6, QxB!), NxQ and wins.

II 24 PxN (best), RxR; 25 QxR, QxQ; 26 RxQ, BxB; 27 P–N3 and the ending is approximately level.

23 P–KR4!   . . . .

White tries a different tack. The following advance can be prevented by 23 ... P–R4, but only at the cost of seriously weakening the King-side.

23 . . . .   K–R2
24 P–R5!   P–KN4

Preferring to slug it out rather than submit to 24 ... PxP; 25 Q–K2, Q–KN3; 26 N–N3, P–R5; 27 N–R5, followed by R–KR3, when Black can resort only to passive resistance against the attack.

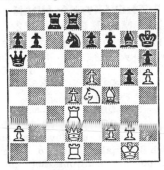

25 B–N3!?   . . . .

The alternative 25 BxP was **very** tempting and can probably be analysed to a win; yet in over the board play with a clock, the simpler text has its merits. After 25 BxP, PxB (or 25 ... NxP; 26 PxN, RxR; 27 QxR, QxQ; 28 RxQ, PxB; 29 NxPch, K–R3; 30 NxPch, KxP; 31 R–KN3! as indicated by Fine, and White should win); 26 NxPch, K–N1; 27 P–K6!, N–B1!; 28 P–R6! White should win: 28 ... BxRP; 29 R–KR3!, BxN; 30 QxBch, N–N3; 31 R–K1! with the double threat of Q–R6 or PxPch. There might follow 31 ... R–B3; 32 PxPch, K–N2; 33 RxP, R–KB1; 34 Q–R6ch, K–B3; 35 R–K8 and wins. This variation is analysis by Fine.

25 . . . .   R–B5

Rather slow for such a critical

position. Here one would expect 25 ... P–B4; 26 PxP e. p., NxP; 27 N–B5, Q–B3 and the position is delightfully unclear!

26 P–B4!   P–B4

Now this move has lost much of its sting, as White need not capture in passing.

27 N–B3!   PxP

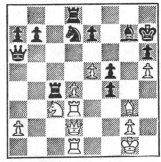

Black was confronted with an unenviable choice. If 27 ... P–N5 the King-side is blocked, but the center is available for a powerful advance, thus: 28 N–Q5, P–K3; 29 N–K3, R–R5; 30 P–Q5! and White should win.

28 BxP   . . . .

Stronger than 28 QxP, the idea being to make room for the shift of the Rook to the King-side.

28 . . . .   P–K3?

This is a triple blunder, partly because it shuts off Black's Queen from the defense of the King-side, partly because it weakens the black squares, and partly because it neglects the most aggressive defense, as pointed out by Fine: 28 ... N–N3!; 29 P–Q5 (... N–Q4 must not be permitted), N–R5! with some counterplay. This course would have been the logical fulfillment of Black's basic strategic plan of the game: counterattack against White's center and Queen-side as

a means of diverting White from
his King-side attack.

    29 R–N3   ....

Now the threat of RxBch is very
definitely in the air.

    29 ....   **N–B1??**

This repeats the previous error
in aggravated form, for now he
cuts off the Rook from the defense!
29 ... Q–B3 or ... R–KN1 w o u l d
have staved off the sacrifice, although White could then play 30
Q–K3, continuing to strengthen his
position or playing P–Q5. The winning chances would have been all
on White's side.

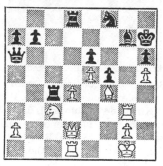

    30 RxBch!   **KxR**
    31 BxPch   **K–R2**

Or 31 ... K–B2; 32 Q–N5 with
decisive effect.

    32 Q–N5   **R–Q2**
    33 BxN   **RxN**
    34 Q–N6ch   **K–R1**
    35 Q–K8   **R(6)–B2**

The position is hopeless. If 35
... Q–B3; 36 B–K7ch, K–N2; 37 Q–
N6ch, K–R1; 38 B–B6ch and mate
next move. On 35 ... R–N2; 36 Bx
Rch, KxB; 37 Q–N6ch, K–R1 (if 37
... K–B1; 38 P–R6 etc.); 38 Q–
B6ch!; K–N1 (or 38 ... K–R2; 39
Q–B7ch, K–R1; 40 P–R6); 39 P–R6,
R–B2; 40 Q–Q8ch etc.

    36 B–K7ch   **K–N2**
    37 Q–N6ch   ....

A time pressure inexactitude.
Quicker is 37 B–B6ch, K–R2; 38
Q–N6 mate.

    37 ....   **K–R1**
    38 Q–R6ch   **K–N1**
    39 Q–B8ch   **K–R2**
    40 Q–B7ch   **Resigns**

For it is mate next move. A very
hard game!

98.

RESHEVSKY–KASHDAN
5th Match Game, 1942

NIMZOINDIAN DEFENSE

Reshevsky   I. Kashdan
WHITE   BLACK

    1 P–Q4   N–KB3
    2 P–QB4   P–K3
    3 N–QB3   B–N5
    4 P–QR3   ....

The sharpest continuation, one
which invariably leads to critical
positions and confronts both players with the gravest problems.

    4 ....   BxNch
    5 PxB   ....

Now it remains to be seen whether White's strong center and two
Bishops will outweigh the weakness of his doubled QBPs. It may
well be that Kashdan's faith in
the two Bishops handicaps him in
this variation.

    5 ....   P–B4!

After this move I knew that I
would be submitted to a stern test;
the advance of the QBP is stronger
than 5 ... P–Q4 (often played here),
because Black retains the option
of ... P–Q3 or ... P–Q4, depending
on which course seems preferable.

    6 P–K3   O–O
    7 B–Q3   N–B3
    8 N–B3   ....

The alternative is 8 N–K2, P–

Q3; 9 O-O followed in due course by P-K4 and P-B4. But meanwhile Black can play ... P-QN3, ... B-R3 and ... N-QR4, concentrating on the weak QBP.

      8 . . . .   P-Q3
      9 Q-B2   . . . .

A finesse. If 9 O-O, P-K4; 10 P-Q5, P-K5! and Black has a fine game.

      9 . . . .   P-K4
      10 P-Q5   N-K2

This retreat is a matter of taste. 10 ... N-QR4 is inviting, but Kashdan feels that his QN will be useful on the King-side.

      11 O-O   . . . .

      11 . . . .   K-R1?

An inexplicably passive move, possibly due to the fact that Black had so many promising continuations:

I 11 ... B-N5 followed by ... B-R4-N3. White must either exchange Bishops, depriving his Pawn at QB4 of valuable support, or he must play P-K4, consigning his KB to permanent inactivity.

II 11 ... P-KN3; 12 N-K1, N-R4; 13 P-B4, PxP; 14 PxP, N-N2 followed by ... B-B4.

III 11 ... B-Q2; 12 N-K1, Q-B1; 13 P-B4, PxP; 14 PxP, B-B4 or 13 P-N3, B-R6; 14 N-N2, N-N3; 15 P-B4, PxP; 16 NPxP, N-K1 and

in either case Black has an excellent game.

White is greatly handicapped by the weakness of his QBPs, which gives his intended attack a "do-or-die" character.

      12 N-K1   N-K1

This explains the ultra-elaborate character of Black's previous move. The KRP cannot be captured with check, so that if 13 BxP??, P-KN3 etc.

      13 P-B4   PxP

13 ... P-B4 would allow White to open up the game favorably with 14 P-K4!

      14 PxP   . . . .

A difficult decision. 14 RxP might have been better, as it would have prevented the subsequent exchange of Bishops. On the other hand, Black would be able to occupy the strong square K4 sooner or later.

      14 . . . .   P-KN3
      15 N-B3   B-B4

At last he has completed the plan initiated with his 11th move.

      16 BxB   NxB

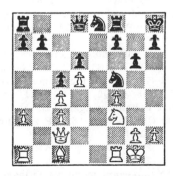

Black has achieved his objective. If left to his own devices, he will develop in normal fashion and play for a combined policy of trying to attack the weak Pawns and occupy the important central square K5.

White therefore feels justified in throwing caution to the wind and staking everything on a speculative attack to maintain the initiative. The attack may not be foolproof, but a game of chess is played over the board and not at the analyst's desk.

    17 P–N4!?   **N–R3**

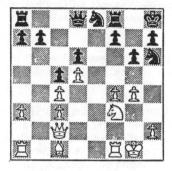

    18 P–B5!?   **. . . .**

See the previous note. Quieter moves such as 18 Q–KN2 would give Black time to consolidate with 18 ... P–B4.

    18 . . . .   **NxNP**
    19 P–R3!   **N–K4**

As good as forced. If 19 ... N(5)–B3; 20 PxP, RPxP (if 20 ... R–KN1; 21 N–N5, RxP; 22 QxR!, BPxQ; 23 N–B7ch with the exchange ahead); 21 B–R6, R–KN1 (if 21 ... N–N2; 22 N–N5 with a winning position); 22 N–N5, Q–Q2; 23 QR–K1 and Black is helpless against the threat of 24 QRxN, NxR; 25 RxP winning.

    20 NxN   **PxN**
    21 B–R6   **R–KN1**
    22 P–B6!   **. . . .**

An important move which leaves Black very cramped.

    22 . . . .   **P–KN4!**

Of course, 22 ... NxP??; 23 B–N5 would be fatal for Black.

    23 Q–B5!   **R–N3**

Forcing White's reply, for if 24

BxP??, P–KR3 wins a piece.

    24 B–B8   **. . . .**

Is this a retreat or an advance?!

    24 . . . .   **N–Q3**

This is weak, but by no means fatal.

24 ... RxP would have been unsatisfactory because of 25 QxKP, K–N1; 26 B–K7, RxRch; 27 RxR, Q–Q2; 28 QxPch, K–R1 (if 28 ... N–N2?; 29 B–B6 wins); 29 RxP and wins, as the threats of R–B8 mate and B–B6ch cannot be met.

However, 24 ... NxP! was much better. White's best course would then have been 25 QxKP, QxB; 26 RxN, RxR; 27 QxRch, Q–N2; 28 Q–B3 and his position is probably worth a Pawn. However, after 24 ... NxP!; 25 BxP would be inferior because of 25 ... N–Q2! If then 26 B–K3, P–N5!; 27 PxP, Q–R5! or 26 B–B2, P–N5!; 27 PxP, Q–N4! with a good game (White dare not play 28 QxN? because of 28 ... R–Q1).

    25 B–N7ch   **K–N1**

If 25 ... RxB; 26 PxRch, KxP; 27 QxKPch, P–B3; 28 Q–K6 followed by 29 QR–K1 with a quick win.

    26 QxKP   **Q–Q2?**

Fine recommends 26 ... NxP; 27 Q–K2, N–Q3; 28 QR–K1, N–K1; 29 Q–K7, QxQ; 30 RxQ, P–N3 as adequate to hold the position. The text loses valuable time. But after 30 ... P-N3; 31 R-Q7, NxB; 32 Px N, RxP; 33 R-B6, White stands better.

27 QR-K1!   . . . .

27 . . . .   P-KR4??

A very difficult position for Black, He must not play 27 ... QR-K1?? because of 28 QxN!

27 ... QxP is insufficient because of 28 QxN, Q-N5ch; 29 K-B2, Q-B4ch; 30 K-N3, Q-Q6ch; 31 R-B3 putting an end to the checks.

Fine's recommendation of 27 ... N-K1!; 28 Q-K7, QxQ; 29 RxQ, P-N3; 30 R-Q7, NxB; 31 PxN, RxP; 32 P-Q6, P-B3! would have held the position. But after 31 ... RxP; 32 R-B6! would have been uncomfortable for Black.

28 Q-K7!   . . . .

Forcing the exchange of Queens under the most favorable circumstances: White's Rooks are posted aggressively, his passed Pawn is a menace, Black's Rooks are disconnected, his King is in a quasi-mating position and the Knight is rather helpless for defense.

28 . . . .   QxQ
29 RxQ   R-Q1

To guard against 30 R-Q7.

If instead 29 ... NxP; 30 RxNP, N-K6?; 31 KR-N1!, RxB; 32 R-

N8ch, RxR; 33 RxRch, K-R2; 34 PxR, KxP; 35 P-Q6 and wins; or 29 ... N-K1; 30 RxNP, NxB; 31 PxN, RxP; 32 R-B7 obtains two connected passed Pawns with an easy win.

30 KR-K1   K-R2

In order to be able to move the Knight without succumbing to R-K8ch. If 30 ... P-R4; 31 R-B7, P-N3; 32 R(1)-K7 and wins.

31 K-N2?   . . . .

Both sides are in arrears on the clock. 31 K-B2 or K-R2 was more exact, for if then 31 ... P-N5; 32 R(1)-K5 is immediately decisive.

Another course, and perhaps the simplest alternative, was 31 R-B7 etc.

31 . . . .   P-N5
32 R(1)-K5!   PxPch
33 KxP   R-N8
34 PxPch   K-N3
35 R(7)-K5!   . . . .

Only the delightful prospect of R-R6 mate could drag this Rook away from the seventh rank!

35 . . . .   R-R8ch
36 K-N4   . . . .

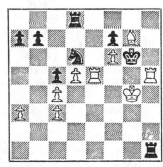

36 . . . .   N-K5?

A "blitz" move in terrible time pressure. The best chance was 36 ... R-N8ch; 37 K-B3, R-B8ch; 38 K-N2 (if 38 K-N3?, N-B4ch; 39 K-N4, R-N8ch), R-B4; 39 R-R6ch,

K–N4; 40 R–K3 and while the position is in White's favor, Black has a fighting chance (if 40 ... NxP?; 41 R–N3ch, K–B5; 42 R–R4ch winning the Knight).

But the text is fatal.

| 37 RxR | N–B7ch |
| 38 K–B4 | Resigns |

For if 38 ... NxR; 39 R–N5ch, K–R2; 40 R–R5ch, K–N3; 41 R–R6 mate.

99.

RESHEVSKY–KASHDAN
7th Match Game, 1942

NIMZOINDIAN DEFENSE

Reshevsky	I. Kashdan
WHITE	BLACK
1 P–Q4	N–KB3
2 P–QB4	P–K3
3 N–QB3	B–N5
4 Q–B2	....

After the "alarums and excursions" of the fifth game, I felt that the more sedate text move would not be amiss.

| 4 .... | P–Q4 |
| 5 PxP | QxP |

Lately Botvinnik has been retaking with the Pawn, with a fair measure of success.

| 6 N–B3 | P–B4 |
| 7 B–Q2 | BxN |

Best, as Queen moves would lose valuable time.

8 BxB	N–B3
9 P–K3	O–O
10 R–Q1	....

This move, the result of analysis during the AVRO tournament, had been considered quite good, as Black's Queen is subjected to some pressure, and 10 ... QxRP would obviously be bad. As a consequence of my experience in this game, I have concluded that the old move

10 PxP (as in Game 92) is preferable.

| 10 .... | QxRP! |

Bravo! Kashdan plays the "obviously bad" move and gets an excellent game with it! In the AVRO tournament, Fine played 10 ... P–QN3 against Capablanca, getting a miserable game after 11 P–QR3!, B–N2; 12 PxP!, QxP; 13 P–QN4!, Q–KR4; 13 BxN and managing to draw only by wonderfully resourceful play.

Note, by the way, the exactitude of Black's last move: if he plays 10 ... PxP; 11 NxP, NxN; 12 RxN, QxP??; 13 B–B4, Q–R8ch; 14 R–Q1 the Queen is lost!

| 11 PxP | N–Q4! |

An important point: if White could retain the two Bishops, he might well secure and maintain the advantage. Therefore Kashdan at once sees to it that a White Bishop disappears.

| 12 B–K2 | .... |

If instead 12 B–Q2, QN–N5; 13 Q–B1, Q–N6 (threatening ... N–B7ch); 14 N–Q4, N–Q6ch etc.

12	QN–N5!
13 Q–Q2	NxB
14 QxN	N–Q4
15 Q–Q2	P–QN3!

Very discreet. After 15 ... B–Q2; 16 N–K5, B–K1; 17 O–O White

would be threatening 18 B–B4, Q–
R5; 19 R–R1 winning the Queen!

16 PxP   PxP?

After playing the opening so
magnificently, Kashdan f a l t e r s
here. The right move was 16 . . .
NxP and if 17 O–O, B–N2; 18 N–Q4,
P–K4; 19 R–R1, Q–Q4; 20 B–B3,
Q–Q2 and Black's Queen has made
a successful escape.

17 O–O   B–N2
18 R–B1   KR–B1
19 N–K5   . . . .

Highlighting the faulty nature of
Black's 16th move. White threatens
N–B4 followed by P–K4, winning
the weak QNP.

19 . . . .   N–B3?

He should have tried 19 . . . RxR;
20 RxR, R–QB1. The text soon
leads to loss of the weak QNP.

20 N–Q4!   R–N4

Or 20 . . . P–QN4; 21 N–N6 and
the Pawn must fall.

21 Q–Q4!   R–B3

If 21 . . . P–QN4 White can win
the QNP with 22 N–Q6, RxR (or
22 . . . R–Q1; 23 Q–K5); 23 RxR etc.

If 21 . . . N–Q4; 22 N–Q6! is
strong (but not 22 P–K4, N–B5; 23
B–B3?, QxB!).

22 N–Q6!   . . . .

Perhaps Kashdan had overlooked
that 22 . . . R–Q1 is now refuted by
23 NxB!, RxQ; 24 RxR and the
mating threat enables White to win
the other Rook as well!

22 B–B3 would have been by no
means so forcing as the text, for
after 22 . . . N–Q4; 23 BxN, PxB; 24
QxQP, QR–QB1 White is in trouble.

22 . . . .   RxR
23 RxR   Q–Q4

Resigning himself to the loss of
the QNP. If 23 . . . B–Q4; 24 P–K4
wins at least a Pawn (24 . . . P–K4;
25 QxKP etc.); or if 23 . . . R–Q1;

24 NxB and Black cannot capture
the Queen!

24 QxQ   BxQ
25 R–B8ch!   . . . .

At last forcing the annexation of
the QNP.

25 . . . .   RxR
26 NxR   K–B1

26 . . . N–Q2 is futile because of
27 B–N5.

27 NxP   . . . .

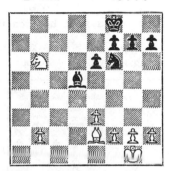

With an outside passed Pawn,
the road to victory is routine:
White brings his King to the center and supports the advance of the
QNP. However, he has been playing
"rapid transit" from his 21st move
on — with only six minutes for 24
moves (the time limit was 45
moves in the first 2¼ hours) and
errors soon creep in.

27 . . . .   B–N2
28 P–B3   K–K2
29 K–B2   N–K1
30 N–B4   P–B3
31 K–K1   P–K4
32 K–Q2   N–B2
33 B–Q3   . . . .

White indulges in some harmless
moves to complete his stint to the
45th move.

33 . . . .   P–R3
34 N–R5   B–B1
35 B–B4   K–Q3
36 K–B3   N–Q4ch

Simplifies White's task, **but** Kashdan always feels better with a Bishop against a Knight.

   37 BxN   KxB
   38 P–K4ch   K–K3
   39 N–B4   B–R3
   40 N–K3?   . . . .

The first slip. There was an easy win with 40 K–N4, P–N3; 41 K–B5, P–B4; 42 P–QN4, PxP; 43 PxP, B–N2; 44 N–Q6 etc.

   40 . . . .   P–R4

Black sees a faint hope on the King-side.

   41 K–N4   P–N3
   42 K–B5   P–B4

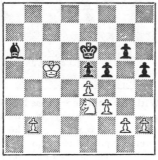

   43 P–QN4??   . . . .

Allowing Black to draw. There was a clear and simple win with 43 N–B4, PxP; 44 PxP, B–N2; 45 N–Q2 followed by the advance of the QNP.

   43 . . . .   PxP
   44 PxP   B–Q6!

This was the move I had missed. Now Black regains his Pawn.

   45 P–N5   BxKP
   46 P–N3   . . . .

The adjourned position. Black must give up his Bishop for the passed Pawn, but he can force a draw with best play.

   46 . . . .   B–B6
   47 P–R3   B–R8
   48 P–N6   B–R1

   49 N–B4   . . . .

Black can no longer mark time, 50 N–Q6 and 51 P–N7 being threatened.

   49 . . . .   K–B4
   50 K–Q6   . . . .

Or 50 N–Q6ch, K–N4; 51 P–N7, BxP; 52 NxB, P–R5; 53 P–N4, K–B5 and Black has at least a draw.

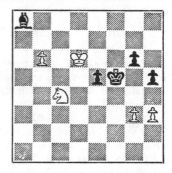

   50 . . . .   P–R5??

50 . . . P–K5 draws: 51 N–K3ch, K–B3!

I 52 K–B7, K–K4; 53 P–N7, BxP; 54 KxB, K–Q5 and Black has at least a draw.

II 52 K–B5, K–K3; 53 K–Q4, K–B3 and White can make no progress, as Black merely moves his King from B3 to K3 and K4.

III 52 P–R4, P–N4; 53 K–B7 (or 53 PxPch, KxP; 54 K–K5, P–R5, after which Black clears up the King-side and has nothing to fear on the other wing), PxP; 54 PxP, K–K4; 55 P–N7, BxP; 56 KxB, K–B5 and White can just barely draw.

It must be admitted that the faulty text move looks very plausible.

   51 PxP!!   . . . .

This must have come as a great surprise to Kashdan, as he had probably figured on 51 P–N4ch, K–B5; 52 NxP, K–N6; 53 NxP, KxP; 54 N–K5, K–N6; 55 P–N5, P–R6;

56 P-N6, P-R7; 57 P-N7, P-R8(Q);
58 P-N8(Q)ch, K-B7 and the Bishop is protected by Black's Queen,
with a likely draw in prospect.

Ordinarily the Pawn capture in
the text would be bad because it
doubles the Pawns, making them
easily susceptible to capture. That
would explain why Kashdan did
not consider this variation.

| 51 . . . . | P-K5 |
| 52 K-K7! | B-B3 |

And here—luckily for White—52
... K-B5 loses after 53 K-B6:

I 53 ... K-N6; 54 K-N5!, KxP;
55 N-K5!, P-K6; 56 NxP, K-N6
(if 56 ... P-K7; 57 N-B4ch wins
the dangerous Pawn); 57 N-B4 and
the RP marches on to queen.

II 53 ... P-K6; 54 NxP, KxN; 55
KxP, K-B5; 56 P-R5 and the Bishop is helpless against the two
passed Pawns.

| 53 K-B7! | B-Q4ch |

If 53 ... P-N4; 54 P-R5! wins.

| 54 K-N7 | B-R1 |

Or 54 ... BxN; 55 P-N7 etc.

| 55 K-R6 | B-B3 |

If 55 ... K-B3; 56 P-R5, PxP;
57 KxP. Black's King must retreat,
(else the RP marches on to queen),
whereupon White's King returns to
the center and wins the KP.

| 56 N-R5 | B-Q4 |

Or 56 ... P-K6; 57 NxB, P-K7

(if 57 ... K-K5; 58 P-N7, P-K7;
58 P-N8 (Q), P-K8(Q); 59 Q-K8ch
etc.), 58 N-Q4ch and wins.

57 P-N7	BxP
58 NxB	P-K6
59 N-B5	K-K4
60 N-Q3ch	K-K5
61 N-K1	K-B4
62 K-N7	P-K7
63 N-B2	Resigns

100.

KASHDAN–RESHEVSKY
10th Match Game, 1942

GRUENFELD DEFENSE

I. Kashdan	Reshevsky
WHITE	BLACK
1 P-Q4	N-KB3
2 P-QB4	P-KN3
3 N-QB3	P-Q4
4 B-B4	B-N2
5 P-K3	P-B3

Satisfied that my opponent has
analysed this variation in detail
and seeing no reason for jeopar-
dizing my lead, I avoid the "gambit" continuation 5 ... P-B4.

6 N-B3	O-O
7 Q-N3	PxP
8 BxP	QN-Q2
9 O-O	. . . .

Too passive. After 9 P-K4! White
has a fine center with the initiative,
and Black's pieces lack good
squares.

9	N-N3
10 B-K2	B-K3
11 Q-B2	QN-Q4
12 B-K5	B-B4
13 Q-N3	. . . .

In Game 84, with the White
pieces, I played 13 Q-Q2. 13 P-K4?
would of course be a mistake because of 13 ... NxN.

| 13 . . . . | Q-N3 |

14 B–QB4   . . . .

14 N–Q2 might have been tried
here. Certainly the text offers
Black no difficulty.

14 . . . .   **NxN**

If Black was interested in a quick
draw, 14 . . . QxQ would have answered the purpose.

15 PxN   . . . .

15 QxN, N–K5; 16 Q–R3, BxB;
17 NxB, N–Q3 gives Black an easy
game.

15 . . . .   **N–K5**

Threatening to win a Pawn with
. . . QxQ and . . . NxQBP.

16 Q–R3!   . . . .

A good move—but he fails to
follow it up properly.

16 . . . .   **BxB**

If now 17 PxB, Q–B4; 18 QxQ,
NxQ and Black has the better ending.

17 NxB   **Q–B2**

17 . . . N–Q7 followed by . . . NxB
would have been more exact. The
text should have involved Black in
difficulties.

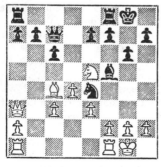

18 QR–Q1   . . . .

Routine play. Correct was 18 P–
B3!, N–Q3; 19 P–K4 (or 19 B–K2
first) with a very strong center.
If 18 . . . N–Q7; 19 BxPch!, RxB;
20 R–B2, NxPch (if 20 . . . N–N8; 21
Q–N3); 21 RxN with a considerably
superior game.

18 . . . .   **N–Q3**

19 B–N3   . . . .

Another thoughtless move. 19 P–
B3 should have been played, and
even 19 B–K2 was preferable to the
text.

19 . . . .   **P–QR4!**

20 Q–B1   **P–R5**

21 B–B2   **P–B4**

Black has greatly improved his
position: he has at last made the
freeing advance . . . P–QB4, and if
left to his own devices, he will gain
ground steadily on the Queen-side.
White must therefore counter energetically in the center and on the
King-side. This explains White's
next move.

22 BxB   **NxB**

23 P–K4   **PxP!**

A challenge for White. After 24
PxN, QxN; 25 PxNP, QPxP; 26 Px
RPch, K–R1 Black's formidable
Queen-side Pawns will decide the
issue. Or 24 PxP, QxQ; 25 RxQ,
NxP and wins.

24 N–N4?   . . . .

He should have played 24 Q–B4,
N–Q3; 25 PxP, KR–B1! (. . . Q–B7
is risky and gives White practical
chances); 26 R–Q2. Black would
then have a strategically won game
with his Queen-side majority of
Pawns and command of the QB
file; but White's healthy center
and good placement of his pieces
might have offered some attacking
chances.

24 . . . .   **N–Q3**

25 RxP   . . . .

Leaving himself with a feeble
QBP which is not long for this
world; but if 25 P–K5, N–B4; 26
PxP, QxQ; 27 RxQ, NxP; 28 R–B7,
P–QN4; 29 RxP, P–N5 and Black's
Queen-side Pawns decide the issue.

25 . . . .   **QR–B1**

25 . . . KR–B1 is too risky: 26 Q–

R6, QxP; 27 RxN!, PxR; 28 P-K5! and wins.

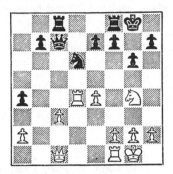

26 N-K3? . . . .

Hoping for 26 ... QxP?; 27 QxQ, RxQ; 28 N-Q5. But Black has a better line.

26 Q-R6 would have been answered by 26 ... QxP; 27 RxN, PxR: 28 P-K5, P-B4; 29 PxP e.p., RxP and wins.

26 RxP is recommended by Fine as "undeniably enough to draw." But Black plays 26 ... Q-Q2; 27 Q-Q1 (or 27 N-R6ch, K-N2; 28 R-Q4, Q-K3; 29 P-B3, P-B4! and despite White's temporary Pawn to the good, his position is very difficult), Q-K3 and White must lose one of his weak Pawns with plenty of play remaining in the position; for example 28 P-K5, N-N4 etc.

26 . . . .   N-N4!

Here also this move is very strong.

If now 27 RxP?, NxP wins. If 27 N-Q5, NxR; 28 NxQ, N-K7ch etc.

27 R-B4   Q-K4

Continuing the attack on the QBP and leaving White no choice.

28 P-B4   Q-K3

29 P-B5   . . . .

A desperate move in a desperate position. If 29 RxR, RxR; 30 P-B4, QxKP winning easily.

29 . . . .   Q-N3

30 RxR   . . . .

30 K-R1, RxR; 31 NxR, Q-B4 is equally hopeless.

30 . . . .   RxR

31 P-B4   N-Q3

Now the Pawns begin to fall.

32 K-R1   NxKP

33 N-Q5   Q-Q3

Politely declining 33 ... N-B7ch?; 34 RxN, QxR; 35 NxPch etc.

34 PxP   RPxP

35 Q-N1   . . . .

White has run out of moves. If 35 Q-B2?, QxN wins a piece. If 35 R-K1, Black can simply play 35 ... P-QN4, for if 36 RxN, QxN.

35 . . . .   RxP

36 QxP   N-B7ch!

37 K-N1   N-N5

If now 38 P-N3, Q-B4ch; 39 K-R1 (or 39 K-N2, QxNch), R-B7 and wins.

38 NxPch   K-N2

39 Q-N2ch   . . . .

Since his game is hopeless, White might just as well have some fun with 39 RxPch?!, KxR; 40 N-B8ch (if 40 N-B5ch, K-B3; 41 NxQ, R-B8 mate), Q-B2! and the attack is over. However, if 40 ... K-N1? (instead of 40 ... Q-B2!); 41 Q-B7ch!, KxQ; 42 NxQch followed by 43 NxR.

39 . . . .   P-B3

Resigns

He cannot prevent the mate and save his Knight at the same time.

101.

RESHEVSKY–KASHDAN
11th Match Game, 1942

QUEEN'S GAMBIT DECLINED

Reshevsky	I. Kashdan
WHITE	BLACK
1 P–Q4	P–Q4
2 P–QB4	P–QB3
3 N–KB3	N–B3
4 N–B3	PxP
5 P–K3	....

This move offers some relief from the all too familiar variation ; which result from 5 P–QR4; in addition, it seemed useful to adopt the text in view of the fact that Kashdan himself thinks well of it.

5	P–QN4
6 P–QR4	P–N5
7 N–R2	P–K3
8 BxP	QN–Q2

The problem presented by this variation is an extremely interesting one: Black has driven back White's QN with gain of time. In the process Black has weakened his Queen-side Pawns, on which White will later train his guns. In doing this, however, he is bound to be hampered by the fact that the mobilization of his Queen-side forces will be very tardy.

9 O–O	B–N2
10 Q–K2	P–B4
11 R–Q1	PxP

The book move is 11 ... Q–N3; but then comes 12 P–K4!, PxP (if 12 ... BxP? or 12 ... NxP?; 13 P–Q5! with a powerful attack); 13 NxP, B–B4; 14 N–N3, O–O; 15 NxB, NxN; 16 B–K3, KR–Q1; 17 P–B3 and White has the better game.

| 12 KNxP | .... |

A difficult choice. The text avoids an isolated QP and keeps the Q file open for White's KR, but it does nothing for the development of White's Queen-side. 12 PxP, on the other hand, would open up the diagonal of the QB, but would leave White with an isolated QP, reduce his KR to a passive role, and would leave Black an ideal post for his pieces at Q4.

12	B–B4
13 N–N3	....

At first sight 13 BxP, PxB; 14 NxKP, Q–N3; 15 NxPch, K–B2; 16 N–B5 looks promising, but the three Pawns are not sufficient value for the piece because White's Queen-side forces cannot be developed for some time to come.

13 P–QN3 followed by B–N2 looks attractive, but the weaknesses of the QNP and of QB3 may be serious in the endgame.

The text is therefore played as the beginning of the play against Black's QNP.

13	B–K2
14 P–R5	....

A useful move in such situations: it isolates Black's QNP by preventing ... P–QR4. It also renders QN3 inaccessible to Black's pieces.

14	O–O
15 B–Q2	Q–N1!

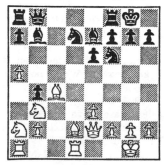

16 P–R6   ....

Black's last move just manages to prevent the loss of a Pawn. If instead 16 BxP, BxB; 17 NxB, BxP; 18 KxB (or 18 N–R6, Q–N2), QxN and Black stands well.

If 16 Q–K1, N–K4; 17 B–K2, B–Q4; 18 N–Q4, P–N6; 19 N–QB3 (Horowitz), Q–N2 and the position is difficult to appraise properly.

If 16 P–B3, B–Q3; 17 P–R3, B–R7ch; 18 K–R1, N–R4; 19 B–K1, N–K4 and the position is very complicated.

16 ....   **B–Q4**

16... B–B3 can be answered by 17 N–R5, but 16... B–K5; 17 P–B3, B–N3 was worth considering here. Black has promising continuations in 18... N–K4 or 18... B–Q3.

17 BxB   **PxB**

Leaving himself with an isolated QP, which, however, will have the important function of protecting a Knight at QB5. After the plausible 17... NxB; 18 P–K4, KN–B3; 19 QR–B1 Black would be at a loss for a good move. For example:

I   19... R–Q1; 20 N–R5 threatening N–B6.

II 19... Q–N3; 20 B–K3 and the Queen must retreat to N1.

III 19... B–Q3; 20 P–R3 and Black cannot continue with 20... N–K4 because of 20 P–B4 followed by 21 P–K5 winning a piece.

18 N–Q4   ....

White could have won the Pawn here with 18 Q–K1, Q–N3; 19 BxP, BxB; 20 NxB, QR–N1; 21 R–Q4. But in that event, his pieces would have been posted very awkwardly, and his Queen-side Pawn formation would make it unlikely that the extra Pawn could be put to good use.

18 ....   **Q–N3**
19 N–B1   **N–B4**
20 N(1)–N3   **KR–Q1**

Judging from his next move, the Rook could have played directly to QB1.

21 N–R5   ....

The position of this Knight has improved considerably during the last few moves; nevertheless 21 R–R5 deserved consideration here. The continuation might have been 21... NxN (virtually forced because of the threat of 22 R–N5); 22 NxN, QR–B1; 23 B–K1 followed by P–B3 and B–B2.

21 ....   **KR–QB1**

21... QxP? would be refuted by 22 QxQ, NxQ; 23 N(5)–B6 winning a piece. 21 ... QR–B1 might have been tried, although 22 DxP, QxB; 23 N(5)–B6, RxN; 24 NxR, Q–K5; 25 NxR, BxN; 26 QR–B1 seems to favor White.

22 KR–QB1   ....

Here 22 BxP, QxB; 23 N(5)–B6, RxN; 24 NxR, Q–K5 would definitely be advantageous for Black.

22 ....   **B–B1**
23 N(5)–N3   ....

The QRP had to be guarded.

23 ....   **KN–K5**

Kashdan has come to the conclusion that his QP is stronger than White's QRP, and he therefore plays for simplification to reach what he hopes will be a favorable position.

24 B–K1	NxN
25 NxN	N–B4
26 N–Q4	N–K3

Fine suggests . . . QR–N1 followed by . . . Q–N3 and . . . R–N3 with intensive "observation" of the QRP. However, White would have sufficient counterplay against Black's weak Pawns.

| 27 N–N3 | R–B2 |
| 28 RxR | . . . . |

Else Black doubles on the QB file.

| 28 . . . . | NxR |

Attacking the QRP and at the same time defending the QP.

| 29 Q–Q3 | R–Q1 |
| 30 Q–Q4 | Q–N1 |

30 . . . QxQ; 31 NxQ (threatening N–B6) would be unfavorable for Black. There might follow 31 . . . R–Q3; 32 BxP, RxP; 33 RxR, NxR; 34 BxB, KxB; 35 N–B6 winning the QRP.

| 31 P–R3 | . . . . |

In such positions, where a later crisis may be anticipated, it is good policy to prepare a flight square for the King. The text turned out to be extremely valuable later on.

31	N–K3
32 Q–Q3	Q–K4
33 N–Q4	NxN

A hasty move. He should have played 33 . . . R–B1, possibly continuing 34 R–Q1, NxN; 35 QxN, QxQ; 36 RxQ, R–B8; 37 K–B1, R–R8; 38 RxQP, RxP with a likely draw.

34 QxN	QxQ
35 PxQ	R–B1
36 R–R5	R–B7?

This is a case where a Rook can be used more effectively in a defensive capacity. 36 . . . R–B3 was the move, after which the ending would very probably have wound up in a draw. The more natural

text soon loses a Pawn.

37 RxP	RxNP
38 R–Q7!	R–N8
39 K–B1	P–N6

All this looks very threatening. 39 . . . R–Q8 would not do because of 39 K–K2, driving the Rook off the file.

| 40 RxRP | P–N3 |

40 . . . B–N5 is of course answered by 41 R–R8ch.

41 R–N7	R–R8
42 RxNP	RxP
43 R–N8	. . . .

White has won a Pawn, but further progress will not be easy, as Black can blockade the QP.

| 43 . . . . | K–N2 |
| 44 K–K2 | R–R7ch |

The checks only help White. 44 . . . B–Q3 followed by . . . K–B3 was a more efficient defense.

45 K–Q3	R–R6ch
46 B–B3	B–Q3
47 R–N2	. . . .

| 47 . . . . | B–K2 |

Eases White's task. With 47 . . . K–B1, bringing the King to the center, he could have made the win much more difficult. If then 48 R–N7 (he cannot try to cut off the King with 48 R–K2, for then 48 . . . B–N5 forces 49 R–B2), R–R3; 49 K–B4 (if 49 K–K4, R–B3; 50 B–N2, R–B7 with counter-chances), R–B3ch and the King must retreat.

White's best plan would have been 49 P–Q5, K–K1; 50 K–B4 etc.

48	K–B4	R–R5ch
49	K–N5	R–R8
50	P–Q5ch	....

Now the win is fairly easy. If 50 ...B–B3; 51 BxBch, KxB; 52 R–K2! and the Pawn must queen. Or 50...P–B3; 51 R–K2, R–N8ch; 52 K–B6, K–B2; 53 P–Q6, B–Q1; 54 K–Q7, R–N1 (if 54...B–N3; 55 R–K7ch, K–N1; 56 K–K8 followed by P–Q7); 55 R–K8, R–N2ch; 56 KxB, R–N1ch; 57 K–B7, RxR; 58 P–Q7 and wins.

| 50 | .... | K–B1 |
| 51 | K–B6 | R–R1 |

If 51...R–QB8; 52 R–N8ch, B–Q1; 53 K–Q7, RxB; 54 RxBch, K–N2; 55 R–QB8 and wins.

| 52 | B–K5 | .... |

The win is now quite easy.

52	....	R–B1ch
53	B–B7	B–B3
54	R–N8	RxR
55	BxR	B–Q5
56	B–Q6ch	K–N2
57	B–B5	Resigns

RETIREMENT AND COMEBACK

A S I HAVE frequently remarked elsewhere in this book, it is a difficult task to make a living from chess. Only if a chessmaster is single can he come even close to scraping by. The married chess professional soon learns the disadvantages of his calling. Since tournaments alone are not sufficiently remunerative, the master finds that he must go afield to give simultaneous exhibitions. This incessant and exhausting travel coupled with tournament play (essential to maintain his reputation) leaves him little or no time for his family. I was determined that this gypsy life was not to be my fate. I wanted to be with my wife and infant daughter, Sylvia. If I couldn't do it by playing chess, then I'd do it some other way. So, after my match with Kashdan, I decided to concentrate on my business career.

Among the tasks I set myself was becoming a certified public accountant. I might remark, in passing, that I have found these C.P.A. examinations far more difficult than most of the chess games I've played. When the 1944 U.S. Championship tournament came along, I was engrossed in studying for these tests. I could not see the wisdom of passing up an opportunity to take them in favor of defending my title. Much to the surprise of the chessworld, I announced that I was not going to play in the tournament. This left the championship in the midst of a free-for-all scramble among the leading masters.

As might be expected, however, as soon as a favorable opportunity presented itself, I was back in competition. When one has been playing chess almost all of his life, it seems unnatural not to face the problems of tournament chess now and then. Still I am determined to follow the dictates of prudence. Henceforth, I will confine my chess activity to vacations and occasional leaves-of-absence. Never again will I permit chess to interfere with the more important business of caring for my family.

U. S. OPEN CHAMPIONSHIP
BOSTON, 1944

D URING the summer of 1944, I happened to be in Boston on a vacation just at the time the U.S.C.F. Open Championship was being held. There didn't seem to be any harm in competing in this one tournament so, after a brief argument with my conscience concerning the wisdom of spending a vacation playing chess, I entered.

Although the field was not particularly distinguished, many of the contestants were dangerous. My long absence from the board had not left me as rusty as I supposed and I bowled my adversaries over one by one. Only Walter Suesman of Providence caught me off guard and won a closely calculated ending from me. Despite this setback, I easily clinched first prize before the tournament was over.

My last round game with Vasconcellos confounded the critics who frequently said I didn't and couldn't play imaginative chess. I cut loose with a hair-raising sacrificial attack which had the spectators (and my opponent) gasping. I consider it one of my best games.

102.

DALY–RESHEVSKY
U. S. Open Championship
Boston, 1944

QUEEN'S PAWN OPENING

H. Daly	Reshevsky
WHITE	BLACK
1 P–Q4	P–Q4
2 P–K3	N–KB3
3 B–Q3	P–B4

Another good continuation is 3 ...N–B3; 4 P–KB4 (if 4 P–QB3, P–K4), N–QN5 and White can hardly avoid the exchange of his KB.

4 P–QB3	QN–Q2
5 P–KB4	P–KN3!

The fianchetto virtually nullifies any attacking chances for White.

6 N–Q2	....

The prospect for White's QB is dark indeed!

6	B–N2
7 N–R3	....

It would have been more logical to play KN–B3, giving the QP additional protection and exerting pressure on K5.

7	O–O
8 O–O	Q–B2
9 Q–B3	Q–B3
10 N–B2	....

10 P–K4? costs a Pawn. With the advance of the KP rendered impossible, it is a superhuman task for White to get his forces working effectively.

10	N–K1!

The Knight can exert pressure on K5 just as well from Q3, and meanwhile the KB is unmasked for powerful action along the diagonal.

11 P–KN4	....

As so often happens when a player cannot complete his development by normal means, White undertakes an attack which will ultimately turn out to his opponent's advantage.

11	N–Q3
12 P–B5	P–K3!

Thus White's impetuous advance is utilized to open lines for Black's pieces.

13 N–R3	KPxP
14 NPxP	N–B3!

Virtually decisive, as the following forced capture will open the KB file for Black.

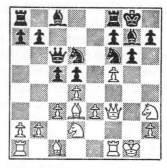

15 BPxP	KBPxP!

This is one instance where the rule about capturing toward the center may be safely violated.

16 Q–N2	B–B4

Enhancing his grip on K5 no matter how White replies.

17 BxB	NxB

With the open K and KB files at the disposal of Black's Rooks, he is well prepared for the final assault.

18 N–B3	N–K5
19 N(R3)–N5	P–R3
20 N–R3	....

Or 20 NxN, PxN; 21 N–K1, N–R5 and the exchange of Rooks will give Black complete control of the KB file.

20	P–KN4!
21 N–B2	NxN
22 RxN	QR–K1

23 R–K2   R–K5

Black's excellent placement of his pieces must soon pay dividends.

24 P–KR3   ....

He cannot very well allow ... P–N5 followed by ... N–R5–B6ch.

24 ....   Q–KN3!

Now ... P–N5 looms up as a tremendous threat.

25 B–Q2   P–N5
26 R–KB1   ....

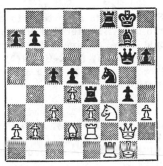

26 ....   Q–R4

The logical culmination of the attack.

27 N–R2   PxP
28 Q–B3   ....

28 Q–B2, Q–N3ch; 29 K–R1, N–N6ch leads to the same conclusion.

28 ....   Q–N3ch
Resigns

White resigns, as decisive material less cannot be avoided.

103.

JACKSON–RESHEVSKY
U. S. Open Championship
Boston, 1944

R U Y L O P E Z

E. S. Jackson, Jr.   Reshevsky
WHITE   BLACK

1 P–K4   P–K4
2 N–KB3   N–QB3
3 B–N5   P–QR3

4 B–R4   N–B3
5 O–O   B–K2
6 R–K1   P–QN4
7 B–N3   P–Q3
8 P–B3   N–QR4
9 B–B2   P–B4
10 P–Q4   Q–B2
11 P–KR3   O–O

All this is very economical on one's clock.

12 QN–Q2   BPxP
13 PxP   N–B3
14 N–N3   ....

For the more customary 14 P–Q5, N–QN5; 15 B–N1, P–QR4 see Game 94 and the notes to Game 74.

14 ....   P–QR4

White was threatening B–Q2 followed by P–Q5 and B–R5.

15 B–K3   ....

In Game 91, Pinkus played 15 P–Q5. In the present game, White plans to defer this advance and keep the center fluid, but eventually he succumbs to the temptation to play P–Q5, thus giving Black's Knights a valuable square at QB4.

15 ....   P–R5
16 QN–Q2   B–Q2

16 ... N–QN5; 17 B–N1, P–R6; 18 Q–N3, RPxP; 19 QxP(2) would be distinctly inferior for Black.

However, 16 ... P–R6 at once is quite playable, for if 17 NPxP (after 17 P–QN3, N–QN5; 18 B–N1, B–Q2 followed by ... KR–B1 Black would have a fine game), RxP; 18 B–N3, N–QR4 and White cannot win the exchange with 19 N–N1 because of 19 ... NxB.

17 QR–B1   KR–B1
18 N–N1   ....

N–B1 was doubtless better. At first sight, the text (intending N–B3–Q5) looks quite formidable; as a matter of fact, Black is able to defeat this plan only by the most careful kind of counterplay.

18 . . . .   Q–R4!

So as to answer 19 N–B3 effectively with 19 . . . P–R6!

19 P–R3   P–N5
20 P–Q5   . . . .

White changes his plan because
he overestimates the strength of
the following pin. 20 PxNP? would
be bad because of 20 . . . QxP.

20 . . . .   N–N1

The only move to save the QNP.

21 B–Q2   N–R3

22 Q–K2   . . . .

22 B–Q3 looks stronger than it
is in reality, as Black gets a satis-
factory game with 22 . . . B–N4; 23
BxB, QxB; 24 RxRch, RxR; 25 PxP,
NxNP; 26 N–B3, Q–N2; 27 QxP (if
27 NxRP, N–Q6 followed by . . . Nx
NP — but this may have been
White's best course!), N–Q6; 28
R–N1, N–B4 and Black must win
the KP, for on either 29 Q–B4 or
Q–B2 comes . . . N(4)xP.

22 . . . .   Q–N3
23 B–K3   N–B4

See the note to White's twentieth
move.

24 B–Q3   QR–N1

Black gives the QNP additional
protection, as he has other plans
for his Queen.

25 QN–Q2   . . . .

An inglorious end to the Knight's
wanderings.

25 . . . .   Q–R2

But not 25 . . . PxP; 26 PxP, Q–
N7?; 27 BxN, PxB; 28 N–B4!, QxQ;
29 RxQ and White wins the KP.

26 N–B4   B–K1
27 KN–Q2   . . . .

Contemplating the advance of the
BP, but it is much too late to be
of any real value.

27 . . . .   KN–Q2
28 P–KN3   Q–R1
29 PxP   . . . .

Should White have tried to preserve his KB? After 29 B–N1, Black
would have continued 29 . . . PxP;
30 PxP, N–N6; 31 R–B2, N(2)–B4
followed by . . . B–N4 with a strong
initiative.

29 . . . .   RxP
30 R–R1   . . . .

Seeking counterplay. If 30 P–B4,
P–B3; 31 PxP, QPxP (or even . . .
BPxP) and White has accomplished
nothing.

30 . . . .   NxB
31 QxN   N–B4
32 BxN   . . . .

An unpleasant choice. However,
if 32 Q–B3 (or Q–R3), Q–N1 threatening . . . NxP or . . . N–N6. Or if 32
Q–K2, B–QN4 pinning the Knight.

32 . . . .   RxB
33 P–N3   . . . .

This turns out badly, but White
was already in difficulties because
of the threat of . . . B–QN4.

33 ....   Q–B1!

This leaves White without a satisfactory reply. Thus if 34 N–K3, PxP; 35 NxP? R–B6 winning a piece. White must either lose the QNP or surrender two pieces for a Rook, hence 34 PxP, R(5)xN; 35 NxR, RxN; 36 P–R5 was relatively best.

34 KR–N1	PxP
35 R–R7	....

Or 35 RxP, R(5)xN; 36 NxR, RxN; 37 QR–N1, R–B8ch and wins.

35	K–B1
36 RxP	....

After 36 N–K3 Black's QNP would decide the game in his favor.

36	R(5)xN
37 NxR	RxN
38 R(3)–N7	R–B6

In addition to having two Bishops for a Rook, Black has a strong attack.

39 Q–Q2	B–Q1
40 K–N2	Q–B5
41 Q–K1	R–B8

42 Q–N4   ....

If 42 Q–K3, Q–B8ch; 43 K–B3, Q–R8ch; 44 K–N4, P–R4ch and mate next move.

42	Q–B8ch
43 K–B3	Q–Q8ch
44 K–K3	B–N4ch

45 P–B4	PxPch
46 PxP	Q–N8ch
	Resigns

White resigns, as there is a forced mate: 47 K–Q3 (if 47 K–B3, Q–B8ch; 48 K–K3, BxPch; 49 K–Q4, Q–B7ch; 50 K–Q3, Q–K6 mate), Q–B8ch; 48 K–Q4, Q–B7ch; 49 K–Q3, Q–B6ch; 50 K–Q4 (if 50 K–Q2, BxP mate), B–B3ch; 51 P–K5, QxBPch; 52 K–Q3, Q–B6ch; 53 K–Q4, BxP mate.

104.

RESHEVSKY–HAMMERMESH
U. S. Open Championship
Boston, 1944

NIMZOINDIAN DEFENSE

Reshevsky	M. Hammermesh
WHITE	BLACK
1 P–Q4	N–KB3
2 P–QB4	P–K3
3 N–QB3	B–N5
4 P–QR3	BxNch
5 PxB	P–B4
6 P–K3	P–Q4
7 BPxP	....

There is a subtle argument in favor of 7 N–B3, for if 7 ... O–O (or 7 ... QPxP; 8 BxP, Q–B2; 9 Q–K2, O–O; 10 O–O, N–B3; 11 P–K4 and White's position is freer); 8 BPxP, NxP; 9 P–B4, N–B3 and now White can develop his KB to Q3 instead of to K2 as in the text continuation.

7 ....   NxP

For 7 ... QxP see Games 37 and 90. 7 ... KPxP and its consequences are well exemplified in Game 88.

8 P–QB4   N–KB3

8 ... N–N3 might have been tried here, with the idea of concentrating on the QBP right from the start.

8 ... N–B6? would lose a piece, however: 9 Q–B2, PxP; 10 PxP, QxP; 11 B–K3, Q–K4 (if 11 ... Q–

B3; 12 R–B1 wins the Knight); 12
N–B3, Q–QR4; 13 B–Q2 and the
Knight is lost.

      9 N–B3   N–B3

Now B–Q3 cannot be played because the QP would be left unprotected; nor would the idea of
playing 10 B–N2 (in order to prepare for B–Q3) serve the purpose,
for then 10 ... Q–R4ch would be
troublesome.

Hence White has to develop his
KB to the modest square K2. His
center is somewhat insecure, but
his Bishops have a promising future.

      10 B–K2   O–O
      11 O–O   PxP
      12 PxP   Q–Q3

Black wants to prevent the pin
at KN5, but it would have been
more to the point to prevent B–
KN5 altogether. Hence ... P–KR3
would be simpler and safer.

      13 B–N5   . . . .

B–N2 was the obvious move, but
the text has its points.

      13 . . . .   P–QN3?

This leads to a poor game, which
would also be the case after 13
... N–Q2; 14 B–Q3, P–KR3; 15 B–
R4, P–QN3; 16 B–N3, Q–K2; 17 R–
K1 threatening P–Q5.

However, the logical move was
13 .. R–Q1! and if 14 BxN (or 14

B–K3, P–QN3 with a fair game for
Black), PxB; 15 Q–N3, P–N3 (not
15 ... NxP??; 16 NxN, QxN; 17
either R–Q1 and wins) with a playable game for Black.

      14 BxN   PxB

Now Black is burdened with a
somewhat exposed King-side without having any real counterchances
in the center.

      15 Q–Q2!   . . . .

Threatening Q–R6 and at the
same time preventing ... Q–B5.

      15 . . . .   N–K2?

This can wait. It was more to
the point to play ... K–N2, preventing Q–R6.

      16 KR–Q1   . . . .

16 Q–R6 would have been more
exact, as it would have prevented
... K–N2, which was still in order.

      16 . . . .   B–N2
      17 Q–R6   N–N3
      18 P–N3   . . . .

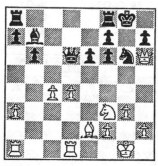

Black is not permitted to play
... Q–B5.

      18 . . . .   KR–Q1
      19 P–KR4   Q–B1
      20 Q–K3   P–KR4?

Waste of time, as the Pawn is
very weak on this square. It would
have been somewhat better to play
20 ... Q–N2 and if 21 P–R5, N–K2;
22 Q–B4, R–Q2 (to prevent Q–B7)
—although White would still have

retained the better game.

| 21 N–K1 | Q–N2 |

This has the drawback of removing the Queen from contact with the Queen-side. ... QR–B1 would have been somewhat better.

| 22 K–R2 | .... |

BxP would be answered by ... NxP.

| 22 .... | K–R1 |

White prefers to avoid the complications resulting from 23 BxP, although they would turn out satisfactorily for him: 23 ... NxP; 24 PxN, R–KN1; 25 P–B4, Q–R3; 26 B–K2, R–N2 (if 26 ... QxRPch; 27 Q–R3); 27 N–B3, QR–KN1; 28 R–KN1 etc.

The simple text move forces the elimination of Black's Bishop, with results that are soon apparent.

| 23 .... | QR–N1 |

23 ... BxB? would lose a Pawn.

| 24 R–Q2 | .... |

24 BxB, RxB; 25 Q–KB3, R(2)–Q2; 26 QxPch, Q–R2; 27 Q–B3 was also possible — but not 27 QxQch, KxQ; 28 N–B3, N–K4! and Black regains his Pawn.

| 24 .... | B–R3 |

If 24 ... BxB; 25 QxB, R–Q2; 26 QxPch, Q–R2; 27 QxQch, KxQ; 28 QR–Q1 and Black has no hope of regaining his Pawn.

| 25 R–B1 | QR–B1 |

Too late.

| 26 P–B5! | .... |

Forcing a passed Pawn which is all the more powerful because of the absence of Black's Queen and Knight.

| 26 .... | PxP |

Refraining from the capture would have been somewhat better, for now White is able to simplify effectively on the Q file.

27 PxP	N–K4
28 RxRch	RxR
29 P–B6	N–N5ch

Black cannot stop the passed Pawn.

| 30 BxN | QxB |

Or 30 ... PxB; 31 P–B7, R–QB1; 32 QxRP, B–K7; 33 R–N1, Q–B1; 34 R–N8 followed by Q–N7.

31 P–B7	R–QB1
32 Q–R6ch	K–N1
33 QxBP	Q–K7
34 R–B5	Resigns

Black is helpless against the crushing threat of 35 R–N5ch, K–B1; 36 Q–Q8ch.

105.

MAGRI–RESHEVSKY
U. S. Open Championship
Boston, 1944

ENGLISH OPENING

Magri	Reshevsky
WHITE	BLACK
1 P–QB4	P–K4

I find the somewhat uncharted lines resulting from this move more interesting than the more stereotyped lines resulting from a transposition into the Queen's Gambit.

| 2 N–QB3 | N–KB3 |
| 3 P–K4 | .... |

A favorite move with Nimzovich, played to assure White a strong

hold on the center, particularly Q5.
Either 3 P–KN3 or 3 N–B3 is more
customary.

    3 . . . .   **B–N5**

Since Black naturally does not
want this Bishop to be blocked by
. . . P–Q3, he must choose between
the text and the equally aggressive
3 . . . B–B4, after which a likely continuation would have been 4 P–B4,
P–Q3; 5 N–B3, N–B3; 6 P–B5, B–
Q2; 7 P–Q3, P–KR3 (to prevent
the pin at N5) and White's pressure in the center is just about
offset by his KB's lack of scope and
his inability to castle.

    4 P–Q3   **O–O**
    5 P–B4   **PxP**

Sooner or later Black will have
to reckon with the possibility of
P–KB5.

    6 BxP   **P–KR3**

This prevents a nasty pin on N5,
and also creates a retreat for the
KN in case of need.

    7 B–K2   . . . .

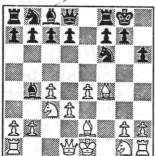

    7 . . . .   **P–Q4!!**

This dynamic freeing move came
as a complete surprise to my opponent.

    8 P–K5   . . . .

The win of the Pawn would be
of doubtful value:

  I 8 KPxP, P–B3; 9 PxP, NxP; 10
N–B3, B–QB4 and Black's superior
development (White's inability to

castle is a prime factor) is sufficient compensation for the Pawn.
  II 8 BPxP, P–B3; 9 P–Q6, BxP;
10 P–K5, B–B2; 11 P–Q4, B–B4; 12
N–B3, N–K5; 13 NxN, BxN; 14
O–O, P–B3 and Black has at least
equality.

    8 . . . .   **P–Q5**
    9 P–QR3   . . . .

Best. If 9 PxN, PxN and White
is in difficulties. If 9 Q–N3, N–B3;
10 PxN, PxN; 11 NPxP, QxP with
advantage.

    9 . . . .   **BxNch**

Black's reply is likewise best.
If 9 . . . PxN; 10 PxB, PxP; 11 R–N1,
Q–Q5; 12 B–N3, KN–Q2; 13 N–B3
with advantage; or 9 . . . B–R4?; 10
P–QN4, PxN; 11 PxN, QxBP; 12
Q–B1, N–B3; 13 B–K3, R–K1; 14
N–B3, B–N5; 15 K–B2.

    10 PxB   **N–R2**

The Knight is very badly posted
temporarily, but this state of affairs is soon remedied.

    11 N–B3   **P–QB4**

Black must maintain the Pawn
at Q5 so as to keep White's KP
artificially isolated.

    12 PxP   **PxP**
    13 O–O   **N–QB3**

White has emerged from the
opening with two Bishops, but they
have little mobility. In addition,
White's KP is far more easily subject to attack than is Black's QP.
We may safely conclude that Black
has come out of the opening with
a clear positional advantage.

    14 R–R2!   . . . .

A good move under the circumstances. White makes room for an
eventual Q–R1 (keeping Black's
QP under observation) and also
prepares to bring the QR to the
King-side.

    14 . . . .   **R–K1**
    15 B–N3   **N–B1**

Already threatening to win the KP with ... N–N3.

16 Q–R1   B–B4

The KP cannot be captured at once: if 16 ... N–N3; 17 K–R1, KNxP; 18 BxN, NxB; 19 QxP etc. Black must bide his time.

17 R–K1   N–N3

Note how the position of this Knight has improved since the retreat to KR2.

18 B–B1   Q–Q2
19 R–KB2   B–N5!

Decisive. Once the Knight is removed, the KP becomes untenable.

20 R(2)–K2   R–K2
21 P–R3   . . . .

White is powerless in the face of Black's contemplated doubling of the Rooks.

21 . . . .   BxN
22 PxB   Q–B4!

Much stronger than 22 ... QR–K1; 23 P–B4, Q–B4; 24 R–K4 and White's chances have improved considerably.

23 P–B4   . . . .

The loss of a Pawn was unavoidable.

23 . . . .   NxBP
24 BxN   QxB
25 R–KB2   Q–N4ch
26 R–N2   Q–R4
27 R–K4   RxP
28 B–K2   Q–B4

Stronger than 28 ... QxP; 29 RxR, NxR; 30 QxP and White's Queen has come into the game.

29 B–N4   Q–B3
30 R–KB2   Q–K2
31 Q–KB1   RxR
32 PxR   N–K4
Resigns

106.

RESHEVSKY-VASCONCELLOS
U. S. Open Championship
Boston, 1944

F R E N C H   D E F E N S E
Reshevsky   A. Vasconcellos
WHITE   BLACK

1 P–K4   . . . .

This game was played in the last round, and I sat down with the firm intention of enjoying myself!

1 . . . .   P–K3

Once more (see Game 80) my opponent does not care to see how I would answer 1 ... P–K4.

2 P–Q4   P–Q4
3 P–K5   . . . .

I adopted this favorite move of Nimzovich because I felt that the advanced KP would have a hampering effect on Black's development.

3 . . . .   P–QB4
4 PxP   N–Q2
5 N–KB3   BxP
6 B–Q3   N–K2

Black's manipulation of the Knights is unorthodox but not bad. On the other hand, 6 ... P–B3 would be inferior because of 7 PxP, KNxP; 8 Q–K2, Q–K2; 9 B–KB4, O–O; 10 O–O and White has pressure on the KP and on K5.

7 O–O   N–QB3

... N–KN3 would prevent White's next move, but then the Knight would be driven away later on by P–KR4–5.

8 B–KB4   Q–B2

A safer course was 8...B–K2 followed by...O–O; but not 8...O–O? 9 BxPch!, KxB; 10 N–N5ch, K–N1 (if 10...K–N3; 11 Q–Q3ch, P–B4; 12 Q–KN3 and wins); 11 Q–R5, R–K1; 12 QxPch, K–R1; 13 Q–R5ch, K–N1; 14 Q–R7ch, K–B1; 15 Q–R8ch, K–K2; 16 QxP mate.

9 N–B3   P–QR3

And not 9...NxP?; 10 NxN, Nx N; 11 Q–R5 winning a piece (11 ...B–Q3; 12 N–N5).

10 R–K1   Q–N3?

A grievous loss of time. Safer was 10...N–N3 followed by...B–Q2 and...O–O–O.

11 B–N3   ....

After 11 Q–K2, N–Q5 (but not 11...QxP?; 12 NxP! PxN; 13 P–K6 etc.); 12 NxN, BxN; 13 QR–N1, N–B4 followed by...NxB, Black would have a satisfactory position.

11 ....   QxP?

Otherwise his previous move is meaningless. But what now follows is a classic instance of the perils resulting from the capture of the QNP in an undeveloped condition.

12 NxP!!   PxN

13 R–N1   ....

The Rook will eventually find the open QN file very useful.

13 ....   Q–R6

14 P–K6!   N–B3

As good a move as Black has. If 14...PxP; 15 N–N5, N–B1 (if 15...P–K4; 16 Q–R5ch, P–N3; 17 BxPch, PxB; 18 QxRch, K–K2; 19 Q–N7ch, K–Q3; 20 N–B7ch, K–B2; 21 NxP etc.); 16 Q–B3, N–Q1; 17 QxP with innumerable attacking possibilities.

15 PxPch   KxP

16 B–R4   ....

After 16 N–N5ch, K–B1; 17 Q–K2, P–QN4 followed by...B–KN5 Black would have an opportunity to catch up in development.

16 ....   N–QN5?

If 16...P–QN4; 17 BxN, PxB (if 17...KxB; 18 Q–Q2, P–R3; 19 Q–B4ch etc.); 18 N–N5ch! PxN (if 18...K–N2; 19 Q–R5 wins); 19 Q–R5ch, K–B3 (or 19...K–N2; 20 QxNPch, K–B2; 21 QxPch etc.); 20 Q–R6ch, K–B2; 21 QxN with many serious threats.

Black's best chance was 16...B–K2 and if 17 BxN, PxB (not 17...BxB; 18 N–N5ch, BxN; 19 Q–B3ch, B–B3; 20 B–N6ch winning the Queen); 18 N–R4 (if 18 N–N5ch, PxN; 19 Q–R5ch, K–N2 and Black has nothing to fear), N–K4; 19 Q–R5ch, K–N2 and Black is safe.

However, after 16...B–K2 White would have continued with 17 P–B4, P–Q5; 18 N–N5ch, K–B1 (if 18...K–K1; 19 N–K4, NxN; 20 BxN,

BxB; 21 BxNch, K–Q1; 22 QxPch and Black is in serious difficulties): 19 Q–K2, P–R3; 20 N–K4, NxN; 21 QxN and White's attack has great chances of success because Black will have considerable trouble in developing his pieces.

17 N–K5ch   K–B1

If 17 ... K–N1; 18 BxN, NxB (or 18 ... PxB; 19 Q–B3, NxB; 20 Qx QPch, K–N2; 21 Q–B7ch, K–R3; 22 QxBPch, K–R4; 23 NxN with the decisive threats of R–K5ch and QxR); 19 QxN, QxQ; 20 NxQ, Bx Pch; 21 KxB, PxB; 22 R–K7 and White wins the ending.

After the text, the game ends amidst thunder and lightning!

18 BxN   NxB

If 18 ... PxB; 19 Q–R5! PxN (or 19 ... B–K3 and White can choose between 20 N–N6ch and 20 Q–R6ch); 20 RxP and wins.

19 BxPch!   ....

Beginning the final assault.

19 ....   KxB

20 RxPch!!   ....

The point of the sacrifice is another sacrifice, which my opponent admitted that he had not foreseen.

20 ....   B–K2

If 20 ... BxR; 21 Q–N4ch, K–B3; 22 Q–B3ch, K–K2 (if 22 ... K–N2; 23 Q–B7ch, K–R3; 24 Q–B6ch, K–R4; 25 P–N4 mate); 23 Q–B7ch, K–Q3; 24 Q–Q7 mate.

Or 20 ... K–R3; 21 N–B7ch, K–N2; 22 NxRch, KxN; 23 R–K8ch, B–B1; 24 Q–R1ch, N–N7; 25 Qx Nch, QxQ; 26 RxB mate.

21 Q–R5!   R–B1

If 21 ... BxR; 22 Q–B7ch, K–R3; 23 N–N4ch, K–N4; 24 Q–N7ch, K–B4 (if 24 ... K–R4; 25 Q–R6ch, Kx N; 26 P–R3ch and mate next move; or 24 ... K–R5, 25 Q–R6ch, KxN, 26 P–R3ch, K–B4; 27 P–N4 mate); 25 N–R6ch, K–B5; 26 Q–N3 mate.

22 Q–N5ch   K–R1

23 N–N6ch!   ....

Crushing. Note that all of White's pieces are en prise!

23 ....   PxN

24 Q–R6ch   K–N1

25 QxPch   K–R1

26 R(7)xB   Resigns

He cannot stop mate. An enjoyable game.

PAN-AMERICAN CHAMPIONSHIP
HOLLYWOOD, 1945

THE tremendous growth of chess interest has had far-reaching effects. Even so hectic a place as Hollywood has fallen under the spell of this ancient pastime. Many film stars are passionately devoted to the game. They snatch precious moments between "takes" to play it on the set. Some, like Humphrey Bogart, have been instrumental in having chess presented in films with more dignity than formerly was the case.

The Pan-American tournament was enthusiastically supported by the chessplaying celebrities of Hollywood. Many attended the event daily to watch the play. In this respect, no other chess tournament has been quite so colorful.

The entry list included players from Argentina, Brazil, Cuba and Mexico. Of these, only Argentina's Herman Pilnik was a serious contender for first place.

107.

RESHEVSKY–PILNIK
Pan-American Championship
Hollywood, 1945
CATALAN SYSTEM
(in effect)

Reshevsky / H. Pilnik
WHITE / BLACK

	White	Black
1	P–Q4	P–Q4
2	P–QB4	PxP
3	N–KB3	N–KB3
4	Q–R4ch	....

As the acceptance of the Gambit is a great favorite with me when I have the Black pieces, I prefer to avoid the beaten track when I have White against this line of play.

4 .... QN–Q2

4...Q–Q2; 5 QxBP, Q–B3; 6 N–R3, QxQ; 7 NxQ is too passive for Black; but 4...B–Q2; 5 QxBP, B–

B3 is simpler than the text.

| 5 | QxBP | P–K3 |
| 6 | P–KN3 | .... |

Now we have a real Catalan formation.

6	....	P–QR3
7	B–N2	P–QN4
8	Q–B6	QR–N1

In my Nottingham game with Capablanca, I played the more exact 8...R–R2!, enabling me to answer 9 B–B4 with 9...B–N2!

9	B–B4	N–Q4
10	B–N5	B–K2
11	BxB	QxB
12	O–O	....

12 P–K4 would be out of place because of 12...N–N5. Black appears to have a good game, but there is a weak spot in his position: the Queen-side Pawns.

12	....	B–N2
13	Q–B2	QR–B1
14	P–QR4!	....

This brings Black's Pawns into disarray no matter how he replies.

14 . . . .   PxP?

But this is a serious strategical error, leaving him with a fatally weak QRP. 14 . . . P-N5 was the lesser evil.

15 QxQRP   O-O
16 N-B3   P-QB4

After 16 . . . NxN; 17 PxN White's coming occupation of the QN file would be very embarrassing for his opponent.

17 NxN   BxN

The more conservative 17 . . . Px N would not do, for then Black's Bishop would be buried and his Pawn position would be weaker than ever.

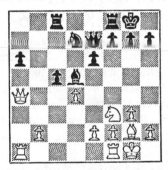

18 KR-B1   . . . .

If 18 QxP, R-N1 regains the Pawn, since 19 Q-R3 is answered by 19 . . . R-N6; while 19 QR-N1 or 19 KR-N1 is answered by 19 . . . B-K5.

18 . . . .   PxP

Now 18 . . . R-N1 would not do because of 19 PxP!, NxP; 20 Q-R3 with a very strong game.

19 NxP   BxB

The unavoidable exchange of the Bishop weakens Black's QRP and his white squares on the Queenside.

20 KxB   N-N1

A melancholy retreat, but if 20 . . . R-R1?; 21 R-B7 is immediately decisive.

21 Q-N3!   . . . .

Beginning a series of maneuvers which soon leave Black with an unbearable position.

21 . . . .   QR-Q1

If 21 . . . P-K4; 22 N-B5, Q-B3; 23 P-K4 and the Knight threatens to land on the mighty square Q5 via K3.

22 P-K3   R-Q2
23 R-R5   R-N2
24 Q-R3   Q-N5

After 24 . . . QxQ; 25 PxQ the occupation of the QB file would soon prove a decisive weapon in White's hands.

25 R-B2   P-N3
26 R(5)-QB5   N-Q2
27 R-QR5   N-N1
28 R-R4   Q-N1

28 . . . Q-K2 would be answered in the same way.

29 R(4)-B4   P-K4

At last he drives away the obnoxious Knight, but he still does not get the anticipated relief.

30 N-B3   P-B3

The opening up of the second rank gives Black a bit more maneuvering space; but in the end even this circumstance turns out in White's favor!

31 R-B8   . . . .

The beginning of the decisive encirclement; if now 31 . . . RxR; 32 RxRch, K-B2; 33 Q-B8ch, K-K3; 34 P-K4 and Black can resign.

31 . . . .   Q-N5
32 Q-Q3!   . . . .

Threatening 33 Q-Q5ch with devastating effect.

32 . . . .   R-KB2
33 P-K4   Q-N2
34 RxRch   . . . .

R–B7, Q–N4; 38 Q–K8!, Q–R5; 39
N–Q2, Q–N4; 40 N–B4 and wins—
or 36 ... N–B3; 37 Q–N8ch, K–R3;
38 RxN!

34 . . . .   RxR

34 ... KxR also loses quickly: 35
Q–Q8ch, K–N2; 36 R–B8, N–Q2; 37

35 Q–Q6!	**Q–Q2**

If 35 ... QxKP; 36 R–B7 wins
easily.

36 Q–N6	**Q–KB2**

He is helpless against the coming penetration on the seventh
rank.

37 R–B7	**Q–K1**
38 Q–N7	**R–B2**
39 RxR	**QxR**
40 QxNch	**Resigns**

SIXTH U. S. CHAMPIONSHIP TOURNAMENT NEW YORK, 1946

THERE were two distinctive features of the 6th U. S. Championship tournament. First of all, it was presented in a
more lavish and showman-like fashion than ever before. The
spectators could sit in a comfortable theater following the
play from wallboards or they could visit the playing room to
watch the competitors in action. It was a rare treat for chess
fans and a notable precedent in American chess.

The second point of interest was the initiation of a zonal
plan to give players all over the country an equal chance to
compete. Each of seven geographical areas was allowed a
specified number of representatives. These, with seven seeded
players—masters of recognized ability, made up the list. Unfortunately, the plan was not strikingly successful. Many of
the "unknown" entrants were far below master-class. However, this defect can be corrected. With the increase in local
competition, each section will be able to put forth players
worthy to compete for the country's highest chess honor.

For me, this was the easiest U. S. championship to date.
Although often in terrible time-pressure and sometimes with
an inferior game, I made my most impressive score in this
event.

108.

FINK–RESHEVSKY
U. S. Championship, 1946

Brilliancy Prize Game

RUY LOPEZ

A. Fink	Reshevsky
WHITE	BLACK
1 P–K4	P–K4
2 N–KB3	N–QB3
3 B–N5	P–QR3
4 B–R4	N–B3
5 O–O	P–QN4
6 B–N3	P–Q3
7 P–B3	....

7 N–N5, P–Q4; 8 PxP, N–Q5 gives Black a powerful initiative.

7	B–K2
8 P–Q4	O–O
9 P–KR3	PxP

A variation with which I have been experimenting of late.

10 NxP	....

10 PxP, P–Q4; 11 P–K5, N–K5 leads to a position full of play, with Black enjoying his share of it.

10	N–QR4
11 B–B2	P–B4

Deliberately assuming a backwards QP in order to drive White's Knight from the center, obtain freedom of action and play against the KP.

12 N–B3	....

Better is 12 N–K2. There would follow 12...B–N2; 13 N–N3, R–K1; 14 N–Q2, B–KB1; 15 P–KB4, with possibilities for both sides.

12	B–N2
13 R–K1	R–K1
14 B–B4	Q–N3
15 QN–Q2	P–N3

To head off White's Knight from the square KB5 via N–B1–N3 and to swing Black's KB to KN2 or KR3 where its scope is enhanced.

16 R–K2	....

This leads to a cramped position. A better plan seems to be 16 N–B1–N3 with King-side prospects in view.

16	B–KB1
17 Q–KB1	N–R4
18 B–R2	B–R3
19 QR–K1	....

White has reduced the issue to the attack and defense of the KP. It is now defended four times.

19	R–K2
20 K–R1	QR–K1
21 P–KN4	....

But this is an about face. He now seeks material gain. Should White temporize, a timely ...N–B5 will net at least the advantage of the Bishops.

21	N–B5!
22 P–N5	NxR
23 PxB	....

And the Knight is trapped–but ...

23	P–B4!

Recovering a Pawn and establishing a firm bind on the position.

24 RxN	PxP
25 Q–K1	P–Q4
26 N–KN1	Q–KB3
27 B–KN3	P–N4

Assuring the return of a second Pawn to keep material in balance.

Positional superiority favors Black.

28	K–R2	QxRP
29	P–B3	. . . .

He is anxious to free his KB for action. But the march of the Pawn to the sixth is of threatening proportions. 29 N–B1 is indicated.

29	. . . .	P–K6
30	N–N3	NxN
31	PxN	P–Q5
32	P–N4	. . . .

Evidently White banks on this move to destroy the center.

32	. . . .	P–N5!

Thereby inaugurating divers positional and mating threats.

33	B–K4	. . . .

If 33 KBPxP, Q–QB3; 34 B–B4, R–KB1; 35 K–N3, R(2)–KB2 and White's position collapses.

33	. . . .	BxB
34	PxB	RxP
35	PxQP	PxQP
36	Q–Q1	. . . .

The QP must be blockaded.

36	. . . .	Q–K3
37	PxP	. . . .

37 P–N3, followed by Q–Q3 offers greater resistance. Now, in addition to staving off the Pawns, he must guard his King.

37	. . . .	RxP
38	R–N2	R–K2
39	N–K2	R(2)–N2
40	Q–QN1	. . . .

Not 40 NxP, Q–R3ch and White's Bishop falls.

40	. . . .	P–KR4

The final assault.

41	R–N1	P–R5
42	B–B4	RxR
43	NxR	Q–N5
44	Q–R2ch	. . . .

If 44 Q–KB1, R–KB2; 45 N–R3, P–K7; 46 Q–B2, RxB; 47 NxR, Q–N6ch and Black queens by force.

44	. . . .	K–R1

Resigns

109.

RESHEVSKY–STEINER
U. S. Championship, 1946

NIMZOINDIAN DEFENSE

Reshevsky	H. Steiner
WHITE	**BLACK**
1 P–Q4	N–KB3
2 P–QB4	P–K3
3 N–QB3	B–N5
4 P–K3	P–Q4
5 P–QR3	BxNch

5...B–K2 is an interesting alternative at this point.

6 PxB	O–O
7 B–Q3	P–B4
8 BPxP	KPxP
9 N–K2	N–B3

Reaching a position over which much midnight oil has been spent. White enjoys the advantage of the Bishops, play in the center and King-side; Black has a free game.

10 P–B3	R–K1
11 O–O	Q–B2
12 R–N1	. . . .

Aiming for maximum mobility of the forces before a positive campaign is launched.

12	B–Q2

Despite Black's freedom of movement, he cannot fix upon a vulnerable target.

13 Q–K1   QR–Q1

One of those so-called mysterious Rook moves. Its object is probably to restrain P–K4 by placing indirect pressure against White's QP and at the same time complete Black's development.

14 P–KN4   . . . .

Black has temporarily restrained the center advance. But he is ill prepared for the wing advance.

14 . . . .   P–KR3

Projecting a target in the King's camp. The patent threat of P–N5, however, needed to be parried.

15 K–R1   B–B1
16 R–N1   P–KN4

Otherwise P–N5 smashes open the Knight file with devastating effect.

17 Q–N3   . . . .

Because of the advantage of the Bishops, White enjoys better end-game prospects and can afford to trade Queens.

17 . . . .   Q–K2
18 Q–B2   K–N2
19 N–N3   R–R1
20 B–B5   . . . .

Threatening 21 BxB, followed by N–B5ch, etc.

20 . . . .   B–K3

As Black's forces are diverted to the wing and less potent in the center, White institutes the "big push."

21 P–K4!   . . . .

Admitting the QB into the final assault.

21 . . . .   K–B1

The QP is immune after 21 . . . QPxP; 22 BPxP, PxP; 23 PxP. For if 23 . . . NxQP; 24 B–N2, the attack on the long diagonal is decisive.

22 P–K5   N–K1
23 BxB   PxB

Forced. Otherwise the NP goes.

24 P–KB4   . . . .

Exposing the adverse King to withering blows.

24 . . . .   NPxP
25 QxPch   K–N1
26 N–R5   . . . .

With 27 P–N5 in view.

26 . . . .   R–R2
27 P–N5   PxNP
28 RxPch   K–R1
29 RxP!   N–B2

29 . . . QxR(2); 30 Q–B8 mate.

30 RxN   Resigns

30 . . . QxR; 31 Q–B6ch, etc.

110.

RESHEVSKY–KASHDAN
U. S. Championship, 1946
QUEEN'S GAMBIT DECLINED

Reshevsky	I. Kashdan
WHITE	BLACK
1 P–Q4	N–KB3
2 P–QB4	P–B3
3 N–KB3	P–Q4
4 PxP	. . . .

The exchange is deceptive; it simplifies and appears to give the game a drawish aspect. In reality it avoids alternate Black lines of play and maintains the initiative of the first move.

4 . . . .   PxP
5 N–B3   P–K3

Sooner or later the symmetry is impaired as Black cannot afford to develop his QB. If, for instance, 5 . . . B–B4; 6 Q–N3 poses a problem of defense for the NP.

6 B–B4   P–QR3
7 P–K3   B–K2
8 B–Q3   P–QN4

To create a post for Black's QB as well as to institute a wing demonstration.

9 R–QB1   B–N2
10 P–QR4   . . . .

Loosening up the Pawn structure

and consequently allowing possibilities on both wings.

10 ....   P–N5
11 N–QN1   N–B3
12 QN–Q2   O–O
13 O–O   N–KR4

Kashdan's predilection for Bishops gives the game an interesting turn.

14 B–K5   ....

Not 14 N–N5, NxB; 15 BxPch, K–R1; 16 PxN, BxN and wins.

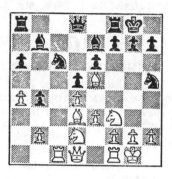

14 ....   P–B3

If 14 ... NxB, White has a choice of two good lines: 15 PxN, P–N3; 16 N–Q4 with prospects on both wings, or 15 NxN, N–B3; 16 N–B6, Q–Q2; 17 NxBch, QxN; 18 N–N3–B5 with a bind on the Queen side.

15 N–N5!   ....

Good for a draw with opportunity for Black to go wrong.

15 ....   Q–K1

15 ... PxB; 16 QxN, BxN; 17 Qx Pch is complicated. Yet Black might squirm out with a draw. White could play 16 BxPch, K–R1; 17 NxP, Q–K1; 18 NxR, BxN; 19 B–N1, and bring about the same position as in the text.

16 BxPch   K–R1
17 B–N1   PxB

17 ... PxN; 18 Q–B2 wins.

18 NxP   PxP

18 ... P–K5; 19 NxR, BxN; 20 P–B3 with good attacking prospects.

19 NxR   ....

Now 19 N–B7 brings home the game perforce: 19 ... Q–B2; 20 Nx R, BxN; 21 RxN, BxR; 22 Q–B2, threatening mate and Bishop and netting a valuable Pawn on the transaction.

19 ....   BxN
20 PxP   N–B3

Not 20 ... NxP; 21 R–K1, Q–B2; 22 R–B7 winning.

21 R–K1   Q–R4
22 QxQch   NxQ
23 N–B3   ....

With Rook and two Pawns for two minor pieces, the position is difficult for both sides.

23 ....   N–B3
24 R–K6   ....

This gives Black d r a w i n g chances. To be considered: 24 N–K5 and if 24 ... NxP; 25 N–N6ch, K–N1; 26 R–B7, R–N1; 27 NxB; KxN; 28 R(1)–K7 and White wins.

24 ....   R–B1
25 B–B5   ....

25 ....   N–K2

Kashdan should run for the draw with 25 ... NxP; 26 RxR, NxNch; 27 PxN, BxR; 28 RxN, PxR; 29 Bx B. Though White remains with a Pawn to the good, Bishops of opposite colors militate against the win.

26 RxR	NxR

Not 26 ... BxR; 27 RxN(7), BxB; 28 R–R7, winning the RP and obtaining an irresistible, passed RP.

27 N–K5	K–N1
28 N–N6	N–Q3

Against passive defense, White resorts to his extra King-side Pawns to make headway. Temporizing, nevertheless offered the best chance.

29 B–R3	N–B5

If 29 ... N(B3)–K1; 30 RxN, NxR; 31 B–K6ch followed by NxB.

30 P–QN3	N–QR4
31 R–N6	. . . .

After which the NP falls and the game is over.

31	K–B2

32 NxB	KxN
33 RxNP	B–B3
34 R–N6	B–K1
35 RxP	NxP
36 P–R5	K–K2
37 R–K6ch	K–Q1
38 P–R6	K–B2
39 P–R7	K–N2
40 R–N6ch!	Resigns

Reshevsky's Tournament & Match Record

Tournaments

	RANK	WON	LOST	DRAWN	TOTAL
NEW YORK 1922 _____3-6		1	2	2	5
DETROIT 1924					
(Western Championship) _____5		10	4	2	16
KALAMAZOO 1927					
(Western Championship) _____3-5		4	2	2	8
TULSA 1931					
(Western Championship) _____1		6	0	3	9
MINNEAPOLIS 1932					
(Western Championship) _____2		8	1	2	11
PASADENA 1932 _____3-5		5	4	2	11
DETROIT 1933					
(Western Championship) _____2		9	0	4	13
CHICAGO 1934					
(Western Championship) _____1-2		6	0	3	9
SYRACUSE 1934 _____1		10	0	4	14
MARGATE 1935 _____1		7	0	3	10
YARMOUTH 1935 _____1		10	1	0	11
NEW YORK 1936					
(1st U. S. Championship) _____1		10	2	3	15
NOTTINGHAM 1936 _____3-5		7	2	5	14
SEMMERING-BADEN 1937 _____3-4		4	3	7	14
KEMERI 1937 _____1-3		10	3	4	17
STOCKHOLM 1937 _____*		6	3	7	16
HASTINGS 1937-8 _____1		5	0	4	9
NEW YORK 1938					
(2nd U. S. Championship) _____1		10	0	6	16
AVRO 1938 _____4-6		3	3	8	14
LENINGRAD-MOSCOW 1939 _____2		7	3	7	17
NEW YORK 1939					
(U. S. Open Championship) _____2		9	0	2	11
NEW YORK 1940					
(3rd U. S. Championship) _____1		10	0	6	16
HAMILTON 1941					
(N. Y. State Championship) _____2-4		4	0	6	10
NEW YORK 1942					
(4th U. S. Championship) _____1-2		10	0	5	15
BOSTON 1944					
(U. S. Open Championship) _____1		15	1	1	17
HOLLYWOOD 1945 _____1		9	0	3	12
NEW YORK 1946					
(6th U. S. Championship) _____1		14	0	4	18
		209	34	105	348

*International Team Tournament

Matches

	WON	LOST	DRAWN	TOTAL
vs. I. HOROWITZ				
(U. S. Championship, 1941) _____	3	0	13	16
vs. I. KASHDAN				
(U. S. Championship, 1942) _____	6	2	3	11
TOTALS	9	2	16	27

ABOUT THE AUTHOR

T HE story of Sammy Reshevsky is a success story made possible not only by phenomenal genius but also by determination, perseverance, and courage. There have been other child prodigies in chess; there have been other great chess masters. But with the exception of the great Capablanca, no other child prodigy has ever become a grandmaster and maintained that position for years. It is the combination of Reshevsky's ability and his personal qualities which has enabled him to succeed so brilliantly where others have failed.

Reshevsky was born in 1911 in the little Polish village of Ozierkov, the sixth child of orthodox Jewish parents. His remarkable mental powers manifested themselves at the age of two, but he did not learn to play chess until he was four years old. His father was fond of chess as a means of whiling away long winter evenings, Little Sammy's interest first took the form of interfering in his father's games, moving pieces from their squares and the like. Instead of becoming irritated, the father taught the boy how to play.

It goes without saying that Sammy learned very quickly, and soon became vociferous in his demand for opponents. There is an echo of a famous anecdote about Capablanca in the story that once, when his father was faced with apparently inevitable defeat, Sammy intervened with a subtle move which saved the day.

In a few months, the child played so well that he could find no worthy opponents in the little village. His family then moved to Lodz, where the Polish master Salve was fascinated by the child prodigy. In 1917 Sammy was taken to Warsaw, where his appearance in the chess club aroused so much interest that the great Akiba Rubinstein decided to play a game with him. Naturally the child lost, but after the game Rubinstein said to him, "You will be World Champion some day." It is worth noting (and very characteristic!) that when Rubinstein showed him the famous game that he had won from Lasker at St. Petersburg in 1909, Sammy pointed out a way of winning two moves earlier!

The score of the game played by Sammy against Rubinstein appears below. It is taken from a book on chess written in Yiddish by Endewelt and Weisblatt and published in Warsaw in 1917. Judged by objective standards, Sammy's play is of course weak, but the game is of extraordinary historical interest. Rubinstein played blindfold.

GIUOCO PIANO

Reshevsky	A. Rubinstein
WHITE	BLACK
1 P-K4	P-K4
2 N-KB3	N-QB3
3 B-B4	B-B4
4 O-O	N-B3
5 N-B3	P-Q3
6 P-KR3	P-KR3
7 P-Q3	P-KN4
8 N-Q5	P-N5
9 N-N5	NxN
10 PxN	PxN
11 PxN	PxBP
12 PxP	P-Q4
13 Q-K2	Q-B3
14 B-N3	Q-R3
15 QxPch	B-K3
16 QxRch	QxQ
17 BxNP	K-Q2
18 P-B3	R-KN1
19 B-K3	BxP
20 B-Q1	B-KR6

21 P-KN3	....
21	RxPch
22 PxR	BxBch
23 R-B2	Q-N2
24 B-N4ch	....

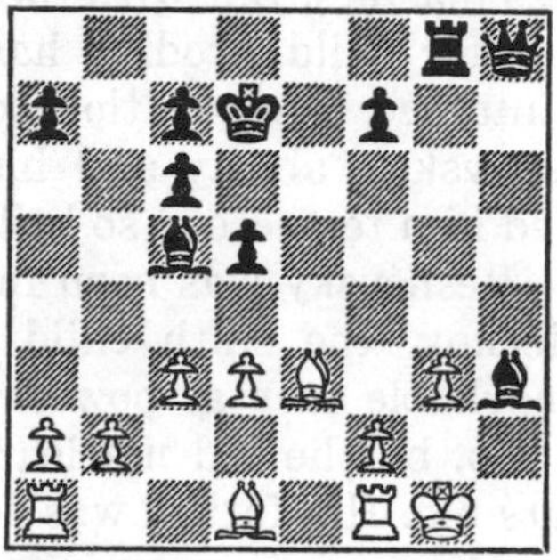

A note here says that Sammy called out "check" exhuberantly delighted with the idea of checking Rubinstein.

24	QxB
Resigns	

A dramatic game took place the same year, when the German Governor of Poland invited the *wunderkind* for a game at his residence. The six-year-old scored once by winning the game and then a second time by telling the hated oppressor: "You can shoot, but I can play!"

In January, 1920, his parents came to a momentous decision: Sammy was to tour the great capitals of Europe to display his skill. The outcome was a triumphal march through Berlin, Vienna, Paris, London, and other great chess centers. Everywhere the general public, as well as chess fans and scientists, took a great interest in the tiny boy who defeated whole groups of greybeards with such astonishing ease.

Fortunately for students of chess and for those interested in child prodigies, young Sammy was examined by **Dr.** Franziska Baumgarten, a Berlin psychologist. The boy was not interested in chocolate or toys, but the psychologist had better luck when he produced a stopwatch. Having won the boy's interest and confidence, he proceeded to test him.

Sammy had had no schooling and had never seen a picture book in his life. Hence he was quite poor at recognizing pictures, an important part of the test. He failed to recognize a lion, a monkey, a tiger, or a camel. He knew that the day was a Wednesday, but hadn't the slightest idea of the date. He was below standard for his age in arithmetic. Thus far the results of the test were disappointing.

There was a different story to tell when he was tested for his powers of visualizing space and forms. One test was to combine irregular shapes so as to form a regular shape, much as in selecting fitting pieces for a jigsaw puzzle. Another test was to cut an irregular shape with a single line in such a way as to divide it into pieces which could then be combined to form a regular shape, such as a rectangle. Sammy solved problems which were considered difficult for children of thirteen (twice his age). He also solved one such problem which had never been worked out by *any* child!

The story became even more remarkable when the young Reshevsky's memory was tested. He was allowed four minutes to examine forty figures, each drawn in a special square on a sheet of paper. The paper was then removed. The boy was able to restate the figures without a single mistake, and in the correct order. Moreover, he was able to fill in the figures correctly on a blank sheet divided into squares. This was a much better result than experimental psychology had ever previously obtained even with adults!

The seven-year-old child impressed the psychologist not only by performing such feats of memory and visualization but also by his independence. He would not allow any kind of assistance in his endeavors. When asked what he would do if the curtain suddenly caught fire, he replied: "I'd get a bucket of water and throw it on the flame." Asked why he wouldn't call the fire brigade, he answered: "I'd want to see to it myself."

These tests and the boy's feats at the chess table were impressive, but did not provide for the child's future. With this problem in mind, his parents brought him to the United States in 1920.

On the evening of Sammy's arrival in New York, he paid a visit to the new quarters of the Marshall Chess Club. Here is how Hermann Helms described the occasion:

> . . . . As the conversation became general, with the boy's achievements as a chief topic, Hodges seized the opportunity to set up three problems of his own making on the table in front of Rzsechewski.* The first, a two-mover, was solved by the wonder child almost at sight. The second, a three-mover took a little longer. The third, another three-mover, was somewhat more difficult and puzzled him a bit.
>
> Resting his chin on one small gloved hand and pointing with the other at the squares to which the King might escape, he reasoned out the steps of the solution so completely, albeit he uttered not a word, that one felt sure that he was on the right track. And indeed he was, for the coming move was foreseen soon after. Someone in the group who had pulled out a watch when the last problem was set up announced that it had taken him three and a quarter minutes to solve it.

In the following weeks, Sammy gave a series of exhibitions in New York which fully confirmed and even exceeded the reports of his phenomenal genius. Two exhibitions took place at the Lenox Theater and one at West Point, where his convincing defeat of the future masters of military strategy seemed to tickle the popular fancy.

In the winter of 1920-21, Sammy undertook a countrywide tour of the United States which lasted well into 1922. Everywhere he went he was greeted by huge crowds and enormous enthusiasm. Few players realize what a huge debt of gratitude American chess owes to Reshevsky: many moribund clubs revived, many new ones were founded—all on the wave of enthusiasm created by the child prodigy's feats. In return, Sammy was rewarded with fame, but not with fortune.

Sammy's sternest test as a child prodigy came in October, 1922, when he played in a tournament arranged by the Chess Club International in New York. His score was superficially disappointing: he beat Janowski, drew with Bernstein and

---

* The Polish spelling of his name.

Jaffe, and lost to Edward Lasker and Bigelow. As a matter of fact, his showing was really an excellent one: every game was hard-fought (it took Lasker 70 moves to beat him!). What really beat Sammy was not lack of ability, but lack of knowledge. His game with Janowski (see Game 10) is surely one of the greatest feats in the history of chess.

But Sammy's days as a child prodigy were drawing to a close. It was time to think of his education and his future. In 1924, the late Julius Rosenwald invited Sammy to his home in Chicago. Rosenwald immediately took a keen interest in the gifted child and promised to provide for Sammy's future if he settled down and devoted himself to acquiring an education.

Sammy's parents readily consented, and he was sent to the home of Morris Steinberg in Detroit. Steinberg, an able businessman and active in the Detroit Chess and Checker Club, was Sammy's friend, companion, and counsellor until he returned to tournament chess. To this day the relationship between Steinberg and Sammy remains a very close one.

Sammy had a private tutor for about six months; then he passed a high school examination and entered Northern High School about the end of 1924. He also devoted himself to the study of singing and Hebrew. In 1929 he graduated from Northern High School with "fairly good marks."

During this whole period he played no serious chess, with the rare exception of a few simultaneous performances. In fact, chess was forbidden, so that he would have all the necessary time and opportunity to live a normal boy's life. He played tennis, baseball, swam, went dancing, mixed with boys and girls. He made friends readily, and did his best to hide his fame. Every summer he would spend a few days at the Rosenwalds' summer home, where he would give one of his rare chess performances: a blindfold game against two of the younger Rosenwalds.

In 1929, Sammy entered the University of Detroit, majoring in accounting. In 1931 he moved to Chicago, where he completed his studies and obtained his degree.

In 1931, Samuel Factor, Chicago's best player, was about to set out for Tulsa to participate in the Western Championship. "Why not come along in my car?" He suggested to Sammy. It was a tempting offer: the summer vacation gave Sammy ample time; he was beginning to be interested once more in the game; he wondered whether he could repeat the fabulous triumphs of his childhood. Sammy's decision to play was justified: he went through the tournament without loss of a game, taking first place half a point ahead of Factor and Whitaker.

Sammy was too level-headed to be too enthusiastic about this victory. It was reassuring, but it did not fully settle the question of whether he still retained his old-time skill. He returned to Chicago and resumed his studies, waiting for another opportunity to test his powers.

The opportunity came with the Western Championship of 1932, held at Minneapolis. Lacking practice and proper theoretical preparation, Sammy was severely handicapped and had to play himself into form. His opening play was generally poor and his success was based on masterly defensive play in difficult positions, supplemented by excellent handling of the endgame.

In the Pasadena Tournament, which followed on the heels of the Minneapolis tourney, the picture remained unchanged. Sammy had to adjourn all of his first five games, and the average length of his games was much greater than that of his competitors. Thus he had to work much harder than all the other players. The fighting character of his play is indicated by his 96-move loss to Alekhine, as well as the low number of draws in his score: five wins, four losses (to Alekhine, Kashdan, Borochow, and Reinfeld), and two draws. The number of losses is abnormally high, and may be directly attributed to poor positions resulting from inferior opening play. Luckily, the tournament was so hard-fought that Sammy's score earned him a very respectable tie for third prize with Arthur Dake and Herman Steiner.

If Sammy was to continue with tournament chess, he would have to polish his opening play. Thus far he had neglected it because of uncertainty about his future course. As Kashdan commented in the May 1933 issue of CHESS REVIEW:

Sammy is at the cross-roads. If he continues in chess, he has every prospect of repeating his triumphs as a child wonder. But as a young man looking for his place in the business world, he would have little time for serious chess playing. The time is at hand when he must choose. The chess world is keenly interested in his decision, as it must be in following the career of its most famous prodigy.

Sammy did not make the choice in 1933—in fact, he has deferred it to this day! He has burdened himself with the tiring task of carrying on two professions simultaneously, with the result that he has never had an opportunity to prepare himself properly for the rigors of tournament and match play with the world's outstanding experts.

However, from 1933 on, Sammy made a determined and successful effort to eliminate the one serious defect in his play—inadequate knowledge of the openings.

The results were immediately apparent in his next tournament, the Western Championship, held in 1933 in Detroit. He played here with new confidence; fortified by careful study of the openings, his play was sure, decisive and particularly rich. Once more the chief feature of the tournament was a race for first between Fine and Reshevsky. Fine carried off the prize, although Sammy had the satisfaction of winning their individual encounter.

The Western Championship in 1934 as Chicago presented a similar picture: Fine and Sammy again slugged it out for first prize, this time tying with 7½ - 1½, ahead of Dake, Denker, and Kashdan. In these tournaments, Sammy was not only a consistent contender for first prize—he had the rewarding knowledge that his chess was improving all the time. These tendencies were to reach their fruition in the Syracuse Tournament, which came shortly after Chicago. The Syracuse event was particularly formidable, but Reshevsky won the tournament without loss of a game.

In 1935 Sammy had the longed-for opportunity to follow in the footsteps of the immortal Morphy, Pillsbury and Marshall: he participated in two international tournaments. His steady, thoroughly competent play in both contests assured him easy victories at Margate and at Great Yarmouth, impressing the chess world and enhancing his reputation considerably. The Margate Tournament was particularly useful in this respect because his chief rival for top honors was ex-World Champion Jose Capablanca. Sammy's masterly victory in this vital struggle was proof to even the most dubious that he retained all the wizardry of his childhood days.

In 1936, Reshevsky faced his sternest test to date: the first American Championship Tournament. From the very start, the tournament took a course which was as remarkable as it was exciting. After a catastrophic start, Reshevsky had to win nine games and draw two to capture the championship!

A few months later, at Nottingham, Sammy proved (if proof were needed) that his victory in the United States Championship was no accident or flash in the pan. The Nottingham Congress is often termed the strongest tournament ever held. Reshevsky began the tournament with a laborious effort to play himself into form: it took him five rounds to amass a plus score! But his victories over Alekhine and Bogolyubov soon put him among the leaders, and he finished only a half point out of first place.

1937 was a busy year for Reshevsky, since he took part in three important international contests: Kemeri, Stockholm, and Semmering-Baden. In 1938 he successfully defended his United States Championship, took part in the AVRO tournament, and met most of the Soviet Union's outstanding masters in the Leningrad-Moscow Tournament. He then played in the United States Open Championship, and once again successfully defended his U. S. Championship in 1940.

From this point on, the paucity of tournaments and the growing demands of his accounting career combined to reduce Reshevsky's active chess playing to a minimum. After the match with Kashdan in 1942, Reshevsky dropped out of serious chess for more than a year and a half. Then, after winning the U. S. Open, he dropped out again for a full year.

Now, after fifteen years of intensive struggle against the great and the near-great of the international chess world, Reshevsky is apparently out to return to serious chess in the effort to win the world championship. But even if he were never to play again, the chess world, chess literature, and the lives of thousands of chess players have been enriched by his magnificent games.

INDEX of PLAYERS

[Bold face indicates Black — Numbers refer to pages]

INDEX of OPENINGS

[Numbers refer to pages]

A CATALOGUE OF SELECTED DOVER BOOKS
IN ALL FIELDS OF INTEREST

AMERICA'S OLD MASTERS, James T. Flexner. Four men emerged unexpectedly from provincial 18th century America to leadership in European art: Benjamin West, J. S. Copley, C. R. Peale, Gilbert Stuart. Brilliant coverage of lives and contributions. Revised, 1967 edition. 69 plates. 365pp. of text.

21806-6 Paperbound $3.00

FIRST FLOWERS OF OUR WILDERNESS: AMERICAN PAINTING, THE COLONIAL PERIOD, James T. Flexner. Painters, and regional painting traditions from earliest Colonial times up to the emergence of Copley, West and Peale Sr., Foster, Gustavus Hesselius, Feke, John Smibert and many anonymous painters in the primitive manner. Engaging presentation, with 162 illustrations. xxii + 368pp.

22180-6 Paperbound $3.50

THE LIGHT OF DISTANT SKIES: AMERICAN PAINTING, 1760-1835, James T. Flexner. The great generation of early American painters goes to Europe to learn and to teach: West, Copley, Gilbert Stuart and others. Allston, Trumbull, Morse; also contemporary American painters—primitives, derivatives, academics who remained in America. 102 illustrations. xiii + 306pp. 22179-2 Paperbound $3.00

A HISTORY OF THE RISE AND PROGRESS OF THE ARTS OF DESIGN IN THE UNITED STATES, William Dunlap. Much the richest mine of information on early American painters, sculptors, architects, engravers, miniaturists, etc. The only source of information for scores of artists, the major primary source for many others. Unabridged reprint of rare original 1834 edition, with new introduction by James T. Flexner, and 394 new illustrations. Edited by Rita Weiss. 6⅝ x 9⅝.

21695-0, 21696-9, 21697-7 Three volumes, Paperbound $13.50

EPOCHS OF CHINESE AND JAPANESE ART, Ernest F. Fenollosa. From primitive Chinese art to the 20th century, thorough history, explanation of every important art period and form, including Japanese woodcuts; main stress on China and Japan, but Tibet, Korea also included. Still unexcelled for its detailed, rich coverage of cultural background, aesthetic elements, diffusion studies, particularly of the historical period. 2nd, 1913 edition. 242 illustrations. lii + 439pp. of text.

20364-6, 20365-4 Two volumes, Paperbound $6.00

THE GENTLE ART OF MAKING ENEMIES, James A. M. Whistler. Greatest wit of his day deflates Oscar Wilde, Ruskin, Swinburne; strikes back at inane critics, exhibitions, art journalism; aesthetics of impressionist revolution in most striking form. Highly readable classic by great painter. Reproduction of edition designed by Whistler. Introduction by Alfred Werner. xxxvi + 334pp.

21875-9 Paperbound $2.50

A CATALOGUE OF SELECTED DOVER BOOKS
IN ALL FIELDS OF INTEREST

VISUAL ILLUSIONS: THEIR CAUSES, CHARACTERISTICS, AND APPLICATIONS, Matthew Luckiesh. Thorough description and discussion of optical illusion, geometric and perspective, particularly; size and shape distortions, illusions of color, of motion; natural illusions; use of illusion in art and magic, industry, etc. Most useful today with op art, also for classical art. Scores of effects illustrated. Introduction by William H. Ittleson. 100 illustrations. xxi + 252pp.

21530-X Paperbound $2.00

A HANDBOOK OF ANATOMY FOR ART STUDENTS, Arthur Thomson. Thorough, virtually exhaustive coverage of skeletal structure, musculature, etc. Full text, supplemented by anatomical diagrams and drawings and by photographs of undraped figures. Unique in its comparison of male and female forms, pointing out differences of contour, texture, form. 211 figures, 40 drawings, 86 photographs. xx + 459pp. 5⅜ x 8⅜.

21163-0 Paperbound $3.50

150 MASTERPIECES OF DRAWING, Selected by Anthony Toney. Full page reproductions of drawings from the early 16th to the end of the 18th century, all beautifully reproduced: Rembrandt, Michelangelo, Dürer, Fragonard, Urs, Graf, Wouwerman, many others. First-rate browsing book, model book for artists. xviii + 150pp. 8⅜ x 11¼.

21032-4 Paperbound $2.50

THE LATER WORK OF AUBREY BEARDSLEY, Aubrey Beardsley. Exotic, erotic, ironic masterpieces in full maturity: Comedy Ballet, Venus and Tannhauser, Pierrot, Lysistrata, Rape of the Lock, Savoy material, Ali Baba, Volpone, etc. This material revolutionized the art world, and is still powerful, fresh, brilliant. With *The Early Work,* all Beardsley's finest work. 174 plates, 2 in color. xiv + 176pp. 8⅛ x 11.

21817-1 Paperbound $3.00

DRAWINGS OF REMBRANDT, Rembrandt van Rijn. Complete reproduction of fabulously rare edition by Lippmann and Hofstede de Groot, completely reedited, updated, improved by Prof. Seymour Slive, Fogg Museum. Portraits, Biblical sketches, landscapes, Oriental types, nudes, episodes from classical mythology—All Rembrandt's fertile genius. Also selection of drawings by his pupils and followers. "Stunning volumes," *Saturday Review.* 550 illustrations. lxxviii + 552pp. 9⅛ x 12¼.

21485-0, 21486-9 Two volumes, Paperbound $10.00

THE DISASTERS OF WAR, Francisco Goya. One of the masterpieces of Western civilization—83 etchings that record Goya's shattering, bitter reaction to the Napoleonic war that swept through Spain after the insurrection of 1808 and to war in general. Reprint of the first edition, with three additional plates from Boston's Museum of Fine Arts. All plates facsimile size. Introduction by Philip Hofer, Fogg Museum. v + 97pp. 9⅜ x 8¼.

21872-4 Paperbound $2.00

GRAPHIC WORKS OF ODILON REDON. Largest collection of Redon's graphic works ever assembled: 172 lithographs, 28 etchings and engravings, 9 drawings. These include some of his most famous works. All the plates from *Odilon Redon: oeuvre graphique complet,* plus additional plates. New introduction and caption translations by Alfred Werner. 209 illustrations. xxvii + 209pp. 9⅛ x 12¼.

21966-8 Paperbound $4.00

DESIGN BY ACCIDENT; A BOOK OF "ACCIDENTAL EFFECTS" FOR ARTISTS AND DESIGNERS, James F. O'Brien. Create your own unique, striking, imaginative effects by "controlled accident" interaction of materials: paints and lacquers, oil and water based paints, splatter, crackling materials, shatter, similar items. Everything you do will be different; first book on this limitless art, so useful to both fine artist and commercial artist. Full instructions. 192 plates showing "accidents," 8 in color. viii + 215pp. 8⅜ x 11¼. 21942-9 Paperbound $3.50

THE BOOK OF SIGNS, Rudolf Koch. Famed German type designer draws 493 beautiful symbols: religious, mystical, alchemical, imperial, property marks, runes, etc. Remarkable fusion of traditional and modern. Good for suggestions of timelessness, smartness, modernity. Text. vi + 104pp. 6⅛ x 9¼.
20162-7 Paperbound $1.25

HISTORY OF INDIAN AND INDONESIAN ART, Ananda K. Coomaraswamy. An unabridged republication of one of the finest books by a great scholar in Eastern art. Rich in descriptive material, history, social backgrounds; Sunga reliefs, Rajput paintings, Gupta temples, Burmese frescoes, textiles, jewelry, sculpture, etc. 400 photos. viii + 423pp. 6⅜ x 9¾. 21436-2 Paperbound $4.00

PRIMITIVE ART, Franz Boas. America's foremost anthropologist surveys textiles, ceramics, woodcarving, basketry, metalwork, etc.; patterns, technology, creation of symbols, style origins. All areas of world, but very full on Northwest Coast Indians. More than 350 illustrations of baskets, boxes, totem poles, weapons, etc. 378 pp.
20025-6 Paperbound $3.00

THE GENTLEMAN AND CABINET MAKER'S DIRECTOR, Thomas Chippendale. Full reprint (third edition, 1762) of most influential furniture book of all time, by master cabinetmaker. 200 plates, illustrating chairs, sofas, mirrors, tables, cabinets, plus 24 photographs of surviving pieces. Biographical introduction by N. Bienenstock. vi + 249pp. 9⅞ x 12¾. 21601-2 Paperbound $4.00

AMERICAN ANTIQUE FURNITURE, Edgar G. Miller, Jr. The basic coverage of all American furniture before 1840. Individual chapters cover type of furniture— clocks, tables, sideboards, etc.—chronologically, with inexhaustible wealth of data. More than 2100 photographs, all identified, commented on. Essential to all early American collectors. Introduction by H. E. Keyes. vi + 1106pp. 7⅞ x 10¾.
21599-7, 21600-4 Two volumes, Paperbound $11.00

PENNSYLVANIA DUTCH AMERICAN FOLK ART, Henry J. Kauffman. 279 photos, 28 drawings of tulipware, Fraktur script, painted tinware, toys, flowered furniture, quilts, samplers, hex signs, house interiors, etc. Full descriptive text. Excellent for tourist, rewarding for designer, collector. Map. 146pp. 7⅞ x 10¾.
21205-X Paperbound $2.50

EARLY NEW ENGLAND GRAVESTONE RUBBINGS, Edmund V. Gillon, Jr. 43 photographs, 226 carefully reproduced rubbings show heavily symbolic, sometimes macabre early gravestones, up to early 19th century. Remarkable early American primitive art, occasionally strikingly beautiful; always powerful. Text. xxvi + 207pp. 8⅜ x 11¼. 21380-3 Paperbound $3.50

ALPHABETS AND ORNAMENTS, Ernst Lehner. Well-known pictorial source for decorative alphabets, script examples, cartouches, frames, decorative title pages, calligraphic initials, borders, similar material. 14th to 19th century, mostly European. Useful in almost any graphic arts designing, varied styles. 750 illustrations. 256pp. 7 x 10. 21905-4 Paperbound $4.00

PAINTING: A CREATIVE APPROACH, Norman Colquhoun. For the beginner simple guide provides an instructive approach to painting: major stumbling blocks for beginner; overcoming them, technical points; paints and pigments; oil painting; watercolor and other media and color. New section on "plastic" paints. Glossary. Formerly *Paint Your Own Pictures*. 221pp. 22000-1 Paperbound $1.75

THE ENJOYMENT AND USE OF COLOR, Walter Sargent. Explanation of the relations between colors themselves and between colors in nature and art, including hundreds of little-known facts about color values, intensities, effects of high and low illumination, complementary colors. Many practical hints for painters, references to great masters. 7 color plates, 29 illustrations. x + 274pp. 20944-X Paperbound $2.75

THE NOTEBOOKS OF LEONARDO DA VINCI, compiled and edited by Jean Paul Richter. 1566 extracts from original manuscripts reveal the full range of Leonardo's versatile genius: all his writings on painting, sculpture, architecture, anatomy, astronomy, geography, topography, physiology, mining, music, etc., in both Italian and English, with 186 plates of manuscript pages and more than 500 additional drawings. Includes studies for the Last Supper, the lost Sforza monument, and other works. Total of xlvii + 866pp. 7⅞ x 10¾. 22572-0, 22573-9 Two volumes, Paperbound $10.00

MONTGOMERY WARD CATALOGUE OF 1895. Tea gowns, yards of flannel and pillow-case lace, stereoscopes, books of gospel hymns, the New Improved Singer Sewing Machine, side saddles, milk skimmers, straight-edged razors, high-button shoes, spittoons, and on and on . . . listing some 25,000 items, practically all illustrated. Essential to the shoppers of the 1890's, it is our truest record of the spirit of the period. Unaltered reprint of Issue No. 57, Spring and Summer 1895. Introduction by Boris Emmet. Innumerable illustrations. xiii + 624pp. 8½ x 11⅝. 22377-9 Paperbound $6.95

THE CRYSTAL PALACE EXHIBITION ILLUSTRATED CATALOGUE (LONDON, 1851). One of the wonders of the modern world—the Crystal Palace Exhibition in which all the nations of the civilized world exhibited their achievements in the arts and sciences—presented in an equally important illustrated catalogue. More than 1700 items pictured with accompanying text—ceramics, textiles, cast-iron work, carpets, pianos, sleds, razors, wall-papers, billiard tables, beehives, silverware and hundreds of other artifacts—represent the focal point of Victorian culture in the Western World. Probably the largest collection of Victorian decorative art ever assembled—indispensable for antiquarians and designers. Unabridged republication of the Art-Journal Catalogue of the Great Exhibition of 1851, with all terminal essays. New introduction by John Gloag, F.S.A. xxxiv + 426pp. 9 x 12. 22503-8 Paperbound $4.50

A HISTORY OF COSTUME, Carl Köhler. Definitive history, based on surviving pieces of clothing primarily, and paintings, statues, etc. secondarily. Highly readable text, supplemented by 594 illustrations of costumes of the ancient Mediterranean peoples, Greece and Rome, the Teutonic prehistoric period; costumes of the Middle Ages, Renaissance, Baroque, 18th and 19th centuries. Clear, measured patterns are provided for many clothing articles. Approach is practical throughout. Enlarged by Emma von Sichart. 464pp. 21030-8 Paperbound $3.50

ORIENTAL RUGS, ANTIQUE AND MODERN, Walter A. Hawley. A complete and authoritative treatise on the Oriental rug—where they are made, by whom and how, designs and symbols, characteristics in detail of the six major groups, how to distinguish them and how to buy them. Detailed technical data is provided on periods, weaves, warps, wefts, textures, sides, ends and knots, although no technical background is required for an understanding. 11 color plates, 80 halftones, 4 maps. vi + 320pp. 6⅛ x 9⅛. 22366-3 Paperbound $5.00

TEN BOOKS ON ARCHITECTURE, Vitruvius. By any standards the most important book on architecture ever written. Early Roman discussion of aesthetics of building, construction methods, orders, sites, and every other aspect of architecture has inspired, instructed architecture for about 2,000 years. Stands behind Palladio, Michelangelo, Bramante, Wren, countless others. Definitive Morris H. Morgan translation. 68 illustrations. xii + 331pp. 20645-9 Paperbound $3.50

THE FOUR BOOKS OF ARCHITECTURE, Andrea Palladio. Translated into every major Western European language in the two centuries following its publication in 1570, this has been one of the most influential books in the history of architecture. Complete reprint of the 1738 Isaac Ware edition. New introduction by Adolf Placzek, Columbia Univ. 216 plates. xxii + 110pp. of text. 9½ x 12¾. 21308-0 Clothbound $10.00

STICKS AND STONES: A STUDY OF AMERICAN ARCHITECTURE AND CIVILIZATION, Lewis Mumford.One of the great classics of American cultural history. American architecture from the medieval-inspired earliest forms to the early 20th century; evolution of structure and style, and reciprocal influences on environment. 21 photographic illustrations. 238pp. 20202-X Paperbound $2.00

THE AMERICAN BUILDER'S COMPANION, Asher Benjamin. The most widely used early 19th century architectural style and source book, for colonial up into Greek Revival periods. Extensive development of geometry of carpentering, construction of sashes, frames, doors, stairs; plans and elevations of domestic and other buildings. Hundreds of thousands of houses were built according to this book, now invaluable to historians, architects, restorers, etc. 1827 edition. 59 plates. 114pp. 7⅞ x 10¾. 22236-5 Paperbound $3.50

DUTCH HOUSES IN THE HUDSON VALLEY BEFORE 1776, Helen Wilkinson Reynolds. The standard survey of the Dutch colonial house and outbuildings, with constructional features, decoration, and local history associated with individual homesteads. Introduction by Franklin D. Roosevelt. Map. 150 illustrations. 469pp. 6⅝ x 9¼. 21469-9 Paperbound $4.00

THE ARCHITECTURE OF COUNTRY HOUSES, Andrew J. Downing. Together with Vaux's *Villas and Cottages* this is the basic book for Hudson River Gothic architecture of the middle Victorian period. Full, sound discussions of general aspects of housing, architecture, style, decoration, furnishing, together with scores of detailed house plans, illustrations of specific buildings, accompanied by full text. Perhaps the most influential single American architectural book. 1850 edition. Introduction by J. Stewart Johnson. 321 figures, 34 architectural designs. xvi + 560pp.

22003-6 Paperbound $4.00

LOST EXAMPLES OF COLONIAL ARCHITECTURE, John Mead Howells. Full-page photographs of buildings that have disappeared or been so altered as to be denatured, including many designed by major early American architects. 245 plates. xvii + 248pp. 7⅞ x 10¾. 21143-6 Paperbound $3.50

DOMESTIC ARCHITECTURE OF THE AMERICAN COLONIES AND OF THE EARLY REPUBLIC, Fiske Kimball. Foremost architect and restorer of Williamsburg and Monticello covers nearly 200 homes between 1620-1825. Architectural details, construction, style features, special fixtures, floor plans, etc. Generally considered finest work in its area. 219 illustrations of houses, doorways, windows, capital mantels. xx + 314pp. 7⅞ x 10¾. 21743-4 Paperbound $4.00

EARLY AMERICAN ROOMS: 1650-1858, edited by Russell Hawes Kettell. Tour of 12 rooms, each representative of a different era in American history and each furnished, decorated, designed and occupied in the style of the era. 72 plans and elevations, 8-page color section, etc., show fabrics, wall papers, arrangements, etc. Full descriptive text. xvii + 200pp. of text. 8⅜ x 11¼.

21633-0 Paperbound $5.00

THE FITZWILLIAM VIRGINAL BOOK, edited by J. Fuller Maitland and W. B. Squire. Full modern printing of famous early 17th-century ms. volume of 300 works by Morley, Byrd, Bull, Gibbons, etc. For piano or other modern keyboard instrument; easy to read format. xxxvi + 938pp. 8⅜ x 11.

21068-5, 21069-3 Two volumes, Paperbound $10.00

KEYBOARD MUSIC, Johann Sebastian Bach. Bach Gesellschaft edition. A rich selection of Bach's masterpieces for the harpsichord: the six English Suites, six French Suites, the six Partitas (Clavierübung part I), the Goldberg Variations (Clavierübung part IV), the fifteen Two-Part Inventions and the fifteen Three-Part Sinfonias. Clearly reproduced on large sheets with ample margins; eminently playable. vi + 312pp. 8⅛ x 11. 22360-4 Paperbound $5.00

THE MUSIC OF BACH: AN INTRODUCTION, Charles Sanford Terry. A fine, nontechnical introduction to Bach's music, both instrumental and vocal. Covers organ music, chamber music, passion music, other types. Analyzes themes, developments, innovations. x + 114pp. 21075-8 Paperbound $1.25

BEETHOVEN AND HIS NINE SYMPHONIES, Sir George Grove. Noted British musicologist provides best history, analysis, commentary on symphonies. Very thorough, rigorously accurate; necessary to both advanced student and amateur music lover. 436 musical passages. vii + 407 pp. 20334-4 Paperbound $2.75

JOHANN SEBASTIAN BACH, Philipp Spitta. One of the great classics of musicology, this definitive analysis of Bach's music (and life) has never been surpassed. Lucid, nontechnical analyses of hundreds of pieces (30 pages devoted to St. Matthew Passion, 26 to B Minor Mass). Also includes major analysis of 18th-century music. 450 musical examples. 40-page musical supplement. Total of xx + 1799pp.

(EUK) 22278-0, 22279-9 Two volumes, Clothbound $17.50

MOZART AND HIS PIANO CONCERTOS, Cuthbert Girdlestone. The only full-length study of an important area of Mozart's creativity. Provides detailed analyses of all 23 concertos, traces inspirational sources. 417 musical examples. Second edition. 509pp.

(USO) 21271-8 Paperbound $3.50

THE PERFECT WAGNERITE: A COMMENTARY ON THE NIBLUNG'S RING, George Bernard Shaw. Brilliant and still relevant criticism in remarkable essays on Wagner's Ring cycle, Shaw's ideas on political and social ideology behind the plots, role of Leitmotifs, vocal requisites, etc. Prefaces. xxi + 136pp.

21707-8 Paperbound $1.50

DON GIOVANNI, W. A. Mozart. Complete libretto, modern English translation; biographies of composer and librettist; accounts of early performances and critical reaction. Lavishly illustrated. All the material you need to understand and appreciate this great work. Dover Opera Guide and Libretto Series; translated and introduced by Ellen Bleiler. 92 illustrations. 209pp.

21134-7 Paperbound $2.00

HIGH FIDELITY SYSTEMS: A LAYMAN'S GUIDE, Roy F. Allison. All the basic information you need for setting up your own audio system: high fidelity and stereo record players, tape records, F.M. Connections, adjusting tone arm, cartridge, checking needle alignment, positioning speakers, phasing speakers, adjusting hums, trouble-shooting, maintenance, and similar topics. Enlarged 1965 edition. More than 50 charts, diagrams, photos. iv + 91pp. 21514-8 Paperbound $1.25

REPRODUCTION OF SOUND, Edgar Villchur. Thorough coverage for laymen of high fidelity systems, reproducing systems in general, needles, amplifiers, preamps, loudspeakers, feedback, explaining physical background. "A rare talent for making technicalities vividly comprehensible," R. Darrell, *High Fidelity*. 69 figures. iv + 92pp. 21515-6 Paperbound $1.25

HEAR ME TALKIN' TO YA: THE STORY OF JAZZ AS TOLD BY THE MEN WHO MADE IT, Nat Shapiro and Nat Hentoff. Louis Armstrong, Fats Waller, Jo Jones, Clarence Williams, Billy Holiday, Duke Ellington, Jelly Roll Morton and dozens of other jazz greats tell how it was in Chicago's South Side, New Orleans, depression Harlem and the modern West Coast as jazz was born and grew. xvi + 429pp.

21726-4 Paperbound $2.50

FABLES OF AESOP, translated by Sir Roger L'Estrange. A reproduction of the very rare 1931 Paris edition; a selection of the most interesting fables, together with 50 imaginative drawings by Alexander Calder. v + 128pp. 6½x9¼.

21780-9 Paperbound $1.50

AGAINST THE GRAIN (A REBOURS), Joris K. Huysmans. Filled with weird images, evidences of a bizarre imagination, exotic experiments with hallucinatory drugs, rich tastes and smells and the diversions of its sybarite hero Duc Jean des Esseintes, this classic novel pushed 19th-century literary decadence to its limits. Full unabridged edition. Do not confuse this with abridged editions generally sold. Introduction by Havelock Ellis. xlix + 206pp. 22190-3 Paperbound $2.00

VARIORUM SHAKESPEARE: HAMLET. Edited by Horace H. Furness; a landmark of American scholarship. Exhaustive footnotes and appendices treat all doubtful words and phrases, as well as suggested critical emendations throughout the play's history. First volume contains editor's own text, collated with all Quartos and Folios. Second volume contains full first Quarto, translations of Shakespeare's sources (Belleforest, and Saxo Grammaticus), Der Bestrafte Brudermord, and many essays on critical and historical points of interest by major authorities of past and present. Includes details of staging and costuming over the years. By far the best edition available for serious students of Shakespeare. Total of xx + 905pp. 21004-9, 21005-7, 2 volumes, Paperbound $7.00

A LIFE OF WILLIAM SHAKESPEARE, Sir Sidney Lee. This is the standard life of Shakespeare, summarizing everything known about Shakespeare and his plays. Incredibly rich in material, broad in coverage, clear and judicious, it has served thousands as the best introduction to Shakespeare. 1931 edition. 9 plates. xxix + 792pp. (USO) 21967-4 Paperbound $3.75

MASTERS OF THE DRAMA, John Gassner. Most comprehensive history of the drama in print, covering every tradition from Greeks to modern Europe and America, including India, Far East, etc. Covers more than 800 dramatists, 2000 plays, with biographical material, plot summaries, theatre history, criticism, etc. "Best of its kind in English," New Republic. 77 illustrations. xxii + 890pp. 20100-7 Clothbound $8.50

THE EVOLUTION OF THE ENGLISH LANGUAGE, George McKnight. The growth of English, from the 14th century to the present. Unusual, non-technical account presents basic information in very interesting form: sound shifts, change in grammar and syntax, vocabulary growth, similar topics. Abundantly illustrated with quotations. Formerly Modern English in the Making. xii + 590pp. 21932-1 Paperbound $3.50

AN ETYMOLOGICAL DICTIONARY OF MODERN ENGLISH, Ernest Weekley. Fullest, richest work of its sort, by foremost British lexicographer. Detailed word histories, including many colloquial and archaic words; extensive quotations. Do not confuse this with the Concise Etymological Dictionary, which is much abridged. Total of xxvii + 830pp. 6½ x 9¼. 21873-2, 21874-0 Two volumes, Paperbound $6.00

FLATLAND: A ROMANCE OF MANY DIMENSIONS, E. A. Abbott. Classic of science-fiction explores ramifications of life in a two-dimensional world, and what happens when a three-dimensional being intrudes. Amusing reading, but also useful as introduction to thought about hyperspace. Introduction by Banesh Hoffmann. 16 illustrations. xx + 103pp. 20001-9 Paperbound $1.00

POEMS OF ANNE BRADSTREET, edited with an introduction by Robert Hutchinson. A new selection of poems by America's first poet and perhaps the first significant woman poet in the English language. 48 poems display her development in works of considerable variety—love poems, domestic poems, religious meditations, formal elegies, "quaternions," etc. Notes, bibliography. viii + 222pp.

22160-1 Paperbound $2.00

THREE GOTHIC NOVELS: THE CASTLE OF OTRANTO BY HORACE WALPOLE; VATHEK BY WILLIAM BECKFORD; THE VAMPYRE BY JOHN POLIDORI, WITH FRAGMENT OF A NOVEL BY LORD BYRON, edited by E. F. Bleiler. The first Gothic novel, by Walpole; the finest Oriental tale in English, by Beckford; powerful Romantic supernatural story in versions by Polidori and Byron. All extremely important in history of literature; all still exciting, packed with supernatural thrills, ghosts, haunted castles, magic, etc. xl + 291pp.

21232-7 Paperbound $2.50

THE BEST TALES OF HOFFMANN, E. T. A. Hoffmann. 10 of Hoffmann's most important stories, in modern re-editings of standard translations: Nutcracker and the King of Mice, Signor Formica, Automata, The Sandman, Rath Krespel, The Golden Flowerpot, Master Martin the Cooper, The Mines of Falun, The King's Betrothed, A New Year's Eve Adventure. 7 illustrations by Hoffmann. Edited by E. F. Bleiler. xxxix + 419pp. 21793-0 Paperbound $3.00

GHOST AND HORROR STORIES OF AMBROSE BIERCE, Ambrose Bierce. 23 strikingly modern stories of the horrors latent in the human mind: The Eyes of the Panther, The Damned Thing, An Occurrence at Owl Creek Bridge, An Inhabitant of Carcosa, etc., plus the dream-essay, Visions of the Night. Edited by E. F. Bleiler. xxii + 199pp. 20767-6 Paperbound $1.50

BEST GHOST STORIES OF J. S. LEFANU, J. Sheridan LeFanu. Finest stories by Victorian master often considered greatest supernatural writer of all. Carmilla, Green Tea, The Haunted Baronet, The Familiar, and 12 others. Most never before available in the U. S. A. Edited by E. F. Bleiler. 8 illustrations from Victorian publications. xvii + 467pp. 20415-4 Paperbound $3.00

MATHEMATICAL FOUNDATIONS OF INFORMATION THEORY, A. I. Khinchin. Comprehensive introduction to work of Shannon, McMillan, Feinstein and Khinchin, placing these investigations on a rigorous mathematical basis. Covers entropy concept in probability theory, uniqueness theorem, Shannon's inequality, ergodic sources, the E property, martingale concept, noise, Feinstein's fundamental lemma, Shanon's first and second theorems. Translated by R. A. Silverman and M. D. Friedman. iii + 120pp. 60434-9 Paperbound $1.75

SEVEN SCIENCE FICTION NOVELS, H. G. Wells. The standard collection of the great novels. Complete, unabridged. *First Men in the Moon, Island of Dr. Moreau, War of the Worlds, Food of the Gods, Invisible Man, Time Machine, In the Days of the Comet.* Not only science fiction fans, but every educated person owes it to himself to read these novels. 1015pp. 20264-X Clothbound $5.00

LAST AND FIRST MEN AND STAR MAKER, TWO SCIENCE FICTION NOVELS, Olaf Stapledon. Greatest future histories in science fiction. In the first, human intelligence is the "hero," through strange paths of evolution, interplanetary invasions, incredible technologies, near extinctions and reemergences. Star Maker describes the quest of a band of star rovers for intelligence itself, through time and space: weird inhuman civilizations, crustacean minds, symbiotic worlds, etc. Complete, unabridged. v + 438pp. 21962-3 Paperbound $2.50

THREE PROPHETIC NOVELS, H. G. WELLS. Stages of a consistently planned future for mankind. *When the Sleeper Wakes*, and *A Story of the Days to Come*, anticipate *Brave New World* and *1984*, in the 21st Century; *The Time Machine*, only complete version in print, shows farther future and the end of mankind. All show Wells's greatest gifts as storyteller and novelist. Edited by E. F. Bleiler. x + 335pp. (USO) 20605-X Paperbound $2.50

THE DEVIL'S DICTIONARY, Ambrose Bierce. America's own Oscar Wilde—Ambrose Bierce—offers his barbed iconoclastic wisdom in over 1,000 definitions hailed by H. L. Mencken as "some of the most gorgeous witticisms in the English language." 145pp. 20487-1 Paperbound $1.25

MAX AND MORITZ, Wilhelm Busch. Great children's classic, father of comic strip, of two bad boys, Max and Moritz. Also Ker and Plunk (Plisch und Plumm), Cat and Mouse, Deceitful Henry, Ice-Peter, The Boy and the Pipe, and five other pieces. Original German, with English translation. Edited by H. Arthur Klein; translations by various hands and H. Arthur Klein. vi + 216pp. 20181-3 Paperbound $1.00

PIGS IS PIGS AND OTHER FAVORITES, Ellis Parker Butler. The title story is one of the best humor short stories, as Mike Flannery obfuscates biology and English. Also included, That Pup of Murchison's, The Great American Pie Company, and Perkins of Portland. 14 illustrations. v + 109pp. 21532-6 Paperbound $1.25

THE PETERKIN PAPERS, Lucretia P. Hale. It takes genius to be as stupidly mad as the Peterkins, as they decide to become wise, celebrate the "Fourth," keep a cow, and otherwise strain the resources of the Lady from Philadelphia. Basic book of American humor. 153 illustrations. 219pp. 20794-3 Paperbound $1.50

PERRAULT'S FAIRY TALES, translated by A. E. Johnson and S. R. Littlewood, with 34 full-page illustrations by Gustave Doré. All the original Perrault stories—Cinderella, Sleeping Beauty, Bluebeard, Little Red Riding Hood, Puss in Boots, Tom Thumb, etc.—with their witty verse morals and the magnificent illustrations of Doré. One of the five or six great books of European fairy tales. viii + 117pp. 8⅛ x 11. 22311-6 Paperbound $2.00

OLD HUNGARIAN FAIRY TALES, Baroness Orczy. Favorites translated and adapted by author of the *Scarlet Pimpernel*. Eight fairy tales include "The Suitors of Princess Fire-Fly," "The Twin Hunchbacks," "Mr. Cuttlefish's Love Story," and "The Enchanted Cat." This little volume of magic and adventure will captivate children as it has for generations. 90 drawings by Montagu Barstow. 96pp. (USO) 22293-4 Paperbound $1.95

THE RED FAIRY BOOK, Andrew Lang. Lang's color fairy books have long been children's favorites. This volume includes Rapunzel, Jack and the Bean-stalk and 35 other stories, familiar and unfamiliar. 4 plates, 93 illustrations x + 367pp.
21673-X Paperbound $2.50

THE BLUE FAIRY BOOK, Andrew Lang. Lang's tales come from all countries and all times. Here are 37 tales from Grimm, the Arabian Nights, Greek Mythology, and other fascinating sources. 8 plates, 130 illustrations. xi + 390pp.
21437-0 Paperbound $2.50

HOUSEHOLD STORIES BY THE BROTHERS GRIMM. Classic English-language edition of the well-known tales — Rumpelstiltskin, Snow White, Hansel and Gretel, The Twelve Brothers, Faithful John, Rapunzel, Tom Thumb (52 stories in all). Translated into simple, straightforward English by Lucy Crane. Ornamented with headpieces, vignettes, elaborate decorative initials and a dozen full-page illustrations by Walter Crane. x + 269pp.
21080-4 Paperbound $2.50

THE MERRY ADVENTURES OF ROBIN HOOD, Howard Pyle. The finest modern versions of the traditional ballads and tales about the great English outlaw. Howard Pyle's complete prose version, with every word, every illustration of the first edition. Do not confuse this facsimile of the original (1883) with modern editions that change text or illustrations. 23 plates plus many page decorations. xxii + 296pp.
22043-5 Paperbound $2.50

THE STORY OF KING ARTHUR AND HIS KNIGHTS, Howard Pyle. The finest children's version of the life of King Arthur; brilliantly retold by Pyle, with 48 of his most imaginative illustrations. xviii + 313pp. 6⅛ x 9¼.
21445-1 Paperbound $2.50

THE WONDERFUL WIZARD OF OZ, L. Frank Baum. America's finest children's book in facsimile of first edition with all Denslow illustrations in full color. The edition a child should have. Introduction by Martin Gardner. 23 color plates, scores of drawings. iv + 267pp.
20691-2 Paperbound $2.50

THE MARVELOUS LAND OF OZ, L. Frank Baum. The second Oz book, every bit as imaginative as the Wizard. The hero is a boy named Tip, but the Scarecrow and the Tin Woodman are back, as is the Oz magic. 16 color plates, 120 drawings by John R. Neill. 287pp.
20692-0 Paperbound $2.50

THE MAGICAL MONARCH OF MO, L. Frank Baum. Remarkable adventures in a land even stranger than Oz. The best of Baum's books not in the Oz series. 15 color plates and dozens of drawings by Frank Verbeck. xviii + 237pp.
21892-9 Paperbound $2.25

THE BAD CHILD'S BOOK OF BEASTS, MORE BEASTS FOR WORSE CHILDREN, A MORAL ALPHABET, Hilaire Belloc. Three complete humor classics in one volume. Be kind to the frog, and do not call him names . . . and 28 other whimsical animals. Familiar favorites and some not so well known. Illustrated by Basil Blackwell. 156pp.
(USO) 20749-8 Paperbound $1.50

EAST O' THE SUN AND WEST O' THE MOON, George W. Dasent. Considered the best of all translations of these Norwegian folk tales, this collection has been enjoyed by generations of children (and folklorists too). Includes True and Untrue, Why the Sea is Salt, East O' the Sun and West O' the Moon, Why the Bear is Stumpy-Tailed, Boots and the Troll, The Cock and the Hen, Rich Peter the Pedlar, and 52 more. The only edition with all 59 tales. 77 illustrations by Erik Werenskiold and Theodor Kittelsen. xv + 418pp. 22521-6 Paperbound $3.50

GOOPS AND HOW TO BE THEM, Gelett Burgess. Classic of tongue-in-cheek humor, masquerading as etiquette book. 87 verses, twice as many cartoons, show mischievous Goops as they demonstrate to children virtues of table manners, neatness, courtesy, etc. Favorite for generations. viii + 88pp. 6½ x 9¼. 22233-0 Paperbound $1.25

ALICE'S ADVENTURES UNDER GROUND, Lewis Carroll. The first version, quite different from the final *Alice in Wonderland,* printed out by Carroll himself with his own illustrations. Complete facsimile of the "million dollar" manuscript Carroll gave to Alice Liddell in 1864. Introduction by Martin Gardner. viii + 96pp. Title and dedication pages in color. 21482-6 Paperbound $1.25

THE BROWNIES, THEIR BOOK, Palmer Cox. Small as mice, cunning as foxes, exuberant and full of mischief, the Brownies go to the zoo, toy shop, seashore, circus, etc., in 24 verse adventures and 266 illustrations. Long a favorite, since their first appearance in St. Nicholas Magazine. xi + 144pp. 6⅝ x 9¼. 21265-3 Paperbound $1.75

SONGS OF CHILDHOOD, Walter De La Mare. Published (under the pseudonym Walter Ramal) when De La Mare was only 29, this charming collection has long been a favorite children's book. A facsimile of the first edition in paper, the 47 poems capture the simplicity of the nursery rhyme and the ballad, including such lyrics as I Met Eve, Tartary, The Silver Penny. vii + 106pp. 21972-0 Paperbound $1.25

THE COMPLETE NONSENSE OF EDWARD LEAR, Edward Lear. The finest 19th-century humorist-cartoonist in full: all nonsense limericks, zany alphabets, Owl and Pussycat, songs, nonsense botany, and more than 500 illustrations by Lear himself. Edited by Holbrook Jackson. xxix + 287pp. (USO) 20167-8 Paperbound $2.00

BILLY WHISKERS: THE AUTOBIOGRAPHY OF A GOAT, Frances Trego Montgomery. A favorite of children since the early 20th century, here are the escapades of that rambunctious, irresistible and mischievous goat—Billy Whiskers. Much in the spirit of *Peck's Bad Boy,* this is a book that children never tire of reading or hearing. All the original familiar illustrations by W. H. Fry are included: 6 color plates, 18 black and white drawings. 159pp. 22345-0 Paperbound $2.00

MOTHER GOOSE MELODIES. Faithful republication of the fabulously rare Munroe and Francis "copyright 1833" Boston edition—the most important Mother Goose collection, usually referred to as the "original." Familiar rhymes plus many rare ones, with wonderful old woodcut illustrations. Edited by E. F. Bleiler. 128pp. 4½ x 6⅜. 22577-1 Paperbound $1.25

TWO LITTLE SAVAGES; BEING THE ADVENTURES OF TWO BOYS WHO LIVED AS INDIANS AND WHAT THEY LEARNED, Ernest Thompson Seton. Great classic of nature and boyhood provides a vast range of woodlore in most palatable form, a genuinely entertaining story. Two farm boys build a teepee in woods and live in it for a month, working out Indian solutions to living problems, star lore, birds and animals, plants, etc. 293 illustrations. vii + 286pp.

20985-7 Paperbound $2.50

PETER PIPER'S PRACTICAL PRINCIPLES OF PLAIN & PERFECT PRONUNCIATION. Alliterative jingles and tongue-twisters of surprising charm, that made their first appearance in America about 1830. Republished in full with the spirited woodcut illustrations from this earliest American edition. 32pp. 4½ x 6⅜.

22560-7 Paperbound $1.00

SCIENCE EXPERIMENTS AND AMUSEMENTS FOR CHILDREN, Charles Vivian. 73 easy experiments, requiring only materials found at home or easily available, such as candles, coins, steel wool, etc.; illustrate basic phenomena like vacuum, simple chemical reaction, etc. All safe. Modern, well-planned. Formerly *Science Games for Children*. 102 photos, numerous drawings. 96pp. 6⅛ x 9¼.

21856-2 Paperbound $1.25

AN INTRODUCTION TO CHESS MOVES AND TACTICS SIMPLY EXPLAINED, Leonard Barden. Informal intermediate introduction, quite strong in explaining reasons for moves. Covers basic material, tactics, important openings, traps, positional play in middle game, end game. Attempts to isolate patterns and recurrent configurations. Formerly *Chess*. 58 figures. 102pp. (USO) 21210-6 Paperbound $1.25

LASKER'S MANUAL OF CHESS, Dr. Emanuel Lasker. Lasker was not only one of the five great World Champions, he was also one of the ablest expositors, theorists, and analysts. In many ways, his Manual, permeated with his philosophy of battle, filled with keen insights, is one of the greatest works ever written on chess. Filled with analyzed games by the great players. A single-volume library that will profit almost any chess player, beginner or master. 308 diagrams. xli x 349pp.

20640-8 Paperbound $2.75

THE MASTER BOOK OF MATHEMATICAL RECREATIONS, Fred Schuh. In opinion of many the finest work ever prepared on mathematical puzzles, stunts, recreations; exhaustively thorough explanations of mathematics involved, analysis of effects, citation of puzzles and games. Mathematics involved is elementary. Translated by F. Göbel. 194 figures. xxiv + 430pp.

22134-2 Paperbound $3.00

MATHEMATICS, MAGIC AND MYSTERY, Martin Gardner. Puzzle editor for Scientific American explains mathematics behind various mystifying tricks: card tricks, stage "mind reading," coin and match tricks, counting out games, geometric dissections, etc. Probability sets, theory of numbers clearly explained. Also provides more than 400 tricks, guaranteed to work, that you can do. 135 illustrations. xii + 176pp.

20338-2 Paperbound $1.50

MATHEMATICAL PUZZLES FOR BEGINNERS AND ENTHUSIASTS, Geoffrey Mott-Smith. 189 puzzles from easy to difficult—involving arithmetic, logic, algebra, properties of digits, probability, etc.—for enjoyment and mental stimulus. Explanation of mathematical principles behind the puzzles. 135 illustrations. viii + 248pp.
20198-8 Paperbound $1.75

PAPER FOLDING FOR BEGINNERS, William D. Murray and Francis J. Rigney. Easiest book on the market, clearest instructions on making interesting, beautiful origami Sail boats, cups, roosters, frogs that move legs, bonbon boxes, standing birds, etc. 40 projects; more than 275 diagrams and photographs. 94pp.
20713-7 Paperbound $1.00

TRICKS AND GAMES ON THE POOL TABLE, Fred Herrmann. 79 tricks and games—some solitaires, some for two or more players, some competitive games—to entertain you between formal games. Mystifying shots and throws, unusual caroms, tricks involving such props as cork, coins, a hat, etc. Formerly *Fun on the Pool Table*. 77 figures. 95pp.
21814-7 Paperbound $1.00

HAND SHADOWS TO BE THROWN UPON THE WALL: A SERIES OF NOVEL AND AMUSING FIGURES FORMED BY THE HAND, Henry Bursill. Delightful picturebook from great-grandfather's day shows how to make 18 different hand shadows: a bird that flies, duck that quacks, dog that wags his tail, camel, goose, deer, boy, turtle, etc. Only book of its sort. vi + 33pp. 6½ x 9¼.   21779-5 Paperbound $1.00

WHITTLING AND WOODCARVING, E. J. Tangerman. 18th printing of best book on market. "If you can cut a potato you can carve" toys and puzzles, chains, chessmen, caricatures, masks, frames, woodcut blocks, surface patterns, much more. Information on tools, woods, techniques. Also goes into serious wood sculpture from Middle Ages to present, East and West. 464 photos, figures. x + 293pp.
20965-2 Paperbound $2.00

HISTORY OF PHILOSOPHY, Julián Marías. Possibly the clearest, most easily followed, best planned, most useful one-volume history of philosophy on the market; neither skimpy nor overfull. Full details on system of every major philosopher and dozens of less important thinkers from pre-Socratics up to Existentialism and later. Strong on many European figures usually omitted. Has gone through dozens of editions in Europe. 1966 edition, translated by Stanley Appelbaum and Clarence Strowbridge. xviii + 505pp.   21739-6 Paperbound $3.00

YOGA: A SCIENTIFIC EVALUATION, Kovoor T. Behanan. Scientific but non-technical study of physiological results of yoga exercises; done under auspices of Yale U. Relations to Indian thought, to psychoanalysis, etc. 16 photos. xxiii + 270pp.
20505-3 Paperbound $2.50

Prices subject to change without notice.
Available at your book dealer or write for free catalogue to Dept. GI, Dover Publications, Inc., 180 Varick St., N. Y., N. Y. 10014. Dover publishes more than 150 books each year on science, elementary and advanced mathematics, biology, music, art, literary history, social sciences and other areas.